D0364856

THE ORIGINS OF

PSYCHO-ANALYSIS

On his early papers what did F mean
by neurasthenia

p 170
connection. FJ "one of souls
behind unconscious
189
alchemy

The Origins of Psycho-Analysis

LETTERS TO WILHELM FLIESS,

DRAFTS AND NOTES: 1887–1902

BY

SIGMUND FREUD

EDITED BY MARIE BONAPARTE, ANNA FREUD,

AND ERNST KRIS

AUTHORIZED TRANSLATION BY ERIC MOSBACHER

AND JAMES STRACHEY

INTRODUCTORY ESSAY BY STEVEN MARCUS

INTRODUCTION BY ERNST KRIS

Basic Books, Inc., Publishers   New York

CONTENTS

INTRODUCTORY ESSAY

BY STEVEN MARCUS

The letters that Sigmund Freud wrote to Wilhelm Fliess between 1887 and 1902, along with the notes, drafts, and other material that Freud included with those letters, make up an extraordinary account. They constitute a singular record of creative discovery in Western thought, and are indispensable to our understanding of how psychoanalysis—itself a unique development of Western civilization—was brought into being. That development may be appropriately regarded as a culmination of the particular tradition of introspection which began with the adjuration of the oracle at Delphi to "Know thyself." This rationally governed method of self-examination takes as its principal objects of scrutiny everything within us that is not rational—our affects, our instinctual strivings, our fears, fancies, dreams, and nightmares, our sexual obsessions, our uncontrollable aggressions. And it is more than a fortunate accident that this most highly developed form of Western secular introspection should have returned at one of its moments of climactic breaking-through to its cultural origins. When Freud, in October of 1897, writes that "I have found love of the mother and jealousy of the father in my own case too, and now believe it to be a general phenomenon of early childhood," and then goes on at once to discuss *Oedipus Rex,* one senses reverberations of profound historical depth. An organic line of cultural evolution is being brought to a decisive moment of conclusion. That conclusion represents the attainment of a new degree of consciousness in Western civilization. Yet this new or higher degree of

does it?

consciousness resumes what has gone before, incorporates and re-integrates its past and intervening history, and by thus returning to its original point of departure simultaneously moves forward into a future that has been significantly altered.

The Freud we meet in these documents is the person within whom this historical drama of development first occurred. At the outset he was certainly not consciously prepared for the direction in which such a development would lead him. He was a young neurologist or neuropathologist with a generous range of interests and high ambitions. He had already published scientific papers on a variety of topics—including the use of cocaine—and had in Paris come under the influence of Charcot, whose notions about hysteria and sexuality he had accepted. He was also interested in the new discoveries that were taking place in the study of the anatomy of the brain and the nervous system, and in such related pathologies as aphasia and the battery of afflictions that accompanied syphilis in its advanced stages. One large connection between these pathologies and the neuroses, in particular hysteria, was that they tended to mimic each other. Hysterically distorted speech or hysterical loss of speech functions often was indistinguishable from the reduced or deformed speech functions of persons who had, from one cause or another, incurred damage of the brain, and vice-versa. The blindnesses, paralyses, tics, lamenesses, spasms, pains, and phantom sensations of hysteria were all produced as well by syphilis in its tertiary phase. Indeed the nineteenth-century epidemics of venereal disease and hysteria were connected in a number of intimate ways. Not only was their symptomatology often convertible and interchangeable, but they often tended as well to occur coincidentally or in tandem, and in the same persons.

The other conditions with which neurologists largely occupied themselves—apart from what today are regarded as actual neurological illnesses—were obsessions, phobias, depressions of certain magnitudes, paranoia in its milder forms, and a variety of symptoms that were bundled together to form the syndromes of neurasthenia and anxiety neurosis. These conditions had a number of attributes

loss or impairment of ability to use language due to brain lesion

in common—apart from the circumstance that no one understood them. One such attribute was essentially negative: they were all in some sense residua, left behind or overlooked by German psychiatry, which at that time and point in its historical development was almost exclusively concerned with psychoses and other more florid and spectacular conditions of mental disorder. Such conditions all seemed, in addition, sooner or later to have something to do with sexuality, but this common feature too was understood, if that is the right word, in a primitive and unformed sense. The store of therapeutic measures available to the young Freud was equally rudimentary. The traditional pharmacopia was of very limited use. Other current resources or treatments of choice were electrogalvanic sessions, hydropathic or water cures, and rest cures of differing descriptions. Hypnotism was relied on by some, and Freud experimented with it, as he did with just about everything else. In addition to hypnotism accompanied by suggestion, there was also therapy by suggestion alone, and Freud seemed at the outset to rely on these two procedures as much as on any others. As he observes to Fliess in one of the early letters, "Talking people into and out of things . . . is what my work consists of." Occasionally some of these methods worked, but no one knew why. More often they failed to make any difference, but again it was generally beyond anyone's power of explanation to say why a particular treatment didn't work in particular cases. As Freud's remark suggests, it was by no means a satisfactory state of affairs—neither therapeutically nor theoretically.

It was by no means a satisfactory state of affairs culturally either. Situated as he was, Freud could not help but observe and be struck by what appears to have been the plague that had settled upon the sexual lives of the middle classes in the latter part of the nineteenth century. The early letters to Fliess, like other medical writings about sexuality of the same period, and like much contemporary literature —such as the novels of Hardy and Gissing or the plays of Ibsen— all refract the same sexual climate of gloom, frustration, fear, and muted despair. For example, quite early on, Freud connects neurasthenic impotence in men with a history of masturbation, and then connects in turn hysteria in women with neurasthenic sexual inadequacy in men: if men excite but cannot satisfy women, hysteria is

a functional disorder characterized by feelings of weakness & a general lowering of bodily & mental tone — not organic nor deficiency

the result. It is not to the point to say that Freud was mistaken; the
value of these early formulations lies in what they suggest to us
about the material that Freud was observing. In a similar way Freud
was at first concerned with the adverse effects that *coitus interruptus*
seemed to have on both middle-class men and women, and collaterally
the even wider adverse effects that the absence of any innocuous
form of contraception seemed to threaten. "In the absence of such a
solution," he wrote at the beginning of 1893, "society seems doomed
to fall a victim to incurable neuroses which reduce the enjoyment of
life to a minimum, destroy the marriage relation and bring hereditary
ruin on the whole coming generation." And in the same document
he declares that although neuroses can be prevented, they are at the
same time "completely incurable." Although he was soon to change
his mind on this topic, from the very beginning Freud made and
continued to make a firm connection between his patients' range of
distresses and states of distress in their sexuality. Although he was at
first able to explain very little about either the etiology or the
dynamics of their unhappy circumstances, he was also unable to
overlook what he had observed or had strongly inferred: namely that
the neuroses in all their differences were all connected in some profound but as yet undisclosed way by disturbances of sexuality. Having made this observation and inference, he clung to the connections
they pointed to with what would later prove to be characteristic
tenacity. Others at the time had made similar connections. Yet, the
question remained: what could result from these connections; to
what did they lead; how was one to proceed?

Freud begins by trying to describe and classify the various
afflicted states that come before his attention, and tries at first to
find a simple, physical, causal explanation for the various neuroses.
For example, in 1893 he tried to explain anxiety attacks as a result
of sexual experience, adducing the case "of a gay old bachelor, who
denies himself nothing." This patient, Freud continued, produced
"a classic attack after allowing his thirty-year-old mistress to induce
him to have coitus three times. I have come to the opinion that
anxiety is to be connected, not with a mental, but with a physical
consequence of sexual abuse." And indeed Freud's first psychological
explanation of anxiety as either dammed-up libido or as a trans-

formation of it may be properly regarded as a derivative of this still-earlier view. These physical or physiological theories had to do with notions of stimulus, excitation, building up of hydraulic pressures or electrical charges or sexual substances, and with such other notions as discharge, equilibrium, homeostasis, constancy, and the like. One sees Freud in these letters and drafts beginning again and again with such ideas and being led inexorably away from them by the complexity of the psychic states that he encountered accompanying them. This is to say that the physiological theories that were available to Freud were simply and finally inadequate to deal with the richness of the psychic material produced by his patients. Freud did not move willingly toward the establishment of an independent psychology. He moved slowly and reluctantly, and one of the outstanding achievements of this early period, his long unpublished "Project for a Scientific Psychology" of 1895, is clearly a work of genius. It is an effort to construct a unified systematic theory of the mind, rising in an unbroken set of connected stages from neurons to complex psychic states; it is no less than an effort to solve or transcend the mind-body duality, and it was, of course, abandoned. Nevertheless, after having given up this heroic undertaking and turned toward the slow and laborious construction of an autonomous psychology, Freud never forgot that the mind was in fact in the body; furthermore, by making questions of sexuality central to his psychology he made it certain that his chances of ever transcending this overriding duality remained minimal. And indeed one can say that in no other psychology is the mind-body relation so inclusively and centrally a presence as in Freud's.

Freud's correspondent and interlocutor was admirably qualified to be the witness of such a complex journey of discovery. Wilhelm Fliess was also fascinated by the mind-body relation, and made its mysteries the center of all his researches and theories. With his hypotheses of nasal reflex neuroses and of the arithmetical periodicities that governed the course of all human—and even nonhuman—existence, Fliess was precisely the right kind of person on whom Freud could securely try out his new insights, theoretical flights, and systematic wild hunches. The careful reader of this volume can hardly escape the realization that for many of the years covered by these letters, Freud was something of a scientific wild man, a "conquistador or adventurer," as he described his own temperament. Great creative geniuses often are, and it was a necessity of Freud's nature that he needed a male companion to accompany him on his forays into the darker regions of mental existence. His friendship and professional alliance with Josef Breuer had come to an end on just these grounds; Breuer was unable to go along with Freud's embarrassing insistence upon the central importance of sexuality. Fliess took Breuer's place as Freud's confidante and alter ego. He was much younger than Breuer and two years younger than Freud. He was quite unembarrassed by considerations of sexuality; in fact he led Freud to place the notion of the bisexuality of all human beings close to the center of his theoretical system. Fliess was a scientific wild man as well; he was not, however, a genius, and his theories were not transmuted under the influence of new insight and experience, as Freud's were, and thereby made to conform more adequately to the differentially relative requirements of science, medicine, or psychology. Fliess' theories remained wild, were elaborated in ever more flamboyant displays of explanatory epicycles, and ended up as a kind of monomania. The occasion that provided the impetus for the final breakup of this most important friendship of Freud's life was, appropriately, a profound theoretical difference; Fliess insisted upon believing that the arithmetical and numerological laws of periodicity governed everything, including psychopathology. Such a belief was clearly incompatible with Freud's developing notions of psychic determinism—notions that asserted that whatever might *ultimately* be true about the physical laws that govern all phenomena, in our present state of knowledge mental existence has certain autonomous functions, and most mental activities can be traced no farther than to antecedent determinations that are themselves psychic. When Fliess remarked accusingly of Freud (and to him) that "the thought-reader [Freud] reads only his own thoughts in those of others," the time to break had come. It was an appropriate pretext to end a relationship that had been going downhill for some time. Freud parted company with Fliess when his friend was no longer able adequately to sustain the mind-body duality, and when

odd – Friendships, so many, Should break up over these!

he insisted upon depriving one side of that relation of its due importance and complexity.

Freud's friendship with Fliess was close, intense, richly personal as well as intellectual, and deeply intimate. Though the two men met at irregular intervals, at what Freud liked to call "congresses," the relationship was sustained in large measure through their correspondence. Of the two hundred and eighty-four letters written by Freud to Fliess that have survived, all but forty were written in the years 1893–1900, the period of highest intensity in their friendship. Looking back upon that friendship from the perspective that Freud's own discoveries have enabled us to achieve, we can perceive that it was in the main constituted out of transference-like characteristics. Freud overvalued and idealized the intelligence, originality, and powers of judgment of his friend. He consulted Fliess about his own health, and submitted to Fliess' medical advice as if his ear, nose, and throat friend in Berlin were Aesculapius himself. He kept his own critical faculties in abeyance as far as Fliess was concerned. He looked to him for approval, and he dreamed about him—some of the dreams are included in *The Interpretation of Dreams*. Naturally and unavoidably certain neurotic processes were involved in this relationship, and among the many things these letters permit us to observe are the points of connection between such processes and Freud's creativity during this period. They also allow us to observe the gradual disentanglement of the two. Freud's relation with Fliess was an essential and enabling part of that creativity. His resolution of that relation brings this major phase of his career to a close. With the publication in 1900 of *The Interpretation of Dreams*, Freud had reached a new plateau, an intellectual elevation from which he could regard large parts of the human world afresh.

The path he followed to reach that goal was not direct but circuitous, as these letters amply demonstrate. Freud was only gradually to be convinced of the primary independence of psychic reality. He began with materialist views and physicalist assumptions, and he was in no hurry to abandon them. The first stage in that evolution was represented by the "Project" of 1895—and by the fact that Freud gave it up. The second, and more dramatic, stage occurred in 1897. In working with his neurotic patients, Freud kept continually coming across accounts produced by them that pointed to certain sexual experiences in childhood, in particular among his female patients with accounts that pointed to experiences of seduction perpetrated upon them by their fathers. Freud took these accounts at face value, and proceeded thereupon to construct a theory of neuroses which had at its genetic center the actual experience of sexual seduction in childhood; at one of its dynamic centers was the idea that such patients were unable adequately to react to, or "abreact," the traumatic excitement of those experiences. This incapacity to somehow achieve a "discharge" of such highly stimulated states, even though such states remained behind as mental representations, such as memories and dreams, was itself based on a physical model, and indeed the same states in question converted themselves into the bodily symptoms of hysteria. In September 1897, Freud wrote to Fliess that he had to give up this theory that he had been building up for some years. The letter merits quoting at length:

> Let me tell you straight away the great secret. . . . I no longer believe in my *neurotica*. That is hardly intelligible without an explanation; you yourself found what I told you credible. So I shall start at the beginning and tell you the whole story of how the reasons for rejecting it arose. The first group of factors were the continual disappointment of my attempts to bring my analyses to a real conclusion, the running away of people who for a time had seemed my most favourably inclined patients, the lack of the complete success on which I had counted, and the possibility of explaining my partial successes in other familiar ways. Then there was the astonishing thing that in every case . . . blame was laid on perverse acts by the father, and realization of the unexpected frequency of hysteria, in every case of which the same thing applied, though it was hardly credible that perverted acts against children were so general. . . . Thirdly, there was the definite realization that there is no "indication of reality" in the unconscious, so that it is impossible to distinguish between truth and emotionally-charged fiction. (This leaves open the possible explanation that sexual phantasy regularly makes use of the theme of the parents.)

Freud's response to this reversal, to the overthrow of a theory on which he had placed such weight, is as remarkable as the reversal itself. "Were I depressed, jaded, unclear in my mind," he writes, "such doubts might be taken for signs of weakness. But as I am in just the opposite state, I must acknowledge them to be the result of honest and effective intellectual labor, and I am proud that after penetrating so far I am still capable of such criticism. Can these doubts be only an episode on the way to further knowledge?" And toward the end of the letter, he adds, "In the general collapse only the psychology has retained its value. . . . It is a pity one cannot live on dream-interpretation. . . ."

It is characteristic of Freud's personal and intellectual courage that he should have regarded such a defeat as a partial victory and that he should appear altogether undeterred by it. As the reader of these documents will soon perceive, the years 1893–1900 are the *anni mirabili* of Freud's life and career. During this period, living in relative isolation, Freud was literally a man possessed and driven. He had found, he wrote, what he needed in order to live—"a consuming passion—in Schiller's words a tyrant. I have found my tyrant, and in his service I know no limits. My tyrant is psychology; it has always been my distant, beckoning goal and now, since I have hit on the neuroses, it has come so much the nearer." The Freud of these years is possessed by a creative demon. He describes the demands he is making on his own mind as "superhuman," and speaks of psychology as "an incubus." When he writes to Fliess in December, 1895 that "we cannot do without men with the courage to think new things before they can prove them," he is describing himself. Ideas, insights, partial theories were coming to Freud faster than he could handle them, set them down, or reflect upon them. Several months after he had written the "Project" he could write to Fliess that "I no longer understand the state of mind in which I concocted the psychology." There is no reason to doubt the candor or truthfulness of this observation. For a large part of this period, Freud appears to have inhabited states of creative possession; his ambitions were of a magnitude that, fortunately for him, bore some plausible correspondence with the extent of his powers. On New Year's day, 1897, he writes: "Give me another ten years and I shall finish the neuroses and the new psychology. . . . When I am not afraid I can take on all the devils in hell. . . ." These documents are the firsthand record of how Freud took on those devils, most of which arose from the hell that was within himself as well as his patients. In May, 1897, he says: "No matter what I start with, I always find myself back again with the neuroses and the psychical apparatus. It is not because of indifference to personal or other matters that I never write about anything else. Inside me there is a seething ferment, and I am only waiting for the next surge forward." He speaks regularly of things "fermenting" in him and of the "turbulence of my thoughts and feelings." Like a great poet, he had during this period exceptional access to his own unconscious, and parts of the turbulence he refers to has to do with the heroic efforts he had to make to bring structure, organization, and meaning to this mysterious, dark, and threatening material. When he turns to the composition of *The Interpretation of Dreams,* he enters a state of creative transport and withdrawal. Having worked over a draft of one section, he writes to Fliess, "it is nearly finished, was written as if in a dream, and certainly not in a form fit for publication." Three weeks later, having finished work upon another section of the book, he sent it to Fliess with the following comments:

> It was all written by the unconscious, on the principle of Itzig, the Sunday horseman. "Itzig, where are you going?" "Don't ask me, ask the horse!" At the beginning of a paragraph I never knew where I should end up. It was not written to be read, of course—any attempt at style was abandoned after the first two pages. In spite of all that I of course believe in the results. I have not the slightest idea yet what form the contents will finally take.

And Freud's son, Ernst, later recalled how during this period his father used to come into meals, from the place where he had been writing, "as if he were sleepwalking." Freud's own comments on this material—almost certainly the great seventh chapter, "On the Psychology of the Dream-Processes"—including his slightly benumbed incomprehension, suggest something of the depths at which he had been seized. Even after *The Interpretation of Dreams* had been finished and published, he still could write: "The big problems are still unsettled. It is an intellectual hell, layer upon layer of it, with everything fitfully gleaming and pulsating; and the outline of Lucifer-Amor coming into sight at the darkest centre." If we are led in the context created by such allusions to think of Dante, Milton, Goethe, and Blake, we are not bringing in material that is irrelevant.

The creative discoveries of Freud during these years were simply of the highest order.

Those discoveries were legion. There is scarcely a notion that Freud was to elaborate upon in the course of his long subsequent career that is not touched upon, hinted at, presented in abbreviated, elliptical or nuclear form in these letters and drafts. The writing itself is on occasion obscure and even incomprehensible, for Freud is moving about in darkness. Nevertheless, the main features of the mental terrain that he is exploring gradually come into focus and clarity. With a sure sense of intellectual priorities we see Freud fairly deliberately concentrated his attention upon areas of major discovery: first, the meaning of dreams and the construction of a psychology of unconscious mental functioning; second, the occurrence and development of infantile and childhood sexuality; and third, the central place in that development occupied by the Oedipal experience. The major vehicle through which these discoveries were made was also an unprecedented occurrence. I am referring of course to Freud's self-analysis, a process in which, as I have already suggested, the classical instruction to know thyself was brought into historical and momentous conjunction with *Oedipus Rex*. That this process also fulfilled in part the quizzical injunction, "Physician, heal thyself," is only one further demonstration of the centrality of Freud's discoveries to the history and traditions of Western civilization. It also serves to remind us that the Freud who appears at the end of this correspondence is not entirely the same man who wrote the bulk of it. He is still to be sure a great genius and is on his way to becoming a great man, but he is not the wildly driven, creatively tormented, fitfully inspired and demonic creature of the largest part of this book. Although Freud is a central figure in the European tradition of Romanticism, and one of its last important legatees, there is a classical side to his achievements and character as well. This side comes into view when we observe that the making of this genius coincided with the maturing of it. He was not afraid that the rational understanding of his own nature would undo the creative energies that had sustained him. And he was equally unafraid that the achievement of personal integration was incompatible with the continuation of a creative and useful life.

The expression "Physician, heal thyself" occurs within and is part of the dominant religious tradition of our civilization. Freud belongs to that group of writers and thinkers who during the last two hundred years have undertaken the major task of transforming that tradition by secularising it. Freud himself was not religious in either temperament or sympathy. Nevertheless, like the other great modern figures he retained one belief, albeit in secular form, that belongs to that tradition. This is the belief in *meaning*. In the instance of Freud it was a belief that all human thought and behavior had a meaning and meanings—that they were understandable, purposeful, had structure, and rose to significance. For example, in 1897 he writes: "Perverted actions are always alike, always have a meaning, and are based on a pattern which can be understood." And in the same year, he also states: "Phantasies arise from an unconscious combination of things experienced and heard, constructed for particular purposes. These purposes aim at making inaccessible the memory from which symptoms have been generated." Discussing the distortions that are built into phantasies that masquerade as memories, he remarks: "I am learning the rules which govern the formation of these structures, and reasons why they are stronger than real memories." And he follows his discovery of "love of the mother and jealousy of the father," with the following observations. "If that is the case, the gripping power of *Oedipus Rex*, in spite of all the rational objections to the inexorable fate that the story presupposes, becomes intelligible, and one can understand why later fate dramas were such failures. Our feelings rise against any arbitrary, individual fate . . . but the Greek myth seizes on a compulsion which everyone recognizes because he has felt traces of it in himself. Every member of the audience was once a budding Oedipus in phantasy, and this dream-fulfillment played out in reality causes everyone to recoil in horror, with the full measure of repression which separates his infantile from his present state." This deep belief in the meaningfulness of human experience and the equally deep belief in the power of the human mind to effect coherent explanations of that experience acted as general motives in the work of Freud. Without divine sanction and without a theodicy, the story of each human life could yet be rendered into some measure of intelligibility.

There might even be moments of surpassing clarity. Such a moment occurred on January 16, 1898, when Freud wrote: "Happiness is the deferred' fulfillment of a prehistoric wish. That is why wealth brings so little happiness; money is not an infantile wish." If there is such a thing as secular wisdom, such a statement, it seems to me, approximates the form it is likely to take. The paths by which such knowledge was attained are imperishably recorded in this volume.

EDITORS' NOTE

This book consists of a selection of letters from Sigmund Freud to Wilhelm Fliess, a Berlin physician and biologist, written between the years 1887 and 1902. The letters, with other documents left by Fliess, came into the hands of a second-hand dealer during the Nazi period in Germany and thus into the editors' possession.[1] Fliess's letters to Freud have not been found.

The preliminary work of preparing the German edition for the press was done by Marie Bonaparte. The work of detailed selection was undertaken by Anna Freud and Ernst Kris. Ernst Kris is responsible for the Introduction and notes.[2]

The correspondence consists in all of 284 items—postcards, picture postcards, letters, notes, drafts. The selection was made on the principle of making public everything relating to the writer's scientific work and scientific interests and everything bearing on the social and political conditions in which psycho-analysis originated; and of omitting or abbreviating everything publication of which would be inconsistent with professional or personal confidence.

Similarly all letters and passages in letters have been omitted which are mere repetitions, or refer to the two correspondents' frequent appointments to meet or to their intended or actual meetings; as well as a good many passages relating to purely family matters or events in their circle of friends. The table on the next page shows the proportion of published to unpublished material.

This volume contains nothing sensational, and is principally intended for the reader and serious student of Freud's published works. In the Introduction and notes an attempt is made to facilitate

---

[1] Draft I in the present volume is the property of Dr. Robert Fliess, into whose possession it came after his father's death. He took it with him as a souvenir when he emigrated from Berlin to New York several years before the Fliess household was broken up.

[2] Translators' notes are enclosed in square brackets [. . .]

understanding of the letters and drafts and to establish their connection with Freud's contemporary and subsequent works. In the English edition references to recent publications have been added, and the editors express their gratitude to James Strachey and A. Winterstein for a number of suggestions and corrections which have been adopted.

The published letters are numbered in order of date, and the notes and drafts are designated by letters of the alphabet. The letters are nearly all dated by the author, or alternatively the date is established by the postmark. In the few cases where drafts or notes are undated they have been inserted by the editors in what appears to be the correct chronological order by reason of their contents. Omissions have been indicated by dots.

The author of the material in this volume would not have consented to the publication of any of it. It was Freud's habit to destroy all notes and preliminary drafts as soon as they had served their purpose, to publish nothing incomplete or unfinished, and to publish material of a personal nature only when it was essential for the purpose of demonstrating unconscious connections. These letters were brought to light by chance, and the editors feel justified in publishing them in spite of the hesitation which respect for the author's attitude in the matter inevitably imposes. They amplify the prehistory and early history of psycho-analysis in a way that no other available material does, provide insight into certain phases of Freud's intellectual processes from his first clinical impressions until the formulation of his theory, throw light on the blind alleys and wrong roads into which he was diverted in the process of hypothesis-building, and furnish a vivid picture of him during the difficult years during which his interest shifted from physiology and neurology to psychology and psychopathology.

Since the publication of the German original of this volume (London, Imago Publishing Co. 1950), certain readers seem to have gained the impression that the "secrets" of Freud's personal life have now become accessible. In view of this we should like to make it clear that the material here published supplements to some extent data on Freud's life and experiences familiar from *The Interpretation of Dreams* and other works of his; but neither the letters to Fliess nor what Freud felt compelled to record about himself in his published works reveal more than certain aspects of his interests and preoccupations at the time.

MARIE BONAPARTE	ANNA FREUD	ERNST KRIS
Paris	London	New York

TRANSLATORS' NOTE

Though the translators are jointly responsible for this volume as a whole, the translation of the bulk of the letters is the work of Eric Mosbacher, while James Strachey is mainly responsible for the "Project" at the end of the book, the "Drafts" and the more technical passages in the correspondence. They have had the advantage of being able, through the kindness of Miss Anna Freud, to consult the original MSS. where difficulties or obscurities have arisen.

J.S.
E.M.

NUMERICAL TABLE

Year		Total number of letters, etc.		Letters, etc., here published.
1887	...	2	...	2
1888	...	3	...	3
1889	...	—	...	—
1890	...	2	...	2
1891	...	4	...	2
1892	...	7	...	4
1893	...	15	...	6
1894	...	18	...	9
1895	...	37	...	21
1896	...	29	...	15
1897	...	39	...	29
1898	...	35	...	21
1899	...	44	...	26
1900	...	27	...	14
1901	...	17	...	11
1902	...	5	...	3
		284		168

THE ORIGINS OF

PSYCHO-ANALYSIS

INTRODUCTION

BY ERNST KRIS

I

WILHELM FLIESS'S SCIENTIFIC INTERESTS

Freud's letters to Fliess give us a picture of him during the years in which he applied himself—tentatively at first—to a new field of study, psychopathology, and acquired the insight on which psychoanalysis, both as a theory and a therapy, is based. They enable us to see him grappling with "a problem that had never previously been stated",[1] and struggling with an environment whose rejection of his work endangered his livelihood and that of his family; and to follow him along part of the road during his effort to deepen his newly-acquired insight against the resistance of his own unconscious impulses.

The letters cover the period from 1887 to 1902, from Freud's thirty-first to forty-sixth year, from when he had just set up in practice as a specialist in nervous and mental diseases until he was engaged in his preliminary studies for *Three Essays on the Theory of Sexuality*. To the years of this correspondence there belong, besides his first essays on the neuroses, the *Studies on Hysteria* (1895d), *The Interpretation of Dreams* (1900a), *The Psychopathology of Everyday Life* (1901b), and *Fragment of an Analysis of a Case of Hysteria* (1905e).

Reading these letters is rather like listening to someone speaking on the telephone: you can hear only what one party to the conversation is saying; the rest you have to guess. As in this case the listener is interested only in what is being said by the party whom he can

---

[1] The phrase is from *Studies on Hysteria*.

hear, he may at first be inclined to dismiss from his mind the speaker at the other end of the line. But very soon he finds he cannot follow satisfactorily unless every now and then he reconstructs the dialogue as a whole.

Freud's friendship with Wilhelm Fliess (1858-1928) was, so far as we know, the closest of his life-time, and it was so closely bound up, both as a helping and a hindering element, with the development of his theories in the nineties that it seems desirable to start with a brief outline of Fliess's scientific interests. If Fliess's letters to Freud were available, we should be in a position, not only properly to follow the exchange of ideas between the two men, but to obtain a reliable impression of Fliess's personality. As it is we have had to fall back on the little that we have been able to gather from Fliess's writings and from questioning those who knew him. All who knew him emphasize his wealth of biological knowledge, his imaginative grasp of medicine, his fondness for far-reaching speculation and his impressive personal appearance; they also emphasize his tendency to cling dogmatically to a once-formed opinion. These character-istics are partially perceptible in his published works.

Fliess was trained as a nose and throat specialist, but his medical knowledge and scientific interests extended over an area far wider than this comparatively restricted field. He was a consultant with a big practice in Berlin, which he continued to the end of his life, but otolaryngological therapy was merely the hub of his wide medical and scientific interests, which took him outside the field of medicine into that of general biology. The first of his more important published works, which he decided to write at Freud's suggestion (see Letter 10), was concerned with a clinical syn-drome.

Fliess's interest was early roused by the fact that he found he was able to clear up a number of symptoms by the administration of cocaine to the nasal mucous membrane. On the basis of this discovery he convinced himself that he was confronted with a clinical entity, a reflex neurosis proceeding from the nose.[1] This, in Fliess's words, was to be regarded as "a complex of varying

---

[1] See Fliess (1892) and (1893).

symptoms, as we find to be the case in Menière's complex."[1] Fliess distinguished symptoms of three different types: head pains; neuralgic pains (in the arm, at the points of the shoulder-blades or between them, in the area of the ribs or the heart, the xiphoid process, the stomach, the spleen, the small of the back in the area of the kidneys; but "gastric neuralgias" in particular); and finally disturbed functioning, particularly of the digestive organs, the heart and the respiratory system. "The number of symptoms adduced is great," Fliess says, "and yet they owe their existence to one and the same locality—the nose. For their homogeneity is demonstrated, not only by their simultaneous appearance, but by their simultaneous disappearance. The characteristic of this whole complex of complaints is that one can bring them temporarily to an end by anaesthetizing with cocaine the responsible area in the nose."[2]

Fliess maintained that the aetiology of the nasal reflex neurosis was a double one. It could arise from organic alterations, for example "the after-effects upon the nose of infectious diseases", or it could be the result of functional, purely vasomotor disturbances. It was the latter that explained why "neurasthenic complaints, in other words the neuroses with a sexual aetiology, so frequently assume the form of the nasal reflex neurosis."[3] Fliess

---

[1] This comparison was suggested by Freud. See Draft C.

[2] It is significant, though it is not mentioned in the correspondence, that Fliess indirectly owed his diagnostic criterium, the administration of cocaine to the nasal mucous membrane, to Freud, who had early drawn attention to the importance of the coca plant; Freud's investigations were continued by the oculist Koller. (See page 30, footnote 2, and *An Autobiographical Study*, 1925d.) See also the paper by Bernfeld (1953) on the subject.

[3] The value of Fliess's clinical writings is still disputed. German clinical literature contains a number of discussions of his work on nasal troubles. These are more or less summarized by G. Hoffer, who says in connection with the nasal asthmas that Fliess paid insufficient attention in his monographs on the nasal reflex neurosis to the work of others in the same field. The result was that at first "a number of enthusiastic followers . . . were opposed by a small circle of sceptics, which quickly grew, however". In Hoffer's opinion there existed "no justification whatsoever for attributing any special priority to nasal complaints as compared with nervous irritations in any other area of the body". ("Die Krankheiten der Luftwege und der Mundhöhle" in Denker and Kahler, Part III, page 263 *sqq.*) Other contributors to Denker and Kahler adopt a similar attitude, though several confirm the appearance of the syndrome described by Fliess and express a favourable opinion of the effectiveness of his therapeutic proposals.

In American m.dical literature Fliess's work was, so far as we are aware,

explained this frequency by assuming a special connection between the nose and the genital apparatus. He recalled the phenomenon of vicarious nose bleeding in place of menstruation, recalled that "the swelling of the turbinate bone during menstruation is to be observed with the naked eye," and reported cases in which the administration of cocaine to the nose led to miscarriage. He maintained that a special connection between the nasal and genital areas existed in men also. In his later works he developed this alleged connection further, basing it at first on purely clinical evidence.

From the clinical observation that "certain parts of the nose played an important part in the origin of two complaints (gastric neuralgia and dysmenorrhoea)" he concluded that "hyperplastic exogenous alterations in the nose" led to "lasting cure of the secondary phenomena when the nasal disturbance was removed," and that "vasomotor endogenous alterations in the nose" arose "essentially from the sexual organs".[1] Fliess was concerned with the problems of human sexual life in general, and Freud, at a time when he was only imperfectly informed about the work that Fliess was doing and projecting, was able to assume that he had solved "the problem of conception", *i.e.*, the problem of at what period likelihood of conception was smallest. Fliess's interests, however, were directed elsewhere.

In the spring of 1896 he sent to Freud his manuscript on "the relations between the nose and the female sex organs from the biological aspect", which was published at the beginning of the following year.[2] In it Fliess elaborates in several respects the theory that he had put forward in his previous work, namely that of a connection between the nose and the female genitals. He states that alterations in the nose are regularly to be observed during menstruation, and he discusses the diagnostic and therapeutic value of administering cocaine to the nose. He claims that this is considerable, because menstruation is "the prototype of numerous phenomena in sexual

---

not mentioned. *Cf.* the discussion of the nasal neuroses by R. A. Fenton in Jackson (1945); and in Sluder (1927). For more recent references to his work and its contributions to the field which today is covered by the term "psychosomatic medicine" see Holmes *et al.* (1951).

[1] Fliess (1895).
[2] Fliess (1897).

life . . . childbed and the act of birth more particularly being both in time and in their essential nature nothing but a transmutation of the menstrual process". "The real pains of delivery" and "nasal dysmenorrhoea, regarded morphologically", are "homologues".

These "facts", which Fliess sought to establish by numerous observations, led him to far-reaching hypotheses about the role of periods in human life. In his introduction he expresses his ideas more pointedly than in the often clumsy language of the monograph:

"Woman's menstrual bleeding", he says, is the expression "of a process which affects both sexes and the beginning of which goes back beyond puberty. . . .

"The facts before us compel us to emphasize another factor. They teach us that, apart from the menstrual process of the twenty-eight day type, yet another group of periodic phenomena exists with a twenty-three day cycle, to which people of all ages and both sexes are subject.

"Consideration of these two groups of periodic phenomena points to the conclusion that they have a solid inner connection with both male and female sexual characteristics. And if both—only with different emphasis—are present both in man and woman, that is only consistent with our bisexual constitution.

"Recognition of these things led to the further insight that the development of our organism takes place by fits and starts in these sexual periods, and that the day of our death is determined by them as much as is the day of our birth. The disturbances of illness are subject to the same periodic laws as are these periodic phenomena themselves.

"A mother transmits her periods to her child and determines its sex by the period which is first transmitted. The periods then continue in the child, and are repeated with the same rhythm from generation to generation. They can no more be created anew than can energy, and their rhythm survives as long as organised beings reproduce themselves sexually. These rhythms are not restricted to mankind, but extend into the animal world and probably throughout the organic world. The wonderful accuracy with which the period of twenty-three, or, as the case may be, twenty-eight whole days is observed permits one to suspect a deeper connection between astronomical relations and the creation of organisms."

These are the broad principles of Fliess's period theory, which he continued to develop for many years, notably in his principal work *Der Ablauf des Lebens* ("The Course of Life"), of which the first edition appeared in 1906 and the second in 1923.[1] He supplemented the first statement of his theory in 1897 with a number of other monographs devoted to the subject of bisexuality, but he laid the chief emphasis on working out the mathematical "proofs" of his theory with an obstinacy and lack of objectivity which ignored all inconsistencies and inconvenient facts.

Some of Fliess's clinical findings have been adopted into modern gynaecology and otolaryngology, but his period theory, which roused critical interest at the time of publication, has been almost unanimously rejected by modern biologists; in particular, his period calculations, which were based on false inferences, have long since been recognised as fallacious.[2]

At the time of his meeting with Freud none of Fliess's works had appeared, but a capacity for bold thinking must already have characterized him. In the autumn of 1887 he paid a visit to Vienna for purposes of professional study, and Breuer advised him to attend Freud's lectures on neurology. He took the opportunity of discussing with Freud the new views which the latter was forming on the anatomy and functioning of the central nervous system. The projects which they discussed were only partially completed and published. The correspondence that followed began as that of two specialists who passed patients on to each other; and from 1893 onwards it became a regular exchange of ideas between two friends drawn together by common scientific interests, who continually

---

[1] See also his later, shorter and to an extent more popular works. (Fliess, 1924a, b and c.)

[2] A detailed criticism of the mathematical assumptions in Fliess's period theory was made by J. Aelby, a physician (Aelby, 1928). Fliess's researches were continued on a sounder basis by the gynaecologist Georg Riebold, whose writings on the subject from 1908 onwards were collected into a single volume (Riebold, 1942). In Riebold's view "some truth lurks" in Fliess's fundamental idea "that life follows a periodic rhythm . . . and the periods of twenty-three and twenty-eight days that he discovered are of frequent occurrence, but the claim made by Fliess, who in his vanity puts himself on a par with Kepler" is rejected as belonging to the realm of the psychopathological. The efforts of Riebold, Fliess and others to establish a relation between menstruation and other periodic

looked forward to but never attained their aim of jointly publishing their scientific work. The progress of their friendship was facilitated by the circumstance that in 1892 Fliess married a Viennese girl who belonged to the circle of Breuer's patients; the result of this was that in the early years the two men met frequently. Soon, however, they started arranging meetings outside the circle of their family and friends in Vienna, at which they exchanged their scientific ideas and findings. Freud called these meetings "congresses". Many of his letters fill in the gaps between the "congresses" and are full of references to what had passed between the two men in conversation.[1]

In the first years of their friendship they had a great deal in common. Both were the sons of Jewish middle-class business men, specialists devoted to scientific research, concerned with setting up a family and establishing a practice. In 1886, the year before he met Fliess, Freud, who was the older by two years, had married and opened a consulting room at 8 Maria Theresienstrasse. During the years covered by the correspondence we see Freud's family increase from one to six; we hear of the removal to the flat at 19 Berggasse, which Freud was to leave forty-seven years later, after the Nazi occupation of Austria, to emigrate to England. We hear of Fliess's marriage to a Fräulein Ida Bondy, of Vienna, of the birth of their three children, and of the life of the two families in so far as this is reflected in the correspondence of two friends.

The resemblance of their outer circumstances was supplemented by the resemblance in the two men's intellectual background. Their

---

phenomena have been critically examined by Knaus (Knaus, 1938, p. 47): "With the advance of our knowledge of the functional connection between the glands related to the uterus and the organ of menstruation there disappears . . . belief in any deep cosmic connection between menstruation and its periodicity, and therewith the scientific repute of Riebold's period laws". Outside Germany no attention has been paid to Fliess's biological theories.

Apart from Aelby and Riebold, several otolaryngologists have observed a mystical tendency in Fliess's clinical writings. "To obtain a picture of the mental attitude underlying the whole, one should not confine oneself only to Fliess's rhinological writings, but also take into account his other works, which contain a number mystique which could quite well have been a product of the end of the Middle Ages." (F. Blumenfeld's article on "Die Krankheiten der Luftwege" in Denker and Kahler, Part II, page 51.)

[1] The result is that numerous passages and remarks, of which only a few are here reproduced, remain unintelligible in spite of all efforts.

scientific interests rested on a firm foundation of the humanities.
They shared an admiration for the masterpieces of world literature,
and exchanged quotations which fitted in with their trend of thought.
Freud referred continually to Shakespeare as well as to Kipling and
other contemporary English writers,[1] and owed to Fliess a closer
acquaintance with the works of the Swiss writer Conrad Ferdinand
Meyer, who remained a permanent favourite of his.

The things they mentioned betrayed the two men's predominant
interests. Among Freud's books is a two-volume edition of Helmholtz's lectures, which Fliess sent him as a Christmas present in
1898. Freud, who followed medical literature closely in the nineties,
kept sending hurried postcards[2] to his friend in Berlin drawing his
attention to articles on otolaryngolical matters which Fliess might
have missed in the German, French and English medical press. He
also mentions his study of the works of contemporary psychologists,
his growing interest in prehistoric and archaeological studies of the
first modest beginnings of Greek and Roman civilization, which
was a substitute for his long-desired and long-postponed journey to
Italy in a Goethean mood. Among the few contemporary events
to which Freud drew particular attention was Sir Arthur Evans's
discoveries in Crete; he mentions the first newspaper report of this
event, which led to the reconstruction of an unknown civilization
from the rubble of the past.

There was a sharper contrast in the physical environment in
which the two men lived. The contrast between the tired, cramped
Vienna of Franz Josef and the lively, go-ahead Berlin of Wilhelm
II is often vividly reflected in Freud's letters. The contrast extended
into the economic sphere. In Vienna medical practice, "right to the
very top of the tree", was severely affected by every economic
recession, every one of which, in addition to the effects of the ups-
and-downs in Freud's reputation with his colleagues and the public,
was reflected in his household's welfare. Fliess's letters betray no
such anxieties. His practice seems to have grown rapidly and unin-
terruptedly. In any case, after his marriage he was exempt from
financial worries.

---

[1] In postcards or letters not reproduced here.
[2] Not reproduced here.

The contrast between Vienna and Berlin extended into the political field. Freud reports the defeat of the Liberals in Vienna, the victory of the anti-Semites, who took over the city administration, and the anti-Semitic tendencies in the Vienna Medical Society, the medical faculty and the academic administration which for a long time withheld from him the title of professor. Freud had every right to expect that the title of professor would act as a stimulus to his practice, as the Viennese public at that time awarded its confidence to specialists according to their academic status.[1] The two friends followed the news of the Dreyfus trial and Zola's "battle for justice" with understandable interest; in this connection Fliess seems to have extolled the progressive spirit prevalent in Berlin and Germany.

However, the true motive of the correspondence was not provided by the similarity in the two men's origin, intellectual background and family situation or, indeed, by anything personal. Even in the years of their closest friendship the relations between the two families were never close, and plans for them to meet in the summer holidays never came to anything. All Freud's letters that have come down to us go to show that the true motive behind the correspondence was the two men's common scientific interests.

We may connect the increasing frequency with which they exchanged ideas,[2] and the increasing confidence and friendship reflected in the change from the use of the formal *Sie* to the familiar *Du*, with a significant change in Freud's personal and scientific relationships—his estrangement from Josef Breuer (1842-1925).[3] Freud had been in close contact with this important personality ever since his student days. Breuer, who was Freud's senior by thirteen years, had described the cathartic treatment of a patient to

---

[1] Appointments of this kind were connected with neither duties nor privileges. The designation *Privatdozent mit dem Titel eines ausserordentlichen Professors* corresponds approximately to that of associate clinical professor in American medical schools.

[2] See page xi.

[3] Freud frequently described his relations with Breuer and thus "certainly did not under-estimate the debt of psycho-analysis" to him. See *On the History of the Psycho-Analytic Movement* (1914d), the obituary of Josef Breuer (1925g), and *An Autobiographical Study* (1925d).

him[1] as early as the beginning of the eighties, and ten years later the two men agreed to write a book on hysteria together.

Differences of opinion which led to their eventual estrangement soon arose, however. Freud's thought advanced by leaps and bounds, and the older and more timid Breuer could not reconcile himself to the position of a follower. In a letter to Fliess (No. 11) Freud reports conflicts with Breuer in connection with their first jointly written paper;[2] and during their work on their joint book, *Studies on Hysteria*, which appeared in 1895, the difficulty of co-operation constantly increased. When the book finally appeared the two authors specifically drew attention in the introduction to the divergence of their views.

Breuer willingly followed Freud in his early assumptions; he took over from him the conceptions of defence and conversion, though he clung to the French psychiatric assumption that a special condition, designated as hypnoid, was responsible for the origin of hysterical phenomena. Freud's fundamental assumption about the functioning of the psychical apparatus, which he formulated as the principle of constancy of psychical energy (pp. 21 and 135), was also accepted by Breuer and elaborated by him. Differences seem to have arisen when Freud's clinical experiences and first theoretical reflections pointed towards the importance of sexuality in the aetiology of the neuroses.[3] At the time of the appearance of *Studies on Hysteria* it was still just possible in public to bridge over the gulf between the two men. If the restraint with which the problem of sexuality is dealt with in *Studies on Hysteria* is compared with what Freud says in a paper on the anxiety neurosis published before the book appeared,[4] and if one takes into consideration the wealth of insight which Freud, as these letters testify, had already obtained, one will have some idea of the difficulties he must have had to contend with. His older friend and mentor, who years before had

---

[1] The case of Anna O. in *Studies on Hysteria*.

[2] "Vorläufige Mitteilung über den psychischen Mechanismus hysterischer Phänomene." It was later reprinted as the introductory chapter of *Studies on Hysteria*.

[3] *Cf.* Freud's account in *On the History of the Psycho-Analytic Movement* (1914d).

[4] "On the Grounds for Detaching a Particular Syndrome from Neurasthenia under the Description 'Anxiety Neurosis'" (Freud 1895b).

introduced him to the problem of hysteria, now refused him his encouragement and support.

No support was to be expected from the official representatives of psychiatry and neurology at the university. Meynert, Freud's former teacher, had already rejected his first essays on hysteria, and Krafft-Ebing regarded him with indifference and reserve. His immediate circle of medical friends was entirely under Breuer's influence. But what Freud found burdensome seems to have been, not so much Breuer's rejection of his discoveries, as his oscillation between criticism and admiration. (See, for example, Letters 24, 35, 135.)[1]

Freud's friendship with Fliess filled the gap left by his estrangement from Breuer and provided a substitute for a friendship and intellectual relationship that had ceased to be viable.[2] He had lost confidence that he would be understood in his own immediate circle, and his Berlin colleague became, in Freud's own words, his only audience.

In the early years of their correspondence Freud kept Fliess informed of his work in progress and sent him copies of everything he wrote. Fliess soon became the confidant to whom he communicated clinical material, his latest findings, and the first formulations of new theories. Thus we find among Freud's letters, not only half-thought-out outlines of new ideas and plans for future research, but some finished essays that were scarcely to be surpassed in his later works. The result was that Freud subsequently asked for a number of drafts sent to Fliess to be returned to him to be used for purposes of publication. Also some of the phases in the development of Freud's theories, and some of the detours he made before arriving at them, are ascertainable only through the material published here.

We do not know what was the effect of all this on the mind of the recipient. We can conclude from Freud's letters that he occasionally

---

[1] A passage in an accidentally preserved letter from Breuer to Fliess, dating from the summer of 1895, several months after the appearance of *Studies on Hysteria*, says: "Freud's intellect is soaring; I struggle along behind him like a hen behind a hawk."

[2] F. Wittels concluded correctly, in our opinion, from the dreams reported by Freud in *The Interpretation of Dreams* that Fliess's role was to replace his lost friend. Wittels also found an ambivalent attitude to Fliess in Freud's dreams— a conclusion which Freud drew himself (Letter 119). (Wittels, 1924, pp. 88 *sqq.*)

expressed doubts or remonstrances, but frequently approved and agreed. The material became richer in content only when differences of opinion became pronounced and Fliess insisted more and more emphatically that his own period theory must be regarded as the basis of Freud's theory of the neuroses.

The letters give us plenty of information about Freud's attitude to Fliess's work. At least for the first ten years he followed it with extreme interest and was full of admiration for it. It is significant that his enthusiasm for Fliess's work was always greater immediately after he had met him, or after Fliess had written to him about it; in his comments on the scientific papers that Fliess sent him he is noticeably restrained.

This circumstance lends support to the suspicion that his over-rating of Fliess's personality and scientific importance corresponded to an inner need of his own. He made of his friend and confidant an ally in his struggle with official medical science, the science of the high-and-mighty professors and university clinics, though Fliess's contemporary writings show that such a role was remote from his thoughts. Freud, to bind his friend closer to him, tried to elevate him to his own level, and sometimes idealized his picture of his assumed ally into that of a leader in the world of science.

No doubt the over-estimation of Fliess reflected in these letters had an objective as well as a personal basis. Freud not only needed Fliess as an audience and an ally, but looked to his association with him to provide answers to questions with which he had been occupied for years—questions about the border-line between the physiological and psychological approaches to the phenomena which he was studying.

II

PSYCHOLOGY AND PHYSIOLOGY

"I was not always a psychotherapist, but was trained in local and electrical diagnosis like other neuropathologists, and I still find it a very strange thing that the case histories I describe read like short stories and lack, so to speak, the serious imprint of science. I must console myself with the thought that it is obviously the nature of the material itself that is responsible for this rather than my own choice. In the study of hysteria local diagnosis and electrical reactions do not come into the picture, while an exhaustive account of mental processes, of the kind we are accustomed to having from imaginative writers, enables me, by the application of a few psychological formulas, to obtain a kind of insight into the origin of a hysteria."

These are the words with which Freud introduces his discussion of the case history of Elisabeth von R., apparently the last that he contributed to *Studies on Hysteria.* They point to an intellectual conflict which had a decisive influence on his ideas in the nineties. A new and unprecedented vista was opening out before him—that of stating in scientific terms the conflicts of the human psyche. It would have been tempting to base his excursion into this territory on intuitive understanding, to trace all case histories to their biographical roots, and to base all the insight gained on intuition "of the kind we are accustomed to having from imaginative writers". The sureness of the literary touch with which he handled biographical material, which he fully demonstrated for the first time in *Studies on Hysteria,* must have been a great temptation. We know from the letters that he had already acquired the ability to subject works of literature to psychological analysis; his analysis of two stories by C. F. Meyer are the first attempts of this nature.[1] We know from later years what his attitude was to the artist's intuition, to the creations of those to whom "it is vouchsafed with hardly an effort to salve from the whirlpool of their own emotions the deepest truths, to which we others have to force our way ceaselessly groping amid torturing uncertainties".[2] The conflict of which he speaks in this passage—he was already concerned with it at the time of *Studies on Hysteria*—is that between intuitive understanding and scientific explanation. There was never any doubt on which side Freud stood. He had been through the school of science, and it became his life work to base the new psychology on scientific methods.

---

[1] Letters 90 and 91.
[2] *Civilization and its Discontents* (1930a).

Let us now briefly recall what is known about Freud's professional training. The sources are his *Autobiographical Study* and other works.[1] In 1882, while still a student in the physiological institute of Vienna university, he abandoned biology for medicine after six years' study; he did this unwillingly and on the explicit advice of his teacher, the physiologist Ernst Brücke [1819-1892], yielding only to practical considerations.[2] In choosing his speciality he continued the direction of his biological work, which had set out from a study of the roots of the nerves and spinal ganglia of the petromyzon.[3] At the suggestion of Theodor Meynert [1832-1892] he devoted himself to neurology and, prompted by a developing "tendency to exclusive concentration", he wrote six monographs in the field of histology, pharmacology and medicine[4] which gained him a lecturership in neuropathology in the spring of 1885, when he was twenty-nine.

A travelling fellowship, for which he was recommended by Brücke, enabled him to go to Paris and study at Charcot's Salpêtrière. He stayed in Paris from the autumn of 1885 to the end of February, 1886.[5] From Paris he went to Berlin "in order to gain a little knowledge of the general disorders of childhood" from Adolph Baginsky, for he could not look forward to a position in the psychiatric-neurological clinic in Vienna, entry to which was barred to him then, as later. Instead the children's specialist Max Kassowitz offered him a post as head of the new neurological department of "the first public hospital for children", a private and unofficial institution from the point of view of the official academic world. Freud worked there for several years.[6]

---

[1] See Bernfeld, 1949 and 1951.
[2] In a letter to a friend (Wilhelm Knöpfmacher) dated August 6th, 1878, Freud said: "During this vacation I went over to another laboratory, where I am preparing for my true calling . . . flaying animals or torturing human beings . . . and I more and more favour the former alternative".
[3] Freud 1877a and 1878a.
[4] Freud. 1884,a, d, e; 1885 a, c, d.
[5] According to a remark of Freud's in a footnote to his German translation (1886f) of Volume III of Charcot's *Lecons sur les maladies du système nerveux* (1887).
[6] This institution, founded in the reign of the Emperor Josef II in 1787, was not modernized till the eighties of last century. Freud's work there occupied him for several hours three times a week. See Kassowitz (1890), Vol. I, introduction.

The letters permit us fleeting glimpses into the period that followed his return to Vienna, his marriage, and his setting up in practice. His interests lay in several fields. In his published papers his predominant interest was at first neurology, and his earliest papers represent a direct continuation of his old interests in the clinical, histological, pharmacological and anatomical fields.[1]

But he soon took up the challenge of the new clinical material he found at his disposal. A study of hemianopia in earliest childhood[2] was the first of a series of works in the field of child neurology. It was followed by a monograph, written jointly with Rie, on unilateral cerebral paralysis in children,[3] and two years later his monograph on the cerebral diplegias[4] appeared; his study of this subject led several years later to the reluctant fulfilment of a long-standing promise to deal exhaustively with cerebral paralysis in children for Nothnagel's handbook of special pathology and therapy.[5] The letters show that this work made Freud feel "like Pegasus yoked to the plough". This is understandable enough when we consider that he had to sacrifice to it his work on the problem of dreams.

However, this labour, which to Freud represented merely the fulfilment of a burdensome and oppressive obligation, still occupies, according to the testimony of R. Brun,[6] a secure place in modern neurology. Freud's monograph, Brun writes, is "the most complete and thorough study of the cerebral paralysis of children that has yet appeared. . . . When one considers that the index alone fills fourteen-and-a-half pages, it will give one an idea of the consummate mastery of the enormous mass of clinical material that is here collected and critically surveyed".

Between 1886 and the winter of 1892–93 there also appeared, almost incidentally, the translations of four large volumes—two volumes of Charcot's lectures and two books of Bernheim.[7] He

---

[1] Freud 1886a, b, c, and 1887d.
[2] Freud 1888a.
[3] Freud and Rie, 1891a.
[4] Freud 1893b.
[5] Freud 1897a.
[6] Brun, 1936.
[7] Charcot 1887 and 1892-3a. Bernheim 1886 and 1890.
These were not Freud's only translations. In his student days he translated a volume of J. S. Mill (see page 343, footnote 2). In later life, in 1922, he

provided two of these volumes with notable introductions, and in addition he provided his translation of Charcot's *Leçons du Mardi à la Salpêtrière* with innumerable references to recent clinical literature, as well as with critical notes, some of which are the earliest statements of Freud's theories in the field of the neuroses.

The reputation which Freud's work in the field of children's neurology earned him made little or no impression on him. (See Letter 18.) His real interest lay elsewhere, in two fields—or rather in two manifestations of a single problem—which alternately occupied the first place in his mind. These were anatomy of the brain and research into hysteria.

The idea of writing on the anatomy of the brain was suggested in the course of his work for Villaret's medical dictionary.[1] As articles in this were unsigned, Freud did not allow his contributions to be included in his bibliography; he also thought that his article on the anatomy of the brain had been ruined by cuts. Freud's monograph on the interpretation of the aphasias,[2] which was dedicated to Breuer, originated from his studies of the same subject. In this[3] he for the first time expressed "doubt about the localization of speech centres". In its place he put forward a theory which placed in the foreground the manner of functioning of the parts of the brain involved. In Freud's opinion the localization theory underrated the play of forces, the dynamics of the thing, and he emphasized the contradiction between dynamic centres and definite localization

---

translated the chapter on Samuel Butler in the German edition, edited by Anna Freud, of Israel Levine's *The Unconscious* (Levine 1926); and finally, in his old age, when he was waiting for a permit to leave Vienna after the Nazi occupation of Austria, he translated Marie Bonaparte's little book *Topsy*, jointly with Anna Freud.

[1] Villaret 1888 and 1891.

[2] "Zur Auffassung der Aphasien" (1891b).

[3] Brun (1936) says of this work: "Freud makes a sharp distinction between the peripheral (and spinal) projection and the central cortical representation of the parts of the body in the central organ and says that the peripheral areas of the body are not locally but exclusively functionally represented in the higher quarters of the brain. Moreover he firmly declines to localize ideas in locally circumscribed areas of the brain ("centres") and instead explains the function of speech genetically (on the basis of its gradual acquisition in childhood) as the result of the restimulation of a widespread visual, acoustic, tactile, kinaesthetic, etc., network of association. It was the breaking of this network of association and not the destruction of any special motor, sensory or 'understanding' centres which led to 'crippling' of the functions of speech and so produced the

points. There can be no doubt that Bernfeld is right when he speaks of the work on aphasia as the first Freudian book.[1]

Freud's interest in hysteria developed slowly. In the early eighties, presumably soon after he left the physiological institute, Breuer told him about a patient whom he treated from 1880 to 1882. This patient is known to us from *Studies on Hysteria* as Anna O., and it was her case that led Breuer to the discovery of the principle of cathartic treatment. When Freud took it upon himself "to inform Charcot of these discoveries ... the great man showed no interest in my first outline of the subject". The result was that Freud's interest, as he himself testifies, was temporarily diverted from the problems which Breuer had opened up.

After his return from Paris, while he was engaged on the translation of Charcot's lectures, Freud took advantage of an external circumstance to discuss the subject of hysteria again. He was under an obligation to report to the Vienna Medical Society on what he had learned in Paris, and on October 15th, 1886, he delivered his report in the form of a lecture on Charcot's recent work in the field of male hysteria. What he said found no credence with his audience, however, and Meynert called on him "to describe to the society cases in which the somatic symptoms of hysteria, the stigmata of hysteria" by which Charcot characterized this neurosis "were to be observed in clear outline". Freud responded on November 26th

---

various forms of aphasia. Finally, he was again the first to lay special emphasis on the work of Hughlings Jackson and the theory of the functional 'disinvolution' of that highly organized apparatus under pathological conditions which had been introduced into pathology by that brilliant English physician but had unfortunately been ignored. In this fruitful work Freud finally put forward the conception of agnosia (to describe disturbance of the capacity to recognize objects, which had previously been lumped together with the 'asymbolia' of Finkelnburg); this idea is well known to have subsequently been a very fruitful one in the pathology of the brain and has been generally accepted. When we consider the clarity with which Freud step by step developed all these modern points of view in his outstanding pathological study of the brain as early as 1891, we need not hesitate to describe him as Monakow's most important predecessor. It seems to me to be an act of historical justice and scientific duty to state this specifically today".

[1] In 1939 Freud declined to have "Zur Auffassung der Aphasien" included in the first volume of the complete German edition of his works on the ground that it belonged to his neurological and not to his psycho-analytic works. On the other hand in his letters he mentions it with greater warmth than his other neurological papers.

by lecturing, jointly with the oculist L. Königstein, on a case of "pronounced hemianaesthesia in a hysterical man".[1] The lecture was applauded, but the rejection of the views of Charcot for which Freud stood remained. Meynert's opposition remained unbroken, and he countered Charcot's theory with an anatomical theory[2] which Freud found totally inadequate.[3] The result of this conflict with Meynert was that Freud's former place of work, the university neurological institute, was closed to him, and his contacts with the medical faculty diminished.

After this first purely clinical report in the autumn of 1886, Freud published nothing on hysteria for more than five years. But his interest in the subject was not dead. From the autumn of 1887 onwards he used hypnotic therapy (Letter 2), and from the spring of 1889 onwards he used hypnosis for the examination of his patients;[4] in the summer of the same year he went to Nancy to see Bernheim and supplement his clinical impressions, and Breuer's interest in the subject received a fresh stimulus from Freud's.

Three years later, in 1892, Freud and Breuer collaborated in a preliminary study "of the psychical mechanism of hysterical phenomena". This was published at the beginning of 1893 and was reprinted more than two years later as the introductory chapter of *Studies on Hysteria*.

Freud's interest in the new field was at first exclusively clinical. Observation of his cases soon forced upon him a recognition of certain important factors which Breuer was unwilling, or only reluctantly willing, to share. The insight that Freud gained was

---

[1] Freud, 1886e. For a detailed account see S. and S. C. Bernfeld (1952), who show that Freud's admiration for Charcot was considered a betrayal of the Viennese medical tradition.

[2] *Wiener Klinische Wochenschrift*, 1889.

[3] See Freud's footnote to page 100 of his translation of Charcot (1892-3a). In his *Interpretation of Dreams* he mentions that when he went to see Meynert on his death-bed, Meynert described himself as a typical case of male hysteria.

[4] According to a passage in the *Studies*, the case of Frau Emmy von N. was the first in which he used these new methods. He reports other applications of hypnosis for therapeutic purposes in "A Case of Successful Treatment by Hypnotism" (1892-93b). But he describes his attitude to hypnotic therapy during those years as follows: "Neither patient nor physician can tolerate for long the contradiction between the emphatic denial of the illness in suggestion and the necessary recognition of it outside suggestion". (Charcot (1892-3a), footnote to page 286).

into the defensive character of symptoms, their over-determination, and the function of resistance. Simultaneously with the acquisition of this clinical insight, or rather in advance of it, he completely altered his technique. He abandoned Breuer's technique for the "concentration technique" described in the *Studies*, and a little later, between 1895 and 1898, he abandoned the remaining elements of suggestion in it and developed the psycho-analytic technique proper.[1]

The clinical and technical parts of the *Studies*—four of the five case-histories and the technical part—were written by Freud, while the theoretical part was signed by Breuer. But much of what Breuer wrote, and in particular the fundamental assumptions he took as his point of departure, was unquestionably Freud's intellectual property, or joint property.[2] We possess a draft of the preliminary study written by Freud in 1892 which anticipates several of Breuer's important formulations.[3] In this Freud put forward the proposition that "the nervous system endeavours to keep constant something in its functional condition that may be described as the sum of 'excitation'. It seeks to establish this necessary precondition of health by dealing with every sensible increase of excitation along associative lines or by discharging it by an appropriate motor reaction".

This theoretical assumption, borrowed from the world of physics, found its way into Breuer's account as the theory of "intra-cerebral excitation", and enabled him to compare events in the central nervous system with those in an electric circuit. In Freud's mind, however, it led to various speculations of which we are informed in

---

[1] Freud's account in the *Studies* suggests that the change in technique preceded the formulation of his findings. A similar sequence played a decisive role in the later development of psycho-analysis. Freud's technical work in the second decade of the twentieth century laid the foundations for his conceptions of the structure of the psyche and contained many elements of what later became the psycho-analytic ego-psychology.

[2] See Bernfeld, 1944.

[3] *Cf.* "On the Theory of Hysterical Attacks" (1940d). Similar formulations are to be found in a letter of Freud's to Breuer of June 29th, 1892 and in a footnote, possibly written earlier, to Charcot (1892-3a) which states : "I have attempted to tackle the problem of hysterical attacks other than descriptively, and from the examination of hysterics in a hypnotic state I have arrived at new results, some of which I shall describe here : the nucleus of a hysterical attack, whatever form it may take, is a memory, the hallucinatory reliving of the scene which was significant for the illness. It is this process which expresses itself manifestly in the phase of *attitudes passionnelles*, but it is also present where the attack appears to include only motor phenomena. The content of the memory is as a

the letters, and eventually to theories about the regulating mechanism of the psyche which belong to the fundamental assumptions of psycho-analysis.

Bernfeld has demonstrated the origin of these ideas in a brilliant essay, which we shall follow here. They stem directly from the physiological ideas of Brücke. Both Freud and Breuer were Brücke's pupils—they first met at the physiological institute. These ideas were widely accepted in the circle of Viennese physiologists, among the leading figures of which were Brücke and his assistants Ernst von Fleischl-Marxow [1846-1891] and Sigmund Exner [1846-1925] (both of whom are mentioned in the letters, though in different contexts). Only now are we able fully to understand what Freud had in mind when in his old age he described Brücke as the teacher who had made the biggest impression on him. Brücke's physiology, firmly based on ideas taken from the world of physics and having the measurability of all phenomena as its ideal, was the point of departure from which psycho-analytic theory was built up.

Brücke was no solitary figure among the physiologists of his time. He was one of a group of men who shared a similar outlook, were pupils of Johannes Müller and had founded the Berlin Physical Society in 1845. In 1847 Helmholtz lectured to this society on the principle of the conservation of energy. Helmholtz (1821-94) and Du Bois-Reymond (1818-92) were close contemporaries and close friends, and regarded Brücke as their "ambassador in Vienna".

The closeness of relations between the Viennese and Berlin physiologists, convincingly described by Bernfeld, provided part of the background of the relationship between Freud and Fliess. When Fliess came to Vienna the scientists on whom he called were

---

rule either the psychical trauma, which because of its intensity was sufficient to provoke the patient's outbreak of hysteria, or the event which, because it occurred at a particular moment, turned into a trauma.

"In cases of so-called 'traumatic' hysteria this mechanism is evident even to the most casual observation, but it can also be demonstrated in hysteria in which there is no single major trauma. In such cases one finds successive minor traumas, or frequently, if there is a strong predisposition, memories, indifferent in themselves, elevated into traumas. A trauma might be defined as an increase in excitation in the nervous system with which the latter is unable to deal adequately by motor reaction.

"The hysterical attack is perhaps to be regarded as an attempt to complete the reaction to the trauma."

men with whom he inevitably felt closely linked. His works leave no doubt that he came of the same school as they, and it was no accident that, as we have already mentioned, he made a present to Freud of Helmholtz's collected works. The ideal of establishing biology on a firm physical-mathematical foundation showed itself more and more plainly in his works. His inclination to mathematics is clearly deducible from the correspondence; it played an unhappy role in his later works, and expressed itself in the sub-title of his principal work, *Der Ablauf des Lebens* ("The Course of Life") (1906) with which he looked forward to "laying the foundations for an exact science of biology".

Fliess's interest in Freud's researches must be seen against this background. He supported Freud in his need to preserve a connection between psychological conceptions on the one hand and physiological and physical conceptions on the other; and finally he offered his own hypotheses as a foundation for Freud's findings; an action which was provoked by his sense of rivalry to Freud and led inevitably to their eventual estrangement.

But in the early years of their friendship the factors which led to their estrangement acted as a mutual stimulus. Fliess's theory of the nasal reflex neurosis touched on one of Freud's liveliest interests, the problem of the differential diagnosis of hysterical and somatic disturbances, with which he had already been concerned in Paris. But he did not deal with the subject till 1893, seven years after his return from Paris, when he published an article in French on one aspect of the problem and demonstrated with unsurpassed clarity that hysterical paralysis conducted itself "as if no anatomy of the brain existed", but had to do with "the general reactivity of a definite group of ideas".[1]

The problem of differential diagnosis also played a notable role in Freud's clinical works at that time. It was natural for him to think that it would be necessary to differentiate "more sharply than had hitherto been possible between neurasthenia proper and various kinds of pseudo-neurasthenia, such as the clinical picture of the

---

[1] "Some Points for a Comparative Study of Organic and Hysterical Motor Paralysis" (1893c). The article was based on a suggestion of Charcot's. See Freud's footnote to page 268 of Charcot (1892-3a).

organically determined nasal reflex neurosis, the nervous disorders of the cachexias and arteriosclerosis, the early stages of general paralysis of the insane and of some psychoses".[1] He regarded it as all the more necessary to make this differentiation because the growing insight he was obtaining from his clinical work seemed to be throwing new and unexpected light on the nature of neurasthenia as an actual-neurosis (anxiety neurosis). We can watch the development of this insight in the letters, in which it is occasionally too sharply formulated, until it was finally published in the paper "On the Grounds for Detaching a Particular Syndrome from Neurasthenia under the Description 'Anxiety Neurosis'". The important discovery that the mechanism of anxiety neurosis lay "in the diversion of somatic sexual excitation from the psyche and the resultant abnormal utilization of that energy" was expressed by Freud in the formula: "Neurotic anxiety is transmuted sexual libido".[2]

This idea was mentioned only briefly in the *Studies on Hysteria*, which were published later, but had important consequences for the history of psycho-analysis. Until the theory of anxiety was revised by the publication in 1926 of *Inhibitions, Symptoms and Anxiety*, the "toxicological" theory, which regarded anxiety as the result of dammed-up libido, held the field. This revision simultaneously revived another important idea which Freud had had in the early nineties;[3] the idea of putting the function of defence in the centre of the theory of the neurosis. After an interval of more than thirty years part of the psycho-analytic ego-psychology was based on this concept of defence.

The views that caused Freud to desire to establish the anxiety neurosis as a clinical entity were not wasted either; they found a secure but modest place in psycho-analytic theory and practice. There can be no doubt of the clinical importance of what we nowadays call the actual-neurotic factor in neurotic conflict and interpret

---

[1] "On the Grounds for Detaching a Particular Syndrome from Neurasthenia under the Description 'Anxiety Neurosis' " (1895b).

[2] Freud 1897b.

[3] In "On the Grounds for Detaching a Particular Syndrome from Neurasthenia under the Description 'Anxiety Neurosis' " (1895b) Freud unquestionably pointed the way to this revision. "The psyche develops the affect of anxiety when it feels itself incapable of dealing (by an adequate reaction) with a task (danger) approaching it externally", he wrote.

as an enhancement of the danger situation of the ego; but sexual frustration is only one among several conditions which give rise to such actual-neurotic situations. The difference between this and Freud's original conception clearly illustrates the development of Freud's hypotheses. While we, on the basis of our knowledge of the role of genetic conditions in the aetiology of the neuroses, are accustomed to deriving the reaction to frustration and instinctual tension from the history of the individual, but do not believe that frustration in the attainment of sexual objectives produces neurotic anxiety in adults, it was the latter idea which Freud originally considered to be of decisive importance. The idea that "the anxiety that underlies the phenomena of neurosis cannot admit of a psychological derivation" promised to lead from the uncertainty of psychological insight on to the firm ground of physiological processes, and at least to establish a link between the explanation of a group of psychopathological phenomena and the realm of physiological theory. It was in this field, that of sexual aetiology, that Breuer had followed Freud, if at all, with so much hesitation, and it was here that Freud felt the need for advice and encouragement. There were innumerable puzzles to be solved; the letters give one the impression of the observer's continual struggle with his clinical impressions. Freud tried at first to push the significance of his new start too far and to explain the physiology and psychology of the sexual function on a single pattern which interpreted all disturbances as quantitative displacements (Draft G.) Fliess obviously supplied the stimulus for this undertaking, which Freud repudiated only a few years later.

In those years the dominant idea in Freud's mind was to make physiological changes and the physically measurable the basis of all psychological discussion; in other words his aim was the strict application of ideas derived from Helmholtz and Brücke. He had been busying himself with the attempt to paint a picture of this kind at least since the beginning of 1895. It is worth recalling in this connection that Breuer was simultaneously engaged in writing the theoretical part of the *Studies on Hysteria*, in which he expressed the view that in the contemporary state of knowledge no link could be established between psychological conceptions and conceptions concerning the physiology of the brain. But it was precisely this that Freud set out to do. He first thought of writing a "psychology for neurologists", but obviously kept altering and modifying his first drafts. One draft dating from the autumn of 1895 has come down to us. The greater part of it was written in a few days immediately after a meeting with Fliess, and the rest in the weeks that followed. No sooner had it been sent off to Fliess than a stream of explanations and corrections went off in its wake. The ideas it contained were kept alive in the correspondence for months, and then gave way to new ideas, and above all to new insights.

The "Project for a Scientific Psychology" printed as an appendix (p. 347) enlightens us on only one phase of Freud's attempt to gain an inclusive view of psychology and the anatomy of the brain, but its historical value is nevertheless considerable. No attempt at a systematic appreciation of it will be made here, but the ideas it contains will be described. It is a coherent attempt to describe the functioning of the psychical apparatus as that of a system of neurones and to conceive of all the processes concerned as in the last resort quantitative changes. These processes are not confined merely to perception and memory but include thought, emotional life, psychopathology and normal psychology, as well as a first restricted but in some respects well-rounded theory of dreams. The idea of fusing the theory of the neuroses and normal psychology with the physiology of the brain was bold in itself. Even more impressive to the present-day reader is the consistency with which Freud holds his objective in mind in spite of all difficulties and contradictions. Each section, whether on the physiology of the brain or psychopathology, defence or thought, contains a wealth of new observations and hypotheses, of which some were only fleetingly utilized in Freud's later works. Some of them point to the future development of psycho-analysis. For example the ego is represented as an organism distinguished by the possession of a constant cathexis of energy—a hypothesis which a quarter of a century later became the cornerstone of the psycho-analytic theory of psychical structure. With Freud's rejection of the system of ideas on which he based this hypothesis in 1895—when he regarded the ego as a group of neurones with special characteristics—the idea seemed temporarily to lose its significance. Other fundamental ideas contained in the "Project" did not have to wait so long before finding a place in psycho-analysis. The idea that biological exigencies, which necessitated adaptation, ran counter to the individual's striving after pleasure was later revived in the form of the pleasure principle and the reality principle. However, the examples with which Freud illustrates these problems in the "Project" come partially from a field the importance of which his clinical work had still only imperfectly revealed to him. They are taken from earliest childhood. One of the most important deals with the relation between the suckling and the breast.

This wealth of ideas, which extends from the physiology of the brain to metapsychology in the later meaning of the term, necessarily makes the "Project" difficult to follow, even for the reader who approaches it with some preparation. Also it contains a number of obvious inconsistencies which Freud himself points out in subsequent letters. We can only partially guess Fliess's reactions to the "Project" from Freud's letters. They appear to have been a mixture of reserve and admiration.

Freud's object in sending it to Fliess, for whom it was written, was to obtain from him detailed suggestions for improving the parts dealing with the physiology of the brain. But Fliess was obviously busy with other matters, and Freud's interest in his all-too-bold undertaking was not sustained. He put away his notes and revolted against the "tyrant" who had been dominating his thoughts. New clinical impressions demanded his attention.

III

INFANTILE SEXUALITY AND SELF-ANALYSIS

The problem which occupied Freud in 1896 and the first half of 1897 had long been heralded. In *Studies on Hysteria* the role of childhood in the aetiology of hysteria was only briefly touched on. In the "Project", written at the same time, he expressed the view that sexual experiences before puberty possessed aetiological significance in the formation of neurosis (see p. 413 *sqq.*). Later he was of the opinion that it was sexual experiences before the period of second dentition that led to neurosis; and he sought to differentiate the individual "forms of neurosis, and paranoia, according to their time of fixation". At first he thought the period was that of later childhood, but the date subsequently grew earlier and earlier, and at the same time he gained the firm impression that the decisive damage was attributable to seduction by adults. "What poets and students of human nature had always asserted", he wrote in his *Autobiographical Study*, "turned out to be true; the impressions of that remote period of life, though they were for the most part buried in amnesia, left ineradicable traces upon the individual's growth and in particular laid the foundations for any nervous disorder that was to follow. But since these experiences of childhood were always concerned with sexual excitations and the reaction against them, I found myself faced by the fact of infantile sexuality; once again a novelty and a contradiction of one of the strongest of human prejudices. . . .

"Before going further into the question of infantile sexuality I must mention an error into which I fell for a while and which might well have had fatal consequences for the whole of my work. Under the pressure of the technical procedure which I used at that time, the majority of my patients reproduced from their childhood scenes in which they were sexually seduced by some grown-up person. With female patients the part of seducer was almost always assigned to their father. I believed these stories, and consequently supposed that I had discovered the roots of the subsequent neurosis in these experiences of sexual seduction in childhood. My confidence was strengthened by a few cases in which relations of this kind with a father, uncle or elder brother had continued up to an age at which memory was to be trusted".[1]

Freud put forward this conception of the genesis of the neuroses in his paper on 'The Aetiology of Hysteria", published in May, 1896, and his letters show that he abided by it for some time; it

---

[1] One of these cases was that of "Katharina" in *Studies on Hysteria*. When this case history was reprinted in Volume I of his Collected Works (*Gesammelte Schriften*, 1924), Freud added a footnote saying that he considered it legitimate after so many years to state that Katherina had fallen ill under the influence of sexual approaches by her father.

later appeared that he did so in spite of a good many misgivings, which he initially suppressed. During the last few months of 1896 and the first half of 1897 Freud studied the luxuriant growth of his patients' phantasy life; not only their day-dreams, but more particularly the infantile phantasies which invariably manifest themselves in the thoughts, dreams and behaviour of adult neurotics under the conditions of psycho-analytic treatment. From these he slowly gained the first hesitant insights into the nature of infantile sexual organization, at first into what was later to be called the anal phase. Later observation was to pile on observation in what was perhaps Freud's boldest undertaking. His observations of adult neurotics enabled him to reconstruct some of the normal stages in the child's growth towards maturity; in the half-century since Freud first discovered them the stages of development of the libido have been the subject of detailed research and systematic observation which have invariably confirmed them afresh.

In the spring of 1897, in spite of accumulating insight into the nature of infantile wish-phantasies, Freud could not make up his mind to take the decisive step demanded by his observations and abandon the idea of the traumatic role of seduction in favour of insight into the normal and necessary conditions of childish development and childish phantasy life. He reports his new impressions in his letters, but does not mention the conflict between them and the seduction hypothesis until one day, in his letter of September 21st, 1897 (Letter 69), he describes how he realized his error. The description of how this came about, and the consequences of the abandonment of the seduction hypothesis, tallies with that given in his published works.[1]

"When this aetiology broke down under its own improbability and under contradiction in definitely ascertainable circumstances, the result at first was helpless bewilderment", he states in *On the History of the Psycho-Analytic Movement.* "Analysis had led by the right paths back to these sexual traumas, and yet they were not true. Reality was lost from under one's feet. At that time I would gladly have given up the whole thing. Perhaps I persevered only because

---

[1] See also Kris, 1950a.

I had no choice and could not then begin again at anything else."

Nearly thirty years later, in his *Autobiographical Study*, Freud pointed to what seems another psychologically important explanation of his mistake. "I had in fact stumbled for the first time upon the Oedipus complex", he wrote. We see from the letters that insight into the structure of the Oedipus complex, and thus into the central problem of psycho-analysis, was made possible by Freud's self-analysis, which he started in the summer of 1897 during his stay at Aussee.[1]

The reader of Freud's works is already familiar with some of the stages of his self-analysis. In his pre-analytic period he had several times conducted experiments on himself, and had quoted the results of self-observation.[2] With his self-analysis, taken in conjunction with his psychological writings, this practice now assumes a new significance. We can regard as the first evidence of this his paper on "Screen Memories",[3] which has been identified by Bernfeld as being essentially autobiographical.[4] After the appearance of *The Interpretation of Dreams* examples multiplied, and they played a notable role in later editions of that work and in the various editions of *The Psychopathology of Everyday Life*. In Freud's later works, published after 1902, autobiographical examples are rarer, but an instance occurs in one of the last things he wrote, the letter to Romain Rolland on the occasion of his seventieth birthday. In this, under the title of "A Disturbance of Memory on the Acropolis (1936a)", he describes the feeling of de-realization that came over him during a visit to Athens in 1904 which he explained as having "something to do with a child's criticism of his father, with the under-valuation which took the place of the over-valuation of earlier childhood". In his introduction to this piece of writing Freud pointed out to Romain Rolland that when he had set out "to throw light upon unusual, abnormal or pathological manifestations of the

---

[1] Freud says in Letter 75 that he started his self-analysis after this summer, but Letters 65 *sqq.* contradict this.

[2] *E.g.* "Über Coca" (1884e, page 84); "Zur Auffassung der Aphasien" 1891b, page 63 (a passage to which Otto Isakower drew attention in the *International Journal of Psycho-Analysis*, vol. XX, 1939, page 340); Über die Bernhardt'sche Sensibilitätsstörung am oberschenkel 1895e, page 491. See also Bernfeld (1946).

[3] Freud (1899a).

[4] Bernfeld (1946).

mind. . . . I began by attempting this upon myself". His letters to Fliess permit us to date his first efforts at this more exactly, and actually enable us to see him at grips with the Oedipus complex. That this was the central theme of his self-analysis is not merely the impression one receives from the letters; it is confirmed by Freud himself when he says in his introduction to the second edition of *The Interpretation of Dreams* that "the book was, I found, a portion of my own self-analysis, my reaction to my father's death— that is to say, to the most important event, the most poignant loss, of a man's life".

The gist of what Freud reports of his self-analysis in his letters to Fliess is concerned with the reconstruction of important events in his childhood, chiefly with the period before he was three. External circumstances caused this period to be sharply marked off from his later life, because when he was three his parents were forced by economic difficulties to leave the small Moravian town of Freiberg. The prosperity of the Freiberg period was followed by the privations of Freud's childhood and youth.

Siegfried and Suzanne C. Bernfeld have attempted to reconstruct from Freud's writings his childhood experiences in the Freiberg period.[1] The material in the letters confirms the Bernfelds' conclusions in many respects and adds a number of details, but on the whole the information on the subject that emerges is far scantier than that which can be gathered and deduced from Freud's published works. Remarks scattered about in them enable us to infer a good deal about his father's household. Jacob Freud was born in 1815, married twice, and his children and grandchildren lived under the same roof. Freud's childhood companions were a nephew a year older than himself—John, the son of his brother Emmanuel, who is frequently mentioned in the correspondence—and a niece, Pauline, who was the same age as he. The two boys, no matter how much they fought on other matters, every now and then united against Pauline (Letter 70). Freud's father remains a shadowy figure in the letters, but rather more light is thrown on him in Freud's other writings. In Freud's early childhood his father was

---

[1] Bernfeld, 1944.

"the wisest, most powerful and wealthiest" man whom the boy knew. Memories of walks in the woods, during which he "used to be able to run away too fast for his father to catch him almost before he could walk", survived for a long time, and may have paved the way for the love of nature to which the letters testify. The figure of Freud's nurse—a clever but ugly old woman—is also known to us through his writings, and important memories were associated with her disappearance: her arrest as a thief; the birth of a sister; impressions of his mother's pregnancy, and of jealousy displaced on to his younger step-brother Philipp (who was, however, twenty years older than he). In his published works Freud used this material in support of several psycho-analytical hypotheses, but the letters give us some information about the analytic work by which it was obtained. Freud's reconstruction of his repressed childhood memories was not effortless, but only succeeded after many vain attempts. To obtain confirmation of a point he asked his mother for information (Letter 71), and her confirmation not only helped him towards understanding his own problems, but also gave him increased confidence in the reliability of his methods. Thus personal and scientific gain reinforced each other.

If references to his self-analysis in his works permit the impression that Freud, studying dreams in the interests of science and concomitantly carrying out part of his self-analysis, obtained insight about himself effortlessly, the letters serve to correct that impression. We can observe him struggling with some of the dynamic effects of his self-analysis; we can see the alternation of progress and resistance; we hear of abrupt changes of mood and of phases in which he felt suddenly plunged back into early childhood. It was, in fact, something far more than a purely intellectual process and bore all the marks of a real analysis. Freud actually appears to have gained full understanding of many of the manifestations of analytic resistance from his own behaviour in this, his "hardest analysis".

We see from the letters how he went on to use the insights gained in his self-analysis in the analysis of his patients; and how in turn he applied what he learned from his patients to further his understanding of his own prehistory. This was not a single process, and was not limited to a brief period of time; it progressed in a series of phases or intermittent advances, each of which yielded important insights. According to the evidence of Freud's works, his self-analysis was not limited to the years of the correspondence; it extended into the early years of the century and at least in isolated instances much further.[1] Many years later, when what had started as Freud's personal experience had long since developed into an institution, and a training analysis had become an essential part of an analyst's professional equipment, Freud returned to the theme of the mutual relationship of analyst and analysand. "We hope and believe", he wrote, "that the stimuli received in the learner's own analysis will not cease to act upon him when that analysis ends, that the processes of ego-transformation will go on of their own accord and that he will bring his new insight to bear upon all his subsequent experience."[2] This process was, however, threatened by the "dangers" to the analysis introduced by the active party, the analyst; to avoid these dangers, in Freud's view, "every analyst ought periodically himself to enter analysis once more". It is legitimate to suppose that this idea was at any rate partially the result of his own experience, and that Freud's self-analysis, perhaps in the modi-fied form of systematic self-observation, was protracted "indefinitely" and acted as a constant check on the observer in his work.[3]

The first and perhaps most significant result of Freud's self-analysis was the step from the seduction theory to full insight into the significance of infantile sexuality. Freud's bewilderment when he recognized his mistake soon gave way to new insights. "If hysterics trace back their symptoms to fictitious traumas, this new fact signifies that they create such scenes in phantasy, and psychical reality requires to be taken into account alongside actual reality. This was soon followed by the recognition that these phantasies were intended to cover up the auto-erotic activity of early childhood,

---

[1] The analysis of "the disturbance of memory on the Acropolis" mentioned above was concerned with an incident in 1904. The analysis of the screen-memory of the disappearance of his nurse was carried further in a later edition of *The Psychopathology of Everyday Life;* and we know from the third edition of *The Interpretation of Dreams* that he investigated the end of his friendship with Fliess by the method of self-analysis. (See page 43).

[2] "Analysis Terminable and Interminable" (1937c).

[3] For an instance of self-analysis late in Freud's life see "The Subtleties of a Faulty Action" (1935b).

parapraxis: generic term for such minor errors in behavior as a slip of the tongue or pen, misplacing articles, memory blockings, small accidents, etc

34 Introduction

Oedipus complex

erotogenic zones in development of libido

to gloss it over and raise it to a higher level; and then, from behind the phantasies, the whole range of the child's sexual life came to light".[1] The development of the idea which Freud here describes in broad outline can be followed in detail in his letters. In the summer and autumn of 1897 his self-analysis revealed the essential features of the Oedipus complex and enabled him to understand the nature of Hamlet's inhibition. Insight into the role of the erotogenic zones in the development of the libido followed. In the spring of 1898 he was at work on a first draft of *The Interpretation of Dreams*, in the summer he solved the problem of parapraxes, and in the autumn he started systematic preparation for *The Interpretation of Dreams* in the form in which we know it; it was written in the summer of 1899. Meanwhile, at the beginning of 1899, after another advance in his self-analysis, he took another decisive step in the development of psycho-analytic insight. Freud had been preoccupied with dreams on the one hand and with clinical questions of neurosis on the other. These had hitherto seemed to be two separate and independent fields of inquiry; he had alternately reported progress in the one and lack of progress in the other. He now recognized that they were part of the same problem and saw that what explained dreams also explained neurotic symptoms (Letters 82 and 105).[2] Two distinct problems merged into a single field of scientific inquiry, and psycho-analysis, as a theory and a therapy, was born. Freud's theoretical and therapeutic interests found expression in the important study "Dreams and Hysteria", read written at the beginning of 1901 but not published till four years later as "Fragment of an Analysis of a Case of Hysteria".[3]

---

[1] *On the History of the Psycho-Analytic Movement* (1914d).

[2] For a more detailed account of the formation of this hypotheses and an attempt to view this process as an example of creative thinking see Kris (1950b).

[3] Attempts to gain insight into the material with which Freud's self-analysis dealt have been current for years. Wittels (1924) used the reinterpretation of dreams reported in the *Interpretation of Dreams* for his later biographical sketch: and Maylan (1930) applied a similar procedure for his anti-Semitic vilifications. More recently Fromm (1952) has undertaken to reinterpret one of Freud's dreams in order to demonstrate the shortcomings of Freudian dream interpretion. For a survey of Freud's self-analysis based on the *Interpretation of Dreams* in conjunction with the letters to Fliess and the material referred to in the notes to the German edition, see Buxbaum (1951), who suggests that "Fliess played an important part in Freud's self-analysis, namely that of a transference figure";

parapraxis — in psychology — psychoanalysis attributed to unconscious conflict.

fugue — on manifestation of neurosis — a long period — which patient has almost complete amnesia for his past altho habits & skills are usually not affected. Usually leaves home & starts a new life, w/ sharply different modes of conduct. Upon recovery earlier events are remembered but those of period of the fuge are forgotten

IV

PSYCHO-ANALYSIS AS AN INDEPENDENT SCIENCE

(End of the Relationship with Fliess)

Freud's self-analysis, which opened the way to understanding of the conflicts of early childhood, brought about a shift in his interests. Insight into the conditions in which individual conflict arose in the course of the interaction between the child and its environment—in other words the intervention of the social aspect—meant that the need to explain psychological processes by immediate physiological factors had lost its urgency. This was a circumstance that could not fail to influence his relationship with Fliess.

Freud had continually turned to Fliess when he wanted information about the "physiological sub-structure", the "foundations", the "*realia*"; henceforth this need declined. Also Fliess had long since developed his own theories to a point at which in his opinion they appeared to supplement Freud's, though in fact they could only hamper them. The first clash between Freud's theory of the neuroses and Fliess's period theory occurred in the spring of 1895, when Ludwig Löwenfeld, a Munich nerve specialist with whom

---

for a supporting view, see Van der Heide (1952), some of whose statements were later corrected by Jones (1952), and for a critical comment see S. C. Bernfeld (1952). In view of these attempts it might be appropriate to re-emphasize that in his *Interpretation of Dreams* Freud did not intend to offer a "complete" analysis of his dreams, but used each example only for definite purposes; similarly we have no reason to assume that in the letters to Fliess all restraint was dropped. On the contrary, it seems evident from the material that the letters to Fliess are concerned only with selected aspects of Freud's interests and preoccupations. That Fliess was not familiar with all phases of Freud's self-analysis is evident. The most detailed report of this kind, contained in Freud's paper "On Screen Memories" (1899a) was published under disguise, a fact which was not communicated to Fliess (see Letter 107). It might in this connection also be restated that Freud remained aware of the limitations of self-analysis. Later in his life he stated his views clearly in a letter to a man whose contributions to the field of psycho-analysis were considerable but who had not undergone analysis. Freud emphasized the crucial importance of a personal analysis for future analytic work and pointed to the fact that he had had to rely on self-analysis himself because he was originally the only analyst and subsequently all analysts were his pupils, a fact which would have made the analytic process impossible.

noxae) — anything physical or mental
nok 'se that is injurious to physical
health

36   *Introduction*

Freud in later years kept up a correspondence based on mutual respect, criticized Freud's conception of the anxiety neurosis.[1] Löwenfeld expressed the view that Freud's theory was inadequate to explain either the diversity of the anxiety states that were to be observed clinically or the unpredictability of their appearance. Freud's reply[2] cleared up a number of Löwenfeld's misunderstandings, drew attention to the quantitative factor, the summation of noxae, and laid down the framework within which discussion of the problem should be conducted. This was provided by the "aetiological formula", in which a "precondition" and several kinds of "causes"—specific, contributory and precipitating—were to be distinguished. Freud discussed the role of heredity as a possible precondition. The precipitating cause could be an event of the day, but sexual experiences and factors such as physical exhaustion had to be taken into account as specific and contributory causes. In Freud's opinion the important field for further investigation was the specific cause. "The form that the neurosis takes, the way in which it breaks out, is determined solely by the specific aetiological factor deriving from sexual life".[3]

Freud's discovery of the significance of infantile sexuality and of conflict in early childhood were destined gradually to yield insight into this specific aetiological factor. But long before he reached that

---

[1] Löwenfeld, 1895.

[2] "A Reply to Criticisms of my Paper on Anxiety Neurosis" (1895f).

[3] Freud himself summarized the contents of his paper on the subject as follows: "It deals with the problem of aetiology in neuropathology; its object is to divide the aetiological factors present into three categories: (a) preconditions; (b) specific causes; (c) subsidiary or contributory causes. The preconditions are those without which the effect could not have been produced but which could not have produced it by themselves unless the specific causes had arisen. The specific causes are differentiated from the preconditions by the fact that they appear only in a few aetiological formulas; while the preconditions play the same role in numerous disorders. Contributory causes are factors which are neither necessarily present in every case nor are sufficient by themselves to produce the effect in question. In the case of the neuroses the precondition is perhaps provided by heredity; the specific cause lies in sexual factors; and all other factors which can be brought forward to explain the aetiology of the neuroses (overwork, emotion, physical illness) are contributory causes and can never completely take the place of the specific factor, though they can replace it quantitatively. The form the neurosis takes depends on the nature of the specific sexual factor; whether neurotic illness take place at all depends on quantitatively effective factors; the effect of heredity is like that of a multiplier introduced into a circuit". (See Freud 1897b).

neuropathology · The sc. P deals w/ diseases
of the nervous system

goal Fliess came forward with his own theory to fill the breach. In his monograph on the connection between the nose and the female sexual apparatus,[1] he specifically recognized the value of Freud's discoveries. He stated on page 142 that his clinical experience had repeatedly confirmed Freud's findings concerning the aetiological significance of undischarged sexual excitation, and went out of his way to demonstrate in detail the mutual consistency of Freud's theories and his own. He emphasized, for instance, that his view of "nasal dysmenorrhoea" did not exclude the influence of conversion as a "magnifying factor" (page 11) and that in the case of real hysterical gastric pains "the nose played no part, as in such cases it was purely a matter of the transmutation of a repressed idea into a physical symptom" (page 110). The seed of future conflict between his period theory and Freud's theory of the neuroses showed itself only in one important point. In the course of his discussion of anxiety "in children, men and women, and the aged" he expressed the view "that the appearance of anxiety attacks was bound up with certain periodic dates". He compared anxiety attacks with certain cases of intoxication, recalled "the anxiety accompanying acute nicotine or colchicum poisoning, or the anxiety stage in diabetic coma" and concluded "that at the time of the periodic days a substance was secreted in the body" which affected the nervous system, and that "with the establishment of the fact that anxiety is released only on definite days"[2] Löwenfeld's objections to Freud's theories collapsed. He observed that "Löwenfeld did not of course know with what exactness his demand for a resemblance between anxiety and epileptic attacks would be fulfilled. Both follow their own determination in time in accordance with the same law".

Thus Fliess answered Löwenfeld's criticism of Freud's conception of the anxiety neurosis with his own theory. Freud had at first been greatly impressed by Fliess's findings. He had been attracted by Fliess's soaring ideas long before the publication of this monograph, and had sent him[3] data on periods from his own case histories, and

---

[1] Fliess (1897).
[2] Fliess's text does not reveal how he arrived at this conclusion.
[3] In letters not printed here. But see Letter 52.

collected dates from the life of his own family. He had also sought to attribute variations in his own health and state of mind to definite dates in accordance with Fliess's ideas. So long as his own ideas were in a state of active development it was easy for him to overlook the latent antagonism between Fliess's theories and his own. Not till his self-analysis taught him to realize the full significance of the past history of the individual did he become aware that Fliess's attempt to explain neurotic conflict by "periodicity" meant shackling the dynamic thinking of psycho-analysis, enriched as it had been by the introduction of the genetic aspect.

Moreover, the conflict was not confined to this one question. Freud's advance from the study of dreams and parapraxes to the further development of his sexual theory was facilitated by an idea that he took over from Fliess. This was the significance of bisexuality. In the introduction to his 1897 monograph Fliess, after proclaiming the existence of both male and female periods, went on to develop the theme of constitutional bisexuality.[1] This problem played an important role in the exchange of ideas between the two men. Freud was fascinated by it, and quickly adopted Fliess's idea that the theory of bisexuality was capable of making an important contribution to the understanding of the neuroses. In *The Psychopathology of Everyday Life* he describes as an example of motivated forgetfulness how the fact that he owed the idea to Fliess faded completely from his memory and only gradually re-emerged.[2] When it came to developing the idea, however, differences arose which

---

[1] The term "bisexuality" was perfectly current in contemporary literature.

[2] "In the summer of 1901 [1900] I one day said to a friend with whom I used to exchange scientific ideas: 'These problems of the neuroses are only to be explained if we base ourselves firmly on the assumption of the initial bisexuality of the individual'. My friend replied: 'That's what I told you two-and-a-half years ago at Br., when we went for that evening walk. But you wouldn't hear of it then!' It is painful to have to surrender one's originality in this way. I could not remember the conversation in question, or that my friend had made any statement of the sort. One of us must have been mistaken, and on the *cui prodest*? principle the one who was mistaken must have been myself. Indeed, in the course of the following week the whole conversation of which my friend had tried to remind me returned to my mind, and I remembered the answer that I had given him at the time. 'I can't accept that', I had exclaimed. 'I don't believe it!' But since that incident I have felt more tolerant when in reading medical literature I have come across any of the few ideas with which my name can be associated quoted without acknowledgment".

brought to the surface the whole latent conflict between the two men. It involved a problem with which Freud was concerned for decades. Twenty years later he stated and discussed it with unsurpassed clarity.[1] He described Fliess's theory[2] as "attractive", and praised its "magnificent simplicity". According to Fliess, he said, "the dominant sex of the person, that which is the more strongly developed, has repressed the mental representation of the subordinated sex into the unconscious. Therefore the nucleus of the unconscious (that is to say, the repressed) is in each human being that side of him which belongs to the opposite sex". Freud's attitude to this idea, which he himself considered for a moment even before Fliess (Letters 52, 63) was at first hesitant (Letter 75 *sqq.*) but he ended by allowing the counter-arguments to prevail. "Such a theory as this can only have an intelligible meaning if we assume that a person's sex is to be determined by his genitals."[3] He rejected it with the words: "I do not think we are justified in sexualizing repression in this way—that is to say, in explaining it on a biological instead of a purely psychological basis".[4] Freud rejected, not the validity of bisexuality as the explanation of many traits of human behaviour, but the claim that biological conditions excluded psychological explanations.

This question of bisexuality had a decisive effect on his relationship with Fliess. In 1901, when the friendship was fading, Freud tried to revive it by once more suggesting that the problem of bisexuality was one which lent itself to harmonious co-operation between them. The effort was vain, however; the gulf could no longer be bridged. Their last meeting at Achensee in 1900 showed that understanding between them was impossible. Something of what took place can be reconstructed from Fliess's subsequent account[5] and from what Freud says in his letters. Fliess seems to

---

[1] "'A Child is being Beaten'" (1919e).

[2] Fliess's name is not mentioned in the passage referred to, but when he discussed Fliess's theories in one of his later works (see below) he referred back to this passage.

[3] "'A Child is being Beaten'" (1919e).

[4] This quotation from one of Freud's last works ("Analysis Terminable and Interminable", 1937c) summarizes the argument contained in several letters (Letters 85 and 146).

[5] See footnote, p. 324.

have asked Freud to accept the validity of his attempt to explain the specific nature of neurotic illnesses by periodic variations resulting from the twenty-eight and twenty-three day cycles. Freud obviously replied that such an assumption excluded the whole psychical dynamism which he was struggling to explain, and that in all the evidence at his disposal he could find nothing to justify it. Fliess thereupon attacked the methods by which Freud's insight into the dynamics of the mind had been obtained and accused Freud of projecting his own ideas into the minds of his patients.

Freud tried to keep the correspondence alive in spite of this onslaught. But Fliess was irreconcilable, and finally admitted the reason. We do not know the terms in which he did so, but we can see from Freud's reply (Letter 146) that Fliess was obviously hurt at the insufficient interest that Freud took in his theories.

Indeed, the interest in Fliess's period theory shown in Freud's letters had been declining since 1897, and more particularly since 1898. The reason is not far to seek. Fliess's theorizing had grown more and more remote from fact and observation; his claim to have discovered a cosmic principle that affected all living things must have developed further in those years. The introduction to his monograph on the connection between the nose and the female sexual apparatus which we mentioned earlier pointed in this direction, and in his later works the drive to rigid, abstract system-building was fully developed.[1]

Meanwhile Fliess had been "refining" his mathematical proofs. The less the observed facts fitted in with his theoretical requirements, the more strained became his calculations. So long as the time-intervals in which he dealt could be explained as parts or multiples of twenty-three and twenty-eight, Freud followed him. But Fliess soon found himself obliged to explain the intervals with which he was confronted by combinations of four figures and to use not only twenty-three and twenty-eight, but five (twenty-eight minus

---

[1] Aelby (1928) concludes his examination of Fliess's work with the observation that anyone with any psychiatric training could not fail to be convinced that Fliess was suffering from over-valuation of an idea. Riebold (1942) calls him "a player with numbers, unfamiliar with the simplest general mathematical principles". O. Frese expresses the opinion that Fliess's nasal reflex neurosis "verges on the mystical". (Denker and Kahler, Part II, page 51).

twenty-three) and fifty-one (twenty-eight plus twenty-three). Freud refused to accompany him in this step, excusing himself on the ground of his lack of mathematical knowledge. But it is legitimate to suspect from the tone of the letters that his interest had been transformed into an understandable reserve.

The tendency of Fliess's that expressed itself in this over-straining of hypotheses led to an epilogue which only very superficially affected his relations with Freud. In 1902 a sensational book called *Sex and Character* appeared, written by a Viennese writer named Otto Weininger, who committed suicide in the autumn of 1903. Weininger made use of Fliess's theory of constitutional bisexuality, as well as of other theories mentioned in his 1897 pamphlet. Weininger had heard of Fliess's work from the Viennese philosopher Hermann Swoboda, who had consulted Freud because of a neurosis and had had his attention drawn to the significance of bisexuality in the course of treatment. He passed on the idea to Weininger, who made use of it in his book without mentioning Fliess's name. In 1904 a monograph by Swoboda appeared entitled "The periods of the human organism and their psychological and biological significance" in which, among other things, he applied the period theory to the interpretation of dreams. Unlike Weininger, he based himself explicitly on the work of Fliess, to whom he devoted a chapter. Weininger's widely-read book and Swoboda's monograph made Fliess feel threatened. He not only wrote a pamphlet in which he defended his own priority, but caused the librarian Richard Pfenning to write a historical study on the question of priority. This appeared in 1906, long after the correspondence with Freud had come to an end.[1]

Fliess's struggle to have his biological system recognized did not come to an end in his life-time. He did not mention Freud's name

---

[1] Pfenning's book was entitled *Wilhelm Fliess und seine Nachentdecker O. Weininger and H. Swoboda*. Its publication led to a literary feud with wide ramifications. See in particular Swoboda's reply *Die gemeinnützige Forschung und der eigennützige Forscher* (1906). Two letters of Freud's dated July 23rd and 27th, 1904, to Fliess, who passed them on to Pfenning for publication, give us information about Freud's relations witn Swoboda and Weininger, as do two letters of Freud's to D. Abrahamsen, dated March 14th, 1938, and June 11th, 1938 (facsimile in D. Abrahamsen, 1946). Abrahamsen had no knowledge of Fliess's works. See Letter 147.

in any of his later works.[1] But he preserved a certain interest in
psycho-analysis, and in the last decades of his life he revived it to a
certain extent in the course of a friendship with Karl Abraham, the
well-known Berlin psycho-analyst. His son Robert, to whom Freud
sends greetings in his letters, became a professional psycho-analyst.

Freud always scrupulously mentioned in his works the debt he
owed to Fliess's theory of bisexuality. In 1910 he started testing the
Swoboda version of the period theory on his own dreams, but after
a year he had found nothing to confirm it.[2] He preserved a certain
amount of interest in Fliess's fundamental ideas. In discussing
developmental inhibitions which might be rooted in the disposition
he referred to Fliess's works. "Since the work of W. Fliess has
revealed the biological importance of periodicity, it has become con-
ceivable that developmental disturbances may be ascribed to modification in the duration of the various stages", he wrote.[3]

When Freud produced his own biological speculations in *Beyond
the Pleasure Principle* he mentioned Fliess again. "According to the
grandiose conception of Wilhelm Fliess", he wrote, "all the vital
phenomena exhibited by organisms—including, no doubt, their
death—are linked with the conception of fixed periods, which
express the dependence of two kinds of living substance (one male
and the other female) upon the solar year. When we see, however,

---

[1] The last mention is in 1902. See Letter 147.

[2] See *The Interpretation of Dreams* (trans. 1953, p. 94). Freud remarks that the
Fliess theory would seem to under-estimate the significance of dreams. "The
subject-matter of a dream, on his view, is to be explained as an assemblage of all
the memories which, on the night on which it is dreamt, complete one of the
biological periods whether for the first or for the nth time".

[3] "The Predisposition to Obsessional Neurosis" (1913i). In 1911, when Karl
Abraham proposed getting in touch with Fliess, Freud encouraged him in the
following terms: "You will meet a highly gifted, fascinating human being, and
incidentally have the opportunity of finding out the scientific grain of truth that
is certainly contained in the period theory, which for personal reasons I am
prevented from doing". (Letter to Karl Abraham of February 13th, 1911.)
After he had met Fliess Abraham reported to Freud as follows: "Since the breach
with you he (Fliess) has cut himself off from all the later developments in psycho-
analysis, but he showed great interest in everything I told him. He did not
make the fascinating impression on me that you foresaw (he may have altered
in recent years), but I had the impression of a keen and original mind. I felt
he lacked any real stature. That is reflected in his scientific work. He sets out
from some valuable ideas; but all the rest of his work is concerned with proving
their correctness or defining them more accurately". (Letter to Freud of
February 26th, 1911.)

how easily and how extensively the influence of external forces is able to modify the date of the appearance of vital phenomena (especially in the plant world)—to precipitate them or hold them back—doubts must be cast upon the rigidity of Fliess's formulas, or at least upon whether the laws laid down by him are the sole determining factors". In other words the period theory occupied a place at the periphery of Freud's interests; it did not contribute to the creation of psycho-analysis.

Freud mentions repeatedly that his relationship with Fliess played a part in his self-analysis (see Letter 66, for instance). Several passages permit one to assume that Freud realized that his relationship with Fliess was connected with the chief problem of the first phase of his self-analysis, his relations with his father (Letter 134), and the progress of the self-analysis seems to have facilitated his estrangement from Fliess.[1] Freud's depression at the initial failure of *The Interpretation of Dreams*, which was increased by financial worries, was the last in his life about which we have information.[2] His visit to Rome, his decision to procure himself the title of professor and thereby assure his livelihood quickly followed. Soon afterwards his first pupils appeared and the psycho-analytic movement was born.

The starting-point of any attempt to estimate in retrospect the significance on Freud's intellectual development of his exchanges with Fliess must be Freud's own conception of the matter. During a period of isolation and estrangement from all colleagues and friends Fliess offered himself as a willing and often enthusiastic listener. His scientific influence was practically exclusively confined to

---

[1] A trace of this analytic work survives in a footnote in the third edition of *The Interpretation of Dreams*. "While I was engaged in working out a certain scientific problem, I was troubled for several nights in close succession by a somewhat confusing dream which had as its subject a reconciliation with a friend whom I had dropped many years before. On the fourth or fifth occasion I at last succeeded in understanding the meaning of the dream. It was an incitement to abandon my last remnants of consideration for the person in question and to free myself from him completely, and it had been hypocritically disguised as its opposite" (*trans.* 1953, p. 145).

We may suspect that the problem with which Freud was occupied was that of bisexuality.

[2] At this time he still had debts which he had incurred in setting up his household. Bringing up six children was no light task in those years for a specialist with no other resources.

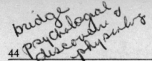

Freud's efforts to establish a bridge between his psychological discoveries and physiology. Freud was concerned with this question before his relations with Fliess became at all close. In *Zur Auffassung der Aphasien* (1891b) he followed Hughlings Jackson: "Physiological processes do not cease when psychical processes begin", he wrote. "On the contrary, the physiological chain continues; but from a certain moment there is a psychical phenomenon corresponding to every link (or several links). Thus the psychical is a parallel process to the physiological".[1]

Freud subsequently posed the question of at what distance from each other these parallel processes were to be studied. French psychiatry showed him the way. German physicians, he says in his introduction to his translation of Charcot (1892-3a) tend "to the physiological interpretation of the state of illness and the complex of symptoms. French clinical observation undoubtedly gains in independence in that it banishes the physiological point of view to second place. . . .That is not negligence, but is done for a specific purpose". Freud attempted in subsequent works to follow these precepts, but in 1894-95, while drafting certain parts of the *Studies on Hysteria*, he was seized with the idea of working psychology and the anatomy of the brain into a single synthesis; an ambitious effort, encouraged perhaps by the fact that Breuer had just completed the theoretical part of *Studies on Hysteria*. Fliess acted as godfather to this enterprise and encouraged it, but Freud soon abandoned it. It is significant that the "Project" of 1895 was found among Fliess's papers, that Freud never asked him to return it, and never again showed any interest in it.

Not till after his self-analysis, when he was able completely to fuse the dynamic and genetic points of view, did Freud succeed in establishing the distance between the physiological and psychological approaches. His first attempt to do so in *The Interpretation of Dreams* was surprisingly successful; the psychical structure sketched in Chapter Seven of that work was the foundation on which all his subsequent work on the question was built. In the next few years

---

[1] "Zur Auffassung der Aphasien", page 56. The phrase corresponding to "parallel process" used by Hughlings Jackson (1879 and 1890) is "dependent concomitant". See also Dorer (1932).

Freud specifically rejected any attempt to use any conceptions taken from the physiology of the brain. He abandoned the idea "of proclaiming cells and fibres or the systems of neurones which nowadays take their place . . . as psychical paths, though it must be possible to represent such paths in terms of organic elements of the nervous system in some not yet assignable way".[1]

Some years later Freud threw light on the problem of the relations between physical and mental processes in his work on psychogenic disturbances of sight (1910i), in which he developed the fundamental principles of what has come to be known in the last two decades as psychosomatic medicine.[2] He subsequently repeatedly spoke of the connection between psychological and biochemical processes as a field still awaiting exploration, and always emphasized that the terminology of psycho-analysis was provisional, valid only until it could be replaced by physiological terminology.[3] What Freud said of the terminology of psycho-analysis obviously applied also to its conceptions. The psychic entities of psycho-analysis are described as organisms and characterized by their functions, just as physiological organs are. This is a direct link with the "Project" of 1895.[4]

The result was that in studying the structure of the psychical apparatus, with the investigation of which Freud had been concerned since the time of his study of cerebral anatomy, it was possible to preserve the connection between the physiological and psychological approaches without hampering psycho-analysis by the closeness of the connection.[5]

After the beginning of Freud's self-analysis in 1897 Fliess's influence could only hinder this development. His attempts to attribute mental events to periodic intoxications or to biologise the

---

[1] *Cf. Jokes and their Relation to the Unconscious* (1905c), where he stated the future task of the physiology of the brain in the terms used by Charcot: "*Je fais la morphologie pathologique, je fais même un peu l'anatomie pathologique, mais je ne fais pas la physiologie pathologique, j'attends que quelqu'un d'autre la fasse*". Regret at the failure of all attempted psychological explanations in the terms of brain physiology are frequently expressed in Freud's works. See the passage quoted on page 349.
[2] See Fenichel (1945).
[3] See Kris (1947).
[4] See Hartmann, Kris and Loewenstein (1947). This was written before the authors were acquainted with the "Project".
[5] For an elaboration see Kris, 1951.

theory of repression could only have the effect of alien bodies. Fliess's allegations that psycho-analysis was incapable of yielding scientific results, that Freud's interpretations were only "projections" of himself, were all the more painful to Freud because of the crucial advances in technique he had made during the years of their closest intellectual contact. In 1898 he wrote a paper in which he reported the alterations he had introduced into his concentration technique.[1] This advance is barely mentioned in the letters, though it was of vital importance and must be counted as one of Freud's great discoveries of the period around the turn of the century. The abandonment of the remnants of the procedure associated with the technique of hypnosis had opened up new possibilities to psycho-analytic therapy; they rapidly revealed to Freud the significance of resistance and transference—conceptions which turned the therapeutic situation into a reliable instrument in the investigator's hands. This goal was reached a few years after Freud's estrangement from Fliess, and psycho-analysis acquired its threefold significance as a therapy, a psychological theory and a new and unique method of observing human behaviour. We owe to the new technique the overwhelming majority of the clinical hypotheses of psycho-analysis, the verification of which by other methods of observation is now in progress. Some of the socially conditioned resistances to the findings of psycho-analysis have simultaneously weakened. Psycho-analysis has given a new sense and a new meaning to psychiatry, has gained an influence over the whole field of medicine through the development of psychosomatic research, has had a big influence on the upbringing and education of children, and has suggested new points of view to the social sciences. The task of the psycho-analytic movement, which had hitherto been to promote the work of psycho-analytic investigation and provide training for psycho-analysts, is now shared with universities and medical research institutions.

In the course of this development some observers have gained the impression that the fundamental principles of psycho-analysis must be out-of-date because a good deal of its terminology derives from

---

[1] "Sexuality in the Aetiology of the Neuroses" (1898a).

the scientific terminology of the eighties and nineties of last century. The fact is not in dispute. The physiology of the brain which Freud took as his point of departure is as out-of-date as Herbart's mechanistic psychology, which Freud frequently took as his point of departure, as M. Dorer[1] has convincingly shown. But the terms thus taken over into psycho-analysis have acquired new meanings which often have little to do with their original meanings. It was the stimulus provided by Herbart that caused Freud to be the first to replace Herbart's mechanistic psychology of association with a new one. The question of the origin of the terminology and fundamental assumptions of psycho-analysis is therefore of only historical interest;[2] it has nothing whatever to do with the question of the value of those assumptions and that terminology for psycho-analysis as a science. There are, however, other questions that remain to be answered. In the first place we must ask ourselves whether the hypotheses which can be based on Freud's assumptions are verifiable and permit the formulation of new hypotheses; and then we must inquire whether there are other assumptions on the basis of which more fruitful hypotheses could be built. These are problems which promise to keep psycho-analytic investigation busy for a long time to come.

From this point of view the material collected in this book acquires importance. It shows Freud gradually shaking himself free from the ideas and conceptions with which he started, or at any rate taking the first steps in that direction. This was at first not desired by him, and it remained unintentional for a long time. It was forced on him by "the nature of the material", by his attempt to take the description and understanding of human conflict out of the realm of art and intuition and to put it into the realm of science.

---

[1] Dorer (1932).
[2] See Hartmann, Kris and Loewenstein (1946) and Kris (1947).

LETTERS

DRAFTS

NOTES

| Neurosis | - Obsolescent term for the activity of
nervous system or of some of its
specific parts - mental disorder- ill
defined in character but milder than
psychoses - functional disorder is
usually meant tho somatic conditions
play a part in neurosis both as factors & cause
& as symptoms. The term, no longer used
for a specific local, organic nerve disorder,
which is called neuropathy. (But see
actual neurosis — which in its older meaning
lingers.) The widely held theory of neurosis
always derived from anxiety should of
incorporated in its def. The manifestation
of neurosis are varied :- Hysteria, obsessions
fugues, phobias anxiety & many minor behavior symptoms. Professional treatment is
needed institutionalization seldom indicated.

Syn: psychoneurosis, nervousness, "nervous breakdown"
the last 2 being lay terms.

| neurosis/actual | a neurosis — which personality is
disordered as a consequence of an organic
difficulty → c.g. person w/ rapid heartbeat enlin or
may become extremely anxious a the whole
personality may be overwhelmed w/ fear

| Neurasthenia | - functional disorder characterized
by feelings o weakness & general lowering
of bodily & mental tone → The term is passing
out of use. But adj neurasthenic still
applies to a neurotic gen defatigability.
It is a misnomer since the disorder
is neither an organic weakness or
deficiency of the nerves.

paraesthesia .par¨es. the ¨zhə wrong or imaginary
localization of such cutaneous sensations as
pricking, tickling, burning

Letter of 24.11.87   51

1

Dear Dr. Fliess,

I have a strictly business motive for writing to you to-day, but I must start with the confession that I hope to remain in contact with you, and that you left a deep impression on me, which might lead easily to my telling you frankly in what class of men I place you.

Since your departure Frau A. has consulted me, and I have had considerable difficulty in making up my mind about her. I have eventually come to the conclusion that her case is not one of neurosis at all; not so much because of the foot clonus (which is not now in evidence) as because I can find no trace in her of what to me are the most significant symptoms of neurasthenia (there can be no question of any other neurosis in her case). In the often so difficult task of differentiating between incipient organic and incipient neurasthenic affections I have always held fast to one distinguishing characteristic. In neurasthenia a ✱ hypochondriacal element, an anxiety psychosis, is never absent, whether admitted or denied, and betrays itself by a profusion of new sensations, *i.e.*, paræsthesias. In our case such symptoms are extremely meagre. Frau A. suddenly found that she could not walk, but, apart from heaviness in the legs, complains of no other sensations; sensations of drawing and pressing in the muscular system, manifold aches and pains, corresponding sensations in other parts of the body, are entirely absent. You know what I mean. The so-called giddiness which occurred years before turns out to have been some kind of fainting fit, not a true vertigo; and I cannot connect it with neurasthenic giddiness.

On the other hand the following occurs to me as pointing in the opposite direction—towards an organic diagnosis. Seventeen years ago she had a post-diphtheritic paralysis of the legs. An infection of the spinal cord of this kind may, in spite of an apparent cure, have left behind a weak spot in the central nervous system, and led to a very slow-spreading malady elsewhere in the body. I have in mind something similar to the connection between tabes and syphilis. You know, of course, that Marie in Paris attributes disseminated sclerosis to acute infections incurred in the past.[1] Frau A. is to all appearances suffering from a slow nutritional decline, which is the fate of our city women after several pregnancies. In such circumstances the point of least resistance in the spinal cord began to revolt.

However, she is doing very well, better than at any time since the beginning of her illness. That is the result of your diet sheet, and there is little left for me to do. I have started electric treatment for the back.[2]

Now for other things. My daughter is flourishing, and my wife is slowly getting better. I am busy writing three papers at the same time, including the one on the anatomy of the brain.[3] The publisher is prepared to bring it out in the autumn.

With cordial greetings,

Your

Dr. Sigm. Freud.

---

[1]Freud was familiar with P. Marie's views of the infectious ætiology of disseminated sclerosis. (Cf. Freud's German translation of Charcot (1892-3a), Vol. I., and Freud's footnote on page 386.)

[2]In *On the History of the Psycho-Analytic Movement* (1914 d). Freud says: "I had already devoted myself to physical therapy, and had felt absolutely helpless after the disappointing results I had experienced with Erb's electrotherapy, which was so full of detailed indications." (The reference is to Erb, 1882).

[3]The paper on the anatomy of the brain, which is repeatedly mentioned in the following letters, never appeared in book form. Some passages in Villaret's medical dictionary (Villaret 1888 and 1891) and the monograph *Zur Auffassung der Aphasien* (1891 b) are obviously the result of this interest. Freud himself refers to "The Anatomy of the Brain" in *On the History of the Psycho-Analytic Movement* (1914 d), in which he observes that a remark of Charcot's might at an early stage have given him a clue to the role of sexuality in the ætiology of the neuroses, had not "brain anatomy and the experimental induction of hysterical paralyses absorbed all available interest". What the other two papers were on which Freud was engaged in 1887 is hard to decide. Only the paper *Bermerkungen über Cocainsucht und Cocainfurcht* was published during this year. In the letter of December 28 he mentions a paper, which was never printed, on the general characteristics of hysterical phenomena. The only work of his to appear in print in 1888 was the paper *Über Hemianopsie im Frühesten Kindesalter* ("On Infantile Hémianopsis"). Freud says of the years 1886-91 in his *Autobiographical Study* that he did little scientific work and wrote scarcely anything. "I was occupied with establishing myself in my new profession and with assuring my own material existence as well as that of a rapidly increasing family." See, however, S. and S. C. Bernfeld (1952) and Introduction, p. 17.

cerebrum — the main div. of brain — vertel consisting of 2 hemispheres — The latest brain to evolve & probably is a critical mental activity of discrimental behavior. Cerebrum is sometimes in for the cortex of the cerebrum, sometimes the entire brain. Both usages are incorrect.

Letter of 28.12.87

Vienna, 28. 12. 87.

My dear Dr. Fliess,

Your friendly letter and magnificent present have roused the pleasantest recollections in my mind, and the thought that lay behind both Christmas gifts makes me look forward to a lively and interesting correspondence. I still do not know how I managed to rouse your interest; my speculative fragment on the anatomy of the brain cannot have satisfied your severe judgment for long. But I am delighted all the same. So far I have always had the luck to choose my friends among the best of men, and I have always been particularly proud of my good fortune in that respect. So I thank you, and beg you not to be surprised if for the time being I have nothing to offer in return for your delightful gift.

I hear about you from time to time—mostly wonderful things, of course. One of my sources is Frau A., who has incidentally turned out to be an ordinary case of cerebral neurasthenia. During the last few weeks I have plunged into hypnotism, and have had all sorts of small but peculiar successes. I am going to translate Bernheim's book on suggestion.[1] Do not advise me not to, because I am already under contract. The two papers on brain anatomy and the general characteristics of hysterical affections[2] are going ahead as a relaxation in my spare time, to the extent that changes of mood and work permit.

paper available ?

My little girl is developing wonderfully and always sleeps the night through—which is every father's greatest pride.

My best wishes, do not let work overwhelm you and, when time and opportunity permit, think of

Your devoted

Dr. Sigm. Freud.

My wife was delighted with your greeting.

---

[1]Bernheim (1890.) A translation of another book of Bernheim's Studies by Freud appeared in 1892. Freud provided the first volume of his translation with a long introduction (it was shortened and amended in the second edition), but did not preface the second volume with any views of his own.

[2]For "The Anatomy of the Brain" see p. 52, footnote 3. The paper on "The General Characteristics of Hysterical Phenomena" was not published.

system & is the organ most critically & differentially involved in behavior & mental processes. But to speak of it as the organ of consciousness is to ignore the many other organs that play imp. roles.

3

Vienna, 4. 2. 88.

My dear Dr. Fliess,

Please consider this letter ante-dated. I should have written to you long ago, but, what with work, tiredness and playing with my daughter, I never did so. First let me give you some news of Frau A., whose sister is now with you. The case has turned out to be perfectly straightforward, an ordinary cerebral neurasthenia—what the pundits call chronic cranial hyperæmia. This was becoming clearer and clearer, and there was steady improvement from the electrical and *demi-bain* treatment. I was expecting that with remedial exercises she would get completely well again—but then something unexpected happened. She missed a period, and worse followed, for when the time for the next period came the treatment stopped too; and now we may certainly speak of expecting, but not of a great improvement. I should have liked to have continued with the treatment, but did not feel sufficiently confident of the result to go on in the face of the lady's anxiety and that of all her family, as well as against Chrobak's[1] advice; so I have associated myself with the prophecy that all will be well after the fourth month, and I am keeping my strong doubts on the subject to myself. Have you any experience of the influence of pregnancy on such neurasthenias?

Perhaps I am partly responsible for the new arrival. I once spoke very strongly in the patient's presence, and not without intention, about the harmfulness of *coitus reservatus*.[2] Perhaps I am wrong about this.

I have little other news to tell you. My little Mathilde is

---

[1] Rudolf Chrobak (1843-1910), professor of gynæcology in Vienna. Freud mentions Chrobak in the *On the History of the Psycho-Analytic Movement* (1914 d) and in his *Autobiographical Study* as one of the men whose medical experience had convinced him of the importance of sexuality in the genesis of neurotic illnesses. In the first of these books Freud also mentions that when Chrobak gave him this clue—obviously in the eighties—he was not yet in a position to appreciate its importance. In fact Freud did not recall what Chrobak said to him on the subject until he committed his memories to paper in *On the History of the Psycho-Analytic Movement*.

[2] The idea that *coitus reservatus* (*interruptus*) played a part in the aetiology of anxiety neurosis appears in Freud's published writings a little later.

thriving, and causes us much amusement. My practice, which, as you know, is not very considerable, has recently benefited somewhat because of the name of Charcot.[1] The carriage[2] is expensive, and visiting, and talking people into and out of things, which is what my work consists of, robs me of the best time for work. The brain anatomy is where it was, but the hysteria is progressing and the first draft is finished.

There was a terrific row at the Medical Society yesterday. They wanted to force us to subscribe to a new weekly which is intended to represent the pure, elevated and Christian views of certain dignitaries who have long since forgotten what work is like. They will naturally carry their proposal through; I feel very inclined to resign.

I must hurry off to a completely unnecessary consultation with Meynert.[3] My kindest regards, and let me have a line from you one Sunday.

Your devoted

Dr. Sigm. Freud.

4

Vienna, 28. 5. 88.
I. Maria Theresienstrasse 8.

My dear Dr. Fliess,

I have a motive for writing to you, though I might have written to you long ago without one. Here it is: Frau A., who since her unmasking as a case of chronic cerebral neurasthenia (if you will accept the term) and since her miscarriage, etc., has made a splendid recovery with a minimum of treatment and is now very well, sees the summer approaching. Her old preferences attract

somatic or not?

---

[1] Freud's translation of Charcot's *Leçons sur les maladies du système nerveux* had appeared in 1886. Freud mentions in the preface that, thanks to Charcot's accommodating attitude, he was in a position to publish the German edition several months before the French. He also added some notes on the author's behalf, mostly supplementing case-histories mentioned in the text.

[2] *I.e.*, carriage hired for visiting patients.

[3] For Meynert's relations with Freud, see page 59.

her to Franzensbad,[1] but I recommended a hydropathic cure in the mountains. She asked me to refer the matter to you, which I am accordingly doing, with every sympathy for you. I thought of somewhere on Lake Lucerne, such as Axenstein. If you agree, will you please jot down the name of a place on a postcard and send it to me by return, and you can rest assured that, whatever place you mention, Frau A. will go to it this summer. But I appeal to you not to pass the decision back to me, because that would not give her any satisfaction, as the magic of your prestige cannot be transferred. Please reply by return, because my promise to write to you is already ten days old. . . .

Life goes on tolerably well here, and our pretensions are constantly abating. When our little Mathilde chuckles we think it the most beautiful thing that could happen to us, and otherwise we are not ambitious and not very industrious. The practice grew a little in winter and spring and is now dropping off again, but it just keeps us alive. Such time and opportunity as there has been for work has gone on a few articles for Villaret,[2] part of the translation of Bernheim's *Suggestion*, and other similar matters not worthy of note. Wait though—the first draft of "hysterical paralyses"[3] is finished—I do not know when the second will be. In short, life goes on, and life is well known to be very difficult and very complicated, and, as we say in Vienna, many roads lead to the Central Cemetery.

My cordial greetings,

Yours ever, in haste,

Dr. Freud.

---

[1] A health resort in Bohemia.

[2] The articles in Villaret's medical dictionary (Villaret 1888 and 1892) are unsigned. The article on brain anatomy can be confidently assigned to Freud, as he mentions it in Letter 5 as having been "severely cut"; so can the article on aphasia, which Freud mentions in his *Autobiographical Study*. The articles on hysteria and paralysis in children, and perhaps also that on paralyses, can also be claimed for him because of their style and content. The article on neurasthenia, however, is obviously not by Freud. Freud's contributions to Villaret were omitted from his bibliography, and no reference is therefore made to them in the evaluation of his neurological work made by R. Brun (1936, pp. 200-207).

[3] Obviously a preliminary draft for the paper "Some Points for a Comparative Study of Organic and Hysterical Motor Paralyses" (1893 c).

5

Vienna, 29. 8. 88.

My dear Fliess,

I have been silent for a long time, but now that I am answering I really have something to show for it: a book, a paper,[1] and a photograph—you cannot expect more with one letter. There was a great deal in your letter which gave me food for thought, and I should very much have liked to discuss it with you. I admit unreservedly that you are right in what you say, and yet I cannot do as you suggest. To go into general practice instead of specialising, to use all the resources of general medicine and treat the patient as a whole, is certainly the only way which promises real satisfaction and material success; but for me it is too late for that now. I have not learned enough for that kind of practice; there is a gap in my medical equipment which it would be hard to close. I was able to learn just enough to become a neuropathologist. And now I lack, not youth, but time and freedom to catch up. Last winter I was quite busy, and that left me with just enough to live on with my very large family, but with no time over for study.[2] During the summer things were very bad; this left me with leisure enough, but with worries that sapped the inclination. Apart from that, the habit of research, to which I have sacrificed a good deal, dissatisfaction with what the student is offered, the need to go into detail and exercise the critical faculty, are obstacles to the study of text-books. The whole atmosphere of Vienna is little adapted to steeling one's will or to fostering that confidence in success which is the prerogative of you Berliners and without which a grown man cannot think of changing the whole basis of his livelihood. So I must stay as I am; but I have no illusions about how unsatisfactory a state of affairs it is.

---

[1] The book was Freud's translation of Bernheim (1886), and the paper *Über Hemianopsie im frühesten Kindesalter* (1888 a).

[2] The reference to Freud's "very large family" at a time when only his first child was born is explained by his having to contribute to the keep of his mother and other members of a very numerous family.

speak the words entendia

As for the enclosures, I am sending you the photograph because I remember your saying you would like to have one when you were in Vienna, when I did not have one for you. As for *Suggestion,* you know all about it. I undertook the work very reluctantly, only to have a hand in something which is certainly going to have a big influence on the practice of nerve specialists in the next few years. I do not share Bernheim's views, which seem to me one-sided, and I have tried to stand up for Charcot[1] in the introduction—I do not know how skilfully, but I am sure unsuccessfully. The suggestion theory, that is to say Bernheim's "intro-suggestion" theory, acts like a charm—the charm of familiarity—on German doctors, who need make no great leap from the simulation theory, on which they stand at present, to arrive at the suggestion theory. Because the attitude of all my friends demanded it, I had to be moderate in my criticism of

---

[1] In this introduction (translated under the title "Hypnotism and Suggestion", 1888-89), Freud offers us a detailed comparison of the theoretical ideas of Bernheim and Charcot, the schools of Nancy and the Salpêtrière. The problem is summed up in the following passage: "How does this affect the antithesis between the mental and physiological phenomena of hypnosis? There was a meaning in it so long as by suggestion was understood a directly mental influence exercised by the physician which forced any symptomatology he liked upon the hypnotised subject. But this meaning disappears as soon as it is realised that even suggestion only releases sets of manifestations which are based upon the functional peculiarities of the subject's nervous system, and that in hypnosis characteristics of the nervous system other than suggestibility make themselves felt. The question might still be asked whether all the phenomena of hypnosis must *at some point* pass through the mental sphere; in other words—for the question can have no other sense—whether the changes in excitability which occur in hypnosis invariably affect only the region of the cerebral cortex. By thus putting the question in this other form we seem to have decided the answer to it. There is no justification for making such a contrast as is here made between the cerebral cortex and the rest of the nervous system: it is improbable that so profound a functional modification of the cerebral cortex would occur unaccompanied by significant alteration in the excitability of the other parts of the brain. We possess no criterion which enables us to distinguish exactly between a mental process and a physiological one, between an act occurring in the cerebral cortex and one occurring in the sub-cortical substance; "consciousness", whatever that may be, is not attached to every activity of the cerebral cortex, nor is it always attached in an equal degree to any particular one of its activities; it is not a thing which is bound up with any locality in the nervous system. It therefore seems to me that the question whether hypnosis exhibits mental or physiological phenomena cannot be accepted in this general form and that the decision in the case of each individual phenomenon must be made dependent upon a special investigation." The greater part of the introduction is, however, devoted to a discussion of the "genuineness" of the hysterical phenomena described by Charcot, and Meynert's position in relation to these problems.

Meynert, who in his usual impudent-malicious manner had delivered himself authoritatively on a subject of which he knew nothing. Even so, they think I have gone too far. I have belled the cat.[1]

At last the hysterical and organic paralysis, which I have quite enjoyed doing,[2] is nearly done. My part in Villaret has turned out to be less substantial than expected. The article on brain anatomy has been severely cut; several other bad articles on neurology are not by me. The scientific value of the whole is not very great.

The anatomy of the brain is still germinating, as when you applied the stimulus. So much for my scientific activities. In other respects all is well. The family has been at Maria-Schutz on the Semmering[3] since the beginning of July, and I hope to spend a week there myself. The little girl thrives marvellously.

I was delighted to hear that you have an assistant. Very likely this letter will not find you in Berlin. Do not work too hard—I should like to remind you of that every day. All best wishes and think kindly of

> Your devoted
> Dr. Sigm. Freud.

6

Reichenau, 1. 8. 90.

Dear Fliess,

I am writing to you to-day to tell you, very much against the grain, that I cannot come to Berlin; not that I care about Berlin or the congress, but I am so disappointed that I shall not be able to see you there. What has upset my plans is not one big thing, but a combination of little ones, as can so easily happen in the case of a doctor and a family man. Going to Berlin would clash with everything. On the professional side my most important

---

[1] See Introduction, pp. 19, 20.
[2] See Letter 4.
[3] A health resort near Vienna.

patient is going through a kind of nervous crisis . . . and on the family side all sorts of things have been going wrong with the children (I now have a son as well as a daughter); and my wife, who generally never objects to my going away for a short time, does not want me to go away just now; and so on and so forth. In short, it cannot be done and, as I look forward to this trip as a great treat, I must be ready to give it up when called upon.

I do so most unwillingly, because I expected a great deal from meeting you. Though otherwise quite satisfied, happy if you like, I feel very isolated, scientifically blunted, stagnant and re-signed. When I talked to you, and saw that you thought some-thing of me, I actually started thinking something of myself, and the picture of confident energy which you offered was not without its effect. I should also have profited professionally from meeting you, and perhaps I should also have benefited from the Berlin atmosphere, because for years now I have been without anyone who could teach me anything and have settled down more or less exclusively to the treatment of the neuroses.

Will there be no chance of seeing you at some time other than that of the congress? Will you not be going away afterwards? Or will you not be coming back here in the autumn? Do not lose patience with me for not having answered you and now for refusing your extremely kind invitation. Let me know that there is some prospect of seeing you for a few days, so that I shall not feel that I am losing your friendship.

With cordial greetings

Your devoted

Sigm. Freud.

7

Vienna, 11. 8. 90.

My dear Fliess,

Magnificent! Can you think of any better place than Salzburg for the purpose? Let us meet there, and walk for a few days wherever you will. The date is all the same to me, so long as it is towards the end of August, so please decide. Because of the obstacles I mentioned it will be only for three or four splendid days, but have them we shall, and I shall do everything possible to avoid being prevented from coming again. If you agree to Salzburg, you will travel *via* Munich and not Vienna.

Yours in pleasurable anticipation,

Sigm. Freud.

8

Vienna, 2. 5. 91.

Dear Fliess,

I am proud indeed of having such a reviewer, and of the result. I imagine the warmth of the review will have contributed not a little to the work's success.[1] In a few weeks I look forward to sending you a paper on aphasia, for which I have a good deal of feeling.[2] I have been very cheeky in it, and have crossed swords with your friend Wernicke, as well as with Lichtheim and Grashey, and have even scratched the high and mighty idol Meynert.[3] I shall be very curious to hear what you think of it. The preferential nature of your relations with the author means that some of the contents will come as no surprise to you. However, the paper is suggestive rather than conclusive.

What else are you doing, apart from reviewing me? In my case "else" is a second boy, Oliver, now three months old. Shall we meet this year?

With cordial greetings,

Your

Dr. Freud.

---

[1] What work this refers to cannot be established.

[2] The monograph *Zur Auffassung der Aphasien. Eine Kritische Studie* (1891 b). An estimate of its value as a contribution to the subject is made by R. Brun (1936). See Introduction, page 17.

[3] The theories of Meynert, Lichtheim, Wernicke and Grashey are critically discussed in this work of Freud's.

[handwritten at top:] reaction – eliminating or weakening a complex or lessening the emotional tension caused by conflict & repression, be relieving

[handwritten:] in ~~thought, feeling~~ feeling action or imagination – the situation that originally caused ~~the~~ conflict.

Vienna, 28. 6. 92.

My Dear Fliess,

. . . . The occasion for writing to you[1] is that Breuer has agreed to joint full publication of the abreaction theory and our other work on hysteria. A part of it,[2] which I at first wanted to write alone, is finished, and in other circumstances I should certainly have sent it to you.

The instalment of Charcot which I am sending you to-day is satisfactory, apart from some irritating uncorrected accents and mistakes in the few French words. Pure carelessness![3]

I hear that you are now expecting a return visit.[4] I hope you will do me the kindness to give me a hint of what to send you for the new household as a token of my wife's and my own heartiest congratulations.

My kindest regards to you, to your Ida, and to her parents, who received me with such undeserved kindness.

Yours

Sigm. Freud.

---

[1] [This is the first letter in which Freud uses the familiar *Du* instead of the more formal *Sie*.]

[2] *I.e.*, of the *Studies on Hysteria*. What part of it was finished in 1892 can no longer be established. [Cf. the posthumously published "Letter to Breuer" (1941 a) written the next day (29. 6. 92).]

[3] The reference is to Freud's German translation of Charcot's *Leçons du mardi à la Salpêtrière*, to which the title *Poliklinische Vorträge* was given. The translation appeared in instalments between 1892 and 1893. In his introduction Freud describes the differences between French and German neuropathology (see Introduction, p. 44). Freud embellished his translation with a large number of footnotes which he intended partly as "elucidations of the text and further bibliographical data, and partly as critical objections and marginal observations which might occur to a listener." He appears to have omitted to have obtained Charcot's permission to do this. In *The Psychopathology of Everyday Life*, where this circumstance is mentioned, Freud conjectures that the author "must have been dissatisfied with this arbitrary behaviour".

[4] *I.e.*, a return visit from Fliess's future wife's parents.

[handwritten notes in top margin: sign catharsis which is now less commonly spoken of — loosely the relief of the emotional tension by thinking about the situation originating]

10

4. 10. 92.

Dr. S. Freud,   IX. Berggasse 19.
Consulting hours 5-7 p.m.

My dear Fliess,

Herewith the first sheet of your reflex neuroses.[1] As it is to be printed in Teschen, it might be better for you to get in touch with the printer yourself. I have only dipped into it, and I hope you will send me the introduction, in which I shall be extremely interested. . . .

For the last week my family have been in Vienna, busily engaged in growing. I am writing paralysis in children part two[2] —yet another part two *si parva licet*, etc.

With heartiest greetings from household to household,

I can now sign myself

Your

Sigm. Freud.

11

IX. Berggasse 19.
18. 12. 92.

Dr. S. Freud,
Consulting hours 5-7 p.m.

My dear Fliess,

I am delighted to be able to tell you that our theory of hysteria (recollection, abreaction, etc.) is going to appear in the *Neurologisches Zentralblatt* for January 1st, 1893, in the form of a

---

[1] Fliess (1893). The words "to the friendly quarter (p. 3) Christmas, 1892" are written on the fly-leaf of the copy in Freud's library. The reference is to a passage in the book which states: "My intention to make the reflex neurosis the object of literary discussion is of extremely recent date, and was the result of a suggestion from a friendly quarter made after I had mentioned that this form of illness was extremely common."

[2] The reference is to Freud (1893 b). Freud refers to this paper as "paralysis in children part two" because it supplements an earlier paper written jointly with Dr. Oscar Rie. (Freud 1891a). ["Part two" is also a playful reference to the second part of Goethe's *Faust*.]

detailed preliminary communication. It has meant a long battle with my collaborator.[1]

What are you doing, happily vanished ones?[2] Shall we be seeing you here at Christmas, as rumour has it?

With best regards

Your

hypnoidal — resembling hypnosis

Sigm. Freud.

Draft A

[Undated. ?End of 1892.]

PROBLEMS[3]

1. Does the anxiety in anxiety neuroses arise from the inhibition of the sexual function or from the anxiety connected with their aetiology?

---

[1] The reference is to Breuer and Freud (1893a). The differences between the authors to which the "long battle with my collaborator" refers can be partially reconstructed by a comparison of the article with Freud's first drafts, posthumously published (1940 d, 1941 a and b). See also Introduction, p. 20. In the introduction to *Studies on Hysteria*, the authors refer to the "legitimate differences of opinion of two observers" who "are in fundamental agreement on facts and principles, but whose conclusions and assumptions do not always coincide". In his *Autobiographical Study* Freud describes the fundamental difference between himself and Breuer as follows: "In answering the question of when it is that a mental process becomes pathogenic, that is, when it is that it becomes impossible for it to find a normal discharge, Breuer preferred what might be called a physiological theory: he thought that the processes which could not find a normal outcome were such as had originated during unusual, 'hypnoid,' mental states. This opened the further question of the origin of these hypnoid states. I, on the other hand, was inclined to suspect the existence of an interplay of forces and the operation of intentions and purposes such as are to be observed in normal life. Thus it was a case of 'hypnoid hysteria' versus 'defence neurosis'." For other methodological comments on the difference between the theories of Breuer and Freud see Hartmann, Kris and Loewenstein (1953).

[2] Fliess had married Fräulein Ida Bondy, of Vienna.

[3] This is the only one of Freud's drafts written throughout in Latin characters. The absence of an accompanying letter may be explained by the fact that Freud and Fliess met several times in the course of 1892 when Fliess came to Vienna to see his fiancée.

In this draft Freud mentions the idea of having his hypotheses checked by systematic clinical observations upon various categories of people, which obviously would be impossible without collaborators. Some of the questions raised seem to point to later works of Freud's. The question of the aetiology of the neuroses, for instance, was dealt with in the paper "A Reply to Criticisms of my Paper on Anxiety Neurosis". (1895 f).

2. To what extent does a healthy person respond to later sexual traumas differently from a person with a predisposition due to masturbation? Only quantitatively? or qualitatively?
3. Does simple *coitus reservatus* (condom) act in any way as a noxa?
4. Is there an innate neurasthenia with innate sexual weakness or is it always acquired in youth? (From nurses, from being masturbated by another person.)
5. Is heredity anything other than a multiplying factor?
6. What is the ætiology of periodic depression?
7. Is sexual anæsthesia in women anything other than a result of impotence? Can it cause neuroses of itself?

Theses

1. No neurasthenia or analogous neurosis can exist without a disturbance of the sexual function.
2. This either has an immediate causal effect or acts as a predisposition for other factors, but always in such a way that without it the other factors cannot produce neurasthenia.
3. On account of its ætiology, neurasthenia in men is accompanied by relative impotence.
4. Neurasthenia in women is a direct consequence of neurasthenia in men, through the agency of the reduction in potency in the latter.
5. Periodic depression is a form of anxiety neurosis, which as a rule takes the form of phobias and anxiety-attacks.
6. Anxiety neurosis is partly a result of inhibition of the sexual function.
7. Simple excess and overwork are not ætiological factors.
8. Hysteria in neurasthenic neuroses indicates a suppression of the concomitant affects.

Categories [for observation]

1. Men and women who have remained healthy.
2. Sterile women in whom preventive traumas in marriage are absent.
3. Women infected with gonorrhoea.
4. Gonorrhoeal men of the world who for that reason have been

sheltered in every way and are aware of their hypospermia.
5. Members of severely tainted families who have remained healthy.
6. Observations from countries in which particular sexual abnormalities are endemic.[1]

Aetiological Factors

1. Exhaustion owing to abnormal gratification.
2. Inhibition of the sexual function.
3. Affects accompanying these practices.
4. Sexual traumas dating back to before the age of understanding.

Draft B

8/2/93[2]

THE AETIOLOGY OF THE NEUROSES

I am writing the whole thing down for you a second time.[3] You will of course keep the draft away from your young wife.

I. It may be taken as common knowledge that *neurasthenia* is a frequent result of an abnormal sexual life.[4] The contention which I am putting forward and desire to test by observations is that neurasthenia is always *only* a sexual neurosis.

I have argued (along with Breuer) in favour of a similar view in regard to hysteria. Traumatic hysteria was familiar. What we

---

[1] This is the earliest occasion in Freud's writings on which he draws attention to the importance of clinical studies under different cultural conditions.
[2] Dated by postmark.
[3] The first draft does not appear to have survived. This draft is mentioned in a letter dated January 5th, 1893 (not included in this volume) in which Freud says: "I am rewriting the thing on the neuroses". The views contained in this draft on anxiety neurosis and the origin of neurasthenia in men and women were later elaborated in the paper "On the Grounds for Detaching a Particular Syndrome from Neurasthenia under the description 'Anxiety Neurosis'" (1895 b).
[4] A. Preyer wrote: "Also perversions in the sexual instincts . . . and further the various kinds of 'mental masturbation' can have ætiological effects. Even in marriage, with otherwise normal sexual intercourse, opportunity for the development of neurasthenic phenomena is provided by *coitus interruptus*" . . . "*Coitus interruptus* is thus by no means an indifferent or harmless thing, but in a large number of cases must be regarded as a secret, unknown and continuously operative source of intense nervousness and irritating nervous weakness, with their innumerable symptoms." (*Der unvollständige Beischlaf (Congressus Interruptus, Onanismus Coniugalis) und seine Folgen beim männlichen Geschlechte. Eine Studie aus der Praxis*).

asserted was that *every* hysteria that is not hereditary is traumatic. In the same way I am now asserting of neurasthenia that *every* neurasthenia is sexual.

We will for the moment leave on one side the question whether hereditary disposition and, secondarily, toxic influences can produce genuine neurasthenia, or whether what appears to be hereditary neurasthenia in fact also goes back to early sexual exhaustion. If there *is* a hereditary neurasthenia, the questions arise whether the *status nervosus* in hereditary cases should not be distinguished from neurasthenia, what relation it has to the corresponding symptoms in childhood, etc.

To begin with, then, my contention is restricted to *acquired* neurasthenia. What I am asserting can be formulated as follows. In the aetiology of a nervous affection we may distinguish (1) the necessary precondition, without which the state cannot arise at all, and (2) the precipitating factors.[1] The relation between these two can be regarded thus: If the necessary precondition operates sufficiently strongly the affection will occur as an inevitable consequence; if it has not operated sufficiently, it will result in the first instance in a predisposition to the affection, which will cease to be latent as soon as a sufficient amount of one of the secondary factors is also present. Thus whatever is lacking in the primary aetiology in order to produce the full effect can be made up for by the secondary aetiology. The secondary aetiology can, however, be dispensed with, while the primary one is indispensable.

If this aetiological formula is applied to our present case, we arrive at this. Sexual exhaustion can by itself provoke neurasthenia. If, however, it fails to achieve this by itself, it has a predisposing effect on the nervous system so great that physical illness, depressing affects or overwork (toxic influences) can no longer be tolerated without neurasthenia. But, unless there is sexual exhaustion, all these factors are incapable of generating neurasthenia. They make the patient normally tired, normally sad, normally weak physically; but they

---

[1] The "aetiological formula" was later expanded. In "A Reply to Criticisms of my Paper on Anxiety Neurosis" (1895 f) and "Heredity and the Aetiology of the Neuroses" (1896 a) Freud distinguishes (*a*) preconditions; (*b*) specific factors; and (*c*) subsidiary contributing factors. See also Introduction p. 36.

only continue to prove "how much of these damaging influences a normal man can bear".

I shall treat neurasthenia in men and women separately.

Neurasthenia in males is acquired at the age of puberty and becomes manifest in the patient's twenties. Its source is masturbation, the frequency of which runs completely parallel with the frequency of neurasthenia in men. One can regularly observe in the circle of one's acquaintances that (at least in urban populations) men who have been seduced by women at an early age escape neurasthenia.

When this noxa is long-continued and intense, it turns the subject into a sexual neurasthenic and his potency is also impaired; and a sufficiently intense cause will correspond to a life-long persistence of the condition. Further evidence of the causal connection lies in the fact that a *sexual* neurasthenic is always at the same time a *general* neurasthenic.

If the noxa has not been sufficiently severe, it has (in accordance with the above ætiological formula) a predisposing effect; so that, if one of the precipitating causes supervenes, neurasthenia is produced, though these latter factors alone would not have been able to produce it. Thus, intellectual work may lead to cerebral neurasthenia, normal sexual effort to spinal neurasthenia, and so on.

In cases of medium severity, we find neurasthenia (typically accompanied by dyspepsia, etc.) beginning and running its course during puberty and terminating at marriage.

A second noxa, affecting men at a later age, is brought to bear on a nervous system which is either intact or predisposed to neurasthenia owing to masturbation. It is a question whether it can lead to detrimental results in the former case; but it probably can. Its effect is manifest in the second case, in which it revives the neurasthenia of puberty and creates new symptoms. This second noxa is *onanismus conjugalis*—incomplete copulation in order to prevent conception. All the different methods of achieving this seem to act similarly in the case of men: they operate with varying intensity according to the subject's predisposition, but they do not actually differ in quality. Where the subject has a strong predisposition or suffers from chronic neurasthenia even normal intercourse cannot be tolerated;

and intolerance is exhibited (in an ascending degree) against the use of the condom, of extra-vaginal coitus and of *coitus interruptus*. A healthy man will tolerate any of these for a considerable length of time but not indefinitely. In the long run he behaves in the same way as a predisposed subject. His only advantage over the masturbator is a more extended period of latency or the fact that he requires the occurrence in every case of precipitating causes. *Coitus interruptus* is found to be the most severe noxa, and produces its characteristic effects even in non-predisposed subjects.

Neurasthenia in females. Girls are normally healthy and not neurasthenic; and the same is true of young married women in spite of all the sexual traumas to which they are subject at that age. Neurasthenia occurs comparatively rarely in its pure form in married women and older girls and must then be regarded as having arisen spontaneously and in the same manner [as in men]. Far more often neurasthenia in a married woman is derived from neurasthenia in a man or produced simultaneously. There is then almost always an admixture of hysteria and this constitutes the common mixed neurosis of women.

The *mixed neurosis* of women is derived from neurasthenia in men in all those not infrequent cases in which the man, being neurasthenic, has lost some of his potency. The admixture of hysteria is an immediate result of the withholding of the excitation of the sexual act. The less the man's potency, the more prominent is the woman's hysteria; so that a sexually neurasthenic man makes his wife not so much neurasthenic as hysterical.

The mixed neurosis arises, along with neurasthenia in males, during the onset of the second sexual noxa, which is of far greater importance than the first so far as the woman is concerned, assuming that she is healthy. Thus we find many more neurotic men during the first ten years after puberty and many more neurotic women during the second ten years. In the latter case this is the result of noxæ involved in contraceptive measures. It is not easy to arrange them in order, and in general none of them can be considered innocuous to women; so that even in the most favourable cases (where a condom is used) women, who are more susceptible than men, will scarcely escape slight neurasthenia. A great deal will of course depend on the predispositions of the two partners: whether (1) she herself was neurasthenic before marriage, and (2) whether she was made hystero-neurasthenic during the time when intercourse occurred without preventives.

II. *Anxiety neurosis.* Every case of neurasthenia no doubt includes a certain loss of self-confidence, some degree of pessimistic expectation and an inclination to "distressing antithetic ideas".[1] But it is a question whether, where these factors are prominent without the other symptoms being particularly developed, we should not detach the case as a specific "anxiety neurosis", especially as such a condition is found no less frequently in hysteria than in neurasthenia.

Anxiety neurosis appears in two forms: as a *chronic state* and as an *attack of anxiety.* The two may easily be combined, and an anxiety attack never occurs apart from chronic symptoms. Anxiety attacks are more often found in those cases of anxiety neurosis which are connected with hysteria—that is, they occur more frequently in women. The chronic symptoms occur more often in neurasthenic males.

The chronic symptoms are: (1) anxiety relating to the subject's own body (hypochondria); (2) anxiety relating to his bodily functioning (agoraphobia, claustrophobia, giddiness on heights); and (3) anxiety relating to his decisions and memory, *i.e.,* to his ideas of his psychical functioning (*folie du doute*, obsessive brooding, etc.). So far I have found no reason for not equating these symptoms. We must further consider whether this condition (1) appears by heredity, without any sexual noxa; (2) whether in hereditary cases it is precipitated by some sexual noxa; and (3) whether it supervenes, as an intensification, on common neurasthenia. There is no question that it may be acquired, both in males and females, during marriage; and this is due to *coitus interruptus* during the second period of sexual noxæ [p. 69]. Predisposition through earlier neurasthenia is not, I believe, necessary; though where predisposition is lacking there is a

---

[1] [For this term see "A Case of Successful Treatment by Hypnotism" (Freud, 1892-3 b), published just before the present draft was written.]

longer latent period. The causal formula is the same as in neurasthenia [p. 67].

The comparatively rare cases of anxiety neurosis outside marriage are found especially in men. They arise from *coitus interruptus* where the emotions are strongly involved and where the women's well-being is a matter of concern. The procedure in such circumstances acts as a greater noxa for the man than does *coitus interruptus* in marriage, which is often corrected, as it were, by normal intercourse outside marriage.

Periodic depression must be regarded as a third form of anxiety neurosis, an attack of anxiety which may last for weeks or months. This is almost always distinguished from melancholia proper by having an apparently rational connection with a psychical trauma. The latter is, however, only the precipitating cause. Moreover, such periodic depressions lack the psychical (sexual) anæsthesia which is characteristic of melancholia. [See pp. 101-102.]

I have been able to trace back a number of such cases to *coitus interruptus;* their onset was a late one, during marriage, after the birth of the last child. In a case of tormenting hypochondria which began at puberty, I was able to discover an assault during the eighth year of life. Another case which began during childhood turned out to be a hysterical reaction to a masturbatory assault. Thus I cannot tell whether in this case there are hereditary forms without sexual causes, nor can I tell whether *coitus interruptus* alone is to be blamed, or whether hereditary disposition can always be dispensed with.

I shall omit occupational neuroses since, as I have told you, alterations in the muscular system can be shown to occur in such cases.[1]

Conclusions.—It follows from what I have said that the neuroses can be completely prevented but are completely incurable. The physician's task is thus wholly concentrated on prophylaxis.[2]

---

[1] In Freud's writings there is no further reference to this point.

[2] The thesis that follows is not stated so explicitly anywhere else in Freud's writings. In *Studies on Hysteria* he said: "I should like to hazard the view that it" (the cathartic method) "is capable—in principle—of getting rid of any kind of hysterical symptoms while it is completely helpless, as can readily be seen against neurasthenic phenomena and can only seldom and indirectly influence the mental consequences of anxiety neurosis."

The first part of this task, the prevention of the sexual noxa of the first period, coincides with prophylaxis against syphilis and gonorrhoea, for these are the noxæ which threaten anyone who gives up masturbation. The only alternative would be free sexual intercourse between young males and respectable girls; but this could only be resorted to if there were innocuous preventive methods. Otherwise the alternatives are: masturbation, with neurasthenia in males and hystero-neurasthenia in females, or syphilis in males, with syphilis in the next generation, or gonorrhoea in males, with gonorrhoea and sterility in females.

The same problem—how to find an innocuous method of preventing conception—is set by the sexual noxa of the second period, for the condom provides neither a safe solution nor one which is tolerable to anyone who is already neurasthenic.

In the absence of such a solution society seems doomed to fall a victim to incurable neuroses which reduce the enjoyment of life to a minimum, destroy the marriage relation and bring hereditary ruin on the whole coming generation. The lower ranks of society know nothing of Malthusianism; but they are following along the same path and will eventually fall a victim to the same fatality.

Thus the physician is faced by a problem whose solution deserves all his efforts.

———

By way of preparation I have begun a collection of one hundred cases of anxiety neurosis; and I should like to make a similar collection of male and female neurasthenias, and the more rare periodical depressions. A necessary complement would be a second series of one hundred nervous cases.

If it were established that the functional nervous disturbances which are acquired through sexual abuse could also be the result of pure heredity, it would give rise to the most far-reaching speculations, the nature of which we are only beginning to suspect.

With heartiest greetings,

Your

Sigm. Freud.

12

Vienna, 30. 5. 93.

My dear Fliess,

.... The fact that you are overwhelmed with patients shows that on the whole people know what they are doing. I am curious to know whether you will accept my diagnosis of the cases I have sent you. I make it often now, and entirely agree with you that the nasal reflex neurosis is one of the commonest disorders. Unfortunately I am never sure of the "executive"[1]. The link with sexuality, too, draws closer and closer; it is a pity that we cannot work on the same cases.

..... I see quite a possibility of filling another gap in the sexual ætiology of the neuroses. I believe I understand the anxiety neuroses of young people who must be regarded as virgins with no history of sexual abuse.[2] I have analysed two such cases, and the cause was an apprehensive terror of sexuality, against a background of things they had seen or heard and only half-understood; thus the ætiology was purely emotional, but still of a sexual nature.

The book I send to-day is not very interesting.[3] The hysterical paralyses will be shorter and more interesting, and will appear at the beginning of June.

Heartiest greetings to you and Ida from the whole household.

Your

Sigm. Freud.

Draft C[4]

REPORT ON WORK IN PROGRESS

Dear Fliess, I do not need to do more than hint at the pleasure of

---

[1] [*Exekutive* in the original. This appears to mean "what practical measures to take".]

[2] This is the first hint of the theory of the role of sexual seduction (in the broadest sense) in the ætiology of the neuroses, which Freud only abandoned in the autumn of 1897.

[3] Freud (1893 b).

[4] Undated, but written between Easter and June, 1893, *i.e.*, between the "Easter talk" mentioned in the text and the medical congress at Wiesbaden, at which Fliess read the paper here discussed.

being able to continue our Easter talks. On the whole I am not de-
tached enough to be the right critic for your work. So I shall only
say that I like it very much, and that I do not think the congress will
produce anything more important. I shall leave it to the congress to
pay you all the compliments that your lecture deserves, and in
accordance with your own wish start picking holes in it and making
suggestions for alterations.

It was not written on an entirely headache-free day, because it
lacks the pregnancy and succinctness with which you can write.
Parts are definitely too long, *e.g.*, *formes frustes*. I have marked
with blue pencil the parts that should go to the barber's. I have tried
to bring out a few key-points more effectively.

Let me recommend you a comparison with Menière's disease.
I hope that the nasal reflex neurosis will soon be generally known
as Fliess's disease.

Now for the sexual question. I think you could express yourself
more graphically on this. The way you refer to sexual aetiology
implies a knowledge on the public's part which it has only in latent
form. It knows, but acts as if it did not know. Preyer, whose merit I
fully recognize, has no claim to be given such prominence in such a
brief account.[1]

So far as I know his works . . . he fails in two fundamental
points: (1) He divides neurasthenia into separate disorders of the
stomach, bowels, bladder, etc., of reflex origin; that is to say, he does
not know our aetiological formula, nor does he know that the sexual
noxa, alongside its direct effect, has a predisposing one which
constitutes latent neurasthenia. (2) He derives the reflexes from minor
anatomical changes in the genitals instead of from changes in the
nervous system. Even if *urethra nostica* should be a reflex organ like
the nose, he cuts himself off from the essential line of approach.

I do not think you can avoid mentioning the sexual aetiology of the
neuroses without tearing the finest leaf out of the wreath.[2] So mention
it straight away in a manner suitable to the circumstances. Announce

---

[1] See Preyer 1884, 1888, 1889, 1891 and 1893.
[2] Freud wrote on the assumption that Fliess had accepted his "aetiological
formula" concerning the origin of neurosis and his views on the role of sexuality,
and wanted Fliess to co-operate in his work. This idea was soon abandoned (see
next letter).

the forthcoming investigations, describe the anticipated result as what it really is, as something new, show the people the key that unlocks everything, the aetiological formula; and, if in the process you again refer to me in the guise of "a friendly colleague", I shall be delighted instead of angry. I have written in such a passage on sexuality merely as a suggestion.[1]

In regard to the therapy of the neurasthenic nasal neuroses, I should not express myself too pessimistically. There may be residual phenomena here which quickly disappear, and, if there are pure cases of vasomotor reflex neuroses, perhaps the pure organic cases are not very frequent and the mixed cases are typical. That is how I look at it. . . .

Now "Go where glory waits thee."[2]

With cordial greetings to you and Ida

Your

Sigm. Freud.

No misunderstanding. Do not mention any names! You do not think me so aspiring.

13

Vienna, 10. 7. 93.

My dear Fliess,

If we had not agreed that there should be no obligations between us, I should have to apologize to you very emphatically to-day. But you have not even remarked on my remissness, which has been due to an abnormal disinclination to put pen to paper after a stiff spell of writing.

You have forestalled me by only a few days with your question of when and where we are to meet this year. The answer is at about the same time; the holidays I have ordered myself begin in the middle of August or a little earlier. So there will be no difficulties in the way of our seeing each other. . . .

The hysterical paralyses should have appeared long ago; they will probably appear in the August number, it is quite a short

---

[1] Fliess appears to have adopted some but not all of Freud's suggestions.
[2] [The words in quotation marks are in English in the original.]

paper[1]. . . . Perhaps you remember that I had the subject in mind when you were my pupil, when I lectured on it.[2] I shall not need to trouble you with the neuroses—I see so many cases of neurasthenia now that I shall be able to manage quite well with my own material for the next two or three years.[3] But in saying this I am not dissolving our partnership. In the first place, I hope you will explain the physiological mechanism of my clinical findings from your point of view; secondly, I want to maintain the right to come to you with all my theories and findings in the field of neurosis; and thirdly, I still look to you as the Messiah who will solve the problem I have indicated by an improvement in technique.[4]

Your work on the nasal reflex was not wasted; you are now realizing that for yourself. Only people need time for everything . . . .

Our work on hysteria has at last received proper recognition from Janet in Paris.[5] It has not been possible to do much with

---

[1] "Some Points for a Comparative Study of Organic and Hysterical Motor Paralyses" (1893 c).

[2] The investigation was prompted by a suggestion of Charcot's.

[3] This was the end of Freud's planned co-operation with Fliess referred to in the letter of 8. 2. 93.

[4] Freud expected from Fliess's researches into the menstrual period a solution of the problem of coitus without contraceptives, which was later approached by Knaus on the basis of different theoretical assumptions. See Introduction, page 6.

[5] "*Mais le travail le plus important qui soit venu confirmer nos anciennes études est sans contredit l'article de MM. Breuer et Freud, récemment paru dans le Neuro- logisches Zentralblatt. Nous sommes très heureux que ces auteurs, dans leurs recherches indépendantes, aient pu avec tant de précision vérifier les nôtres, et nous les remercions de leur aimable citation. Ils montrent par de nombreux exemples que les divers symptômes de l'hystérie ne sont pas des manifestations spontanées idiopathiques de la maladie, mais sont en étroite connexion avec le trauma provocateur. Les accidents les plus ordinaires de l'hystérie, même les hyperesthésies, les douleurs, les attaques banales, doivent être interprétés de la même manière que les accidents de l'hystérie traumatique par la persistance d'une idée, d'un rêve. Le rapport entre l'idée et l'accident peut être plus ou moins direct, mais il existe toujours. If faut cependant constater que souvent le malade, dans son état normal, ignore cette idée provocatrice qui ne se retrouve nettement que pendant les périodes d'état second naturelles ou provoquées, et c'est précisément à leur isolement que ces idées doivent leur pouvoir. Le malade est guéri, disent ces auteurs, quand il parvient à retrouver la conscience claire de son idée fixe. Cette division de la conscience, que l'on a constaté avec netteté dans quelques cas célèbres de double existence, existe d'une façon rudimentaire chez toute hystérique.*"—Janet (1894), *p.* 268.
Janet changed his attitude to Freud's work a few years later. Among other things he vigorously denied the therapeutic effect of abreaction and repudiated several of Freud's clinical findings. See Janet (1898) vol. I., p. 163; vol. II, p. 265.

Breuer since then. His time is taken up with weddings, travel, and his practice.

I see that my writing is becoming scarcely legible, so I shall close by saying that we are all well, that I hope the same is true of you and Ida, in spite of lack of news, and that I am looking forward tremendously to the fulfilment of our plan to meet this year.

With cordial greetings,

Your

Sigm. Freud.

14

Vienna, 6. 10. 93.

My dear Fliess,

. . . Your opinion of the paper on Charcot,[1] and the fact that you read it to Ida, delighted me. . . . Meanwhile things have grown livelier. The sexual business attracts people; they all go away impressed and convinced, after exclaiming: "No one has ever asked me that before!" The complication of the thing increases as more confirmation accumulates. Yesterday, for instance, I saw four new cases the aetiology of which, as shown by the chronological data, could only be *coitus interruptus*. It may perhaps amuse you if I give you a short account of them. They are far from being uniform.

1. Woman, age 41; children, 16, 14, 11 and 7. Nervous
   disorder for the last 12 years; well during pregnancy;
   subsequent recurrence; not made worse by the last pregnancy. Attacks of giddiness with feeling of weakness,
   ⌐agoraphobia⌐ *anxious* expectation, no sign of neurasthenia,
   little hysteria. Aetiology confirmed. A case of simple
   [anxiety neurosis].

---

[1] Freud (1893 f).

2. Woman, age 24; children 4 and 2. Since the spring of '93 attacks of pain at night (from back to sternum) with insomnia; otherwise nothing; well during daytime. Husband a commercial traveller; was at home in the spring as well as for some time recently. In the summer while her husband was away she was perfectly well. *Coitus interruptus* and great fear of having a baby. A case of hysteria therefore.

3. Man, age 42; children, 17, 16 and 13. Well until six years ago; then, on the death of his father, sudden attack of anxiety with heart-failure, hypochondriacal fears of cancer of the tongue; several months later a second attack, with cyanosis, intermittent pulse, fear of death, etc.; since then weakness, vertigo, agoraphobia, some dyspepsia. A case of simple anxiety neurosis accompanied by heart symptoms, following after emotion; whereas *coitus interruptus* seems to have been tolerated easily for ten years. [1]

4. Man, age 34. Loss of appetite for the last three years; dyspepsia during the last year, with loss of 20 kilos [44 lb.] constipation; when these symptoms ceased, violent pressure on the head when a scirocco is blowing; attacks of weakness with associated sensations, hysteriform clonic spasms. In this case, therefore, neurasthenia predominates. One child, age 5. Since then *coitus interruptus* owing to his wife's illness. At about the same time as his recovery from dyspepsia, normal intercourse was resumed.

In view of these various reactions to the same noxa, it requires some courage to insist upon the specific nature of its effects in my sense. Yet it must be so; and there is some supporting evidence to be found even in these four cases (simple anxiety neurosis—simple hysteria—anxiety neurosis with heart symptoms—neurasthenia with hysteria).

In Case 1, that of a very intelligent woman, there was no fear of having a baby; she had a simple anxiety neurosis.

---

[1] [This case appears, with some further details, in Freud's first and second papers on anxiety neurosis (1895 b and 1895 f).]

In Case 2, a nice, stupid young woman, the fear of having a baby was highly developed; after a short time she started hysteria.

Case 3, with anxiety and heart symptoms, was a very potent man, who had been a great smoker.

Case 4, on the contrary, was (without having masturbated) only moderately potent—frigid, in fact.

Now think what would happen if one were a physician like you, able to investigate the genitals and the nose simultaneously so to speak; the riddle would be solved in no time.

But I am too old and lazy and overwhelmed with daily tasks to be able to learn anything new at this stage.

With cordial greetings from us to you all,

Your

Sigm. Freud.

The family returned the day before yesterday in the best of health.

15

Vienna, 17. 11. 93.

Dear Fliess,

. . . The sexual business is becoming more and more firmly consolidated, and the contradictions are fading away, but new material is very meagre because of an unusual shortage of patients. When I undertake a case for radical treatment everything is confirmed, and sometimes the seeker finds more than he bargained for—*anæsthesia sexualis* in particular is ambigious and self-contradictory. The anxiety type X has become quite clear. I have seen a gay old bachelor, who denies himself nothing, produce a classic attack after allowing his thirty-year-old mistress to induce him to have coitus three times. I have come to the opinion that anxiety is to be connected, not with a mental, but with a physical consequence of sexual abuse.[1] I was led to this by a remarkably pure case of anxiety-neurosis, after *coitus interruptus* in a placid and entirely frigid woman. Otherwise the thing does not make sense. . . .

I am on good terms with Breuer, but see little of him. He has put himself down for my Saturday lecture! . . .

The enclosed ("Enuresis") is just a hotch-potch.[2]

With heartiest greetings to all,

Yours

Sigm. Freud.

16

Vienna, 7. 2. 94.

My dear Fliess,

I am so harassed at present that I am answering your letter at once; otherwise it might remain unanswered for a long time. Your acceptance of the theory of obsessional ideas did me good, because I miss you all the time while doing that sort of work.[3] When you come to Vienna in the spring you must drag yourself away from the family for a few hours and devote them to discussion with me. I have something else *in petto* that is just dawning on me. You notice that my last paper[4] dealt with conversion and transposition of affect, but besides that there is its transformation. But I shall not lift the veil more than that yet. [See below p. 84].

Conversion Reaction

---

[1] This theory is several times referred to in cautious terms in Freud's first paper on anxiety neurosis (1895 b), in which he writes: "In the first place it was surmised that we are here dealing with an accumulation of excitation; secondly, there was the exceedingly important fact that the anxiety, which underlies all the clinical symptoms of this neurosis, is not derived from any psychical source."

[2] In the essay referred to (Freud 1 893g) he expresses the opinion that a hypertonia of the lower extremities is present in the cases of nearly half the children who suffer from *enuresis nocturna.*

[3] There seems to be a gap between this and the preceding letters (not all of which are reproduced here). The explanation may be that Freud and Fliess met at Christmas in Vienna.

[4] Freud (1894a).

You are right—the connection between obsessional neurosis and sexuality does not always lie so near the surface. I can assure you that in my case II (compulsive micturition) it was not so easy to find. If it had been sought for by anyone less obstinately wedded to the idea, it would have been overlooked.[1] And in this case, which I have been studying carefully over months of feeding up, sexuality quite simply dominates the whole scene. Your case of the disgusted, divorced woman suggests that closer analysis would yield the same result.

I am busy at present with the analysis of several cases which look like paranoia, and fit into my theory. The book on hysteria I am doing with Breuer is half-finished; a few case histories and two general chapters are still outstanding . . .

I forget if I have already told you that I am going to be secretary of the neurological section of the natural sciences congress in September. I hope to see you there, and sometimes with us.

Billroth's death is the talk of the day here.[2] Happy is he who does not outlive his reputation.

With cordial greetings from us all to you and to your charming wife,

Your

Sigm. Freud.

17

Vienna, 19. 4. 94.

My dear Fliess,

After your kind letter I shall not restrain myself and spare you any longer, and I feel I have a right to write to you about my health. Scientific and personal news will come at the end.

As everyone must have come under someone's suggestive influence, to escape his own criticism, from that time on (three weeks ago to-day) I have had nothing lit between my lips, and I can now actually watch others smoking without envying them,

---

[1] See Freud (1894 a) and (1895c), in which the same case is mentioned.
[2] Theodor Billroth (1822-94), professor of surgery in Vienna.

and can conceive of life and work without it. I have only just reached this point, and the misery of abstinence has been unexpectedly great, but that is obvious, after all.

What is less obvious, perhaps, is my state of health in other respects. For several days after the deprivation I felt moderately well, and started to write down my present position on the neurosis question for you. Then came a sudden cardiac oppression, greater than I had before giving up smoking. I had violent arrhythmia, with constant tension, pressure, and burning in the region of the heart, burning pains down the left arm, some dyspnoea—suspiciously moderate, as if organic—all occurring in two or three attacks extending continuously throughout part of the day, and accompanied by a depression of spirits which expressed itself in visions of death and departure in place of the normal frenzy of activity. The organic discomforts have diminished during the last two days, but the hypomanic state persists, having the civility, however, to relax suddenly (as yesterday evening and at midday to-day), leaving behind a human being who looks forward with confidence again to a long life and undiminished pleasure in smoking.

It is painful for a medical man, who spends all the hours of the day struggling to gain an understanding of the neuroses, not to know whether he is himself suffering from a reasonable or a hypochondriacal depression. In such a situation one needs help. So yesterday evening I betook myself to Breuer, and told him my view that the heart trouble was not due to nicotine poisoning, but that I had a chronic myocarditis, which could not tolerate smoking. I remember arrhythmia occurred rather suddenly in 1889 after my attack of influenza. I had the satisfaction of being told that it might be the one thing or the other, and that I should have myself examined. I promised to do so, but I know that these examinations generally do not result in anything being found. I do not know how far it is possible to differentiate between the two things, but I think myself that it should be possible to do so on the basis of the subjective symptoms and events, and that you people know what to think of it. I am suspicious of you this time, because this heart trouble of mine is the first occasion on which I have ever heard you contradict yourself. Last time you explained it as nasal, and said the percussive signs of a nicotine heart were absent; this time you show great concern over me and forbid me to smoke. I can only explain the inconsistency by assuming that you wish to conceal the true state of affairs from me, and I appeal to you not to do that. If you can tell me anything definite, please do so. I have no exaggerated opinion either of my responsibilities or my indispensability, and I should endure with dignity the uncertainty and the shortened expectation of life to be inferred from a diagnosis of myocarditis; indeed, I might perhaps draw benefit from it in arranging the remainder of my life, and enjoy to the full what is left to me.

As I was so completely unable to work, it was painful to realize that in case of chronic illness I could not count on being able to do scientific work. I have not looked at your excellent case-histories. "The present state of knowledge of the neuroses" was abandoned in the middle of a sentence, and everything is as it was in the Sleeping Beauty's castle when the catalepsy overtook it. As the last few days have undoubtedly brought some relief, I hope to catch up soon and shall then report to you further.

Otherwise, I have nothing new on the theory of the neuroses; but I keep collecting material and something will come of it. . . .

So soon as I am capable of work, I shall send you a set of interesting case histories.

With heartiest greetings to your wife and yourself, and many thanks for your letter.

Your
Sigm. Freud.

18

Vienna, 21. 5. 94.

My dear Fliess,

. . . I am pretty well alone here in tackling the neuroses. They regard me rather as a monomaniac, while I have the distinct feeling that I have touched on one of the great secrets of nature.

There is something comic about the incongruity between one's own and other people's estimation of one's work. Look at my book on the diplegias, which I knocked together almost casually, with a minimum of interest and effort.[1] It has been a huge success. The critics say the nicest things about it, and the French reviews in particular are full of praise. Only to-day I have been looking at a book by Raymond, Charcot's successor,[2] which simply quotes me wholesale in the relevant chapter, of course with complimentary acknowledgments. But for the really good things, like the "Aphasia", the "Obsessional Ideas", which threaten to appear shortly, and the coming aetiology and theory of the neuroses, I can expect no more than a respectable flop. This is bewildering and somewhat embittering. There are a hundred gaps, large and small, in my ideas about the neuroses; but I am getting nearer to a comprehensive picture and some general points of view. I know three mechanisms: (1) conversion of affect (conversion hysteria); (2) displacement of affect (obsessions) and (3) transformation of affect (anxiety neurosis and melancholia). In all these cases what seems to undergo the change is sexual excitation; but what precipitates the change is not always something sexual. That is to say, wherever neuroses are *acquired*, they are acquired owing to disturbances of sexual life; but there are people in whom the behaviour of their sexual affects is disturbed *hereditarily*, and they develop the corresponding forms of hereditary neuroses. The most generalized headings under which I can classify [the ætiology of the] neuroses are the following four:

1. Degeneracy.
2. Senility. (And what does that mean ?).
3. Conflict.
4. Conflagration.

Degeneracy signifies an innately abnormal behaviour of the sexual affects; so that in proportion to the part played by the sexual affects in the course of the subject's life, those affects

---

[1] Freud (1893 b).
[2] Raymond (1894). Raymond, Charcot's successor, and Janet were the joint authors of Vol. II of *Névroses et Idées Fixes* (1898).

are "converted", displaced or transformed into anxiety.

Senility is clear. It is, as it were, a degeneracy that is normally acquired in old age.[1]

Conflict coincides with my concept of defence (or fending off). It comprises the cases of acquired neurosis in people who are not hereditarily abnormal. What is fended off is always sexuality.

Conflagration is a new heading. It signifies states of what may be termed *acute* degeneracy (*e.g.*, severe intoxications, fevers, the preliminary stage of general paralysis)—catastrophes, that is to say, in which disturbances of the sexual affects set in without sexual precipitating causes. Perhaps this might lead further into an elucidation of traumatic neuroses.

The core and mainstay of the whole business remains, of course, the fact that even healthy people can acquire the different forms of neurosis if they are subject to special sexual noxae. And the bridge to the more generalized view is provided by the fact that, where a neurosis develops *without* a sexual noxa, a similar disturbance of the sexual affects can be shown to have been present from the first. "Sexual affect" is, of course, taken in the widest sense, as an excitation with a definite quantity.[2]

I might perhaps give you my latest example in support of this thesis:

A man, age 42, strong and handsome. At the age of 30 he suddenly developed a neurasthenic dyspepsia, with a loss of 25 kilos [55 lb.]. Since then he has lived in a reduced and neurasthenic condition. At the time of this development he was engaged to be married, and suffered an emotional upset as a result of his fiancée's falling ill. Apart from this there were no sexual noxae. He masturbated for not more than a year perhaps, from the age of 16 to 17; from 17 onwards he had normal intercourse; scarcely ever practised *coitus interruptus*; no excesses,

---

[1] The conceptions of degeneracy and conflagration play no further part in Freud's writings, but he deals with the special psychological conditions of old age in his first paper on anxiety neurosis (1895b) in which he says: "Anxiety in ageing men (the male climacteric) requires another explanation. There is no reduction in libido here; but, just as during the climacteric in women, such an increase in the production of somatic excitation occurs that the psyche proves relatively unable to master it."

[2] [The concept of "quantity" is discussed at length in the "Project".]

morphology — biological science P deals w/ bodily forms & structure

no abstinence. He himself attributes the cause of his trouble to the strain he put upon his constitution up to the age of 30; to his having worked, drunk and smoked a great deal and to his irregular life. But this strong man, who was subjected to no more than the stock noxæ, had *never* been properly potent (never from the age of 17 to 30); he could never perform coitus more than once at a time; he always ejaculated quickly; he was never really able fully to use his chances with women; he never found his way into the vagina easily. What was the origin of this limitation? I cannot tell. But it is a remarkable thing that it was present in his particular case. Incidentally, I have treated two of his sisters for neuroses. One of these is among my most successful cures of neurasthenic dyspepsia. . . .

With cordial greetings to you and Ida from your devoted

Sigm. Freud.

Draft D

[Undated.? May 1894.]

ON THE AETIOLOGY AND THEORY OF THE MAJOR NEUROSES[1]

I. CLASSIFICATION

Introduction. Historical. Gradual differentiation of the neuroses—The course of development of my own views.

A. *Morphology of the Neuroses.*
  1. Neurasthenia and the pseudo-neurasthenias.
  2. Anxiety neurosis.
  3. Obsessional neurosis.
  4. Hysteria.
  5. Melancholia, mania.
  6. The mixed neuroses.
  7. Ramifications of the neuroses. Transitions to the normal.

---

[1] "The Aetiology and Theory of the Major Neuroses" is mentioned in Letter 18 (21. 5. 94). This draft may be somewhat earlier.

ephemeral

B. *Aetiology of the Neuroses* (provisionally restricted to acquired neuroses).

   1. Aetiology of neurasthenia—Type of innate neurasthenia.

   2. Aetiology of anxiety neurosis.

   3. Aetiology of obsessional neurosis and hysteria.

   4. Aetiology of melancholia.

   5. Aetiology of the mixed neuroses.

   6. The basic aetiological formula [p. 67]—The thesis of specific aetiologies. The separating out of the medley of neuroses.

   7. Sexual factors and their aetiological significance.

   8. Examination of patients.[1]

   9. Objections and proofs.

  10. Behaviour of asexual persons.

C. *Aetiology and Heredity.*

The hereditary types—Relation of ætiology to degeneracy, to the psychoses and to predisposition.

II. THEORY[2]

the Project

D. *Points of Contact with the Theory of Constancy.*

Internal and external increase of stimulus: constant and ephemeral excitation. — Summation a characteristic of internal excitation. — Specific reaction. [p. 379] —Formulation and elaboration of the theory of constancy. — The part played by the ego and the storing-up of excitation.[3]

E. *The Sexual Process in the Light of the Theory of Constancy.*

Path taken by the excitation in the male and female sexual processes. — Path taken by the excitation under the influence of aetiologically operative sexual noxæ. — Theory of a sexual substance. The schematic picture of sexuality [p. 104 *sqq*].

F. *Mechanism of the Neuroses.*

The neuroses as disturbances of equilibrium due to increased

---

[1] Freud obviously intended to deal with problems of therapeutic technique in addition to clinical and theoretical problems, and in fact did so shortly afterwards in the last chapter of *Studies on Hysteria*.

[2] Freud's plan to base the theory of the neuroses on the psychical regulative principles was carried out in his metapsychological writings (1911-20).

[3] [All these points are developed in Part I of the "Project."]

anything physical or mental P i injurious to physical kind

difficulty in discharge. — Attempts at compensation of limited efficiency. — Mechanism of the different neuroses in relation to their sexual aetiology. — Affects and neuroses.

G. *Parallel between Neuroses of Sexuality and Hunger.*

H. *Summary of the Theories of Constancy, Sexuality and the Neuroses.*
Place of the neuroses in pathology. Factors to which they are subject. Laws governing their combination. — Psychical inefficiency, development, degeneracy, etc.

Draft E

[Undated. ? June 1894.]

HOW ANXIETY ORIGINATES[1]

You have unerringly put your finger on the point which I myself feel is the weak one. So this is all I know about it:—

It quickly became clear to me that my neurotic patients' anxiety had much to do with sexuality; and in particular it struck me how inevitably *coitus interruptus* practised on a woman led to anxiety neurosis. I began by following a number of false scents. I thought that the anxiety from which patients suffer was a prolongation of the anxiety experienced during the sexual act—that it was, in fact, a *hysterical* symptom. And indeed the connections between anxiety neurosis and hysteria are sufficiently obvious. There might be two occasions for anxiety in *coitus interruptus:* in the woman, a fear of becoming pregnant, and in the man, a fear that his device might not succeed. But I then found convincing evidence in a number of cases that anxiety neurosis also appeared where there was no question of these two factors being present, where it was really of no importance to the people concerned whether they had a baby. Thus anxiety neurosis could not be a prolongation of recollected, *hysterical* anxiety.

---

[1] Draft E has been inserted in this place because it seems to fit in by reason of its contents. An envelope bearing the postmark 6. 6. 1894 may possibly belong to it. A substantial part of it agrees with his first paper on anxiety neurosis (1895b) in declaring neurasthenia to be a definite complex of symptoms to be differentiated from anxiety neurosis. Freud mentions his intention of writing this paper in the next letter.

A second, highly important point was established by the following observation. Anxiety neurosis is found in women who are anaesthetic during intercourse no less than in women who have sensations. This is most remarkable and it can only mean one thing: that the source of anxiety is not to be looked for in psychical events. It must lie in physical events; and what generates anxiety must be some physical factor in sexual life. But what can this factor be?

To resolve this question I collected all the conditions under which I found anxiety arising from sexual causes. They seemed at first a most heterogeneous collection:—

1. Anxiety occurring in *virginal* subjects (where sexual observations have been made or sexual information received, or where there are foreshadowings of sexual life). Numerous instances of this have been confirmed, in both sexes, though principally in women. Not infrequently there is a hint at an intermediate link—a feeling in the genitals akin to an erection.

2. Anxiety occurring in subjects who are *deliberately abstinent*—prudes (a neuropathic type). These are men and women characterized by pedantry and a love of cleanliness, who regard anything sexual as an abomination. These people are inclined to work their anxiety over into phobias, obsessive acts or *folie du doute*.

3. Anxiety in subjects who are *abstinent from necessity*: women who are neglected by their husbands or cannot be satisfied owing to their husbands' lack of potency. This form of anxiety neurosis can certainly be acquired, and, owing to subsidiary circumstances, is often combined with neurasthenia.

4. Anxiety in women who are subject to *coitus interruptus*, or (what is very similar) in women whose husbands suffer from *ejaculatio praecox*—in subjects, that is, in whom physical stimulation is not satisfied.

5. Anxiety in men who practise *coitus interruptus*, and still more in men who excite their sexual feelings in various ways but do not employ their erections for intercourse.

6. Anxiety in men who force themselves to carry out intercourse though it is *beyond their desire or strength*.

7. Anxiety in men who are *abstinent from contingent circumstances*: in youngish men for instance, married to women older than themselves, by whom they are in fact disgusted, or in neurasthenics who have been diverted from masturbation by intellectual occupations without compensating for this by intercourse, or in men whose potency is beginning to decline and who abstain from intercourse in marriage on account of [unpleasant] sensations *post coitum*.

In the remaining cases the connection between the anxiety and sexual life was not obvious, though it could be demonstrated theoretically.

How are all these different instances to be combined? The factor of abstinence is the most frequently recurring one. If we bear in mind our observation that anxiety occurs after *coitus interruptus* even in those who are anæsthetic, we may lay it down that what we are dealing with is a physical accumulation of excitation—*an accumulation of physical sexual tension*. The accumulation is due to discharge being held up. Anxiety neurosis is thus, like hysteria, a neurosis due to damned-up excitation, and this explains their similarity. And since there is no sign of anxiety in what is accumulated, the position can be expressed by saying that the anxiety arises from a *transformation* of the accumulated tension.

At this point we may interpolate some information arrived at simultaneously on the mechanism of melancholia. It happens quite particularly often that sufferers from melancholia are anæsthetic. [See p. 101 *sqq*.] They have no need for coitus and no sensations in connection with it; but they have a great longing for love in its psychical form—or, as we might put it, they are subject to great psychical erotic tension. And if this accumulates and remains unsatisfied, melancholia develops. Here, then, we should have the counterpart to anxiety neurosis:—

Where there is an accumulation of *physical* sexual tension, we find anxiety neurosis.

Where there is an accumulation of *psychical* sexual tension, we find melancholia.

But why should this transformation into anxiety occur when there

endogenous — originating from within a structure
or ~~system~~ esp originating from
within the body

is an accumulation of tension? At this point we should have to enter into the normal mechanism for dealing with accumulated tension. What we are here concerned with is the second possibility—the case of endogenous excitation. With exogenous excitation [the first possibility] things are simpler. The source of excitation is outside and sends an increased amount of excitation into the psyche, and this is dealt with according to its quantity. For this purpose any reaction is sufficient which reduces the psychical excitation by the same amount.

But it is otherwise with endogenous tension, the source of which lies within the subject's own body (hunger, thirst or the sexual instinct). In this case only *specific* reactions are of use: reactions which prevent the further production of excitation in the end-organs concerned, whether those reactions can be achieved with a greater or less expenditure of energy.[1] We may suppose that endogenous tension may increase continuously or discontinuously, but that in either case it is only noticed when it has reached a certain *threshold*. It is only above this threshold that it is turned to *psychical* account and that it enters into relation with certain groups of ideas which then set about producing the specific remedies. Thus physical sexual tension, when it rises above a certain degree, arouses psychical libido which then leads to copulation, etc. If the specific reaction does not follow, the physico-psychical tension (the sexual affect) increases to an immeasurable extent; it becomes an interference, but there is still no ground for its becoming transformed. In anxiety neurosis, however, a transformation *does* occur, and this suggests that things have gone wrong in the following fashion. The physical tension increases and reaches the threshold level at which it can arouse a psychical affect. But for some reason the psychical linkage offered to it remains insufficient; a sexual affect cannot be formed, because there is something lacking in the psychical conditions. Accordingly the tension, not being psychically "bound",[2] is transformed into—anxiety.

If we accept our theory up to this point, we shall be obliged to insist that in anxiety neurosis there is a deficiency in sexual affect, in *psychical libido*. And this is confirmed by observation. If we draw the

---

[1] [This whole topic is expanded in the "Project."]
[2] [On the concept of "bound" energy see the "Project", p. 425.]

attention of women patients to this connection, they are always in-
dignant, and declare that on the contrary they have no sexual desires
whatever. Men patients often agree that they have noticed that since
becoming anxious they have experienced no sexual desire.

We will now see how far this mechanism agrees with the different
instances that have been enumerated above.

1. *Virginal anxiety*. Here the field of ideas which ought to take
   up the physical tension is not yet present or it is only present
   insufficiently; moreover there is, as a further factor, a psychical
   repudiation of sexuality, which is a secondary result of upbringing. This class conforms very well to the hypothesis.

2. *Anxiety in prudes*. Here we find defence at work—a complete
   psychical refusal, which makes any working-over of the sexual
   tension impossible. This class includes the common case of
   obsessive ideas; again it conforms very well.

3. *Anxiety from enforced abstinence*. This is essentially the same as
   the last case. For women of this kind usually induce psychical
   refusal in order to avoid temptation. The refusal in the present
   case is a contingent one, while in the former case it is intrinsic.

4. *Anxiety from coitus interruptus in women*. Here the mechanism
   is simpler. What we are dealing with is endogenous excitation
   which does not originate spontaneously but is induced [from
   outside] and is not sufficient in amount to be able to arouse
   psychical affect. An artificial alienation is brought about
   between the physico-sexual act and its psychical working-over.
   If subsequently the endogenous tension is further increased on
   its own account, it cannot be worked over and so generates
   anxiety. Here, then, the place of *psychical refusal* is taken by
   psychical alienation; and in place of tension of endogenous
   origin we have induced tension.

5. *Anxiety in men from coitus interruptus or reservatus*. The case of
   coitus reservatus is the more straightforward. *Coitus interruptus*
   may be regarded partly as equivalent to it. Once again we are
   dealing with psychical diversion, for attention is turned to
   another aim and is diverted from the working-over of the
   physical tension. But this explanation of *coitus interruptus*
   probably stands in need of improvement.

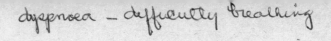
dyspnoea — difficulty breathing

6. *Anxiety from diminishing potency or insufficient libido.* In so far as this is not the transformation of physical tension into anxiety as a result of senility, it is to be explained as being due to the impossibility of summoning up sufficient psychical desire for the performance of some individual sexual act.

7. *Anxiety in men owing to disgust, or in abstinent neurasthenics.* The former case requires no fresh explanation. The latter is perhaps a special attenuated form of anxiety neurosis, for this normally develops fully only in potent men. It may be that the neurasthenic nervous system cannot tolerate an accumulation of physical tension, since masturbation involves becoming accustomed to frequent and complete absence of tension.

The explanation does not fit so badly on the whole. Where there is abundant sexual tension but where it cannot be turned into affect by being worked over psychically—whether on account of insufficient development of psychical sexuality, or of attempts to suppress it (*i.e.,* defence), or of its falling into decay, or of habitual alienation between physical and psychical sexuality—the sexual tension is transformed into anxiety. Thus a part is played in this process by the accumulation of physical tension and by obstacles in the way of its discharge in a psychical direction.

But why is it transformed into *anxiety*? Anxiety is the sensation of an accumulation of another endogenous stimulus—the stimulus towards breathing—which cannot be worked over psychically in any way; anxiety may therefore be capable of being used in relation to accumulated physical tension in general. Furthermore, if we examine the symptoms of anxiety neurosis more closely, we find that it includes the disjointed fragments of a major anxiety attack: simple dyspnoea, simple palpitation, simple feelings of anxiety, and combinations of these. Looked at more precisely, these are the paths of innervation along which the physico-sexual tension normally passed even when it is being worked over psychically. The dyspnoea and the palpitation are concomitants of copulation, and, while normally they are used only as subsidiary paths of discharge, here they serve, so to speak, as the only ways of escape for the excitation. Thus there is a kind of "conversion" at work in anxiety neurosis just as there is in hysteria (once again a similarity between the two); only in hysteria it is a *psychical* excitation which takes a wrong path in an exclusively somatic direction, whereas in anxiety neurosis it is a *physical* tension, which is unable to find a psychical outlet and consequently continues along a physical path. The two are extremely often combined.

later view? [handwritten marginal note]

That is as far as I have got. The gaps sorely need filling in; I think it is incomplete, something is missing, but I believe the foundation is right. It is still completely unsuitable for publication, of course. Suggestions, amplifications, indeed refutations and explanations, will be received with extreme gratitude.

With cordial greetings,

Your

Sigm. Freud.

19

22. 6. 94.

My dear Fliess,

Your letter, which I have just read, has reminded me of an obligation which I intended in any case to fulfil very soon. To-day I withdrew from my meagre practice to jot down some notes, but instead I shall write you a long letter about "theory and life".

Thank you for letting me know what you think of the anxiety paper. Your opinion that it will not do yet is the echo of my own; indeed, no one else has set eyes on it. I am letting it lie until I can get it clearer. But I have got no further yet, and shall have to wait until light dawns on me from somewhere. I should like to produce a preliminary study of the grounds for differentiating anxiety-neurosis from neurasthenia; but that would mean going into theory and aetiology, and so I prefer not to. I have further developed the conversion theory and explained its

conversion theory [handwritten marginal note]

connection with autosuggestion, but that is not yet ready either; I am letting it lie. The book with Breuer will include five case-histories, a chapter by him—from which I dissociate myself—on the theories of hysteria (summarizing and critical), and one by me on therapy[1] which I have not started yet. . . .

The children are flourishing, except that I am rather worried about Mathilde. My wife is all right and cheerful, but does not look very well. We are on the point of getting old, rather prematurely for the children.

I actually spend the whole day thinking about nothing but the neuroses, but since my scientific contact with Breuer has ended I have been thrown back on myself alone, which is why it goes so slowly.

With heartiest greetings to your wife and yourself,

Your devoted

Sigm. Freud.

20

Reichenau, 18. 8. 94.

My dear Fliess,

I am home, after a magnificent reception from the flourishing brood, with the delightful flavour of the days in Munich still lingering in my mind—another of those moments in which one can take pleasure in life. . . .

After I had been back for a few hours a small case of anxiety neurosis presented itself and had to be allowed to stay; I am jotting it down for you at once, not to be read immediately, but some time when you have a free hour, along with many others of my collection.

Heartiest greetings to you and Frau Ida. Yours, with the feeling that our separation is still far from complete,

Sigm. Freud.

---

[1] See last chapter of *Studies on Hysteria*, "On the psychotherapy of hysteria".

Draft F

18. Aug. 94.

COLLECTION III[1]

No. 1.   Anxiety Neurosis: Hereditary
                                                              Disposition.

Herr K., Age 27.

Father treated for senile melancholia. Sister O. well-marked case of complicated anxiety neurosis; thoroughly analysed. All the K.'s neurotic and mentally gifted. Cousin of Dr. K. of Bordeaux.—In good health till recently; has slept badly for the last 9 months; in February and March woke frequently with night-terrors and palpitation; gradually increasing general excitability; intermission owing to army manœuvres, which did him a great deal of good. Three weeks ago in the evening a sudden attack of anxiety with no content, attended by a feeling of congestion from his chest upwards to his head; interpreted by him as meaning that something dreadful must be going to happen; not accompanied by any sense of oppression and only by slight palpitation. Similar attacks followed in daytime as well and at midday meal. Two weeks ago consulted a physician; improved on bromide, though condition is still present, but sleeps well. Besides this, during the last two weeks, short attacks of deep depression, resembling complete apathy, lasting only a few minutes; has improved here in R—. Furthermore, attacks of pressure at the back of the head.

He himself began by volunteering sexual information. A year ago he fell in love with a girl who was a flirt. It was a great shock to him to find she was engaged to someone else. He is no longer in love with her now.—He attached very little importance to this.—Further, between the age of 13 and 16 or 17 he used to masturbate—as a result of being seduced at school—to a moderate extent according to him. He was moderate in sexual intercourse; he had used a condom for the last $2\frac{1}{2}$ years for fear of infection; often felt limp after using it;

---

[1] The two case histories that follow are connected with the ideas on the "aetiological formula" which Freud developed in "A Reply to Criticisms of my Paper on Anxiety Neurosis" (1895 f) and more extensively in "Heredity and the Aetiology of the Neuroses (1896 a). The numbering obviously refers to clinical notes which have not survived.

described this kind of intercourse as "forced"; noticed that his libido had been greatly diminished during the last year. He had been very much sexually excited in his relations with this girl (without touching her, etc.). His first attack at night (in February) was two days after having had intercourse; his first anxiety attack was the same evening after having had intercourse; afterwards (for three weeks) he had been abstinent—a peaceful, affectionate and in other ways normal man.

18. 8. 94.
Discussion of No. 1.

If we attempt to interpret the case of K., one thing in especial forces itself upon us. He had a hereditary disposition: his father suffered from melancholia (possibly an anxious melancholia), his sister, whom I know very well, suffered from a typical anxiety neurosis, which I should otherwise certainly have described as acquired. This gives one ground for thought on the subject of heredity. In the K. family there is probably only a "disposition" (a tendency to fall more and more seriously ill in response to the typical aetiology) and no "degeneracy". It may be presumed therefore, that in Herr K.'s own case the mild anxiety neurosis arose from a mild ætiology. Where would unprejudiced views lead us to look for that ætiology?

It seems to me in the first place that we are faced by an enfeebled condition of sexuality. The man's libido has been diminishing for some time; preparing to use a condom is enough to make him feel that the whole sexual act is forced and that his enjoyment of it is imaginary. This is no doubt the core of the whole matter. After intercourse he feels limp; he notices this, as he says, and then two days later or (as the case may be) during the same evening, has his first attacks of anxiety.

The combination of reduced libido with an anxiety neurosis fits in well with my theory. There is a weakness in the psychical mastery of the somatic sexual excitation [*Cf.* Draft G.]. This weakness has been present for some time and makes it possible for anxiety to appear if there is an incidental increase in somatic excitation.

How was this psychical enfeeblement acquired? A small amount of masturbation in boyhood would certainly not produce such results, and it seems not to have exceeded the usual amount. His relations with the girl, which caused him great sensual excitement, seem much better calculated to cause a disturbance of this kind; indeed, the case resembles the conditions we find in the neurosis so common in men during long engagements. But above all it cannot be doubted that his fear of infection and decision to use a condom formed the basis of what I have called the factor of alienation between the somatic and the psychical. [p. 93]. The effect seems to have been the same as that produced in men by *coitus interruptus*. In short, Herr K. brought psychical sexual enfeeblement on himself because he took a dislike to copulating; and, his physical health and his production of sexual stimuli being unimpaired, the situation led to the generation of anxiety. We may add that his readiness to take precautions instead of finding adequate satisfaction in a safe sexual relationship points to a sexuality which was from the first of no great strength. He had, indeed, a bad heredity; and the aetiological factor observable in his case, though it was *qualitatively* important, would have been tolerated without difficulty by a healthy (that is, by a vigorous) man.

An interesting feature of this case is the appearance of typically melancholic moods in attacks of short duration. This must be of theoretical importance in connection with anxiety neurosis due to alienation; but for the moment I can only draw attention to it.

20. Aug. 94.
No. 2.
Herr von F., Budapest. Age 44.

A healthy man physically. He complained that "he was losing his liveliness and zest, which was not natural in a man of his age". This state—in which everything seems indifferent to him, and in which he finds his work a burden and feels peevish and limp—is accompanied by severe pressure on the top, and also on the back, of his head. Moreover, it is regularly characterized by bad digestion, *i.e.*, by disinclination for food and by flatulence and sluggish stools. He also seems to sleep badly.

But the condition evidently appears only at intervals. Each time it lasts for 4 or 5 days and then gradually passes off. He notices from the flatulence that there is going to be an onset of the nervous weakness. There are intervals of 12 to 14 days; sometimes he is well for as much as several weeks. On occasion, good periods have even lasted for months. He insists that he has been like this for the last 25 years. As so often happens, one has to build up the picture of his symptoms, for he keeps on monotonously repeating his complaints and declares that he has paid no attention to any other events. Thus the indeterminate outline of the attacks forms part of the picture, as well as their complete temporal irregularity. Of course he puts the blame for his condition on to his digestion. . . .

Organically sound; no serious worries or emotional disturbances. As regards his sexuality: Masturbated from the age of 12 to 16; then very regular relations with women, though without any overwhelming urge. Married for the last 14 years; only two children, the younger 10 years ago. In the interval and since then has used a condom and no other technique. His potency has decidedly diminished during the last few years, with intercourse every 12 to 14 days, often with long intervals. Admits that after intercourse with a condom he feels limp and wretched, not immediately afterwards, but two days later. That is, as he puts it, he has noticed that two days later he gets digestive trouble. Why does he use a condom? Well, one mustn't have too many children! ([He has] 2.)

Discussion.

A mild, but very characteristic, case of periodic depression or melancholia.[1] Symptoms: apathy, inhibition, pressure on the head, dyspepsia, disturbance of sleep—the picture is complete.

There is an unmistakable similarity to neurasthenia, and the aetiology is the same. I have actually analogous cases who are masturbators (*e.g.*, Herr A.); and also people with a bad heredity— the von F.'s are notoriously psychopathic. So it is a case of neurasthenic melancholia, and there must be a point of contact here with the theory of neurasthenia.

It is quite possible that the invariable starting-point of a minor melancholia like this may be an act of intercourse. An exaggeration

---

[1] The word "melancholia" is used in the sense in which we would now talk of depression.

of the physiological dictum: *omne animal post coitum triste*. The time-intervals would tally: The man is improved by every course of treatment and every absence from home—that is, by every period of relief from intercourse. Of course he is, as he says, faithful to his wife. His use of a condom is evidence of weak potency; being something analogous to masturbation, it acts as a continuous causative factor of his melancholia.

21

Reichenau, 29. 8. 94.

My dear Fliess,

. . . On this Monday[1] I have collected only a few cases:
No. 3.

Dr. Z., physician. Age 34. Has suffered for many years from irritability of the eyes: phospheum [flashes], dazzle, scotomas, etc. These have increased enormously, to the point of preventing his working, during the last 4 months (since the time of his marriage). Background: masturbation since the age of 14, apparently continued up to the last few years. Marriage not consummated; greatly reduced potency; incidentally, divorce proceedings started.

Typical case of hypochondria relating to a particular organ in a masturbator at a period of sexual excitation. It is interesting to observe to what a superficial depth medical education penetrates.
No. 4.

Herr D. Nephew of Frau A. who died a hysteric. A highly neurotic family. Age 28. Has suffered for some weeks from lassitude, pressure on the head, shaky knees, reduced potency, premature ejaculation, the beginnings of perversion: very young girls attract him more than mature ones.

Alleges that his potency has been capricious from the first; admits masturbation but not for an unduly long time; has a long

---

[1] Obviously the day on which Freud went into Vienna for his consultation hour during the summer holiday.

period of abstinence behind him at present. Earlier, anxiety states in the evening.

Has he made a full confession ? . . .

A monograph by Moebius has appeared, called *Neurologische Beiträge*.[1] It is a collection of previously published little essays, very well done; they are important on the subject of hysteria. His is the best mind among the neurologists; fortunately he is not on the track of sexuality.

Actually I realize I have nothing to say at the moment. When I get back to Vienna my editor[2] will certainly be after me for articles. Might I not offer him a critical article on M's "Migraine" ?[3] You would have to let me have some of your observations. Will you not get your essay on the stomach-menstrual business[4] off your chest as soon as you feel better ? That is the kind of thing the profession is waiting for.

Sigm.

Draft G

[Undated.   ? 7. 1. 1895.[5]]

MELANCHOLIA

I

The facts before us seem to be as follows:

A. There are striking connections between melancholia and

---

[1] Moebius (1894).

[2] Dr. Paschkis, editor of the *Wiener Klinische Rundschau*. Freud was one of his regular contributors.

[3] The reference is presumably to a paper of Meynert's.

[4] This article, frequently mentioned in the correspondence, was submitted to the *Wiener Klinische Rundschau* by Freud on Fliess' behalf and appeared in 1895. See Introduction, p. 6.

[5] This draft, according to the postmark on the envelope that apparently belongs to it, seems to have been written on 7. 1. 1895, after a meeting with Fliess at Christmas. In it Freud follows the practice of the older German psychiatrists and uses the term "melancholia" to describe all states even of mild parathymia and depression. Freud naturally soon found this attempt to derive "melancholia" from a reaction to sexual excitation insufficient. He pointed out in "Further Remarks on the Neuro-Psychoses of Defence" (1896 b) that " 'periodic melancholia' in particular appears to be reducible with unexpected frequency to obsessional affects and obsessional ideas" and hence could be explained by the nature of obsessional-neurotic conflict. A little later he recognized the whole attempt to have been

[sexual] anæsthesia. This is proved (1) by the discovery that so many melancholics have a long history of anæsthesia; (2) by the experience that everything that provokes anæsthesia also encourages the development of melancholia; and (3) by the existence of a type of woman, very demanding psychically, whose desire changes over very easily into melancholia, and who are anæsthetic.

B. Melancholia can arise as an intensification of neurasthenia as a result of masturbation.

---

mistaken. (See also Letter 102). All that survived clinical observation was what could later be translated into the language of the libido theory, especially the comparison between mourning and melancholia. It was used in Freud's conclusion to the "Discussion on Suicide" (1910 g) and in "Mourning and Melancholia" (1917 e), where he refers to Abraham's work on the subject. (Abraham, 1912).

The theoretic assumptions from which Freud proceeds in this draft are known from the first of his two papers on the anxiety neurosis (1895b), which appeared a little later but was written earlier. In this he states: "In the sexually mature male organism somatic sexual excitation is produced—probably continuously—and acts periodically as a psychical stimulus. In order to define this idea more clearly, let us interpolate that this somatic sexual excitation takes the form of pressure on the walls of the *vesiculae seminales* which are lined with nerve-endings; this visceral excitation will then actually develop continuously, but only when it reaches a certain height will it be sufficient to overcome the resistance in the paths of conduction to the cerebral cortex and express itself as a psychical stimulus. Thereupon the group of sexual ideas present in the mind becomes charged with energy and a psychical state of libidinal tension comes into existence, bringing with it an impulse to relieve this tension. The necessary psychical relief can only be effected by what I shall describe as a *specific* or *appropriate action*. For the male sexual instinct this appropriate action consists in a complicated spinal reflex act leading to the relief of the tension at these nerve-endings and in all the preparatory psychical processes necessary to induce this reflex. Nothing but the appropriate action would be effective; for, once it has reached the required level, the somatic sexual excitation is continuously transmuted into psychical excitation; the action which will free the nerve endings from the burdensome pressure and so abolish the whole of the somatic excitation present, thus allowing the subcortical tracts to re-establish their resistance, must absolutely be carried into operation. . . . In women also we must postulate a somatic sexual excitation, and a condition in which this excitation becomes a psychical stimulus, evoking libido and the impulse to a specific action to which voluptuous pleasure is attached. Where women are concerned, however, we cannot state what is the process analogous to the relief of tension in the *vesiculae seminales*."

Draft G carries these considerations further and the schematic picture of sexuality (p. 104) illustrates them. The attempt to explain on a purely physiological basis the difference between the male and female sexual function is also carried a little further, presumably under the influence of Fliess, who may well, here as elsewhere, have pressed for a physiological explanation.

C. Melancholia appears in a typical combination with severe anxiety.

D. The typical and extreme case of melancholia appears to be the periodic or cyclical hereditary form.

II

Before we can do anything with this material we must have some fixed points of departure. These seem to be provided by the following considerations:

a. The affect corresponding to melancholia is mourning or grief—that is, longing for something that is lost. Thus in melancholia there is probably a question of a loss—a loss in the subject's instinctual life.

b. The nutritional neurosis parallel to melancholia is anorexia. The well-known *anorexia nervosa* of girls seems to me (on careful observation) to be a melancholia occurring where sexuality is undeveloped. The patient asserts that she has not eaten simply because she has no appetite and for no other reason. Loss of appetite—in sexual terms, loss of libido.

So it would not be far wrong to start from the idea that *melancholia consists in mourning over loss of libido.*

It now remains to be seen whether this formula explains the occurrence and peculiarities of cases of melancholia. I shall go on to discuss this on the basis of the schematic picture of sexuality. [Fig. 1].

III[1]

I will now discuss, on the basis of the schematic picture of sexuality which I have often used [see Fig 1] the conditions under which the excitation of the psychical sexual group[2] (Ps.S) becomes reduced in

---

[1] Several of the ideas in this section are developed far more clearly in the section of *Three Essays on the Theory of Sexuality* (1905 d) headed "The Problem of Sexual Excitation". Greater light was thrown on the ideas with which Freud is here concerned with the introduction of the concept of libido as the "psychical energy of the sexual instinct".

[2] [*I.e.*, the group of ideas with which the physical sexual tension enters into contact after reaching a certain magnitude, and which then work over the tension and deal with it psychically (see p. 91.) Here as elsewhere in these MSS. (see footnote on p. 355) Freud makes use of numerous abbreviations. These are not always uniform, and their expansion by the editor has not been easy. Thus in this passage Freud himself explains that "Ps. S." stands for "psychical sexual group"; but a few lines lower down he uses the initials "Ps. G." for what appears to be the same term.]

magnitude. There are two possible cases: (1) when the production of somatic sexual excitation (S.S.) diminishes or ceases, and (2) when the sexual tension is diverted from the psychical sexual group (Ps.S.).

Schematic Picture of Sexuality

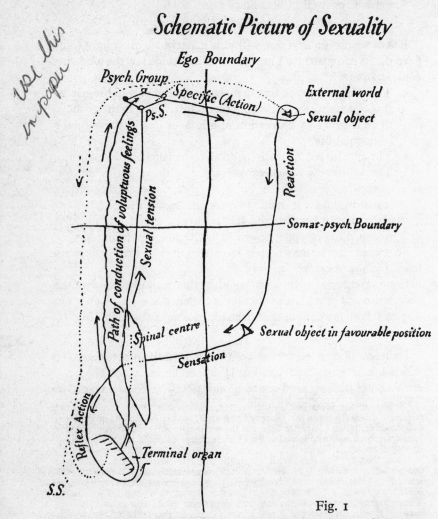

Fig. 1

[In the original all the arrows are in red, except the dotted one on the extreme left.]

The first case, in which the production of somatic sexual excitation (S.S.) ceases, probably characterizes common severe melancholia proper, which recurs periodically, or cyclical melancholia, in which periods of increase and cessation of production alternate. Now, our theory of excessive masturbation assumes that it leads to excessive discharge from the terminal organ (T.) and so produces a low level of stimulus in that terminal organ. We may therefore conclude that excessive masturbation goes on to affect the production of somatic sexual excitation (S.S.) and to bring about a lasting diminution of it, and that it consequently leads to a weakening of the psychical sexual group. Here we should have neurasthenic melancholia.

The second case, in which sexual tension is diverted from the psychical sexual group while the production of somatic sexual excitation (S.S.) remains undiminished, presupposes that the somatic sexual excitation (S.S.) is employed elsewhere—at the boundary [between the somatic and the psychical, see Fig. 1]. This however, is the determinant of anxiety; and this case accordingly coincides with that of anxious melancholia, a mixed form combining anxiety neurosis and melancholia.

In this discussion, then, I have accounted for the three forms of melancholia which have in fact to be distinguished.

IV

How does it come about that anæsthesia plays this part in melancholia ?

According to the schematic picture, we have the following classes of anæsthesia.

Anæsthesia always consists in the omission of the voluptuous feelings (V) which ought to find their way into the psychical sexual group after the reflex action which discharges the terminal organ. The amount of voluptuous feeling corresponds to the quantity of discharge.

a. The terminal organ is insufficiently charged and in consequence the discharge when copulation takes place is slight and V very small. Here we have the case of frigidity.

b. The path from sensation to the reflex action is damaged, so that that action is not sufficiently strong. In that case the discharge and the voluptuous feeling will also be slight. Here we have the case of masturbatory anæsthesia, anæsthesia with *coitus interruptus*, etc.

c. Everything at the lower levels is in order. But the voluptuous feeling is not admitted to the psychical sexual group owing to being linked in another direction (with disgust—defence). Here we have hysterical anæsthesia, which is entirely analogous to hysterical anorexia (disgust).

How far, now, does anaesthesia encourage melancholia?

In case (*a*), that of frigidity, the anæsthesia is not the *cause* of the melancholia but an indication of a predisposition to it. This tallies with Fact A (1) mentioned at the beginning of this paper [pp. 101-102]. In other cases the anæsthesia *is* the cause of the melancholia, since the psychical sexual group is strengthened by the introduction of voluptuous feelings and weakened by their omission. (There is a reference here to the general theory of the "binding" of excitation in the memory.[1]) Fact A (2) [pp. 101-102] is thus taken into account.

Accordingly, it is possible to be anæsthetic without being melancholic; for melancholia is related to the absence of somatic sexual excitation (S.S.), while anæsthesia is related to the absence of voluptuous feelings. Anæsthesia is, however, an indication of or preparation for melancholia; since the psychical sexual group is as much weakened by the absence of voluptuous feelings as by the absence of somatic sexual tension.

V

The question deserves to be raised of why anæsthesia is so predominantly a characteristic of *women*. This arises from the passive part played by women. An anæsthetic man will soon cease to undertake sexual intercourse, but women have no choice. They become anæsthetic more easily for two reasons:

(1) Their whole upbringing aims at not arousing somatic sexual excitation (S.S.) but at translating into psychical stimuli any excitations which might otherwise have that effect—at directing the dotted path from the sexual object (in Fig. 1) entirely into the psychical sexual group. This [is necessary] because, if there were a

---

[1] Some account of this will be found in the "Project" below (p. 425).

vigorous somatic sexual excitation (S.S.), the psychical sexual group would soon from time to time acquire such strength that (as happens in men) it would bring the sexual object into a favourable position by means of a specific reaction. But women are required to omit the arc of the specific reaction and instead to adopt permanent specific actions calculated to entice men to perform the specific action. Their sexual tension is consequently kept low and its access to the psychical sexual group is so far as possible cut off, while the indispensable strength of the psychical sexual group is supplied in another way. If, then, the psychical sexual group gets into a condition of desire, it easily becomes transformed into melancholia, supposing the terminal organ is at a low level.[1] The psychical sexual group is capable in itself of little resistance. Here we have the immature, juvenile type of libido, and the demanding, anæsthetic women mentioned above [Fact A (3), p. 102] merely carry this type into later life.

(2) Women very frequently approach the sexual act (or get married) without any love—that is, with only slight somatic sexual excitation (S.S.) and tension of the terminal organ. In that case they are frigid and remain so.

A low level of tension in the terminal organ seems to constitute the main disposition to melancholia. Where this is present, any neurosis easily takes on a melancholic stamp. Thus, whereas potent individuals easily acquire anxiety neuroses, impotent ones incline to melancholia.

VI

And now, how can the effects of melancholia be explained? They can best be thus described: *psychical inhibition accompanied by instinctual impoverishment, and pain that this should be so.*

We can imagine that, if the psychical sexual group suffers very great loss in the amount of its excitation, this may lead to a kind of *indrawing in the psyche*, which produces an effect of suction upon the adjoining amounts of excitation. [See Fig. 2]. The neurones associated (with the group) are obliged to give up their excitation, and this *produces pain*. The uncoupling of associations is always painful. There sets in an impoverishment of excitation—of

---

[1] That is to say, if the tension in the terminal organ is at a low level.

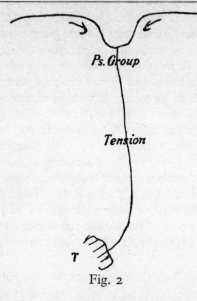

Fig. 2

reserve stock—in a way that resembles *internal bleeding*, and this shows itself in the other instincts and functions. This indrawing process has an inhibiting effect and operates like a wound, in a manner analogous o pan (*citf*. the theory of physical pain).[1]

The counterpart *Ps.S.* to this is afforded by mania, where an overflow of excitation is communicated to all the associated neurones. Here there is a similarity to neurasthenia. In neurasthenia a very similar impoverishment arises owing to the excitation running out, as it were, through a hole. But in that case what is pumped empty is somatic sexual excitation (S.S.) [Fig. 3]; in melancholia the hole is in the psyche. Neurasthenic impoverishment can, however, extend to the psyche. And indeed the manifestations of these conditions are so similar that some cases can only be differentiated with difficulty.

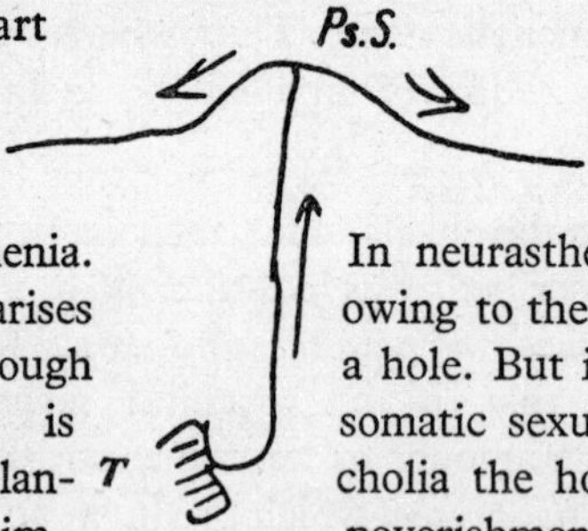

Fig. 3

---

[1] [This subject is touched on in the "Project" but was more fully described many years later in Chapter IV of *Beyond the Pleasure Principle* 1920 g).]

Draft H

(24. 1. 1895)

PARANOIA[1]

In psychiatry delusional ideas stand alongside obsessional ideas as purely intellectual disorders, and paranoia stands alongside obsessional insanity as an intellectual psychosis. If obsessions can be traced back to affective disturbances and their strength can be shown to be due to a conflict, the same view must be applicable to delusions, and they too must be the consequence of affective disturbances and their strength due to a psychological process. A contrary opinion to this is held by the psychiatrists, whereas laymen are in the habit of attributing madness to mental shocks; "a man who does not lose his reason over certain things can have none to lose".[2]

Now it is in fact the case that chronic paranoia in its classical form is *a pathological mode of defence*, like hysteria, obsessional neurosis and states of hallucinatory confusion. People become paranoic about things that they cannot tolerate—provided always that they have a particular psychical disposition.

In what does this disposition consist? In a tendency to something which exhibits the psychical characteristic of paranoia; and this we will consider in an example.

An unmarried woman, no longer very young (about 30), shared a home with her brother and [elder] sister. She belonged to the superior working-class; her brother was gradually working his way up into a small manufacturing business. Meanwhile they let off a room to an acquaintance, a much-travelled, rather mysterious man, very clever

---

[1] This paper was enclosed with a letter of 24. 1. 95 not reproduced here. Part of the material was subsequently used in "Further Remarks on the Neuro-Psychoses of Defence", (1896 b), the second section of which describes the analysis of a case of chronic paranoia which Freud classified in a footnote added in 1924 as dementia paranoides. The paper published in 1896 did not, however, go so far as the material published here. In particular, the detailed discussion of projection and its employment in normal and abnormal psychical processes is only to be found in Freud's later works. A complete, independent description of the mechanism of projection—a subject which is illuminated from many angles in the Schreber case history (1911 c) never appeared. The emphasis on the concept of defence in this paper and the comparison of the effectiveness as defensive mechanisms of the symptoms exhibited in different cases anticipates a good deal of what was to be stated thirty years later in *Inhibitions, Symptoms and Anxiety* (1926 d), when it was put on a new basis.

[2] A quotation from Lessing's play *Emilia Galotti* [IV, 7].

and intelligent. He lived with them for a year and was on the most companionable and sociable terms with them. After this he went away, but returned after six months. This time he stopped only a comparatively short time and then disappeared for good and all. The sisters used often to lament his absence and could speak nothing but good of him. Nevertheless, the younger sister told the elder one of an occasion when he made an attempt at getting her into trouble. She had been doing out his room while he was still lying in bed. He had called her up to the bed, and, when she had unsuspectingly obeyed, put his penis in her hand. There had been no sequel to this scene, and soon afterwards the stranger had gone off.

In the course of the next few years the sister who had had this experience fell ill. She began to complain, and eventually developed unmistakable delusions of observation and persecution to the following effect. She thought the women neighbours were pitying her because she had been jilted and because she was still hoping for the man to come back; they were always making hints to her of this kind and kept on saying all kinds of things to her about the man, and so on. All this, she said, was of course untrue. Since then the patient has only fallen into this state for a few weeks at a time. Her insight then temporarily returns and she explains that it is all due to getting excited; though even in the intervals she suffers from a neurosis which can easily be interpreted as a sexual one. And she soon falls into a fresh bout of paranoia.

The elder sister was astonished to notice that whenever the conversation turned to the scene of seduction, the patient at once denied all knowledge of it. Breuer heard of the case and she was sent to me. I tried to correct the tendency to paranoia by trying to bring her memory back to the scene, but without success.[1] I talked to her twice and got her to tell me all about the lodger in a state of "concentration hypnosis". In reply to my searching enquiries as to whether nothing "embarrassing" had happened, I was met by the most decided negative and—I saw her no more. She sent me a message to say that it upset her too much. Defence! That was obvious. She *wished* not to be reminded of it and consequently deliberately repressed it.

---

[1] [The transitional technique, half way between hypnosis and free association, described in the last chapter of *Studies on Hysteria*.]

There could be no doubt whatever about the defence; but it might just as well have produced a hysterical symptom or an obsession. What was the peculiar nature of the paranoic defence?

She was sparing herself something; something was repressed. And we can guess what that was. She had probably in fact been excited by what she had seen and by recollecting it. So what she was sparing herself was the self-reproach of being "a bad woman". And the same reproach was what reached her ears from outside. Thus *the subject-matter remained unaffected;* what was changed was something in the *placing* of the whole thing. To start with it had been an internal reproach; now it was an imputation coming from outside. The judgment about her had been transposed outwards: people were saying what she would otherwise have said to herself. Something was gained by this. She would have had to accept the judgment from inside; but she could reject the one from outside. *In this way the judgment, the reproach, was kept away from her ego.*

The purpose of the paranoia, therefore, was to fend off an idea that was intolerable to her ego by projecting its subject-matter into the external world.

Two questions arise: (1) How is a transposition of this kind brought about? (2) Does all this apply equally to other cases of paranoia?

(1) The transposition is brought about very simply. It is a question of the abuse[1] of a psychical mechanism which is very commonly employed in normal life: the mechanism of transposition or projection. Whenever an internal change occurs, we can choose whether we shall attribute it to an internal or external cause. If something deters us from accepting an internal origin, we naturally seize upon an external one. In the second place, we are accustomed to our internal states being betrayed to other people (by the expression of emotion). This explains normal delusions of observation and normal projection. For they are normal so long as in the process we remain conscious of our own internal change. If we forget it, and if we are left only with the leg of the syllogism that leads outwards, then we have paranoia, with its exaggeration of what people know about us and of what people have done to us—what people know about us, what we have no

---

[1] [*Missbrauch* in the MS. The 1950 German edition reads, incorrectly, *Ausbruch* ("breaking out").]

knowledge of whatever, what we cannot admit. *This, then, is a misuse of the mechanism of projection for purposes of defence.*

Something quite analogous takes place with obsessions. The mechanism of *substitution*, once again, is a normal one. If an old maid keeps a dog or an old bachelor collects snuff-boxes, the former is finding a substitute for a companion in marriage and the latter for his need for—a multitude of conquests. Every collector is a substitute for Don Juan Tenorio—so too the mountain-climber, the sportsman, and so on. These things are erotic equivalents. Women are familiar with them as well. Gynæcological treatment falls into this category. There are two kinds of women patients: one kind who are as loyal to their physician as to their husband, and the other who change their physicians as though they were lovers. This normally operating mechanism of substitution is misused in obsessions—once again for purposes of defence.

(2) And now, does this view apply equally to other cases of paranoia? I should say to *all* of them. But I will take a roll-call.

The litigious paranoic cannot bear the idea that he has committed an injustice or that he ought to part with his property. Consequently he thinks that the judgment is not legally valid, that he is not in the wrong, etc. (The case is too clear and perhaps not quite unambiguous; maybe it could be explained more simply.)

The "*grande nation*" cannot face the idea that it can be defeated in war. *Ergo*, it was *not* defeated; the victory does not count. It provides an example of mass paranoia and invents the delusion of betrayal.[1]

The alcoholic will never admit to himself that he has become impotent through drink. However much alcohol he can tolerate, he cannot tolerate this knowledge. So the woman is responsible—and there follow delusions of jealousy, etc.

The hypochondriac will struggle for a long time before he has found the key to his feeling that he is seriously ill. He will not admit to himself that it arises from his sexual life; but it gives him the greatest satisfaction to believe that his sufferings are not endogenous (as Moebius says) but exogenous. So he is being poisoned.

The official who has been passed over for promotion needs to believe that persecutors are plotting against him and that he is being

---

[1] [The reference is, of course, to the Franco-Prussian War of 1870.]

spied upon in his room. Otherwise he would have to admit his own shipwreck.

But what develops here need not always be delusions of persecution. Megalomania may be even more successful in keeping the distressing idea away from his ego. Here, for instance, is a cook whose looks have faded and who should accustom herself to the thought that she has lost her chance of happiness in love. This is the right moment for the emergence of the gentleman across the way, who is clearly anxious to marry her and has given her to understand as much in a remarkably bashful but none the less unmistakable fashion.

In every case the delusional idea is clung to with the same energy with which some other intolerable, distressing idea is fended off from the ego. Thus these people love their delusion *as they love themselves*. Herein lies the secret.

Next, let us compare this form of defence and those we already know: (1) hysteria; (2) obsessions; (3) hallucinatory confusion; and (4) paranoia. We have to consider the affect, the content of the idea and the hallucinations. [See Fig. 4].

(1) *Hysteria*. The intolerable idea is not admitted into association with the ego. The content is retained in a segregated condition; it is absent from consciousness; its affect is displaced into something somatic by means of conversion. . . .

(2) *Obsessions*. Here again the intolerable idea is not allowed into association [with the ego]. The affect is retained; a substitute is found for the content.

(3) *Hallucinatory confusion*. The whole of the intolerable idea—both its affect and its content—are kept away from the ego. This is only possible at the price of a partial detachment from the external world. Recourse is had to hallucinations, which are friendly to the ego and give support to the defence.

(4) *Paranoia*. In direct opposition to (3), the content and the affect of the intolerable idea are retained; but they are projected into the external world.—The hallucinations which occur in some forms are hostile to the ego, but nevertheless support the defence.

In *hysterical psychoses*, on the contrary, it is precisely the ideas fended off that gain the mastery. The type of these is the attack and the *état secondaire*. The hallucinations are hostile to the ego.

SUMMARY

	Affect	Content of idea	Hallucinations	Outcome
Hysteria	got rid of by conversion —	absent from consciousness —	—	Unstable defence with satisfactory gain
Obsessions	retained +	absent from consciousness substitute found	—	Permanent defence without gain
Hallucinatory Confusion	absent —	— absent	friendly to ego friendly to defence	Permanent defence brilliant gain
Paranoia	retained +	+ retained projected out	hostile to ego friendly to defence	Permanent defence without gain
Hysterical Psychoses	obtain mastery +	over consciousness +	hostile to ego hostile to defence	Failure of defence

Fig. 4

The *delusional idea* is either a copy of the fended-off idea or its contrary (*e.g.*, in megalomania). Paranoia and hallucinatory confusion are the two psychoses of obstinacy and defiance. The "reference to the self" in paranoia is analogous to the hallucinations in confusional states, which seek to assert the exact opposite of the fact that is being fended-off. Thus the reference to the self always tries to prove the correctness of the projection.

22

Vienna, 4. 3. 95.

My dear Wilhelm,

. . . There is nothing new on the scientific side. I am working hard on the paper on the therapy of hysteria.[1] Hence the delay. . . . I have nothing to send you this time. At best a little parallel to D.'s dream psychosis, which you and I went through. Rudi Kaufmann, Breuer's very intelligent nephew, and a doctor too, is a late riser. He has himself woken by a charwoman in the morning, but he is very reluctant to get out of bed. One morning, as he did not answer, she knocked a second time and called him by name, "Herr Rudi!" He thereupon had the hallucination of a chart-board on a hospital bed (*cf.* the "Rudolf Hospital"!) with the name "Rudolf Kaufmann" on it, and said to himself: "Well, Rudolf Kaufmann's at the hospital in any case, so there's no need for me to go," and went off to sleep again.[2] . . .

Perhaps the short paper on migraine will come into your hands. It contains only two leading ideas.[3] . . .

Best wishes from us all for a speedy recovery.

Your

Sigm.

---

[1] Published as the last chapter of *Studies on Hysteria* under the heading "On the psychotherapy of hysteria."

[2] Quoted in *The Interpretation of Dreams* (*trans.* 1953), p. 125.

[3] This apparently refers to the next draft.

Draft I

[Undated ?4 March 1895.]

MIGRAINE: ESTABLISHED POINTS[1]

1. *A matter of summation.* There is an interval of hours or days between the instigation and the outbreak of the symptoms. One has a kind of feeling that an obstacle is being overcome and that a process can then go forward.

2. *A matter of summation.* Even without an instigation one has an impression that there must be an accumulating stimulus, which is present in a very small quantity at the beginning of the interval but in a greater quantity at the end.

3. *A matter of summation*, in which susceptibility to ætiological factors lies in the height of the level of the stimulus already present.

4. A matter with *a complex ætiology*. Perhaps on the pattern of a "chain aetiology", where one cause after another can be produced directly and indirectly over a period of many months; or of a "summation aetiology", where a specific cause can be helped out by substitutes of quite moderate quantity.

5. A matter on the pattern of menstrual migraine and included in the sexual group. Evidence of this:
   a. Least common in healthy males.
   b. Restricted to the sexual time of life: childhood and old age almost excluded.
   c. If it is produced by summation, sexual stimulus too is a thing produced by summation.
   d. The analogy of there being periodicity [both in migraine and sexuality].
   e. Frequency of its appearance in persons with disturbed sexual discharge (neurasthenia, *coitus interruptus*).

6. Certainty that migraine is produced by chemical stimuli: poisonous emanations from human bodies, scirocco, fatigue,

---

[1] Undated MS. in the possession of Dr. Robert Fliess of New York: it appears to be the paper mentioned in the previous letter.

smells. Sexual stimulus, incidentally, is also chemical.

7. Cessation of migraine during pregnancy, at which time its production is probably diverted in other directions.

It seems to follow from this that migraine represents a toxic effect produced by the stimulus of the sexual substance when this cannot find adequate discharge. And perhaps one should add in this connection that where there is special susceptibility there may be some particular path [of conduction] present whose topography has yet to be determined. The question as to what this path may be is the question of the *localization* of migraine.

8. There are indications for identifying this path in the fact that organic diseases of the cranium, tumours and suppurations (without toxic intermediate links ?) produce migraine or something similar; and also that migraine is unilateral, is connected with the nose and is linked with localized paralytic phenomena. The first of these indications is not unambiguous. The unilaterality of migraine, its localization over the eye, and its complication by localized paralyses are more important.

9. The painfulness of migraine can only suggest the cerebral meninges, since affections of the cerebral *substance* are certainly painless.

10. If migraine seems in this way to approach neuralgia, this harmonizes with the summation, the variations in susceptibility and the production of neuralgias by toxic stimuli. Toxic neuralgia would thus be its physiological prototype. The meninges are the seat of its pain and the trigeminal is its path. Since the change occurring in neuralgia can only be a central one, we must suppose that the logical centre for migraine is a trigeminal nucleus whose fibres supply the dura mater.

Since the pain in migraine is similarly located to that in supra-orbital neuralgia, this dural nucleus must be in the neighbourhood of the nucleus of the first branch. Since the different branches and nuclei of the trigeminal influence one another, all other affections of the trigeminal might contribute to the aetiology (of migraine) as concurrent (but not as "stock")[1] factors.

The Symptomatology and Biological Position of Migraine.

The pain of a neuralgia usually finds its discharge in tonic tension (or even in clonic spasms). Therefore it is not impossible that migraine may involve a spastic innervation of the vascular muscles which are the reflex area of the dural region. We may ascribe to this innervation the general (and, indeed, the local) disturbance of function which does not differ symptomatically from the similar disturbance which arises from vascular constriction. (*Cf.* the similarity of migraine to attacks of thrombosis.) Part of the inhibition is due to the pain in itself. It is presumably the vascular area of the choroid plexus which is first affected by the spasm of discharge. The relation to the eye and nose is explained by their common attachment to the first branch [of the trigeminal].

23

Vienna, 27. 4. 95.

Dear Wilhelm,

Your letter arrived to-day, and gave me great pleasure. It breathes health, work and progress. I am naturally most eager to hear everything new. . . .

This separation and letter-writing is a great trial, but there is no help for it. Particularly for someone who writes so much as I do and suffers from time to time from *horror calami*. . . .

On the scientific side I am in a bad way; I am so deep in the "Psychology for Neurologists" that it quite consumes me, until I have to break off out of sheer exhaustion. I have never been so intensely preoccupied by anything. And will anything come of it ? I hope so, but the going is hard and slow.

Neurotic cases are very scarce at the moment; my practice is getting more intense, but its extent is dropping off. [I am busy

---

[1] [See the discussion on "stock" ("banal") factors in Freud's second paper on the anxiety neurosis (1895 f).]

with] a lot of little things. I shall send you a few pages for Mendel
on a case of sensory disturbance described by Bernhardt; I
suffer from it myself.[1] It is a hotchpotch, of course, only to give
people something to think about. Löwenfeld has attacked me in
one of the March numbers of the *Münchner Medizinische
Wochenshrift*, and I shall answer him in a few pages in Paschkis;[2]
and so on and so forth.

I must make a start on the paralyses of children for Nothnagel,
but my interest lies elsewhere.[3]

My heart is in the coffin here with Cæsar.[4] . . .

That is the *status praesens* in matters scientific and private.
My affectionate regards, a good share of which please pass on to
your wife.

Your

Sigm.

24

Vienna, 25. 5. 95.

Dear Wilhelm,

. . . I have had an inhuman amount to do, and after ten or
eleven hours with patients I have been incapable of picking up
a pen to write you even a short letter, though I had a great deal
to tell you. But the chief reason was this: a man like me cannot
live without a hobby-horse, a consuming passion—in Schiller's
words a tyrant. I have found my tyrant, and in his service I know
no limits. My tyrant is psychology; it has always been my
distant, beckoning goal and now, since I have hit on the neuroses,
it has come so much the nearer. I am plagued with two ambitions: to see how the theory of mental functioning takes shape if

---

[1] *Über die Bernhardt'sche Sensibilitätsstörung am Oberschenkel* (1895 e).

[2] Löwenfeld (1895). Freud answered it with "A Reply to Criticisms of my
Paper on Anxiety Neurosis," (1895 f). Dr. Paschkis was editor of the *Wiener
Klinische Rundschau*.

[3] Freud's *Die infantile Cerebrallähmung* did not appear till 1897, and is frequently referred to in the correspondence as being an oppressive burden.

[4] [This quotation is in English in the original.]

quantitative considerations, a sort of economics of nerve-force, are introduced into it; and secondly, to extract from psycho-pathology what may be of benefit to normal psychology. Actually a satisfactory general theory of neuropsychotic disturbances is impossible if it cannot be brought into association with clear assumptions about normal mental processes. During recent weeks I have devoted every free minute to such work; the hours of the night from eleven to two have been occupied with imaginings, transpositions, and guesses, only abandoned when I arrived at some absurdity, or had so truly and seriously over-worked that I had no interest left for the day's medical work. You must not ask me for results for a long time yet. My reading has been following the same direction. I have been greatly interested in a book by W. Jerusalem on the function of judgment,[1] because it contains two of my main ideas, that judgment consists of a transposition into motor phenomena, and that inner perception can have no claim to be "evidential".

I get great satisfaction from the work on neuroses in my practice. Nearly everything is confirmed daily, new pieces are added, and it is a fine thing to feel certain that the core of the matter is within one's grasp. I should have a whole series of most remarkable things to tell you, but I cannot do it by letter and, what with the pressure of these days, my notes are so fragmentary that they would be of no use to you. . . .

Your news was enough to make me shout for joy. If you have really solved the problem of conception,[2] the only thing left for you to do is to make up your mind what kind of marble you prefer. For me your discovery is a few months too late, but it may come in useful next year. In any case, I am consumed with curiosity to hear more about it. . . .

Breuer, however, is a new man. One cannot help liking him

---

[1] Jerusalem (1895). Jerusalem, who was familiar with hypnotic phenomena and the writings of Charcot, Richet and Bernheim, maintained in this book that there was justification for "belief in unconscious mental phenomena". His remarks about the importance of "observations of the child's mind and of making use of reports on the mental life of undeveloped peoples" (page 19) may also have had a stimulating effect on Freud.

[2] Obviously the question of at what periods there is the greatest and least likelihood that conception will take place.

again without any reservations. He has accepted the whole of
your nose.[1] Not only does he spread your reputation abroad
in Vienna, but he has become fully converted to my theory of
sexuality. He has become quite a different fellow from the one
we have been used to. . . .

   With cordial greetings for you and your wife, and please
do not take my neglect of the last few weeks as a precedent.

Your

Sigm.

25

Vienna, 12. 6. 95.

My dear Wilhelm,

   . . . you are quite right in supposing that I am overflowing
with news as well as theories. The "Defence" has taken an
important step forward, and I shall soon be sending you some
short notes on the subject as an earnest of the fact. The construction of the "Psychology" also looks as if it is going to come
off, which would give me great cause for rejoicing. Of course I
cannot say for certain yet. Saying anything now would be like
sending a six-months female embryo to a ball. . . .

   I have started smoking again, because I still missed it (after
fourteen months abstinence), and because I must treat that mind
of mine decently, or the fellow will not work for me. I am demanding a great deal of him. Most of the time the burden is
superhuman.

   All of us here are very well, and we send cordial greetings to
you and your wife.

Your

Sigm.

---

[1] Fliess's nasal reflex neurosis theory.

26

6. 8. 95.

Dr. Sigmund Freud   Consulting hours 3—5 p.m.
IX. Berggasse 19.

My dear Wilhelm,

Let me tell you that after prolonged thought I believe I have found my way to the understanding of pathological defence, and with it to the understanding of many important psychological processes. Clinically it all fitted in long ago, but the psychological theory I needed yielded only to laborious assaults. I hope it is not "dream-gold".

It is not nearly ready yet, but I can at least talk about it and appeal on many points to your superior scientific equipment. It is bold but beautiful, as you will see. I am looking forward to telling you about it. . . . Your wife will see to it that I stop when I have bothered you too much.

With cordial greetings to the whole of your little family,

Your

Sigm.

27

Bellevue, 16. 8. 95.

My dear Wilhelm,

I spent several days at Reichenau, and then I was undecided for a few days, but now I can tell you my plans.

I am going to Venice with my little brother[1] between the 22nd and the 24th, so unfortunately I shall not be able . . . to be in Oberhof at the same time. I had to make up my mind one way or the other, and what decided me was concern for the young man, who shares with me responsibility for two old people and so many women and children. . . .

---

[1] Alexander Freud (1866-1943).

I have had a remarkable experience with my $\phi\psi\omega$[1]. Soon after I proclaimed my alarming news to you, raising your expectations and calling for your congratulations, I came up against new difficulties; I had surmounted the first foothills, but had no breath left for further toil. So, quickly composing myself, I threw the whole thing aside and persuaded myself that I took no interest in it at all. It makes me very uncomfortable to think that I have got to tell you about it. If I saw you every month, I should certainly avoid you in September. So let it be as you will, but now there is all the more reason to let you do the talking. But about my neurotic novelties I do not propose to be reticent.

My little group is very comfortable here. My wife is naturally not very active, but is otherwise cheerful. Not long ago my son Oliver illustrated beautifully his characteristic of concentrating exclusively on what is immediately ahead. An enthusiastic aunt came to see him the other day. "Oli, what are you going to be?" she asked him. "Five years old next February, auntie," he replied. The children are very entertaining in their several ways.

This psychology is really an incubus—skittles and mushroom-hunting are certainly much healthier pastimes. All I was trying to do was to explain defence, but I found myself explaining something from the very heart of nature. I found myself wrestling with the problems of quality, sleep, memory—in short, the whole of psychology. Now I want to hear no more of it.

The soup is on the table, or I should go on grumbling. . . .

My best wishes for your wife and child and all your hopes,

Your

Sigm.

28

Bellevue, 23. 9. 95.

My dear Wilhelm,

The only reason I write to you so little is that I am writing so much for you. In the train I started writing a short account of the

---

[1] $\phi\psi\omega$ (or W) is an abbreviation for the fundamental hypotheses of the "Psychology". See "Project", p. 347 *sqq.*

ΦΨΩ for you to criticize, and I am now continuing it in my free time and in the intervals between the acts of my gradually increasing practice.[1] It already amounts to a sizeable tome, very rough, of course, but good enough, I hope, to be a groundwork for you to supply the trimmings, on which I set great hopes. My rested brain is now making child's play of the accumulated difficulties, for instance, the contradiction in the fact that actions re-establish their resistance,[2] whereas the neurones in general are subject to facilitation. That now fits in very well, if the smallness of the individual endogenous stimuli is taken into account. Other points are also now falling into line, to my great satisfaction. How much of this progress will dissolve into thin air again on a better view remains to be seen. But you provided the great impulse to take the thing in earnest.

Apart from adapting the theory to the general laws of motion, for which I count on you, I have to test it against the individual facts of the new experimental psychology. The subject fascinates me as much as ever, to the disadvantage of all medical interests and of my children's paralyses—which are supposed to be finished by the New Year!

I hardly know what else to tell you about. I think I may send you the thing in two parts. I hope your refreshed mind will do me the favour of finding the imposition a trifling one. I look with fellow-feelings on your attempts at autotherapy. With me things have gone as you expected they would after the last sinus operation—thoroughly badly, with increasing discomfort. To-day it started to get a little better, if I am not mistaken.

Ida will have told you that in the third electoral district the Liberals were beaten by 46 seats to nil, and in the second district by 32 seats to 14. I voted after all. Our district remained Liberal.[3]

---

[1] See "Project", p. 347 *sqq.* Freud had visited Fliess in Berlin.

[2] [The subject of actions is discussed in the last two pages of the "Project", p. 444.]

[3] This is a reference to the progress towards securing control of the Vienna municipal council being made by the anti-Semitic Christian Social Party led by Karl Lueger, which was unsuccessfully opposed by the Liberals. Lueger was elected burgomaster three times in the years 1895-96, but confirmation of his election was withheld by the Emperor until 1897. For Freud's attitude to Lueger, who remained burgomaster of Vienna until his death in 1910, see Letter 88.

A dream the night before last provided the most amusing confirmation that the motivation of dreams is wish-fulfilment.[1] Löwenfeld has written to me that he is preparing a work on phobias and obsessional ideas on the basis of a hundred cases, and has asked me for various items of information. I have warned him in reply not to take my notions lightly. . . .

I am still waiting . . . for your notes on migraine. The family are well. All my best wishes for you, and Ida—who has made a conquest even of Alexander—and the hoped-for little one.

Your

Sigm.

29

Vienna, 8. 10. 95.

Dear Wilhelm,

. . . I am enclosing all sorts of things for you to-day, including some things I have to return to you, which reminds me of the thanks I owe you; your case-histories of labour pains, and two notebooks of mine. Your notes have reinforced my first impression that a self-contained pamphlet, "The nose and female sexuality" ought to be made of them.[2] I naturally very much missed the concluding observations, with their surprisingly simple explanations.

Now for my two notebooks.[3] I wrote them in one breath since my return, and they contain little that will be new to you. I have a third notebook, dealing with the psychopathology of repression, which I am not ready to send you yet, because it only takes

---

[1] A conclusion reached by Freud in July, 1895. See Letter 137 and "Project", p. 400 *sqq.*

[2] Fliess accepted the suggestion (Fliess, 1897).

[3] See page 349.

the subject to a certain point.[1] From that point I had to start from scratch again, and I have been alternately proud and happy and abashed and miserable, until now, after an excess of mental torment, I just apathetically tell myself that it does not hang together yet and perhaps never will. What does not hang together yet is not the mechanism—I could be patient about that —but the explanation of repression, clinical knowledge of which has incidentally made great strides.

Note that among other things I suspect the following: that hysteria is conditioned by a primary sexual experience (before puberty) accompanied by revulsion and fright; and that obsessional neurosis is conditioned by the same accompanied by pleasure.[2]

But the mechanical explanation is not coming off, and I am inclined to listen to the still, small voice which tells me that my explanation will not do.

Missing you and your company came on rather late this time, but I felt it acutely. I am alone with my mind, in which so much is stirring, and for the time being stirring itself into a muddle. I am finding out the most interesting things, which I cannot talk about and for lack of leisure cannot get down on paper (I send you a torso herewith).[3] I do not want to read, because it stirs up too many thoughts and stints me of the satisfaction of discovery. In short, I am a wretched recluse. Apart from that I am so exhausted that I must lay the whole thing aside for a while. Instead I shall study your migraine.[4] Also I am involved in a controversy by post with Löwenfeld. When I have answered his letter you shall see it. . . .

My best wishes to Ida and little Paul(ine). The children here are well. Martha has settled down happily in Vienna again.

Your

Sigm.

---

[1] This notebook has not survived.
[2] See next letter.
[3] This has not survived.
[4] A manuscript of Fliess's that has not survived.

30

15. 10. 95.

Dr. Sigmund Freud   Consulting hours 3—5 p.m.
IX. Berggasse 19.

Dear Wilhelm,

What a crazy correspondent I am! For two whole weeks I was
in a fever of writing and thought I had found the secret, but now
I know I have not got it yet, and I have laid the thing aside again.
All the same a lot of things have been cleared up, or at any rate
have sorted themselves out, and I am not discouraged. Have I
revealed the great clinical secret to you, either in writing or by
word of mouth? Hysteria is the consequence of a presexual
sexual shock. Obsessional neurosis is the consequence of presexual *sexual pleasure* later transformed into guilt.[1]

"Presexual" means before puberty, before the production of
the sexual substance; the relevant events become effective only
as *memories*.

Cordially your[2]

31

Vienna, 16. 10. 95.

Dear Wilhelm,

.... If on top of the feverish work of recent weeks, the tan-
talizing hopes and disappointments and some real discoveries
—all against a background of feeling wretched physically and
the usual practical irritations and difficulties—I send a you few
pages of philosophical stammering (not that I think they are
successful), I hope I shall have conciliated you again.

---

[1] Cf. previous letter. This is one of the fundamental themes of "Further Remarks on the Neuro-Psychoses of Defence" (1896 b). The moral conflict in the
structure of the obsessional neuroses is specifically recognized in it.
[2] Signature missing.

I am still all at sixes and sevens. I am practically sure I have solved the riddle of hysteria and obsessional neurosis with the formula of infantile sexual shock and sexual pleasure, and I am just as sure that both neuroses are radically curable now—not just the individual symptoms but the neurotic disposition itself. That gives me a kind of flat satisfaction—at having lived some forty years not quite in vain; but it is not real satisfaction, because the psychological gaps in the new knowledge demand the whole of my interest.

Naturally I have not had time for your migraine,[1] but that will come. I have entirely given up smoking again, so as not to have to reproach myself for my bad pulse, and to be rid of the horrid struggle with the craving for a fourth of fifth cigar; better to struggle with the craving for the first. Abstinence is probably another thing that is not very conducive to mental satisfaction.

That is enough about myself. Perhaps the favourable side of all this is that I consider that I have substantially mastered the two neuroses and am looking forward to the struggle with the psychological interpretation.

The Jacobsen (N.L.) has moved me more than anything I have read in the last nine years. The last chapters seem to me classic.[2]

I am delighted to be able to conclude from numerous hints that you are very much better. . . .

At the moment I have on hand a noisy children's party of twenty for Mathilde's birthday.

Last Monday, and the two following, lectures on hysteria at the physicians' society—very boring.[3]

Affectionate regards to you and your wife,

> Your
>
> Sigm.

---

[1] Fliess's notes mentioned in Letter 29.
[2] The reference is to a story, "Niels Lyhne", by the Danish writer Jacobsen.
[3] Fully abstracted in the *Wiener Klinische Rundschau* of Oct. 20th and 27th and Nov. 3rd, 1895.

32

Vienna, 20. 10. 95.

Dear Wilhelm,

. . . . I was of course tremendously pleased with your
opinion of the solution of hysteria and obsessional neurosis.
Now listen to this. One strenuous night last week, when I was
in the stage of painful discomfort in which my brain works best,
the barriers suddenly lifted, the veils dropped, and it was
possible to see from the details of neurosis all the way to the very
conditioning of consciousness. Everything fell into place, the
cogs meshed, the thing really seemed to be a machine which in a
moment would run of itself.[1] The three systems of neurones,
the "free" and "bound" states of quantity, the primary and
secondary processes, the main trend and the compromise trend
of the nervous system, the two biological rules of attention and
defence, the indications of quality, reality, and thought, the
state of the psycho-sexual group, the sexual determination of
repression, and finally the factors determining consciousness
as a perceptual function—the whole thing held together,
and still does. I can naturally hardly contain myself with
delight.

If I had waited a fortnight before setting it all down for you
it would have been so much clearer. But it was only in the process of setting it down that I cleared it up for myself. So it could
not be helped. Now I shall not have much time to write it all out
properly. Treatments are beginning, and the children's paralyses, which do not interest me at all, have got to be done soon.
But I shall put some things down for you—the quantitative
postulates, from which you are to infer the characteristics of
neuronic motion, and a description of neurasthenia and the
anxiety neurosis in accordance with the premises of the
theory. . .

If I could talk to you about nothing else for forty-eight hours

---

[1] The following refers to the "Project".

on end the thing could probably be finished. But that is impossible.

> *Was man nicht erfliegen kann,*
> *muss man erhinken. . . .*
> *Die Schrift sagt, es ist keine Schande zu hinken.*[1]

Confirmation from neurotic material keeps pouring in on me. The thing is really true and sound.

To-day I gave my second lecture on hysteria, making repression the central point.[2] They liked it, but I shall not have it published.

You will not have any objection to my calling my next son Wilhelm! If *he* turns out to be a daughter, *she* will be called Anna.

With cordial greetings,

Your

Sigm.

33

Vienna, 31. 10. 95.

Dear Wilhelm,

I am dead tired, but feel I must write to you again before the month is out. First of all about your last scientific papers, which are a welcome measure of your freedom from headaches.[3]

My first impression was one of amazement at the existence of someone who was an even greater visionary than I, and that he should be my friend Wilhelm. My conclusion was that I must send the papers back to you, to prevent them from getting lost. In between I found them most illuminating, and said to myself that only a universal specialist such as you could have produced them. . . .

---

[1] ["What we cannot reach flying we must reach limping. . . . The Book tells us it is no sin to limp."] A quotation from Rückert's *Makamen des Hariri*, subsequently quoted at the end of *Beyond the Pleasure Principle*.
[2] See footnote 3, p. 128.
[3] Fliess was suffering at this period from continual migraine.

I cannot borrow yet on my own million.¹ I think it hangs together as a whole, but I do not really trust the individual parts. I keep changing them, and do not yet dare submit the whole structure to a wise man. What you have is also partially discredited—it was intended more as a trial run than anything else —but I hope something will come of it. I am now pretty well drained dry, and in any case I have to put it aside for two months while I write the children's paralyses for Nothnagel in time for 1896—not a word of it is yet on paper.

I have started doubting the pleasure-pain² explanation of hysteria and obsessional neurosis which I announced with so much enthusiasm. Unquestionably those are the essential factors. But I have not yet put the pieces of the puzzle in the right place.

Fortunately, for me, all these theories necessarily converge into the clinical field of repression, where I have opportunities daily for correcting mistakes or clearing things up. The end of the year has got to see the end of my "bashful" case, who developed hysteria in youth and later delusions of observation, and whose almost transparent history has got to clear up certain doubtful points for me. Another man (who dares not go out into the street because of homicidal tendencies) has got to help me solve another riddle.

I have been busy recently with a study of the sexual act, in the course of which I have discovered the pleasure pump (not the air pump)³ as well as other *curiosa*, but for the time being shall not talk about them.⁴ Then migraine will come as a separate part; it is on that account that I have made an excursion into the mechanism of the sexual act. . . .

---

¹ "My own million" was a popular catch-phrase. Freud's scepticism followed the period in which he wrote the "Project" in less than three weeks. We see him here reverting from theory to empiricism. He was waiting for the result of one of his cases (perhaps the often-mentioned case of Herr E.) to provide the explanation of the clinical aspects of repression. (See next letter.)

² [Freud here uses the word *Schmerz* ("pain"), not *Unlust* ("unpleasure").]

³ [In German *die Lustpumpe (nicht Luftpumpe)*.]

⁴ The "pleasure-pump" idea does not recur in the present letters, etc., or in any of Freud's published works. [Cf., however, a possible reference above on p. 108.]

"Wilhelm" or "Anna" is behaving very badly and should see the light in November. I hope all is well with your Christmas child.

I recently perpetrated three lectures on hysteria in which I was very impudent. I shall be starting to take pleasure in being arrogant, particularly if you continue to be so pleased with me.

With affectionate greetings to you, Ida, and little Pauline (?)

Your

Sigm.

34

2. II. 95.

Dr. Sigmund Freud   Consulting hours 3—5 p.m.
IX. Berggasse 19.

I am glad I left the letter unposted. To-day I am able to add that one of the two cases has given me what I was waiting for (sexual shock, *i.e.*, infantile abuse in a case of male hysteria!) and at the same time some further working through the doubtful material has strengthened my confidence in the correctness of my psychological assumptions.[1] I am enjoying a moment of real satisfaction.

Meanwhile the time has not yet come to enjoy the climax and then sit back and relax. The later acts of the tragedy will still demand a lot of work from

Your

Sigm.

who sends his cordial greetings.

---

[1] The idea that the aetiology of hysteria was connected with the seduction of children by adults seemed to be confirmed by Freud's analytic work. See Introduction, p. 28.

35

Vienna, 8. 11. 95.

My dear Wilhelm,

Your long letter is a sign that you are well. May both the cause and symptom persevere. As for my own health (so that I do not forget to mention it and shall not have to mention myself again), I have been incomparably better for the last fortnight. I was not able to maintain complete abstinence [from smoking], for with my present burden of theoretical and practical worries the increase in psychical hyperæsthesia was insupportable. Otherwise I am keeping to the prescription, and only over-indulged one day for joy at Lueger's non-confirmation in office.

From now on my letters will be comparatively empty. I have bundled the psychological drafts into a drawer, where they must slumber till 1896. What happened was this. First of all I laid the psychology aside to make time for the children's paralyses, which has got to be finished before 1896. I also started on migraine. The first points that arose led me to my seeing something which reminded me again of the subject I had put· aside and would have required quite a lot of revision of it. At that point I rebelled against my tyrant. I felt overworked, irritated, muddled and incapable of mastering the thing. So I flung it all aside. If you felt called on to form an opinion of those few sheets of paper that would justify my pæan of victory, I am sorry, because you must have found it difficult. Do not trouble yourself about it any further. I hope that in two months' time I may be able to get the whole thing clearer. But the clinical explanation of hysteria still stands; it is beautiful and simple, and perhaps I shall pull myself together and write it down for you soon.

10. xi. I return herewith the case histories on nose and sex.[1] I need not say that I am in entire agreement with what you say. This time you will find I have had little to add—I have only done a little red pencilling. I hope I shall have more to say when I have read the theoretical part. Your sexual-chemical hypotheses

---

[1] These have not survived.

really fascinated me. I hope you will continue with them seriously.

I am fully occupied with the children's paralyses, in which I am not in the least interested. Since putting the psychology aside I have felt depressed and disillusioned—I feel I have no right to your congratulations.

Now I feel that something is missing.

Not long ago Breuer made a big speech to the physicians' society about me, putting himself forward as a convert to belief in sexual aetiology. When I thanked him privately for this he spoiled my pleasure by saying: "But all the same I *don't* believe it!" Can you make head or tail of that? I cannot.

Martha is already suffering pretty badly.[1] I wish it were over.

On the neurotic side there is a lot of interesting material, but nothing new, only confirmation. I wish we could talk about it.

With cordial greetings to you, mother and (child),

Your

Sigm.

36

Vienna, 29. 11. 95.

Dear Wilhelm,

. . . . I am in top working form, nine to eleven hours hard work, six to eight analytical cases a day—most beautiful things, all sorts of new material. For original work I am entirely lost. When I sit down to my desk at 11 p.m. I have to patch the children's paralyses together. In two months I hope to have finished and to be able to resume turning to account the impressions gained from treating my patients.

I no longer understand the state of mind in which I concocted the psychology; I cannot conceive how I came to inflict it on you. I think you are too polite; it seems to me to have been a kind of aberration. The clinical explanation of the two neuroses will probably stand, after some modifications.

---

[1] A reference to his wife's pregnancy.

The children have all been down with colds. Minna[1] came a few days ago for a stay of several months. Of the world I see nothing and hear little, and at such times, when I find writing so difficult, I become acutely aware of the distance between Vienna and Berlin . . .

Wernicke's pupils Sachs and C. S. Freund have produced a piece of nonsense on hysteria (on psychical paralyses), which incidentally is almost a plagiarism of my "Points" in the *Archives de Neurologie*. What is more painful is Sachs's putting forward the principle of the constancy of psychological energy.[2]

I hope soon to hear good news of you, wife, child, and sexuality through the nose.

With heartiest greetings,

Your

Sigm.

---

[1] Minna Bernays, Freud's sister-in-law (1865-1941).

[2] The paper written by C. S. Freund at Breslau (Freund 1895, pp. 938-946) follows the main ideas of Freud's "Some Points for a Comparative Study of Organic and Hysterical Motor Paralyses" (1893 c) without quoting them. About half of the paper is borrowed word for word from Heinrich Sachs's textbook (Sachs, Heinrich, 1893). This states: "The human brain contains quite soon after birth a very large number of molecular waves of the most varied degree of tension as a result of the experiences accumulated during life. Only a small number of these at any one time reach a height sufficient to allow them to break through into consciousness as a composite image. No wave maintains its height for any length of time; each one of them starts losing height and thus disappears from consciousness to make way for others. Thus in the normal brain one idea continually succeeds another." (p. 110). Freund adds: "In Heinrich Sachs's opinion a law underlies this last-mentioned fact, that is to say the 'law of the constant quantity of mental energy', according to which the sum of the tensions of all the molecular waves present within certain temporal limits in the same individual is approximately constant."

Freud had been occupied for years with the principle of the constancy of psychical energy. In a letter to Breuer of 29. 6. 1892 (Freud, 1941 a) he mentions "the theorem which deals with the constancy of the sums of excitation" as the first of their joint theories, and in the first draft of their "Preliminary Communication," which was written at the end of November, 1892 (Breuer and Freud, 1940 d), the idea is taken further. (See also the note in Freud's translation of Charcot's *Lectures* quoted on p. 21). The principle of constancy plays an important role in Freud's "Project" of 1895 (see p. 357) as the "principle of inertia." It then developed in the form of the "pleasure principle" (the tendency of the mental apparatus to maintain a constant tension) and the "Nirvana principle" (the tendency of the mental apparatus to reduce its tension to zero) into one of the regulative principles of psycho-analysis.

37

Vienna, 3. 12. 95.

Dr. Sigmund Freud.   Consulting hours 3-5 p.m.
IX. Berggasse 19.

Dear Wilhelm,

If it had been a son I should have sent you the news by telegram, as he would have been named after you. But as it is a little
girl of the name of Anna, you get the news later. She arrived
to-day at 3.15 during my consulting hours, and seems to be a
nice, complete little woman. Thanks to Fleischmann's[1] care
she did not do her mother any harm, and both are doing well.
I hope it will not be long before similar good news arrives from
you, and that when Anna and Pauline meet they will get on well
together.

                                        Your
                                            Sigm.

38

Sunday, 8. 12. 95.

Dear Wilhelm,

. . . . We like to think that the baby has brought a doubling
of my practice. I have trouble in fitting everything in, and I can
pick and choose and begin to dictate my fees. I am getting confident in the diagnosis and treatment of the two neuroses, and I
think the town is gradually beginning to realize that something
is to be had from me.

Have I already written and told you that obsessional ideas are
invariable *self-reproaches*, while at the root of hysteria there is
always *conflict* (sexual pleasure versus an accompanying unpleasure)? That is a new formula for expressing the clinical
explanation. I have some beautiful mixed cases of the two neuroses at present, and hope to draw closer conclusions from them
about the essential mechanisms involved.

_____
[1] Karl Fleischmann, the well-known gynæcologist.

I always respect your opinion, even about my psychology. What you say makes me look forward to taking it up again in a few months, and this time to giving it patient, critical, detailed work. The best you can say about it so far is that it deserves the commendation *voluisse in magnis rebus*. Do you really mean that I should attract attention to these stutterings by a preliminary article? I think it would be better to keep it to ourselves until we see whether anything comes of it. Perhaps in the end I may have to learn to content myself with the clinical explanation of the neuroses.

As for your discoveries in sexual physiology, I can only promise close attention and critical admiration. My knowledge is too limited for me to be able to intervene. But I look forward to fine and important things, and I hope that when the time comes you will not fail to come out into the open even with hypotheses. We cannot do without men with the courage to think new things before they can prove them.

Many things would be different if we were not geographically separated. I am not worrying myself about the copyright of the "psychical constancy" principle. You are right, the most various things might be understood by it.[1]

Visitors, I must stop.

Cordial greetings from all here to wife and daughter.

Your

Sigm.

Draft J

[Undated. ?1895.]   (1)

FRAU P. J., AGE 27.[2]

She had been married for three months. Her husband, a commercial traveller, had had to leave her a few weeks after their marriage and had already been away for some weeks. She missed him very much

---

[1] See footnote 2, p. 135.

[2] The form in which this case is reported is similar to that used in the case history in the "Project" (p. 410). The handwriting also suggests that it was written in 1895 (perhaps earlier in that year). The case is not quoted in Freud's published works.

and longed for him. She had been a singer, or at any rate had been trained as a singer. To pass the time, she was sitting at the piano singing when she suddenly felt ill—in her abdomen and stomach, her head swam, she had feelings of oppression and anxiety and cardiac paræsthesia; she thought she was going mad. A moment later it occurred to her that she had eaten eggs and mushrooms that morning, and concluded that she had been poisoned. However, the condition quickly passed off. Next day the servant-girl told her that a woman living in the same house had gone mad. From that time on she was never free of an obsession, accompanied by anxiety, that she was going to go mad too.

Such is the outline of the case. I assumed to begin with that her condition at the time had been an anxiety state—a release of sexual feeling which was transformed into anxiety. A condition of that kind, I fear, can appear unaccompanied by any psychical process. Nevertheless, I did not turn my back on the more hopeful possibility that such a process might be found; on the contrary, I decided to make it the starting-point of my work. What I expected had happened was this:—She had felt a longing for her husband—i.e., for sexual relations with him—; she had thus come upon some idea that had excited sexual affect and afterwards a defence against that idea; she had then been frightened and had made a faulty connection or substitution.

I first asked her about the subsidiary details of the event: something must have reminded her of her husband. She said she had been singing Carmen's aria "Près des Remparts de Séville".[1]

I got her to repeat it; but she could not even remember the words exactly.—"At what point do you think you had the attack?"—She did not know.—When I applied pressure [to her forehead] she said it had been after she had finished singing the aria. That seems quite possible: it was a train of thought brought up by the words of the song.—I then insisted that before the attack there had been thoughts in her mind which she might not remember. And in fact she remembered nothing, though pressure [on her forehead] produced "husband" and "longing". After further insistence on my part this was further defined as longing for sexual caresses.—"I'm very ready to

---

[1] [The *seguidilla* from Act I of Bizet's opera.]

believe that: the attack was no more than a state of erotic effusion. Do you know the page's song?—

> '*Voi che sapete che cosa è amor,*
> *Donne, vedete s'io l'ho nel cor . . .*'[1]

But there must have been something besides—a feeling in the lower part of your body, a convulsive desire to micturate."—She proceeded to confirm this. The insincerity of women starts from their omitting the characteristic sexual symptoms in describing their states. So it had really been an *orgasm*.

"Well," I went on, "you can see that a state of longing like that in a young woman whose husband has left her is nothing to be ashamed of?"—On the contrary, she agreed, it was something to be approved of.—Very well; but, if so, I could see no reason for the fright.—"You are certainly not frightened about 'husband' and 'longing'; so there must be some other thoughts missing, which would fit in better with fright." But she would only add that she had all along been afraid of the pains caused by intercourse, but that her desire had been much stronger than her fear of the pains.—At this point we broke off.

II

It was greatly to be suspected that in Scene I (at the piano), besides her longing thoughts about her husband (which she remembered), there had been another, deep-going train of thought, which she did *not* remember and which led to some Scene II. But I did not know its starting-point. To-day she arrived in tears and despair, evidently without any hope of the treatment being a success. So her resistance was already active; and things began to move with much greater difficulty. What I wanted to know, then, was what thoughts there still were that might lead to her being frightened. She produced all kinds of things that could not be relevant: the fact that for a long time her hymen was not perforated (which Professor Chrobak confirmed to her), that she attributed her nervous states to that and for that reason wished it might be done.—This was of course a thought of a later date; up to the time of Scene I she had been in good health.— Eventually I extracted the information that she had already had a

---

[1] [Cherubino's *canzonetta* from the second act of Mozart's *Figaro*.]

similar, but much weaker and more transitory attack with the same feelings. (From this I saw that the path leading down to the deeper layers of her mind lay through her memory-image of the orgasm itself.) We now investigated this earlier scene. At that time—four years back—she had had an engagement at Ratisbon. In the morning she had sung at a rehearsal and given satisfaction. In the afternoon, at home, she had had a "vision"—as if there were something between her (a row) and the tenor of the company and another man, and afterwards she had had the attack, with the fear that she was going mad.

Here then, was a Scene II which had been touched on by association in Scene I. But once again the memory clearly had gaps in it. There must have been still further ideas present, to account for the release of sexual feeling and fright. I enquired for these intermediate links, but instead I was given her motivations. She had disliked the whole of life on the stage.—Why?—The brusqueness of the manager and the actors' relations to one another.—I asked for details of this.— There had been a comic old woman, and the young men had amused themselves by asking her if they might come and spend the night with her.—I asked for something further, about the tenor.—*He* had pestered her as well; at the rehearsal he had put his hand on her breast. Through her clothes or on her bare skin?—She began to say the latter, but then took it back; she had been in outdoor clothes.— Well, what else?—The whole character of their relations—she had found all the embracing and kissing between the actors frightful.— Yes?—Once again the manager's brusqueness; moreover she had only stayed a few days.—Was the tenor's assault made on the same day as your attack?—No; she did not know whether it was earlier or later.—The procedure by pressure showed that the assault had been on the fourth day of her stay and her attack on the sixth day.

Interrupted by the patient's flight.

39

I. I. 96.

My dear Wilhelm,

The first leisure of the new year belongs to you—to shake your hand across the few kilometres between us, and to tell you

how glad I was to hear both your family news and the news about
your work. I am delighted that you have a son,[1] and with him
the hope of other children. While the prospect was still distant
I did not want either of us to have to admit what you would have
missed. . . .

Your letters, such as the last for instance, contain a wealth
of scientific penetration and imagination about which all I can
say, unfortunately, is that I am fascinated and overwhelmed.
The thought that we should both be busy with the same work is
the happiest that I could have just now. I see that you are using
the circuitous route of medicine to attain your first ideal, the
physiological understanding of man, while I secretly nurse the
hope of arriving by the same route at my own original objective,
philosophy. For that was my original ambition, before I knew
what I was intended to do in the world. During the last few
weeks I have tried repeatedly to summarize my latest findings
about the defence neuroses for you, as some recompense for
what you have sent me, but my thinking capacity was so
exhausted last spring that now I cannot do anything. But I shall
pull myself together and send you the fragment.[2] A still, small
voice has warned me again to postpone the description of
hysteria—it contains too much uncertainty. You will probably
be pleased with the obsessional neurosis. The few remarks on
paranoia arise from a recently begun analysis which has already
established beyond doubt that *paranoia is really a defence
neurosis*. Whether this explanation has therapeutic value remains
to be seen.

Your remarks on migraine[3] have led me to an idea which
would result in a complete revision of all my $\varphi\psi\omega$ theories,
on which I cannot venture now. I shall try to indicate it,
however.[4]

I start off from the two species of nerve-endings. The free
nerve-endings receive only quantity and conduct it to ψ by

---

[1] Robert Wilhelm.
[2] See the following Draft K (p. 146), part of which is identical with the paper
"Further Remarks on the Neuro-Psychoses of Defence." (1896 b).
[3] These have not survived.
[4] The following refers to the "Project", p.

summation ; [*Cf.* "Project", p. 377-8] they have no power, however, to evoke sensation—that is, to affect ω. In this connection the neuronic motion retains its genuine character of being monotonous in quality. [*Ibid.*, pp. 371-2]. These are the pathways for all the quantity that fills ψ, including sexual energy, of course.

The nerve-paths which start from terminal organs do not conduct quantity but their particular qualitative characteristic. They add nothing to the sum [of quantity] in the Ψ-neurones, but merely put these neurones into a state of excitation. The perceptual neurones (ω) are those Ψ-neurones which are capable of only a very small quantitative cathexis. The necessary condition for the generation of consciousness is the coincidence of these minimal quantities with the quality which is faithfully transferred to them from the terminal organ. In my new scheme I insert these perceptual neurones (ω) between the Φ-neurones and the Ψ-neurones; so that Φ transfers its quality to ω, and ω transfers neither quality nor quantity to Ψ, but merely excites Ψ—that is, indicates the direction to be taken by the free psychical energy [of attention]. (I do not know if you can make out this double Dutch. There are, as it were, three ways in which neurones can affect one another: (1) they can transfer quantity to one another; (2) they can transfer quality to one another; (3) they can, in accordance with certain rules, have an exciting effect on one another.)

On this view, perceptual processes would *eo ipso* [from their very nature] involve consciousness, and would only produce further psychical effects *after* becoming conscious. The Ψ-processes would in themselves be unconscious, and would only subsequently acquire a secondary, artificial consciousness by being linked with processes of discharge and perception (with speech-associations). A discharge from ω which I had to assume in my other account, now becomes unnecessary. Hallucinations, which were always hard to explain, are no longer a retrogression of excitation to Φ, but only to ω. It is now far easier to understand the rule of defence, which does not apply to perceptions but only to Ψ-processes. The fact that secondary consciousness lags behind makes it possible to give a simple account of the processes in neuroses. I am also relieved of the troublesome problem of how much of the strength of Φ-excitations (sensory stimuli) is transferred to Ψ-neurones. The answer is: none at all, directly; the quantity (Q) in Ψ depends only on how far free Ψ-attention is directed by the perceptual neurones (ωN).

The new hypothesis also fits in better with the fact of objective sensory stimuli being of such minimal size that it is difficult to derive the force of the will from that source in accordance with the principle of constancy. We now see, however, that sensation brings no quantity (Q) whatever to Ψ, and that the source of Ψ-energy is derived from the [endogenous] organic paths of conduction.

I also find an explanation of the release of unpleasure, which I require for the purpose of repression in the sexual neuroses, in the conflict between the purely quantitative organic conduction and the processes that are *excited* in Ψ by conscious sensations.

As regards *your* side of the question, the possibility arises that states of stimulation may occur in organs which produce no *spontaneous* sensations (though they must no doubt exhibit susceptibility to pressure), but which can be excited in a reflex manner (that is, through the effect of equilibrium) by disturbances arising from other neuronic centres. For the notion of there being a mutual "binding" between neurones or neuronic centres also makes it likely that the symptoms of motor discharge are of very different kinds.[1] Voluntary actions are probably determined by a transference of quantity (Q), since they discharge psychical tension. But on the other hand there are pleasurable discharges, convulsive movements and so on, which I explain by supposing that what is happening is not that quantity is being *transferred* to the motor centre but that it is being

---

[1] These modifications of the views stated in the "Project" deserve attention as they are a reformulation of the difference between perceptual stimuli and internal stimuli; they prepare the way to the contrast between conscious and unconscious (but not repressed) mental processes and thus point in the direction of the conception of the structure of the mind at which Freud arrived in later years. Their immediate development is to be seen in Chapter VII of *The Interpretation of Dreams*: the conception of hallucination hinted at here is repeated in it practically unaltered.

liberated in that centre because the binding quantity (Q) in the sensory centre coupled to it may have diminished. This would give us the distinction of which we have so long been in search between "voluntary" movements and "spastic" ones, and at the same time would afford a means of explaining a group of subsidiary somatic effects—in hysteria, for instance.

It is possible for the purely quantitative processes of transference to Ψ to attract consciousness to themselves; if, namely, they fulfil the conditions necessary for producing pain. Of these conditions the essential one is probably the suspension of the process of summation and a continuous influx [of quantity] into Ψ lasting for some length of time. Some of the perceptual neurones then become hypercathected, produce a feeling of unpleasure, and also cause attention to be riveted on this particular spot. Thus "neuralgic changes" would have to be regarded as due to an influx of quantity from some organ being augmented beyond a certain limit, so that summation is suspended, the perceptual neurones are hypercathected and free Ψ energy becomes riveted. As you see, we have arrived at migraine; its determining condition would be the existence in nasal regions of the state of stimulation which was detected by your naked eye. The surplus of quantity would spread out along various subcortical paths before reaching Ψ. When this has once happened, what is now a continuous flow of quantity (Q) forces its way into Ψ and, in accordance with the rule of attention [p. 417], the free Ψ-energy streams to the seat of the eruption.

The question now arises as to the source of the state of stimulation in the nasal organ.[1] The idea suggests itself that the *qualitative* organ for olfactory stimuli may be the Schneiderian membrane and that their disconnected *quantitative* organ may be the *corpora cavernosa*. Olfactory substances, as, indeed, you yourself believe, and as we learn from flowers, are disintegrated products of the sexual metabolism; they would act as stimuli upon both these organs. At times of menstruation and of other

---

[1] Freud obviously wrote the following passage in the hope of building a bridge between Fliess's field and his own. The ideas it contains played no part in the further development of Freud's theories.

sexual processes the body produces an increased number of these substances and therefore of these stimuli. It would have to be decided whether they act on the nasal organ by means of the expiratory air or through the blood-stream; probably the latter since one has no subjective sensation of smell before the migraine. Accordingly, the nose would, as it were, receive information about *internal* olfactory stimuli through the *corpora cavernosa*, just as it does about *external* stimuli by means of the Schneiderian membrane; it could thus come to grief as a result of the products of the subject's own body. These two ways of developing migraine—spontaneously and by smells, poisonous emanations from human bodies, would thus be on a par with each other, and could at any time provide complementary summation in bringing about their effects.

Thus the swelling of the nasal organs of quantity would be a kind of adaptation of the sense organ as a result of increased internal stimulation, analogous in the case of the adaptation of the true (qualitative) sense organs to opening the eyes wide, focusing, straining the ears, etc.

It would not be too hard, perhaps, to adapt this view to the other sources of migraine and to similar conditions, though I cannot yet see how it is to be done. In any case it is more important to test it in relation to the main topic.[1]

By this means a number of obscure and ancient medical ideas acquire life and importance. . . .

That is enough for now. Best wishes for 1896, and let me know soon how mother and child are. You can imagine how greatly all that interests Martha.

Your

Sigm.

---

[1] See Freud's discussion of migraine, p. 116.

Draft K

(1 January 1896)

THE NEUROSES OF DEFENCE

(A Christmas Fairy Tale[1])

There are four types of these, and many forms. My comparison can only be drawn between hysteria, obsessional neurosis and one form of paranoia. They have a number of things in common. They are pathological aberrations of normal psychical states of affect: of *conflict* (in hysteria), of *self-reproach* (in obsessional neurosis), of *mortification* (in paranoia) and of *grief* (in acute hallucinatory amentia). They differ from these affects in that they do not end by being worked off but in permanent damage to the ego. They are brought about by the same precipitating causes as their affective prototypes, provided that two further conditions are satisfied. The precipitating cause must be of a sexual nature and it must occur at a time before sexual maturity has been reached. (The provisos of *sexuality* and *infantilism*.) I have no fresh knowledge on the subject of *personal* determinants; in general I should say that heredity is an extra determinant in so far as it facilitates and increases the pathological affect—the determinant, that is, which in general makes possible the gradations between the normal and the extreme case. I do not believe that heredity determines the choice of the particular defensive neurosis.

There is a normal inclination towards defence—that is, an aversion to directing psychical energy in such a way that unpleasure results. This inclination, which is related to the most fundamental attributes of the psychical mechanism (the law of constancy),[2] cannot be directed against perceptions, for these are able to compel attention (as is shown by their being conscious); it only comes into operation in regard to memories and thoughts. It is innocuous where it is concerned with ideas to which unpleasure was at one time attached but which are unable to acquire any contemporary unpleasure (other

---

[1] In the last section of this draft Freud seeks to bring his ideas into connection with those of the "Project" which he partially repeats. The main ideas stated here were used to some extent in *Further Remarks on the Neuro-Psychoses of Defence* 1896 b).

[2] [Cf. the "Project", p. 358]

than remembered unpleasure); in such cases, too, it can be overridden by psychical interest.

The inclination towards defence is detrimental, however, if it is directed against ideas which are able, in the form of energy, to release fresh unpleasure—as is the case with sexual ideas. Here, indeed, we have the one possibility of a memory subsequently producing a more powerful release than that produced in the first instance by the corresponding experience itself. Only one further condition must be fulfilled, namely, that puberty should have occurred between the experience and its repetition—an event which very greatly intensifies the effect of the revival. The psychical mechanism seems unprepared for dealing with this exception, and it is consequently a *sine qua non* of being free from defensive neuroses that one should have undergone no considerable sexual irritation before puberty, though it is true that an experience of that kind must have its consequences intensified by hereditary disposition before it can reach a height sufficient to make one fall ill.[1]

(At this point a side issue branches off: how does it come about that analogous conditions sometimes give rise to perversion or simple immorality instead of to neurosis?[2])

We shall be plunged deep into the riddles of psychology if we enquire into the origin of the unpleasure which is released by premature sexual stimulation and without which the occurrence of a repression cannot be explained. The most plausible answer will recall the fact that shame and morality are the repressing forces and that the neighbourhood in which nature has placed the sexual organs must inevitably arouse disgust at the same time as sexual experiences.[3] Where there is no shame (as in male persons) or no morality (as in the lower classes of society), there too, infantile sexual stimulation will not lead to repression nor, consequently, to neurosis.[4] Nevertheless

---

[1] See similar arguments in the "Project", p. 409 *sqq.* and Letter 52, (p. 173 *sqq.*)

[2] For further attempts to solve the problem of the choice of neurosis, see Letter 125.

[3] *Inter faeces et urinas nascimur.* Cf. the *Three Essays* (Freud, 1905 d), the case history of "Dora" (Freud, 1905 e), and the arguments in *Civilisation and its Discontents* (1930a) which are partially connected with Bleuler (1913).

[4] These unsatisfactory assertions, which Freud rejects in the next sentence, deserve attention because they show that Freud was already aware of the influence of social circumstances on the development of neurosis; see also Draft A.

I fear that this explanation will not stand up to closer examination. I cannot think that the release of unpleasure during sexual experiences is the consequence of a chance admixture of certain unpleasurable factors. Everyday experience teaches us that if libido is sufficiently great, disgust is not felt and morality is overridden; and I believe that the origin of shame is connected with sexual experience by deeper links. In my opinion there must be some independent source for the release of unpleasure in sexual life: if that source is present, it can activate sensations of disgust, lend force to morality, and so on. I cling to the model of anxiety neurosis in adults, where too a quantity deriving from sexual life causes a disturbance in the psyche when it would normally have been employed in some other way in the sexual process. So long as we have no correct theory of the sexual process, the problem of the origin of the unpleasure operating in repression will remain unsolved.

The course of the illness in the defensive neuroses is, generally speaking, always the same. We find

1. a sexual experience (or series of experiences) which is premature and traumatic and has to be repressed;
2. the repression of this experience on some later occasion which recalls it to memory, and the consequent formation of a primary symptom;
3. a stage of successful defence, which resembles health, except for the existence of the primary symptom; and
4. a stage in which the repressed ideas return and in which, during the struggle between them and the ego, fresh symptoms are constructed, which constitute the illness proper: that is, a stage either of coming to terms, or of being overwhelmed, or of recovery accompanied by a malformation.

The main distinctions between the different neuroses are shown in the manner in which the repressed ideas return; other distinctions lie in the mode in which the symptoms are formed and in the course taken by the illness. But the specific character of the different neuroses resides in the way in which repression is accomplished.

The course of events in obsessional neurosis is the clearest to me, since I have come to know it the best.

Obsessional Neurosis

In this case the primary experience has been accompanied by pleasure. It is either an active one (in boys) or a passive one (in girls), without any admixture of pain or disgust; and this, in general, implies a higher age (about 8) in girls. When this experience is recollected later, it gives rise to a release of unpleasure; and, in particular, what first emerges is a self-reproach which is conscious. Indeed, it appears as though the whole psychical complex—recollection and self-reproach—is conscious at first. Later on, without anything fresh happening, both of them are repressed, and in their place an *antithetic symptom* is formed in consciousness: some *nuance* of *conscientiousness*.

The repression may come about by the pleasurable memory in itself releasing unpleasure when it is reproduced in later years—which we should have to explain in our theory of sexuality. But it may come about in another way. In *all* my cases of obsessional neurosis there had been, at a very early age, years before the pleasurable experience, a *purely passive* experience; and this can scarcely be an accidental fact. If so, we can suppose that it is the later convergence of this passive experience with the pleasurable one that adds the unpleasure to the pleasurable memory and makes repression possible. Thus it would be a necessary clinical condition of obsessional neurosis that the passive experience should occur early enough not to interfere with the spontaneous development of the pleasurable experience. The formula would therefore run:

Unpleasure—Pleasure—Repression

The chronological relations of the two experiences to each other and to the date of sexual maturity would be the determining factors.

We find that at the stage of the return of the repressed the self-reproach returns unaltered. But it seldom happens that it attracts attention to itself, so that it emerges for a while as a pure sense of guilt without any content. It usually becomes linked to a content which is distorted in two ways, in time and in subject-matter: the former in that it relates to a contemporary or future action, and the latter in that it relates not to the real experience but to some analogous substitute. Thus the obsession is a product of compromise, correct as regards affect and category, but falsified by chronological displacement and the substitution of something analogous.

The affect of the self-reproach may be transformed by various psychical processes into other affects, which then enter consciousness more distinctly than the affect itself: *e.g.*, into *anxiety* (concerning the consequences of the action to which the self-reproach applies), *hypochondria* (fear of its somatic effects), *delusions of persecution* (fear of its social effects), *shame* (fear of other people knowing about it), and so on.

The conscious ego regards the obsession as something alien to itself: it withholds belief from it, by the help, it seems, of the antithetic idea of conscientiousness which had been formed long before. But at this stage the ego may from time to time be overwhelmed by the obsession: if, for instance, the ego is affected by an episodic melancholia. Apart from this, the stage of illness is taken up by the ego's defensive struggle against the obsession; and this may itself produce fresh symptoms—the symptoms of *secondary defence*. The obsession, like any other idea, is subjected to logical criticism, though its compulsive force is unshakable; the secondary symptoms consist in an intensification of conscientiousness, and a compulsion to examine things and to hoard them. Other secondary symptoms arise when the compulsion is transferred to motor impulses directed against the obsession: *e.g.*, to brooding, drinking (dipsomania), protective ceremonials, etc. (*folie de doute*).

Accordingly three species of symptoms may be formed:

    a. the primary defensive symptom—*conscientiousness;*

    b. the compromise symptoms of the illness—*obsessions or obsessive affects;*

    c. the secondary defensive symptoms—*obsessive brooding, compulsion to hoard things, dipsomania, obsessive ceremonials.*

Cases in which the content of the memory has not become admissible to consciousness owing to substitution, but in which the affect of self-reproach has become admissible owing to transformation, give one the impression of a displacement having occurred along a chain of inferences: I reproach myself on account of some event—I am afraid of other people knowing about it—consequently I feel ashamed in the presence of other people. The first link in this chain having been repressed, the compulsion jumps on to the second or third link, and the outcome is delusions of reference of two forms, which, however, are in fact part of the obsessional neurosis. The defensive struggle is brought to a conclusion in a generalized doubting mania or by the adoption of a life of eccentricity with an indefinite number of secondary defensive symptoms—that is, if it is brought to a conclusion at all.

It further remains an open question whether the repressed ideas can return of themselves, without the help of any contemporary psychical force, or whether they require such help at every fresh recurrence. My experience points to the latter alternative. It seems as though states of contemporary unsatisfied libido use the force of their unpleasure in awakening the repressed self-reproach. Once this awakening has taken place and a symptom has arisen owing to the impact of the repressed material upon the ego, that material no doubt continues to operate on its own account; but the oscillations in its quantitative power always remain dependent on the amount of libidinal tension present at the moment. Sexual tension which has no time to turn into unpleasure because it is satisfied does no harm. Obsessional neurotics are people who are subject to the danger that eventually the whole of the sexual tension which is daily generated in them may turn into self-reproaches or the symptoms that follow from them—though at the present time they would not admit the *primary* self-reproach.

Obsessional neurosis can be cured if we undo all the substitutions and affective transformations that have taken place, till the primary self-reproach and the experience belonging to it can be laid bare and placed before the conscious ego to be judged afresh. In the course of doing this we have to work through an incredible number of intermediate or compromise ideas which become obsessions temporarily. From this we gain the liveliest conviction that it is impossible for the ego to direct on to the repressed material the part of psychical energy which is attached to conscious thinking. The repressed ideas—so we must believe—enter without inhibition into the most rational trains of thought; and the memory of them is aroused, too, by the barest

allusion. Our suspicion that "morality" is put forward as the repressing force merely as an excuse is confirmed by the experience that
resistance during therapeutic work makes use of every possible
motive for defence.[1]

Paranoia

Here the determining clinical conditions and the chronological
relations of pleasure and unpleasure in the primary experience are
still unknown to me. What I have found is the fact of repression, the
primary symptom and the stage of illness as something determined
by the return of the repressed ideas.

The primary experience seems to be of a nature similar to that in
obsessional neurosis; repression occurs after the recollection of it has
released unpleasure—I do not know how. No self-reproach, however, is formed and afterwards repressed; but the developing unpleasure is turned upon the patient's fellow-men according to the
psychical formula of projection. The primary symptom which is
formed is *distrust* (over-sensitiveness to other people).   In this
process belief is being withheld from a self-reproach.

We can suspect the existence of different forms, according to
whether only the *affect* is repressed by projection or the *content* of the
experience too, along with it. So too what returns may be either the
distressing affect alone or the memory as well. In the latter
case, which is the only one with which I have a fairly close acquaintance, the content of the experience returns either as the occurrence of a thought or as a visual or sensory hallucination. The
repressed affect seems invariably to return in hallucinations of voices
heard.

The returning portions of the memory are distorted by being replaced by analogous images from contemporary life; thus they are
distorted only in one way—by chronological shifting but not by the
formation of a substitute. The voices, just as in the case of obsessions,
present the self-reproach in the form of a compromise symptom; they
are, firstly, distorted in their wording to the point of becoming

---

[1] In "Further Remarks on the Neuro-Psychoses of Defence" (1896 b) Freud
adds a good deal to these considerations and deletes some unessential points.

indefinite and are transformed into a threat, and, secondly, relate not to the primary *experience* but to the distrust—that is, to the primary *symptom*.

Since belief has been withheld from the primary self-reproach, it is at the unrestricted disposal of the compromise symptoms. The ego does not regard these as alien to itself, but is incited by them to make attempts at explaining them which may be termed "delusions of assimilation".

At this point, with the return of the repressed in a distorted form, the defence has failed; and the delusions of assimilation cannot be regarded as secondary defensive symptoms but must be interpreted as the beginning of a *modification of the ego*, an expression of the fact of its being overwhelmed. The process reaches its conclusion either in melancholia (a sense of the littleness of the ego), which, in a secondary manner, attaches to the distortions the belief which has been withheld from the primary process, or—what is more frequent and more serious—it ends in the formation of *protective delusions* (megalomania), until the ego has been completely remodelled.[1]

The determining element in paranoia is the mechanism of projection accompanied by the refusal to believe the self-reproach. Hence follow the general characteristics of the neurosis: the significance attached to the voices, as being the means by which other people affect us, and also to gestures, which reveal other people's mental processes to us; and the importance of the *tone* of their remarks and their allusions—since any direct reference to the repressed memory in the *content* of the remarks is inadmissible to consciousness.

In paranoia repression takes place after a complicated conscious process of thought (the withholding of belief). This may perhaps be an indication that it first sets in at an age later than in obsessional neurosis and hysteria. The underlying basis of the repression is no doubt the same in all three cases. It remains an open question whether the mechanism of projection is entirely a matter of individual disposition, or whether it is picked out by particular temporal and accidental factors.

---

[1] These considerations reappear, but in altered form, only in Freud's later works.

There are four species of symptoms:

a. primary defensive symptoms;
b. the return [of the repressed] with the characteristic of a compromise;
c. secondary defensive symptoms;
d. symptoms of the overwhelming of the ego.

Hysteria

Hysteria necessarily presupposes a primary unpleasurable experience—that is, one of a passive kind. The natural sexual passivity of women accounts for their being more inclined to hysteria. Where I have found hysteria in men, I have been able to trace a large amount of sexual passivity in their anamnesis. A further condition of hysteria is that the primary unpleasurable experience shall not occur at too early a time, while the release of unpleasure is still too slight; for if so, pleasurable events can of course follow later independently, and the result will only be the formation of obsessions. For this reason we often find a combination of the two neuroses in men or the replacement of an initial hysteria by a later obsessional neurosis. Hysteria *begins* with the overwhelming of the ego, which is the *end* of paranoia. The increase of tension is so great in the primary unpleasurable experience that the ego does not resist it and constructs no psychical symptom, but is obliged to allow a manifestation of discharge to occur—usually an excessive expression of excitation. This first stage of hysteria may be described as "fright hysteria"; its primary symptom is a *manifestation of fright* accompanied by a *gap* in the psyche. It is still unknown up to how late an age this first hysterical overwhelming of the ego can take place.

Repression and the formation of defensive symptoms only occur afterwards, in connection with the memory; and thenceforward *defence* and *overwhelming* (that is, the formation of symptoms and the onset of attacks) may be combined to any extent in hysteria.

Repression does not take place by the construction of an excessively strong antithetic idea, but by the intensification of a "boundary idea", which thereafter represents the repressed memory in the processes of thought.[1] It may be termed a "boundary idea" because on the one hand it belongs to the conscious ego and on the other hand forms an undistorted portion of the traumatic memory. Thus, as in the other neuroses, it is the result of a compromise; but this compromise is not manifested in a substitution based upon any similarity of subject-matter but in a displacement of attention along a series of ideas that are connected by having occurred simultaneously. If the traumatic experience found a vent in some motor manifestation it will be this that becomes the frontier idea and the first symbol of the repressed material. There is thus no need to assume that some idea is being suppressed at each repetition of the primary attack; it is a question in the first instance of there being *a gap in the psyche*.

40

Vienna, 6. 2. 96.

Dear Wilhelm,

There has been an unconscionable break in our correspondence. I know you have been occupied with Robert Wilhelm, neglecting nose and sex on his account, and I hope he has rewarded you by thriving. I have been slaving away in one of my bouts of writing, and used it to produce three short articles for Mendel and a general one for the *Revue Neurologique*.[2] It was all sent off yesterday and now I am blowing my own trumpet for lack of anyone else to blow it for me and have decided to rest on my self-awarded laurels and to start writing to you immediately.

I have spared you the draft of my school essay, as it is the same as part of what I sent you as a Christmas story.[3] I am dreadfully sorry that these latest novelties (the real aetiology of hysteria—the nature of obsessional neurosis—insight into

---

[1] The conception of a "boundary idea" found no place in Freud's published works. The part of "Further Remarks on the Neuro-Pyschoses of Defence" (1896 b) which deals with hysteria is far superior to the material here, and rests on a far richer clinical foundation.

[2] The three short articles were "Further Remarks on the Neuro-Psychoses of Defence" (1896 b); the longer "general" one was "Heredity and the Aetiology of the Neuroses" (1896 a).

[3] See p. 146 *sqq.*

paranoia) should have been spoilt for you by the way I presented them. You shall have everything made clear at our private congress in the summer. I am going to Munich for the psychological congress from August 4th to 7th. Will you grant me those days? I am making absolutely no official engagements.

Little Anna is flourishing; Martha took a long time to recover. Mathilde has been isolated for a week with a slight scarlatina. No one else has got it yet. . . .

Our book had a disgraceful notice by Strümpell in the *Deutsche Zeitschrift für Nervenheilkunde*,[1] but in compensation there was a very sensitive article by Freiherr von Berger in the old *Presse* of 2. 2. 96.[2]

We very much look forward to a word from you, when all your anxieties are over, about how your wife and my young friend are.

With heartiest greetings to all three of you,

Your

Sigm.

41

Vienna, 13. 2. 96.

Dear Wilhelm,

I am so isolated, and therefore so delighted with your letter, that I am using the quiet after to-day's consulting hour to answer.

---

[1] Strümpell (1896) said that though Breuer's theoretical arguments included "a number of striking and suggestive ideas," they "were excessively generalized and strained". "The authors' therapeutic views" were based "on a correct and delicate psychological understanding of a number of cases of severe hysteria." But he had doubts about their therapeutic procedure. "This, as the authors emphasize themselves, requires a penetrating investigation, often extending into the most minute details, of the patient's private affairs and experiences. I do not know whether such fathoming of the most intimate private affairs can in all circumstances be considered legitimate, even on the part of the most high-principled physician. When sexual relations are concerned I consider it particularly questionable."

[2] Alfred Freiherr von Berger (1853-1912) was professor of literary history in Vienna University and later director of the Burgtheater. The article referred to, entitled "Soul Surgery", appeared in the *Neue Freie Presse* and was reproduced in part in *Die Psychoanalytische Bewegung*, vol. IV, 1932, p. 73, *sqq.* For an appreciation, see Kris (1952).

First of all, so that you do not think I am withholding anything from you, the latest thing to be printed is an extract from
the so-called Christmas fairy tale I wrote for you, rather more
objective and toned down.

I am naturally very much looking forward to your nose-sex.[1]
Counterblasts against you are being prepared in the clinics
here. That is all I could find out. Criticism will not affect you
any more than Strümpell's criticism affected me. I really do not
need to be consoled on account of it. I am so sure that we have
both laid hands on a fine piece of objective truth, and we can
do without recognition from strangers (strangers to the facts)
for a long time to come. I hope we shall make still more discoveries and go on correcting our own mistakes before anyone
catches up with us. . . .

My health does not deserve to be asked after. . . . I have
grown grey very quickly.

I am continually occupied with psychology—it is really
metapsychology;[2] Taine's book *L'Intelligence*[3] gives me especial satisfaction. I hope something will come of it. It is the
oldest ideas which are the most useful, as I am belatedly finding
out. I hope to be occupied with scientific interests to the end of
my life. Apart from them I am scarcely a human being any
longer. At 10.30 after my practice I am dead tired.

I shall read "Nose and Sex" immediately, of course, and send
it back. I hope you also mention some of our fundamental views
on sexuality in it. . . .

With heartiest greetings to your wife and Robert,

Your

Sigm.

---

[1] This is obviously a reference to the manuscript of Fliess (1897) without the
final chapter.
[2] This is the first use of the term "metapsychology". See also Letter 84.
[3] Taine (1864).

42

Vienna, 1. 3. 96.

Dear Wilhelm,

I read through your draft in a single breath. I liked tremendously its easy assurance, the natural, almost self-evident way in which each point leads to the next, its unpretentious unfolding of riches and—last not least[1]—the wealth of glimpses of new riddles and new explanations. I read it through the first time as if it had been intended for me alone. You will find no red pencilling, except at one place only; there was no need for it. You will forgive my not having checked the case histories again.[2]

If I am to criticize, first I must screw myself up. First of all, then, you should have sent me the last, general, chapter at the same time. It cannot be a mere appendix, because what you have sent me cries out for it urgently and aloud. I am most anxious to see it. Another point is that I think people will not like the way in which the delightful story of I.F.'s period-times in pregnancy, with the associated hypotheses of the two halves of the organ and their transfer of functions and interference, is inserted like a single glimpse of a distant panorama when one is on a low, flat road. It is almost reminiscent of the way in which G. Keller in *Der grüne Heinrich* breaks off his life story to describe the fate of the poor, crazy little princess. I should say that for the common reader of this booklet it would be better to put this piece of interpretation, which goes with the tables, in the general, explanatory section, and that in the context it would be sufficient to add a note to the tables to the effect that it appears from the nasal findings that the menstrual intervals from July onwards vary between 23 and 33 days, and that this will be referred to again later. Also the evidence for a 23-day cycle would then be on another level. Certainly it is just these points which are by far the most interesting to us two. But one

---

[1] [These three words in English in the original.]
[2] The work on which Freud is here commenting is Fliess (1897). See Introduction, p. 6 *sqq.*

should not provide the public with an opportunity of exercising its limited critical faculty, which it generally does to its own detriment, in the chapter devoted entirely to facts.[1] And then what is new and hypothetical in the second part ought to be amplified. Otherwise I fear that readers might jump to the conclusion that it was not the only possible explanation for the periodicity of events in the I.F. case, particularly as the birth did not fit in with it, but was the result of a disturbance. But that can only be seen clearly if the second section is there to back it up.[2]

And now that I have completed the arduous duty of looking at your work through the public's spectacles, which do not suit me, let me add that some of your random observations made a deep impression on me. It occurs to me that the limits of repression in my theory of the neuroses, *i.e.*, the time after which a sexual experience works not posthumously but directly, coincide with the second dentition.[3] I think I am just beginning to understand the anxiety neurosis now; the menstrual period is its physiological pattern, and it is a toxic state the physiological foundation for which is an organic process.[4] It is to be hoped that the unknown organ (the thyroid[5] or whatever it may be) will not remain unknown to you for long. I was also delighted with the idea of the male menopause; in my "Anxiety Neurosis" I boldly stated that it might turn out to be the final conditioning factor for men.[6] You also seem to have provided

---

[1] Fliess seems to have adopted several of Freud's suggestions.

[2] For Freud's attitude to Fliess's period theory see page 40 *sqq*.

[3] In "The Aetiology of Hysteria", written later in the same year (1896 c) Freud writes: "Since in no single instance does the chain of effective experiences break off with the eighth year, I must assume that this time of life, the period of growth in which the second dentition occurs, forms a limit for hysteria, which cannot be caused when once that limit has been passed". See on the other hand the view stated in the "Project", where puberty is taken to be the limit.

[4] This is an attempt to carry a step further the hypothesis of the transformation into anxiety of dammed-up sexual excitation (libido).

[5] Freud took an interest in the functioning of the thyroid gland as early as 1892. See his footnote on p. 237 of his translation of Charcot (1892-3a).

[6] In this (1895 b) Freud enumerates among the conditions that may give rise to anxiety neurosis among men: "Anxiety in ageing men. There are men who have a climacteric like women and who develop anxiety neurosis at the time of their waning potency and increased libido".

the explanation of the periodicity of anxiety attacks for which Löwenfeld asked me. . . .

Affectionate regards to you, Ida and W.R.

Your

Sigm.

43

Vienna, 16. 3. 96.

My dear Wilhelm,

. . . Do not think I am throwing doubt on your period theory just because the observations made by you and your wife are not free of disturbing influences. I only want to stop you from giving the enemy, the public, something on which to exercise its mind —as I unfortunately always do—because it usually revenges itself for such a challenge.[1]

My scientific work is going forward slowly. To-day—just like a budding poet—I wrote at the top of a sheet of paper:

Lectures on the Major Neuroses

(Neurasthenia, Anxiety Neurosis, Hysteria, Obsessional Neurosis).

The fact is that for the moment I am getting no further with the common neuroses, and have nothing to retract. So I may as well strike out and get things down on paper. Behind it there looms another and nobler work to be entitled:

Psychology and Psychotherapy of the Neuroses of Defence

for which I shall allow myself years of preparation and into which I shall put my whole soul.

I have a case of dipsomania I want to tell you about at our next meeting; it resolved itself very obviously in accordance with my theories. I keep on coming back to psychology; it is a compulsion from which I cannot escape. What I have is neither a

---

[1] Fliess's reaction to Freud's previous letter, Letter 42, paved the way to their eventual estrangement. Fliess demanded the unconditional recognition of his period theory. See Introduction, p. 35 *sqq.*

million nor yet a penny, but a lump of ore containing an unknown amount of precious metal. On the whole I am satisfied with my progress, but I am met with hostility and live in such isolation that one might suppose I had discovered the greatest truths.[1]

Our congress will be a great refreshment and relief.

With heartiest greetings to you, your wife and R. W.'s mother,

Your

Sigm.

44

Vienna, 2. 4. 96.

My dear Wilhelm,

Your manuscript goes to Deuticke to-morrow. I have read it through and like it very much. We shall soon be able to discuss it. I am delighted to see that you are able to substitute realities for my incomplete efforts. Perhaps it will lead to an organic explanation of the difference between neurasthenia and anxiety neurosis, at which I arrived by a kind of clinical instinct. I have always regarded anxiety neurosis, and the neuroses generally, as primarily toxic states,[2] and I have often thought of the similarity of the symptoms in anxiety neurosis and Basedow's [Graves'] disease,[3] with which you may perhaps still be able to deal. . . .

On the whole I am getting on very well with the psychology of the neuroses and have every ground to be satisfied. I hope you will lend me your ear for a few metapsychological questions also. . . .

If we are both granted a few more years of quiet work, we shall certainly leave behind something which will justify our

---

[1] Freud speaks in *On the History of the Psycho-Analytic Movement* (1914 d) of "the void which formed itself about me". See also Letter 45. At times he defined the reaction of his environment to his discoveries even more pointedly; he said that, after he had gained an understanding of the functioning of resistance, it was his environment's rejection of him that gave him insight "into the full significance of his discoveries".

[2] See footnote 2, p. 158.

[3] See footnote 5, p. 159.

existence. That feeling strengthens me against all daily cares and worries. When I was young, the only thing I longed for was philosophical knowledge, and now that I am going over from medicine to psychology I am in the process of attaining it. I have become a therapist against my will; I am convinced that, granted certain conditions in the person and the case, I can definitely cure hysteria and obsessional neurosis.

So till our meeting then. We have honestly earned a few good days together.

When you say good-bye to your wife and son for Easter, give them my greetings too.

> Your
>
> Sigm.

45

Vienna, 4. 5. 96.

My dear Wilhelm,

. . . I am still working hard and in solitude at psychology, and, however much I reduce my standards of what is "finished", I cannot yet send you what is only half-finished. I am getting a higher and higher opinion of the chemical neurone theory. The assumptions I started with were similar to those you described, but now I have got stuck, after cudgelling my brains to a standstill over it yesterday.

With consciousness I feel on firmer ground, and I have now got to make an attempt to deal with this most difficult of all things in my course on hysteria. On Saturday I lectured on dream interpretations to the young people of the Jewish academic reading circle; some time you shall hear the gist of what I said.[1] I enjoy talking about my ideas at the moment.

I am as isolated as you could wish me to be . . . because a void is forming round me. So far I bear it with equanimity. What I find less agreeable is that this year for the first time my consulting room is empty, that I see no new faces for weeks on end, that I get no new cases for treatment, and that not one of the

---

[1] No trace of this survives.

old ones is finished yet. Things are so difficult and trying that it needs a strong constitution to deal with them. . . .

17.5 The wedding excitement is just over[1] . . . The best . . . was our little Sophia—with curled hair and a wreath of forget-me-nots.

Your
Sigm.

46

Vienna, 30. 5. 96.

My dear Wilhelm,

Here is the fruit of some tormenting reflections on the ætiology of the psychoneuroses—a solution which still awaits confirmation from individual analyses. Four periods of life have to be distinguished [Fig. 5]:

I*a* up to 4 years	I*b* up to 8	A	II up to 14	B	III up to *x*
Preconscious[2]	Infantile		Prepubertal		Maturity

Fig. 5

A and B (from about 8-10 and 13-17) are the transitional periods during which repression usually takes place.[3]

The awakening at a later period of a sexual memory from an earlier one produces a surplus of sexuality in the psyche which has an inhibitory effect upon thought and gives the memory and its derivatives a compulsive character, so that they cannot be inhibited.

---

[1] The wedding of Freud's sister Rosa.

[2] [The manuscript reads "*praeconsc.*" This term (apparently never used elsewhere by Freud) has, of course, quite a different meaning from *vorbewusst*, for which the standard English translation is also "preconscious".]

[3] This anticipates the conception of the latency period, a term which Freud borrowed from Fliess.

The period I*a* possesses the character of being untranslated [into verbal images]; so that the awakening of a I*a* sexual scene leads, not to psychical consequences, but to realizations [*i.e.*, *physical* consequences] to *conversion*. The surplus of sexuality prevents translation [into verbal images].

Surplus of sexuality alone cannot cause repression; the co-operation of *defence* is necessary. But without a surplus of sexuality defence will not lead to a neurosis.

The different neuroses depend upon the sexual scenes occurring at particular periods. [Fig. 6]:

	I*a* Up to 4	I*b* Up to 8	A	II Up to 14	B	III Up to *x*
Hysteria	Scene			Repression		Repression
Obs. Neur.		Scene		Repression		Repression
Paranoia				Scene		Repression

Fig. 6.

That is to say, in hysteria the scenes occur during the first period of childhood (up to 4), in which memory traces cannot be translated into verbal images. It is a matter of indifference whether these I*a* scenes are awakened in the period after the second dentition (between 8 and 10) or during the period of puberty. Hysteria always results, and in the form of *conversion*, since the combined effect of defence and surplus sexuality prevents translation [into words].

In obsessional neurosis the scenes occur during period I*b* and can be translated into words. When they are awakened either in II or III, psychical obsessional symptoms arise.

In paranoia the scenes occur after the second dentition, in period II, and are awakened in III (maturity). Defence then manifests itself in disbelief.

Thus the periods during which *repression* occurs are of no significance in the choice of neurosis. The periods during which the *event* occurs are decisive. The *nature* of the scenes is of importance in so far as it is able to give rise to defence.

What happens if the scenes extend over several periods? Either the result is determined by the earliest period or combined forms are produced, which it should be possible to demonstrate. There cannot be a combination of paranoia and obsessional neurosis, because the repression of a I*b* scene effected during II would make fresh sexual scenes impossible. [*Cf.* p. 208].

Hysteria is the only neurosis in which symptoms may perhaps be possible even in the absence of defence, for even so the characteristic of conversion would remain. (Pure somatic hysteria.)

It will be seen that paranoia depends least on infantile determinants. It is the defensive neurosis *par excellence* and is independent of morality and aversion to sexuality, which, in A and B, provide the motives of defence for obsessional neurosis and hysteria. . . .

[It is] a disorder of maturity. If there are no scenes in either I*a*, I*b* or II, defence can have no pathological consequences (*i.e.*, [we have] normal repression). Surplus of sexuality is the determinant of *anxiety attacks* during maturity. The memory traces are insufficient to absorb the quantity of sexuality released, which should become [psychical] libido.

The importance of *pauses* in sexual experience will be evident. A continuous series of scenes overlapping the boundary between two periods may perhaps be a means of avoiding repression, since in that case no surplus of sexuality will develop between a scene and the first important memory of it.[1]

We must assume three points about consciousness, or rather the process of becoming conscious:

1. that, as regards memories, it consists for the most part in the appropriate *verbal* consciousness—that is, in access to the associated verbal images;
2. that it is not attached exclusively either to what is known as the "unconscious" sphere or to the "conscious" one, so that these terms should, it seems, be rejected;

---

[1] This suggestion, in conjunction with the views developed in *Three Essays on the Theory of Sexuality* (1905 d) later led to the theory of fixation.

3. that it is determined by a compromise between the different psychical forces which come into conflict with one another when repressions occur.

These forces must be closely studied and inferred from their consequences. They are (1) the *inherent quantitative strength* of an idea, and (2) a freely displaceable *attention,* which is attracted in accordance with certain rules and repelled in accordance with the rule of defence. Symptoms are almost all compromise structures. A fundamental distinction must be made between un-inhibited psychical processes and those which are inhibited by thought. Symptoms arise as compromises between these two—compromises for which the path to consciousness is opened. In neuroses each of the two processes is rational in itself (though the uninhibited one is mono-ideistic—one-sided); while the resultant compromise is *irrational,* like a logical error.[1]

In every case quantitative conditions have to be fulfilled, since otherwise the fending off of the thought-inhibited process will prevent the formation of symptoms.

One species of psychical disorder arises if the power of the un-inhibited processes increases, and another species if the force of the thought-inhibition relaxes (as in melancholia or exhaustion —and dreaming, as a prototype).

An increase in the uninhibited processes to the point of their alone being in possession of the path to verbal consciousness produces *psychoses.*

There is no question of a separation between the two pro-cesses; it is only considerations of unpleasure that put a barrier in the way of various possible associative transitions between them. . . .

In defiance of my colleagues I wrote out in full for Paschkis

---

[1] We can regard this as a first formulation of the theory of the compromise character of symptoms. There is also a suggestion of the structure theory; Freud speaks of psychical forces that come into conflict with each other, and in his con-ception of consciousness anticipates the view, first fully developed in *The Ego and the Id* (1923 b) that the ego plays a part both in consciousness and in the un-conscious, or in other words that some ego-functions are conscious and others not.

It is characteristic of Freud's interests at the time he wrote this letter that he chooses his comparisons from the field of the psychology of the intellectual pro-cesses and compares symptoms to logical errors; the ideas in the "Project" here play an important role. [Cf. the last pages of the "Project".]

the lecture on the aetiology of hysteria. The first instalment appears to-day.[1]

My eldest brother from Manchester has been staying here this week. Next Thursday the family goes to Aussee. . . .

You do not need to express any opinions on the above. I admitted to you that there is more speculation about it than usual, but it would not leave me in peace.

With warmest greetings,

Your

Sigm.

47

4. 6. 96.

My dear Wilhelm,

. . . I have had to put neuroses and psychology aside to write the children's paralyses, which have to be finished by August. But in the meantime I have become convinced of the truth of something in the last piece of theorizing—hysteria up to the age of four—inability to translate into verbal ideas also belongs only to that period. The Löwenfeld affair you know of—you will have read his paper. My remark on "coitus periodicity" is part

---

[1] The lecture (Freud 1896 c) had an unfriendly reception. Krafft-Ebing, as Freud reported in a letter not reproduced here, remarked that "it sounds like a scientific fairy-tale". Freud himself summed up its contents as follows in his early bibliography of his writings (1897b): "Reports in some detail on infantile sexual experiences which have proved responsible for the causation of psychoneuroses. Their contents are to be described as 'perversions'; those concerned are usually to be found among the patient's nearest relatives. A discussion of the difficulties that have to be surmounted in the process of uncovering these repressed memories and of the doubt that may be cast upon the results thus obtained. Hysterical symptoms are shown to be derivatives of memories operating unconsciously. The presence of infantile sexual experiences is an indispensable condition if the efforts at defence (which are also present in normal people) are to succeed in producing pathogenic results, that is, neuroses."

of my reply (pages 9-10).[1] Do not bother too much with it. . . .
Do not leave me too long without your promised letter.
Heartiest greetings to you all,

Your

Sigm.

48

30. 6. 96.

My dear Wilhelm,

. . . My aged father (he is eighty-one) is in Baden in a very
shaky condition with heart-attacks, bladder weakness and so on.
Waiting for news, going to see him, etc., have been the only
things to count in the last fortnight. In the circumstances I
cannot undertake any plans that involve a day's journey from
Vienna. My father is a stalwart fellow, and I hope he may yet be
granted a spell of good health; if so I shall turn it to account for

---

[1] Fliess had come across a remark of Löwenfeld's about the periodicity of
anxiety attacks. In reply Freud pointed to the following passage in his "Reply
to Criticisms of my Paper on Anxiety Neurosis" (1895 f):

"To Löwenfeld's further assertion that anxiety-attacks only appear under
certain conditions and fail to appear when these are avoided, whatever the *vita
sexualis* of those concerned—we may urge in contradiction that Löwenfeld
manifestly has in mind only the anxiety of *phobias*, as is shown by the examples
appended to the part of his essay which I have quoted. He says not a word concerning spontaneous anxiety-attacks, taking the form of dizziness, palpitation,
dyspnoea, trembling, sweating, etc. My theory, however, seems quite equal to
explaining the appearance and disappearance of these anxiety-attacks. The
semblance of periodicity in the onset of anxiety states may be found in a great
number of such cases of anxiety-neurosis, similar to that observed in epilepsy,
only that here the mechanism of this periodicity is more perspicuous. On closer
examination we find with great regularity an exciting sexual occurrence (that is,
one capable of releasing somatic sexual excitation), recurring at definite and often
quite constant intervals of time, to which the anxiety-attack is related. In abstinent
women this part is played by menstrual excitation, and in both men and women
by recurrent nocturnal pollutions and above all by sexual intercourse itself
(injurious when it is incomplete), which transfers its own periodicity to the
anxiety-attacks resulting from it. If anxiety-attacks occur apart from the usual
periodicity, it is usually possible to trace them to an occasional cause of more
rare and irregular incidence, to a single sexual experience, something read, a
visual impression, or the like. The interval I referred to varies from a few hours
up to two days: it is the same as that which in other persons is followed by the
well-known sexual migraine, due to the same causes, which has an undoubted
connection with the symptom-complex of anxiety-neurosis."

Freud's view on this matter actually had nothing whatever to do with Fliess's,
but illuminated the problem of discharge of tension and his theories about it with
particular clarity.

our meeting. I cannot say anything definite to-day; but can you arrange to be free, so that I could let you know by telegram that I could leave to come and see you within twenty-four hours, leaving you time to put me off by wire? Avoiding your period-date, of course.

I am in a rather gloomy state, and all I can say is that I am looking forward to our congress as to a slaking of hunger and thirst. I shall bring with me nothing but a pair of open ears, and shall be all agape. Also I expect great things—so self-centred am I—for my own purposes. I have run into some doubts about my repression theory which a suggestion from you, like the one about male and female menstruation in the same individual, may resolve. Anxiety, chemical factors, etc.—perhaps you may supply me with solid ground on which I shall be able to give up explaining things psychologically and start finding a firm basis in physiology!

I have really been very inactive. The completely uninteresting work on children's paralyses has taken all my time. But I have not been able to help suspecting or finding out one or two things of value, about somnambulism, for instance. I cannot wait to see you and talk to you.

The family are in a paradise at Aussee (Obertressen) and are having a fine time. I only came back myself to-day. I still look forward to making R.W.'s acquaintance in the course of 1896. Meanwhile my heartiest greetings to his mother and to you, and write again soon to

Your

Sigm.

49

Dr. Sigmund Freud,   26. 10. 96.
   IX. Berggasse 19.   Consulting hours 3-5 p.m.

My dear Wilhelm,

No real answer is possible after such an interval, but it shall not remain so.

The old man died on the night of the 23rd, and we buried him yesterday. He bore himself bravely up to the end, like the remarkable man he was. He must have had meningeal hæmorrhage at the last; there were stuporous attacks and inexplicable temperatures, hyperæsthesia and muscular spasms, from which he would awake without temperature. The last attack ended with an oedema of the lungs, and he had an easy death. It all happened in my critical period, and I am really down over it. . . .

Cordially,

Your

Sigm.

50

Vienna, 2. 11. 96.
IX. Berggasse 19.

Dr. Sigmund Freud,
  Lecturer on nervous diseases
    in the University.

My dear Wilhelm,

I find it so difficult to put pen to paper at the moment that I have even put off writing to you to thank you for the moving things you said in your letter. By one of the obscure routes behind the official consciousness the old man's death affected me deeply. I valued him highly and understood him very well indeed, and with his peculiar mixture of deep wisdom and imaginative light-heartedness he meant a great deal in my life. By the time he died his life had long been over, but at a death the whole past stirs within one.

I feel now as if I had been torn up by the roots.

Apart from that I am writing the children's paralyses (Pegasus yoked to the plough!)[1] and I am glad at having seven cases and particularly glad at the prospect of talking to you for several hours. I am completely isolated, but that goes without saying.

---

[1] [The reference is apparently to the title of a poem by Schiller.]

Perhaps I shall have a few odd things to tell you in return for your great findings and theories. Less gratifying is the state of my practice this year. My spirits are always dependent on it. . . .

I recently heard the first reaction to my incursion into psychiatry. "Gruesome, horrible, old wives' psychiatry" were some of the things that were said. That was Rieger in Würzburg. I was extremely amused. And, of all things, about paranoia, which has become so clear!

Your book is not out yet. Wernicke[1] sent me a patient, a lieutenant who is in the officers' hospital.

I must tell you about a very pretty dream I had on the night after the funeral. I found myself in a shop where there was a notice up saying:

> You are requested
> to close the eyes.

I recognized the place as the barber's to which I go every day. On the day of the funeral I was kept waiting, and therefore arrived at the house of mourning rather late. The family were displeased with me, because I had arranged for the funeral to be quiet and simple, which they later agreed was the best thing. They also took my lateness in rather bad part. The phrase on the notice-board has a double meaning. It means "one should do one's duty towards the dead" in two senses—an apology, as though I had not done my duty and my conduct needed overlooking, and the actual duty itself. The dream was thus an outlet for the feeling of self-reproach which a death generally leaves among the survivors.[2] . . .

Heartiest greetings to I.F. and R.W.[3] Perhaps my wife may have joined you by now.

Your

Sigm.

---

[1] Karl Wernicke (1848-1905), a well-known Breslau psychiatrist and neurologist.

[2] Freud described this dream in slightly different terms, obviously with the aid of notes, in *The Interpretation of Dreams* (*trans.* 1953), pp. 317-8.

[3] The initials are those of Fliess's wife and son.

51

4. 12. 96.
IX. Berggasse 19.

My dear Wilhelm,

... I am working at full pressure, with every half-hour occupied. ... I am busy thinking out something which would cement our work together and put my column on your base, but I have a feeling that I ought not to write about it. A fragment, naturally for your eyes only, will be ready in a few days. I am curious to hear what you will say about it. ...

Apart from that the world is full of the most amazing things, as well as stupid ones—human beings are generally responsible for the latter. The first thing I shall disclose to you about my works are the introductory quotations. My psychology of hysteria will be preceded by the proud words: *Introite et hic dii sunt;*

the chapter on summation by:

Sie treiben's toll, ich fürcht' es breche,
Nicht jeden Wochenschluss macht Gott die Zeche;[1]

the symptom-formation by:

Flectere si nequeo superos Acheronta movebo;[2]

and resistance by:

Mach es kurz!
Am jüngsten Tag ist' nur ein . . .[3]

I send my heartiest greetings to you and your little family and look forward to *res novae* about them and your work.

Your

Sigm.

---

[1] ["They are exceeding all bounds, I fear a breakdown; God does not present the reckoning at the end of every week".]

[2] A line from the *Aeneid* quoted on the title-page of *The Interpretation of Dreams*.

[3] ["Cut it short! On doomsday it won't be worth a . . . !"] From Goethe's *Zahme Xenien*. Freud used it in 1914 to introduce Chapter III of *On the History of the Psycho-Analytic Movement*, which deals with schismatic movements.

52

6. 12. 96.

My dear Wilhelm,

As I am dead tired and mentally fresh after completing the day's labour and earning the recompense that I need for my well-being (ten hours and 100 florins), I shall try to summarize the latest bit of speculation for you.

As you know, I am working on the assumption that our psychical mechanism has come about by a process of stratification: the material present in the shape of memory-traces is from time to time subjected to a rearrangement in accordance with fresh circumstances—is, as it were, transcribed.[1] Thus what is essentially new in my theory is the thesis that memory is present not once but several times over, that it is registered in various species of "signs". (I postulated a similar rearrangement some time ago, in my study of aphasia, for the paths leading from the periphery.[2]) I cannot say how many of these registrations

---

[1] The following passage forms a half-way house between the assumptions about the mental apparatus put forward in the "Project" and Freud's ideas as stated in Chapter VII, of *The Interpretation of Dreams*. Freud later returned to them in *Beyond the Pleasure Principle* and in the paper "A Note upon the 'Mystic Writing-Pad'" (1925 a) he stated them in a form that combined the early and the later theories.

"All the forms of auxiliary apparatus which we have invented for the improvement or intensification of our sensory functions are built on the same modes as the sense organs themselves or portions of them; for instance, spectacles, photographic cameras, ear trumpets. Measured by this standard, devices to aid our memory seem particularly imperfect, since our mental apparatus accomplishes precisely what they cannot: it has an unlimited receptive capacity for new perceptions and nevertheless lays down permanent— even though not unalterable—memory-traces of them. As long ago as in 1900 I gave expression in *The Interpretation of Dreams* to a suspicion that this unusual capacity was to be divided between two different systems (or organs of the mental apparatus). According to this view, we possess a system Pcpt.-Cs. which receives perceptions but retains no permanent trace of them, so that it can react like a clean sheet to every new perception: while the permanent traces of the excitations which have been received are preserved in "mnemic systems" lying behind the perceptual system. Later, in *Beyond the Pleasure Principle* (1920g) I added a remark to the effect that the inexplicable phenomenon of consciousness arises in the perceptual system *instead* of the permanent traces."

[2] One of the rare passages in which Freud himself draws attention to the resemblance between his *Zur Auffassung der Aphasien* (1891 b) and his later works.

there may be: at least three and probably more. I have illustrated this in the following schematic picture (Fig. 7), which
assumes that the different transcripts are also separated (though
not necessarily in topography) in respect to the neurones which
are their vehicles. This assumption may not be an essential one,
but it is the simplest and is provisionally admissible.

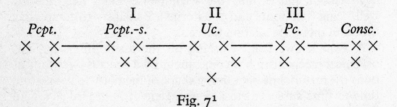

Fig. 7[1]

Pcpt. are neurones in which perceptions appear and to which
consciousness is attached but which in themselves retain no
trace of what happens. For *consciousness and memory are mutually
exclusive*. [*Cf.* the "Project", p. 363].

Pcpt.-s. is the first registration of the perceptions; it is quite
incapable of being conscious and is arranged according to
associations of simultaneity.

Uc. (unconsciousness) is a second registration, or transcription, arranged according to other associations—perhaps
according to causal relations. *Uc.* traces may correspond to
conceptual memories; they too are inaccessible to consciousness.

Pc. (preconsciousness) is the third transcription, attached to
verbal images and corresponding to the official ego. The
cathexes proceeding from this *Pc.* become conscious in accordance with certain rules. This secondary "thought-consciousness"
is subsequent in time and probably connected with the

---

[1] ["*Pcpt.*" = perception; "*Pcpt.-s.*" = perceptual signs; "*Uc.*" = unconscious
(signs); "*Pc.*" = preconscious (signs); "*Consc.*" = consciousness. These abbreviations are the precursors of the familiar "Ucs." etc., which were first used in the
letter to Fliess of May 31, 1897 (No. 64) and were introduced into Freud's
published writings in Section B of the seventh chapter of *The Interpretation of
Dreams* (1900 a).]

hallucinatory activation of verbal images; so that the neurones of consciousness would once again be perceptual neurones and in themselves devoid of memory.

If I could give a complete account of the psychological characteristics of perception and of the three transcriptions, I should have enunciated a new psychology. Some material for this is at my disposal, but that is not my present purpose.

I must emphasize the fact that the successive transcripts represent the psychical achievement of successive epochs of life.[1] At the frontier between any two such epochs a translation of the psychical material must take place. I explain the peculiarities of the psychoneuroses by supposing that the translation of some of the material has not occurred—which involves certain consequences. For I hold firmly to the tendency towards quantitative equalization. Each later transcription inhibits its predecessor and takes over the excitatory process from it. If the later transcription is lacking, the excitation will be disposed of according to the psychological laws governing the earlier psychical epoch and along the paths which were then accessible. Thus an anachronism remains: in a particular province *fueros*[2] are still in force. Relics of the past still survive.

A failure of translation is what we know clinically as "repression". The motive for it is always a release of unpleasure which would result from a translation; it is as though this unpleasure provokes a disturbance of thought which forbids the process of translation.

Within one and the same psychical phase and among transcriptions of one and the same species there can appear a *normal*

---

[1] Freud did not carry on directly in his published writings with the idea of finding a genetic basis for the understanding of the manner of functioning of the mental apparatus, though in "Formulations on the Two Principles of Mental Functioning" (1911 b) he represented that point of view indirectly. Even in recent years Freud's initiative in this direction has not been satisfactorily followed up. But the problem he had in mind in as early as 1896 can now be more exactly stated. It is a matter of connecting the history of individual ego-functions with the development of the mental apparatus. On this problem see Hartmann (1940) and Hartmann, Kris and Löwenstein (1947).

[2] [A *fuero* was an ancient Spanish law, holding good in some particular city or province and guaranteeing that region's immemorial privileges.]

kind of defence against the generation of unpleasure. *Pathological* defence is directed only against memory traces from an *earlier* phase which have not yet been translated.

It cannot depend on the *magnitude* of the release of unpleasure whether the defence succeeds in bringing about repression.[1] We often struggle in vain precisely against memories involving the greatest unpleasure. So we arrive at the following account. If event A, when it was a current one, aroused a certain amount of unpleasure, then the mnemic transcript of it, AI or AII, possesses the means of inhibiting the release of unpleasure when the memory is re-awakened. The more often the memory recurs, the more inhibited does the release ultimately become. But there is *one* case in which the inhibition fails. If A, when it was a current event, released a certain amount of unpleasure and if, when it is awakened, it releases fresh unpleasure, then this cannot be inhibited. The memory behaves as though it were some current event. This case can only occur where the events are sexual; because the magnitude of the excitations which these release increases of itself as time passes (*i.e.*, as sexual development takes place).

Thus a sexual event in one phase acts in the next phase as though it were a current one and is at the same time uninhibitable. The determining condition of pathological defence (*i.e.*, of repression) is therefore *that the event should be of a sexual nature and should have occurred during an earlier phase.*

Not all sexual experiences release unpleasure; most of them release pleasure. Thus the reproduction of most of them is accompanied by uninhibitable pleasure. Uninhibitable pleasure of this kind constitutes a *compulsion*. We are therefore led to the

---

[1] The economic ideas which in the previous year (see "Project") were still stated in the language of the physiology of the nervous system, are here replaced by general assumptions about cathectic intensities. The account of the mental apparatus has accordingly become a good deal more "independent", and can be more easily brought into harmony with clinical observations; the ontogenetic viewpoint is simultaneously introduced.

The next section connects Freud's assumptions about the functioning of the mental apparatus with his assumptions about the special position of repression as a defence against sexual traumas. These assumptions are still based on the foundation of the "seduction" hypothesis. (See Introduction, p. 28 *sqq.*)

following conclusions. When a sexual experience is remembered in a different phase, then, if there is a release of pleasure, the result is compulsion, but, if there is a release of unpleasure, the result is repression. In both cases the translation into the signs of the new phase seems to be inhibited.(?)[1]

Clinical experience makes us acquainted with three groups of sexual psychoneuroses—hysteria, obsessional neurosis and paranoia; and it teaches us that the repressed memories relate to what was actively current in the case of hysteria between the ages of $1\frac{1}{2}$ and 4,[2] of obsessional neurosis between 4 and 8, and of paranoia between 8 and 14. But before the age of 4 there is no repression; so that the psychical periods and sexual phases do not coincide.[3] [Fig. 8].

	$1\frac{1}{2}$	4	8	14-15
Psych.	Ia	Ib	II	III
Sex.		I	II	III

Fig. 8

Another consequence of premature sexual experiences may be perversion, the determining condition of which seems to be that defence either did not occur before the completion of the psychical apparatus or did not occur at all.[4]

(The following diagrammatic sketch overleaf illustrates this [Fig. 9].)

---

[1] [In the MS.]

[2] Cf. Freud's earlier view in Letter 46.

[3] Freud here distinguishes only two "sexual" phases before puberty, separated from each other by the second dentition.

[4] This is Freud's first mention of perversion. [There is a bare allusion to it on p. 147.]

	Pcpt.-s.	Pcpt.-s. +Uc.	Pcpt.-s. +Uc. +Pc.	Ditto.
	up to 4	up to 8	up to 14—15	
Hysteria	current	compulsion	repressed in Pcpt.-s.	
Obs. Neur.		current	repressed in Uc. signs	
Paranoia			current	repressed in Pc. signs
Perversion	current	current	compulsion (current)	repression impossible or not attempted

Fig. 9

So much for the superstructure. Now for an attempt to set it on organic foundations. What has to be explained is why sexual experiences which, when they were current, generated pleasure should, if they are remembered during a later phase, generate unpleasure in some people and persist as compulsion in others. In the former case they must evidently release unpleasure at a later time which was not released earlier.

We have also to trace the origin of the different epochs, both psychological and sexual. You have explained the latter to me as special instances of multiples of the 28-day female period. . . .[1]

In order to explain why the outcome is sometimes perversion and sometimes neurosis, I avail myself of the universal bisexuality of human beings. In a purely male being there would be a surplus of masculine release at the two sexual boundaries [p.38], consequently pleasure would be generated and at the same time perversion; in a purely female being there would be a surplus of *unpleasurable* substance at these two points of time. During the first phases the releases would run parallel (*i.e.*, there would be a normal surplus of pleasure). This explains the preference of true females for the defensive neuroses.

In this way the intellectual nature of males would be confirmed on the basis of your theory.

Finally, I cannot suppress a suspicion that the distinction between neurasthenia and anxiety neurosis, which I detected clinically, is related to the existence of the two 23-day and 28-day substances.[2]

In addition to the two whose existence I here suspect, there may be several others of each kind.

It seems to me more and more that the essential point of

---

[1] In a passage not reproduced here Freud makes an attempt to regard the phases in which the seduction experiences of each group of neurotic illness took effect as multiples of Fliess's periods. The next passage, which is reproduced here, deals with the idea that bisexuality provides the foundation for neurosis, an idea which Fliess later made completely his own. See Introduction, p. 39 *sqq.* In this first formulation, however, Freud's views are already much more far-reaching. He recognizes the significance of the erotogenic zones, and at any rate one sentence points to the importance that processes of maturation possess in this connection.

[2] An assumption from which Freud soon freed himself. It represented the climax of his efforts to connect Fliess's views with his own.

hysteria is that it is a result of perversion on the part of the seducer; and that heredity is seduction by the father. Thus a change occurs between the generations:—

1st generation: Perversion.

2nd generation: Hysteria, and consequent sterility. Incidentally there is a metamorphosis within the individual: he is perverse during the age of his strength, and then, after a period of anxiety, becomes hysterical. Thus hysteria is in fact not repudiated *sexuality* but rather repudiated *perversion*.

Behind this lies the notion of abandoned *erotogenic zones*. That is to say, during childhood sexual release would seem to be obtainable from very many parts of the body; but at a later time they are only able to release the 28-day anxiety substance and none other. This differentiation and limitation would thus underlie advances in culture and the development of morality, both social and individual.

A hysterical attack is not a discharge but an *action;* and it retains the original character of every action—of being a means to reproducing pleasure. (That, at least, is what it is at root; it puts forward all kinds of reasons to the preconscious.)

Thus those patients who had something sexual done to them in their sleep suffer from attacks of sleep. They go to sleep again in order to repeat the same experience; and they often bring on hysterical fainting fits as well.

Attacks of giddiness and fits of weeping—all these are aimed at *some other person*—but most of all at the prehistoric, unforgettable other person who is never equalled by anyone later. Even the chronic symptom of lying in bed has this same explanation. One of my patients still whimpers in his sleep as he did long ago in order to be taken into his mother's bed, who died when he was 22 months old. Attacks never seem to occur as an "intensified expression of emotion".[1]

... I am working at full pressure ten or eleven hours a day and feel well accordingly, but rather hoarse. Is that strain on the

[1] In "The Neuro-Psychoses of Defence" (1894 a), Freud still accepted Oppenheim's belief that hysteria was "an intensified expression of emotion".

vocal cords or anxiety neurosis? The question does not need answering. The best thing is to take Càndide's advice—*travailler sans raisonner*. . . .

I have now adorned my room with plaster casts of the Florentine statues.[1] It was the source of extraordinary refreshment to me. I am thinking of getting rich, to be able to repeat these journeys. Think of a congress on Italian soil! (Naples, Pompeii.)

Cordial greetings to you all,

Your
Sigm.

53

Vienna, 17. 12. 96.

My dear Wilhelm,

. . .[2] Now, without any proper connection with the above, for some psychoneurotic matters. I am very glad you accept the explanation of anxiety as the key-point. Perhaps I have not yet told you the analysis of several phobias. "Fear of throwing oneself out of the window" is a misconstruction by the conscious, or rather the preconscious, and relates to an unconscious content in which window appears and can be dissected as follows:

Anxiety + ... window . . . . .;
explained thus:

Unconscious idea: going to the window to beckon to a man as prostitutes do: sexual release arising from this idea;

Preconsciousness: rejection, hence anxiety arising from the release of sexuality.

The only conscious element in this content is *window*, as this fragment of it can be used as a compromise-formation because of the idea of "falling out of the window", which is consistent with anxiety. So what they are consciously aware of is *fear of the window*, which they interpret in the sense of *falling* out of it;

---

[1] The room was Freud's newly occupied consulting room on the ground floor of 19, Berggasse.

[2] The beginning of this letter, not reproduced here, contains a further attempt to connect Fliess's period theory with Freud's own theories of the neuroses.

this latter is not even always consciously present. In either case their behaviour is the same; they avoid approaching the window. Think of Guy de Maupassant's *faire de la fenètre*. . . .[1]

I have simultaneously come across all sorts of very pretty explanations in my field. I have confirmed, for instance, a long-standing suspicion about the mechanism of agoraphobia in women. You will guess it if you think of prostitutes. It is the repression of the impulse to take the first comer on the streets—envy of the prostitute and identification with her. In other respects I might be pleased also, but not a single case is finished yet: I feel an essential piece is still missing. So long as I have not seen to the bottom of a single case I cannot feel happy. When I have once got to the bottom of a single case I shall be in a state to enjoy a good day between two night-journeys.

The explanation of the "clownism" phase in Charcot's formula of [hysterical] attacks lies in the perversion of the seducers who, under a compulsion to repeat dating from their youth, obviously seek their satisfaction to the accompaniment of the craziest capers, somersaults, and grimaces. Hence the "clownism" in boys' hysteria, the imitation of animals and circus scenes, which are to be understood by the connection between nursery games and sexual scenes. . . .

I send my heartiest greetings to you, your wife and your son.

Your
Sigm.

54

3. I. 97.
IX. Berggasse 19.

S.F.

My dear Wilhelm,

We shall not be shipwrecked. Instead of the passage we are

---

[1] Fear of falling out of the window is also susceptible of other interpretations. In "Dreams and Telepathy" (1922 a) Freud points out its significance as a symbol of childbirth.

seeking, we may find oceans, to be fully explored by those who come after us; but, if we are not prematurely capsized, if our constitutions can stand it,[1] we shall make it. *Nous y arriverons.* Give me another ten years and I shall finish the neuroses and the new psychology; perhaps you will complete your organology in less time than that. In spite of the complaints you refer to, no previous New Year has been so rich with promise for both of us. When I am not afraid I can take on all the devils in hell, and you know no fear at all.

You certainly do not believe that my theories of the neuroses are as flimsily based as my remarks on your organology. I have no material whatever in that field, and can only guess; in my own field I have the most solid foundations for which you could ask. Certainly I still have a great deal to learn; for instance the time limits within which the various neuroses arise will probably have to be corrected when my cases are finished. While the work is in progress the determination of time-limits seems to be hampered at every turn. Everything now points more and more to the first three years of life.[2] This year I have had no further news of my patient with obsessional neurosis, whom I treated only for seven months. Yesterday I heard from F. that he went back to his birthplace to check the genuineness of his memories for himself, and that he got the fullest confirmation from his seducer, who is still alive (she was his nurse, now an old woman).[3] He is said to be feeling very well; he is obviously using this improvement to avoid a radical cure. New valuable evidence of the

---

[1] This is a reference to a story told by Freud in *The Interpretation of Dreams* (p. 195) in connection with one of his own dreams. It is as follows: "An impecunious Jew had stowed himself away without a ticket in the fast train to Karlsbad. He was caught, and each time tickets were inspected he was taken out of the train and treated more and more severely. At one of the stations on his *via dolorosa* he met an acquaintance, who asked him where he was travelling to. 'To Karlsbad', was his reply, 'if my constitution can stand it'."

[2] This is the first reference to the aetiological significance of early childhood. [But see pp. 164 and 177.] But Freud must have had ideas on the subject long before, because in 1895 (see "Project" p. 391) he used the infant's relationship to its nurse and the mother's breast as an example on which to base a discussion of the difference between perception and hallucination.

[3] This is the first attempt to verify a psycho-analytic reconstruction.

soundness of my material is provided by its agreement with the perversions described by Krafft.[1]

At our next congress I hope there will be important things to talk about; I think at Easter at the latest, perhaps in Prague. Perhaps I shall have got a case finished by then. . . .

The quotation preceding the "therapy" chapter will be *Flavit et dissipati sunt;*[2] for that on "Sexuality" "from heaven through the world to hell"—if that is the correct quotation.

I am looking forward to the solution of a case which throws light on two psychoses, that of the seducer and the later illness of the seduced patient. It is also of organological interest, as you will see (oral sexual organs).

My very best wishes for the New Year, and my thanks to your wife and best avuncular greetings to young Robert.

Your

Sigm.

55

II. I. 97.
IX. Berggasse 19.

My dear Wilhelm,

Here are some brand-new notions which occurred to me to-day and seem to be viable. They are, of course, based on analytic findings.

1. The condition that determines the occurrence of a psychosis

---

[1] Krafft-Ebing, author of *Psychopathia Sexualis,* was then professor of psychiatry and neurology in Vienna. His attitude to Freud, to whom he used to send his works, was one of benevolent scepticism.

[2] The inscription on the medal struck to commemorate the destruction of the Spanish Armada; *cf. The Interpretation of Dreams* (page 214) where Freud mentions that he "had thought, half seriously, of using those words as the heading to the chapter on 'Therapy', if ever I got so far as producing a detailed account of my theory and treatment of hysteria". [The quotation which follows is of the last line of the "Prologue in the Theatre" from Goethe's *Faust.* Freud used it later in connection with the perversions in the first of his *Three Essays on the Theory of Sexuality.*]

instead of a neurosis (*i.e.*, of a confusional psychosis or psychosis in which the subject's ego is overwhelmed—as I have described it earlier [p. 154] seems to be that sexual abuse should have taken place before the end of the first intellectual stage has been reached, that is, before the psychical apparatus has been completed in its first form (from $1\frac{1}{4}$ to $1\frac{1}{2}$ years of age). It is possible that the abuse may date back so far that these earlier experiences may be concealed behind the later ones and may be recurred to from time to time.[1]

Epilepsy, I believe, goes back to the same period. . . . I shall have to find some other explanation of *tic convulsif*, which I used to assign to this same stage. This is how I arrived at these views. One of my male hysterical patients . . . caused the eldest of his younger sisters to fall ill of a hysterical psychosis which ended in a state of complete confusion. Now I was able to trace his own seducer, a man of genius who, however, had had attacks of the severest dipsomania from his fiftieth year onwards. These attacks regularly started either with diarrhoea or with catarrh and hoarseness (N.B. the oral sexual system!)—that is, with a reproduction of his own passive experiences. This man had been perverse up to the time of his falling ill, and had consequently been healthy. The dipsomania arose from the intensification (or rather *substitution*) of one impulse for the associated sexual one. (The same was probably true of old F.'s gambling mania.) Now, scenes took place between this seducer and my patient, at some of which his little sister (under a year old) was present. Later on my patient had relations with her, and at puberty she became psychotic. This will show you how it comes about that a neurosis increases into a psychosis in the following generation (this is what people speak of as "degeneracy") simply because someone of a tenderer age becomes involved. Incidentally, here is the heredity in this case (Fig. 10):

---

[1] In these and the following letters we see the "seduction" hypothesis gaining significance in Freud's mind. In spite of this detour, however, he made a number of fruitful incidental discoveries. For instance, the date of the "fixation" of neurotic illnesses grew earlier and earlier, and he obtained the first hints of the phases of libidinal development.

```
            Father                            Uncle
        age 64, healthy                  genius, perverse
              |                       dipsomaniac from age of 50
       Patient, hysteric                        |
              |                            Eldest son
                                     dementia in early youth
         Eldest sister                          |
         hyst. psychosis                     2nd son
              |                         Drinker, still healthy
          2nd sister                            |
        slightly neurotic               Daughter, obsessional
   (slightly involved with patient)             |
              |                          Second marriage
       3rd, 4th & 5th sisters                  Son
        completely healthy                  Crazy poet
        (spared by patient)                    |
                                            Daughter
                                         hyst. psychosis
                                                |
                                         small daughter?
                                           young son?
```

Fig. 10

I hope that I shall be able to tell you many other things of importance on the basis of this particular case, which throws light on three forms of illness.

2. The perversions regularly lead into zoophilia, and have an animal character. They are not to be explained by the functioning of erotogenic zones which have later been abandoned, but by the operation of erotogenic *sensations* which have subsequently lost their force. In this connection it will be remembered that the principal sense in animals (for sexual purposes as well as others) is that of smell, which has been deposed from that position in human beings.[1] So long as the sense of smell (and of taste) is dominant, hair, faeces, and the whole surface of the

---

[1] These considerations concerning the significance of the sense of smell in men and animals are a pointer towards Freud's later hypotheses about the role of the upright stance in onto- and phylogenesis. See Letter 75.

body—and blood as well—have a sexually exciting effect. The increase in the sense of smell in hysteria is no doubt connected with this. The fact that the different groups of sensations have much to do with psychological stratification would seem to follow from the way in which things are distributed in dreams, and no doubt has a direct relation to the mechanism of hysterical anæsthesias.

You can see that I am in the full swing of discovery; otherwise I am feeling very well too. Now I look forward to hearing the same from you.

With heartiest greetings.

Your
Sigm.

56

17. I. 97.
IX. Berggasse 19.

My dear Wilhelm,[1]

You obviously enjoy the turmoil in my head, so I shall keep on writing to you about it whenever there is anything new. I still have a high opinion of my theory of the conditioning of the psychoses, and I shall let you have the material soon. . . . By the way, what have you got to say to the suggestion that the whole of my brand-new theory of the primary origins of hysteria is already familiar and has been published a hundred times over, though several centuries ago? Do you remember my always saying that the mediæval theory of possession, that held by the ecclesiastical courts, was identical with our theory of a foreign body and the splitting of consciousness? But why did the devil

---

[1] This letter and the next contain hints of three important directions in which Freud's work was to develop: (i) the approach to folklore and anthropology, *i.e.*, the extension of the field of observation; (ii) the discovery of the anal-sadistic phase and its manifestations, which plays a big role in the letters during the succeeding months and years; and (iii) the collapse of Freud's view of the role of seduction in the aetiology of the neuroses, of which he was firmly convinced and continued to be convinced until in the course of his self-analysis he suddenly realized the difference between phantasy and reality in what his patients told him.

who took possession of the poor victims invariably commit misconduct with them, and in such horrible ways ? Why were the confessions extracted under torture so very like what my patients tell me under psychological treatment ? I must delve into the literature of the subject. Incidentally, the cruelties practised serve to illuminate some hitherto obscure symptoms of hysteria. The pins which appear in such astonishing ways, the needles for which the poor creatures have their breasts cut open, though they are invisible with X-rays, can all be found in the stories of seduction! . . .

The inquisitors now again search with needles for diabolical stigmata, and the victims again invent the same gruesome stories (aided perhaps by the seducer's disguise). Thus victim and torturer alike recall their earliest youth.

On Saturday I duly gave an account of your nasal work in my course, and on Thursday I shall continue it. The five young men listened attentively. It makes enthralling material.

As you see, things are going very well with me. Why are you not feeling fresh at the moment ?

My heartiest greetings to your wife and son,

Your

Sigm.

Prague at Easter then.

57

24. 1. 97.

IX. Berggasse 19.

My dear Wilhelm,

The parallel with witchcraft is taking shape, and I believe it is conclusive. Details have started crowding in, I have found the explanation why witches "fly"; their broomstick is apparently the great Lord Penis. Their secret gatherings, with dances and other entertainment, can be seen any day in the streets where children play. I read one day that the gold which the devil gave his victims regularly turned into excrement; and next day

Herr E., who reports that his nurse had money deliria, suddenly told me (by way of Cagliostro—alchemist—*Dukatenscheisser*[1] that Louise's[2] money was always excrement. Thus in the witch stories it is only transformed back into the substance of which it originally consisted. If I only knew why the devil's semen in witches' confessions is always described as "cold". I have ordered a *Malleus Maleficarum,* and now that I have put the finishing touches to the children's paralyses I shall study it diligently. Stories about the devil, the vocabulary of popular swear-words, the rhymes and habits of the nursery, are all gaining significance for me. Can you without trouble suggest some good reading on the subject from your well-stocked memory? In connection with the dances in witches' confessions you will recall the dancing epidemics of the Middle Ages. E.'s nurse was a dancing witch of that kind. The memory of her, consistently enough, first returned at the ballet; hence his fear of the theatre.

The gymnastic feats performed by boys in hysterical attacks, etc., belong with flying and floating in the air.

I am toying with the idea that in the perversions, of which hysteria is the negative,[3] we may have the remnants of a primitive sexual cult, which in the Semitic east may once have been a religion (Moloch, Astarte). . . .

Perverted sexual actions are always alike, always have a meaning, and are based on a pattern which can be understood.

I am beginning to dream of an extremely primitive devil religion the rites of which continue to be performed secretly,[4] and now I understand the stern therapy of the witches' judges. The links are abundant.

Another tributary into the main stream is suggested by the

---

[1] [Literally "one who excretes ducats". Figuratively "one who ostentatiously throws his money about", with the possible further implication that the money has been improperly obtained.]

[2] Louise was E.'s "nurse and first love". (See Letter 80.)

[3] Freud later retained this formulation [which is already hinted at above on pp. 180 and 185.] In *Three Essays on the Theory of Sexuality* (1905 d) he wrote: "Thus symptoms are formed in part at the cost of *abnormal* sexuality; *neuroses are, so to say, the negative of perversions*".

[4] The phantasies of the anal-sadistic phase.

consideration that to this very day there is a class of persons who tell stories similar to those of witches and my patients; nobody believes them, though that does not shake their belief in them. As you will have guessed, I refer to paranoiacs, whose complaints that excrement is put in their food, that they are abominably maltreated at night, sexually, etc., are pure memory-content.[1] You know I have made a distinction between delusions of memory and delusions of interpretation. The latter are connected with the characteristic indefiniteness about the identity of the evil-doer, which is cloaked by the defence mechanism.

One more point. In the exacting standards insisted on by hysterics in love, in their humility before the loved one, or in their inability to marry because of unattainable ideals, I recognize the influence of the father-figure. The cause is, of course, the immense elevation from which the father condescends to the child's level. In paranoia compare the combination of megalomania with the creation of myths about the child's true parentage.[2] That is the reverse side of the medal.

Meanwhile one of the notions that I have been fostering, that the choice of neurosis is determined by its time of origin, is beginning to look shaky; it seems much more likely that it is determined in infancy. It is still doubtful whether it depends on the time of origin or the time of repression; (my present tendency is to believe the latter).

Being absorbed in all this, I am left cold by the news that the board of professors have proposed my younger colleague in my speciality for the title of professor, thus passing me over, if the news is true. It leaves me quite cold, but perhaps it will hasten my final breach with the university.

In letters like this I tell you all I have to say before the congress, so I shall be able to listen to your exposition of the facts about periodicity and get the substructure complete from you instead of imagining it.

---

[1] This idea appears in somewhat different form as a hypothesis on the element of truth in psychotic delusions in Freud's later works. Cf. *Moses and Monotheism* (1939 a) and "Construction in Analysis" (1937 d).

[2] This idea was left to be developed by O. Rank (*The Myth of the Birth of the Hero*, 1909).

Write to me again soon.

I think I have now passed the age boundary; I am in a much more stable state.

Cordial greetings to you, your wife and your child,

Your
Sigm.

58

8. 2. 97.
IX. Berggasse 19.

My dear Wilhelm,

. . . I must correct something I recently told you. When I called on Nothnagel the other day to give him a complimentary copy, he told me spontaneously, and as a secret for the time being, that he and Krafft-Ebing were going to propose me for a professorship (with Frankl-Hochwart), and he showed me the document, with their signatures. He added that if the board did not adopt the proposal the two of them would send in the recommendation on their own.[1] Being a sensible man, he also added: "You know the further difficulties. It may do no more than put you on the *tapis*". We all know how slight the chance is that the Minister will accept the proposal.

The proposal may have come up at yesterday's meeting. The pleasing thing about it for me is that I can go on regarding the two men as decent people, because if they had passed me over I should have found it difficult to think well of them.

I have not written anything for a week, because work (eleven and a half to twelve and a half hours a day) has exhausted all my energies. In the evening I drop as if I had been felling timber.

My expectations about this season have been confirmed. I now have ten patients under treatment, including one from Budapest;

---

[1] It was the practice at Austrian universities that before a lecturer in the medical faculty could be granted the title of professor his name had to be put forward by two of his colleagues and accepted by a majority vote. It then went forward to the Minister, who submitted the decree making the appointment for the imperial signature. See also Introduction, p. 11.

another is coming from Breslau. Perhaps it is an hour too much, but otherwise it suits me best to have a lot of work. I earned 700 florins last week, for instance, and you do not get that for nothing. It must be very difficult to get rich.

Work is progressing excellently, but I am naturally still beset with riddles and doubts. I am not going to tell you everything before the congress. Perhaps by then I may have one case completely finished. Until that happens I can feel no certainty.

11.2. I have been interrupted by pressure of work and two period days when I felt poorly—which are rare with me nowadays. I wanted to ask you, in connection with excrement-eating . . .[1] and animals, when disgust first appears in small children and whether there is a period in early infancy when no disgust is felt. Why do I not go to the nursery and —— experiment? Because with twelve-and-a-half hours' work I have no time, and because the womenfolk do not back me in my investigations. The answer would be interesting theoretically. Incidentally theory has receded into the distance. I am postponing all attempts to obtain understanding. Even the time relationships have begun to seem uncertain.[2]

Somnambulism, as we suspected at Dresden, turns out to have been correctly diagnosed. The latest result is the explanation of tonic hysterical spasm. It is the imitation of death with *rigor mortis*, *i.e.*, identification with someone who is dead. If they have actually seen a corpse, they lie with glazed eyes and open mouth; if not, they just lie there quietly and peacefully.

Hysterical cold shudders = being taken out of a warm bed. . . .

At all events I shall have a lot of strange material to tell you about in Prague.

My cordial greetings to you and to your wife and child. My family is flourishing.

Your

Sigm.

---

[1] Word illegible.
[2] A further advance on the way that led to insight into the phases of development of the libido. Freud was obviously starting to feel that his old idea of the traumatic influence of seduction was no longer satisfactory.

59

6. 4. 97.
IX. Berggasse 19.

My dear Wilhelm,

. . . The missing piece in the hysteria puzzle which I could not find has turned up in the form of a new source from which an element in unconscious production flows. I refer to the hysterical phantasies which, I now see, invariably go back to things heard in early infancy and only subsequently understood.[1] The age at which such knowledge is acquired is remarkably early—from six to seven months onwards! . . .

I have written my life-history for Krafft-Ebing, who is writing a report on me.[2] Otherwise I have done very little. The work of recent weeks has taxed my capacity to the limit.

I am delighted that we are to meet in less than a fortnight now.
Heartiest greetings to you, your wife and child,

Your

Sigm.

60

Vienna, 28. 4. 97.

My dear Wilhelm,

I had a dream last night which concerned you. There was a telegram giving your address:

$$(\text{Venice}) \begin{cases} \text{Via} \\ \quad\textit{Casa Secerno} \\ \text{Villa} \end{cases}$$

That way of writing it shows which parts were obscure and which appeared in more than one form. Secerno was the clearest.

---

[1] Another hint of the significance of phantasy life, which, however, for the time being did not shake Freud's belief in the reality of the seduction experiences described to him.

[2] A report by Krafft-Ebing was a necessary step in the recommendation for a professorship.

My feeling about it was annoyance that you had not gone where I had recommended—the Casa Kirsch.[1]

Motivation.—The dream was prompted by events of the previous day. H. came and talked about Nuremberg, saying he knew it very well and had stayed at the Preller. I could not recall it immediately, so asked him about it. "So it's outside the town then." This conversation revived the regret I have felt recently at not knowing your address and having no news of you. I wanted you for my audience, to tell you about some of my ideas and the outcome of my recent work. But I could not risk sending my notes off into the blue; there was some valuable material I should have had to ask you to keep for me. So your telegraphing your address was a wish-fulfilment. All sorts of things lie behind the wording: memory of the etymological feasts you set before me, allusions connected with H.'s "outside the town", as well as more serious things, as soon occurred to me. I felt a sense of irritation with you, as if you were always claiming something special for yourself; I criticized you for taking no pleasure in the Middle Ages,[2] and then there was the persistent reaction against your defence-dream, with the attempt to substitute the grandfather for the otherwise usual father.[3] Added to that was the thought that I am constantly bothering my head about how to remind you to ask I.F.[4] who called her "Katzel"[5] in her childhood as she calls you now. As I am still doubtful myself about matters concerned with the father-figure, my touchiness is intelligible. The dream thus collected all the irritation with you that was present in my unconscious.

Also the wording conveys other things as well:

> Via (Pompeii streets which I am studying).
> Villa (Böcklin's Roman villa).

In other words our talks of travel; Secerno sounds Neapolitan-

---

[1] [A *pension* in Venice.] This dream is reported in *The Interpretation of Dreams* (p. 317).
[2] Apparently a reference to the dislike that Fliess took to Nuremberg.
[3] An unintelligible reference.
[4] *I.e.*, Ida Fliess, Fliess's wife.
[5] ["Kitten."]

Sicilian, rather like Salerno. Underlying that is your promise of a congress on Italian soil.

———

The complete interpretation only occurred to me after a lucky chance this morning brought confirmation of my theory of paternal aetiology. Yesterday I started treatment of a new case, a young woman, whom for lack of time I should have liked to have frightened off. She had a brother who died insane, and her chief symptom—insomnia—dates from the time she heard the carriage driving away from the house taking him to the asylum. Since then she has been terrified of carriage drives and convinced that an accident was going to happen. Years later, while she was out driving, the horses shied and she took the opportunity to jump from the carriage and break a leg. To-day she came and said she had been thinking over the treatment and had found an obstacle. "What is it ?" "I can paint myself as black as necessary, but I must spare other people. You must allow me to mention no names." "Names don't matter. What you mean is your relationship with the people concerned. We can't draw a veil over that." "What I mean is that earlier the treatment would have been easier for me than now. Earlier I didn't suspect it, but now the criminal nature of certain things has become clear to me, and I can't make up my mind to talk about them." "On the contrary, I should say that a mature woman becomes more tolerant in sexual matters." "Yes, there you're right. When I consider that the most excellent and high-principled men are guilty of these things, I'm compelled to think it's an illness, a kind of madness, and I have to excuse them." "Then let us speak plainly. In my analyses I find it's the closest relatives, fathers or brothers, who are the guilty men." "It has nothing to do with my brother." "So it was your father, then."

Then it came out that when she was between the ages of eight and twelve her allegedly otherwise admirable and high-principled father used regularly to take her into his bed and practise external ejaculation (making wet) with her. Even at the time she felt anxiety. A six-year-older sister to whom she talked about it later admitted that she had had the same experiences with her father. A cousin told her that at the age of fifteen she had had to resist the advances of her grandfather. Naturally she did not find it incredible when I told her that similar and worse things must have happened to her in infancy. In other respects hers is a quite ordinary hysteria with usual symptoms.

———

Quod Erat Demonstrandum.

61

Vienna, 2. 5. 97.

My dear Wilhelm,

. . . As you will see from the enclosed, I am consolidating my gains. In the first place I have gained a sure notion of the structure of a hysteria. Everything points to the reproduction of scenes which in some cases can be arrived at directly and in others through a veil of intervening phantasies. The phantasies arise from things *heard* but only understood *later*, and all the material is of course genuine. They are defensive structures, sublimations and embellishments of the facts, and at the same time serve the purpose of self-exoneration. Their contingent origin is perhaps from masturbation phantasies. A second important insight is that the psychical structures which in hysteria are subjected to repression are not properly speaking memories, because no one sets his memory working without good cause, but impulses deriving from the primal scenes. I now see that all three neuroses, hysteria, obsessional neurosis and paranoia, share the same elements (besides the same ætiology), namely, memory-fragments, impulses (deriving from, memory) and *defensive fictions*. But the break-through into consciousness, the compromise or symptom-formation, is different in each case. In hysteria it is memories, in obsessional neurosis perverse impulses, and in paranoia defensive fictions (phantasies), which penetrate to the surface in a distorted form imposed by compromise.

In this I see a big advance in insight, and I hope it will seem the same to you.[1]

... I hope you have at last started enjoying the lakes. I find it hard to forgive your criticisms of Venice, but I understand something of the harmony and proportion in the austere constructions of your mental processes.

Best wishes to you both for an enjoyable holiday,

Your

Sigm.

Draft L

(May 2nd 1897)[2]

NOTES (I)

Architecture of Hysteria

The aim seems to be to hark back to the primal scenes. This is achieved in some cases directly, but in others only in a roundabout way, *via* phantasies. For phantasies are psychical outworks constructed in order to bar the way to these memories.[3] At the same time, phantasies serve the purpose of refining the memories, of sublimating them. They are built up out of things that have been heard about and then *subsequently* turned to account; thus they combine things that have been experienced and things that have been

---

[1] The "big advance" of which Freud speaks subsequently led to a complete revision of his psycho-analytic hypotheses and turned psycho-analysis into a psychology of the instincts. When Freud says that "the psychical structures which in hysteria are subjected to repression are not properly speaking memories, because no one sets his memory working without good cause, but impulses which derive from the primal scenes", he has nearly discovered the "id" (the meaning of instinct.)

[2] Enclosure in the letter of 2.5.97. The following are examples of the notes, generally suggested by clinical observations, which Freud used to jot down in no systematic order. Other notes of this kind follow on pp. 202 and 207. Freud made such notes to the end of his working life. See for instance some posthumously published notes dating from June, 1938 (1941f).

[3] This idea is not stated with comparable pregnancy in any of Freud's published writings: see *The Interpretation of Dreams*. "The study of the psychoneuroses leads to the surprising discovery that these phantasies or day-dreams are the immediate forerunners of hysterical symptoms, or at least of a whole number of them. Hysterical symptoms are not attached to actual memories, but to phantasies erected on the basis of memories." (*trans.* 1953, p. 491.)

heard about past events (from the history of parents and ances-
tors) and things seen by the subject himself. They are related to
things heard in the same way as dreams are related to things seen.
For in dreams we hear nothing, but only see.

The Part Played by Servant-Girls.[1]

An immense load of self-reproaches (*e.g.*, for theft, abortion, etc.)
is made possible for a woman by identification with these people of
low morals, who are so often remembered by her as worthless women
connected sexually with her father or brother. And, as a result of the
sublimation of these girls in phantasies, highly improbable charges
are made in these same phantasies against other people. Fears of
prostitution (fears of walking in the street alone), fears of a man being
hidden under the bed, and so on, also point in the direction of servant-
girls. There is tragic justice in the fact that the action of the head of
the family in stooping to relations with a servant-girl is atoned for by
his daughter's self-abasement.

Mushrooms

There was a girl last summer who was afraid to pick a flower or
even a mushroom, because it was against the will of God; for He
forbids the destruction of any germs of life. This arose from a
memory of religious talks with her mother, who inveighed against
taking precautions during intercourse because they meant the
destruction of living germs. "Sponges"[2] (Paris "sponges") had been
especially referred to among possible preventives. Identification with
the patient's mother was the chief content of her neurosis.

Pains

These are not the direct sensation of a fixation,[3] but an intentional
repetition of it. A child bangs up against a corner of a piece of furni-
ture and so brings its genitals into contact with it, in order that a

---

[1] To understand the following note the social situation of servant-girls in
Viennese bourgeois households of the nineties should be taken into account.
Such part of the ideas put forward here that found a place in Freud's later think-
ing is to be found restated in "On the Universal Tendency to Debasement in the
Sphere of Love" (1912 d).

[2] [The German word *Schwamm* means both "mushroom" and "sponge".]

[3] [*I.e.*, of an experience that becomes unconsciously fixed in the subject's
memory. This seems to be the first use of the term.]

scene may be repeated in which what is now a painful spot was originally pressed against a corner and led to a fixation.

Multiplicity of Psychical Personalities[1]

The fact of identification may perhaps allow of this phrase being taken *literally*.

Wrapping-up

Continuation of the mushroom story. The girl insisted that any objects handed to her must be wrapped up. (Condom.)

Several Versions of the Same Phantasy. Do they connect back [to the original experiences]?

In cases where a patient *wishes* to be ill and clings to his distressing symptoms, this is regularly due to the suffering being regarded as a protective weapon against his own libido—*i.e.*, due to distrust of himself. In this phase the symptom, which is a memory [of the original experience], becomes a defensive symptom as well. The two active currents unite. At an earlier stage the symptom was a product of the libido, a provocative symptom; it may be that between the two stages phantasies serve the purpose of defence.

It is possible to follow the paths, the times and the material of the construction of phantasies. The process bears a close resemblance to the construction of dreams; only there is no regression in the form which they are given, but only *progression*. Observe the relation between dreams, phantasies and reproductions.[2]

Another Wishful Dream

"I suppose you'll say", said E., "that *this* is a wishful dream. I dreamt that just as I was bringing a lady home with me I was arrested by a policeman, who ordered me to get into a carriage. I asked to be given time to put my affairs in order", and so on.—Some more details?—"I had the dream in the morning after I had spent the night with this lady."—Were you horrified?—"No."—Do you know what you were accused of?—"Yes. Of having killed a child."—Was this connected with anything real?—"I was once responsible for the abortion of a child as a result of a *liaison*. I don't like to think about

---

[1] Surely an anticipation of the conception of the super-ego.
[2] Similar ideas are put forward in "Creative Writers and Day-Dreaming" (1908 e).

it."—Well now, did nothing happen during the morning before you had the dream?—"Yes. I woke up and had intercourse."—But you took precautions?—"Yes. By withdrawing."—Then you were afraid you might have begotten a child; and the dream showed the fulfilment of your wish that nothing had gone wrong and that you had nipped the child in the bud. You then made use of the anxiety that arises after this kind of intercourse as material for your dream.[1]

62

16. 5. 97.

My dear Wilhelm,

... I could tell from your letter how refreshed you are. I hope you will now remain your old self for a good long time and allow me to go on taking advantage of your good nature as an indulgent audience, because without such a thing I cannot work. If it suits you, I shall do the same as last time, and send you my notes as I make them, with the request that you return them when I ask for them. No matter what I start with, I always find myself back again with the neuroses and the psychical apparatus. It is not because of indifference to personal or other matters that I never write about anything else. Inside me there is a seething ferment, and I am only waiting for the next surge forward. I cannot bring myself to do the provisional summing up of the present position which you want; I think that what is stopping me is an obscure feeling that very shortly something vital will have to be added. On the other hand I have felt impelled to start writing about dreams, with which I feel on firm ground, and which you feel I ought to write about in any case. I was interrupted straight away by having hurriedly to prepare for the press an abstract of all my publications.[2] The vote is going to take place any day.[3] Now I have finished and can

---

[1] Used in *The Interpretation of Dreams*, pp. 155-6.

[2] A bibliography of Freud's scientific works was published in 1897 (Freud 1897 b).

[3] The board of professors of the medical faculty voted by a majority on June 12, 1897, in favour of Freud's being awarded the title of professor. After this the delay in making the appointment was attributable solely to the (anti-Semitic) policy of the Ministry of Education.

think about dreams again. I have been looking into the literature on the subject, and feel like the Celtic imp: "How glad I am that no man's eyes have pierced the veil of Puck's disguise". No one has the slightest suspicion that dreams are not nonsense but wish-fulfilment.

I do not know if I have already told you, but as a precaution, and to make quite sure, let me repeat that I have discovered the source of auditory hallucinations in paranoia. The origin of the phantasies, as in hysteria also, is things heard but only understood *subsequently*.

A few days after my return a proud ship of mine ran aground. My banker, who had got furthest in his analysis, made off at a critical point, just before he should have produced the final scenes. This has no doubt damaged me materially also, and it has shown me that I do not yet know all the factors that are at work. But, refreshed as I was, I took it in my stride, and told myself that obviously I must wait still longer for a complete cure. It must be possible, and it shall be done. . . .

I wanted to send the children to Aussee on the 18th; Martha would have stayed here until Whitsun. The terrible weather has made us postpone it indefinitely. Martin has had another not-dangerous attack of *poetitis*. . . . He wrote a poem called "Holiday in the Woods", and another on "The Hunt", which is still incomplete. You will conclude that his operation has been done from the following couplet from his "Wise Animals' Conversations":

"Hare", said the roe,

"Does your throat still hurt when you swallow ?"

Oli's indignation at the spelling mistakes with which his brother's poetical effusions abound was exceedingly amusing. . . . Mathilde now has a passion for mythology, and recently wept bitter tears because the Greeks, who used to be such heroes, suffered such heavy blows at the hands of the Turks. They are an amusing crew. . . .

I now have several new listeners and a real pupil from Berlin, a Dr. Gattl who came here to learn from me. I have promised to instruct him, in the old classical fashion (peripatetically) rather than in the laboratory and the ward, and I am curious to see how he will turn out. Incidentally he is half-American. . . .

I had all sorts of other good ideas for you during the last few days, but they have all disappeared again. I must wait for the next drive forward, which will bring them back. In the meantime I should like to hear good and full news of you, Ida and Robert. . . .

My heartiest greetings and good luck in your work,

Your

Sigm.

63

25. 5. 97.

My dear Wilhelm,

I send you herewith *il catalogo delle belle*, etc.[1] The board's decision is still hanging fire; there was fresh opposition and a consequent postponement at the last meeting. Fortunately, my interests lie elsewhere.

The enclosed comes of a surge of guesses, which rouse great hope in me. If anything comes of it I shall make my visit to Berlin. You can count on it that will not happen before next year. . . .

My rabble went off to Aussee yesterday with Minna, and apparently arrived in beautiful weather. Martha is staying here till Whitsun.

Your

Sigm.

Draft M

(25 May 1897)[2]

NOTES (II)

Architecture of Hysteria

Probably as follows. Some of the scenes are accessible directly, but others only by way of superimposed phantasies. The scenes are

---

[1] A playful reference [put in approximately the words of Mozart's Leporello] to the "catalogue" of Freud's works, *i.e.*, the bibliography. See previous letter.

[2] Enclosed with Letter 63.

arranged according to increasing resistance. Those which are more slightly repressed come to light only incompletely to begin with, on account of their association with those which are severely repressed. The path followed by [analytic] work proceeds by a series of downward lines: first down to the scenes or to their neighbourhood, then a step further down from one of the symptoms, and then a step further still.[1] Since most of the scenes converge upon only a few symptoms, our path repeatedly follows a line through the background thoughts of the same symptoms.

Symptoms: our work consists of a series of such stages at deeper and deeper levels. [See Fig. 11].

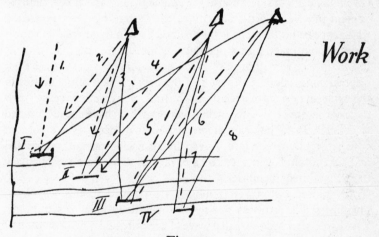

Fig. 11

[All the dotted lines, arrows and figures are in red in the original, as well as the word "Work" and the line accompanying it.]

Repression

It is to be suspected that the essential repressed element is always femininity. This is confirmed by the fact that women no less than

---

[1] The idea that "scenes are arranged according to increasing resistance" and that the work proceeds by a series of downward slants led subsequently to the views of the meaning of resistance stated in Freud's technical writings and thus to the establishment of the psycho-analytic technique.

men admit more easily to experiences with women than with men. What men essentially repress is their pæderastic element.[1]

Phantasies

Phantasies arise from an unconscious combination of things experienced and heard, constructed for particular purposes. These purposes aim at making inaccessible the memory from which symptoms have been generated or might be generated. Phantasies are constructed by a process of fusion and distortion analogous to the decomposition of a chemical body which is combined with another one. For the first kind of distortion consists in a falsification of memory by a process of fragmentation, which involves a disregard of chronological considerations. (Chronological corrections seem to depend precisely on the activity of the system of *consciousness*.) A fragment of a visual scene is then joined up to a fragment of an auditory one and made into a phantasy, while the fragment left over is linked up with something else. This makes it impossible to trace their original connection. As a result of the construction of phantasies of this kind (in periods of excitation) the mnemic symptoms cease. But instead there are now unconscious fictions which have not succumbed to defence. If the intensity of such a phantasy increases to a point at which it would have to force its way into consciousness, it is repressed and a symptom is generated by a backward drive from the phantasy to its constituent memories.

All anxiety symptoms (phobias) are derived in this way from phantasies. Nevertheless this gives a simplified view of symptoms. There may perhaps be a third wave of pressure and a third method of constructing symptoms—originating from *impulses*.[2]

Types of Displacement resulting in Compromise

Displacement on associative lines: hysteria.

Displacement on lines of (conceptual) similarity: obsessional.

---

[1] The idea alluded to here is one which occupied Freud throughout his life (*cf.* Introduction, p. 39). It led to the insight into the general significance of "the tendency to inversion in psychoneurotics" which Freud, according to a footnote in the *Three Essays on the Theory of Sexuality* (1905 d) owed to a suggestion of Fliess's; then to an understanding of the general significance of latent homosexuality; and finally, in the last years of Freud's working life, to an understanding of passivity in infantile life.

[2] [See the discussion of impulses below, p. 207 ff.]

Neurosis. (Characteristic of the place, and perhaps also of the time, at which the defence occurred.)
Displacement on causal lines: paranoia.

Typical Course of Events

There are good grounds for suspecting that the arousing of the repressed material is not left to chance but follows the laws of development. Also, that repression proceeds from recent material backwards and affects the latest events first.

Difference between the Phantasies in Hysteria and Paranoia

In the latter they are systematic and all of them in harmony with one another. In the former they are independent of one another and even contradictory—insulated, that is; they seem to have arisen, as it were, automatically (by a chemical process). This and neglect of the characteristic of time are no doubt essential distinctions between activity in the preconscious and unconscious.

Repression in the Unconscious

It is not enough to take into account the repression between the preconscious and the unconscious; we must also consider the normal repression that occurs within the system of the unconscious itself. This is very important, but still very obscure.[1]

One of our brightest hopes is that we may be able to determine the number and species of phantasies as well as we can those of the "scenes". A romance of being a stranger (*e.g.*, in the family) (*cf.* paranoia) is found regularly, and serves as a means of bastardizing the relatives in question.[2] Agoraphobia seems to depend on a romance of prostitution, which itself goes back to this same family romance. Thus a woman who will not go out by herself is asserting her mother's unfaithfulness.

---

[1] The progress of the idea hinted at here can be followed in Freud's later thought; in the differentiation between what is instinctual and what is repressed in the id ("The Ego and the Id", 1923 b) and in the idea that the repressed may itself be worked off and made to disappear ("The Dissolution of the Oedipus Complex" (1924 d).)

[2] The family romance, which is regarded here and in earlier passages in the letters as a distinguishing mark of paranoia, was later recognized by Freud to be a part of the normal phantasy life, developing under the pressure of the Oedipus complex. His first statement of this was in a passage contributed to Rank's *The Myth of the Birth of the Hero* (Freud, 1909 c).

64

31. 5. 97.
IX. Berggasse 19.

My dear Wilhelm,

I have not heard from you for a long time. Herewith a few fragments thrown up on the beach by the last surge. I have jotted them down for your eyes alone, and hope you will look after them for me. By way of apology or explanation let me add that I know they are only suspicions, but something has come of everything of this kind, and I have only had to withdraw the things I wanted to tack on to the system Pcs.[1] Another presentiment tells me, as if I knew already—though I do not know anything at all—that I am about to discover the source of morality. Thus the whole thing grows in anticipation and gives me the greatest pleasure. If only you were nearer, so that I could tell you about it more easily.

Otherwise the summer mood is very strong. On Friday evening we go to Aussee for Whitsun. I do not know whether I shall have any more ideas worth reporting to you; I do not want to do any more work. I have laid even dreams aside. Not long ago I dreamt that I was feeling over-affectionately towards Mathilde, but her name was "Hella", and then I saw the word "Hella" in heavy type before me. The solution is that Hella is the name of an American niece whose photograph we have been sent. Mathilde may have been called Hella because she has been weeping so bitterly recently over the Greek defeats. She has a passion for the mythology of ancient Hellas and naturally regards all Hellenes as heroes. The dream of course fulfils my wish to pin down a father as the originator of neurosis and put an end to my persistent doubts.

Another time I dreamt that I was walking up a staircase with very few clothes on. I was walking up very briskly, as was emphasized in the dream (heart not affected!) when I suddenly

---

[1] [See footnote p. 174.]

noticed that a woman was coming up behind me, whereupon I found myself rooted to the spot, unable to move, overcome by that paralysis which is so common in dreams. The accompanying emotion was not anxiety but erotic excitement. So you see how the feeling of paralysis peculiar to sleep can be used for the fulfilment of an exhibitionistic wish. Earlier that night I had really climbed the stairs from the flat below, at any rate without a collar, and it had occurred to me that I might meet a neighbour.[1] . . .

With heartiest greetings to your wife and son,

Your

Sigm.

Draft N [2]

NOTES (III)

(31 May 1897)

Impulses

Hostile impulses against parents (a wish that they should die) are also an integral part of neuroses. They come to light consciously in the form of obsessional ideas. In paranoia the worst delusions of persecution (pathological distrust of rulers and monarchs) correspond to these impulses. They are repressed at periods in which pity for one's parents is active—at times of their illness or death. One of the manifestations of grief is then to reproach oneself for their death (*cf.* what are described as "melancholias") or to punish oneself in a hysterical way by putting oneself into their position with an idea of retribution. The identification which takes place here is, as we can see, merely a mode of thinking and does not relieve us of the necessity for looking for the motive.

It seems as though in sons this death-wish is directed against their father and in daughters against their mother.[3] A servant-girl makes a transference from this to the effect that she wishes her mistress to die

---

[1] *Cf.* a fuller description and comment on this dream in *The Interpretation of Dreams* (pp. 238-40).

[2] Enclosed with Letter 64.

[3] First hint of the Oedipus complex.

so that her master can marry her. (*Cf.* Lisel's[1] dream about Martha and me.)

Relation between Impulses and Phantasies

Memories appear to bifurcate: one part of them is set aside and replaced by phantasies, and another and more accessible part seems to lead directly to impulses. Is it possible that later on impulses may also proceed from phantasies?

Similarly obsessional neurosis and paranoia would proceed equally from hysteria—which would explain the incompatibility of these two disorders. (*Cf.* p. 152).

Transposition of Belief

Belief (and doubt) is a phenomenon that belongs wholly to the system of the ego (the Cs.), and it has no counterpart in the Ucs. In the neuroses belief is transposed: it is withheld from the *repressed* material if it forces its way to reproduction, and—as a punishment, one might say—is transposed on to the *defensive* material. So Titania, who refused to love her rightful husband Oberon, was obliged instead to shower her love upon Bottom, the ass of her imagination.

Poetry and Fine Frenzy[2]

The mechanism of creative writing is the same as that of hysterical phantasies. Goethe combined in Werther something he had experienced (his love for Lotte Kastner) and something he had heard of (the fate of young Jerusalem, who killed himself). He probably toyed with the idea of killing himself and found a point of contact in this for identifying himself with Jerusalem, whom he provided with a motive from his own love-story. By means of this phantasy he protected himself against the consequences of his experience.

So Shakespeare was right in his juxtaposition of poetry and madness (the fine frenzy).[3]

Motives for the Formation of Symptoms

Remembering is never a motive, but only a method—a mode. The

---

[1] Governess to the Freud children.

[2] [The words "fine frenzy" are in English in the original.]

[3] In later works Freud used these ideas again in connection with different material and developed them further; particularly in *The Interpretation of Dreams*, in his study of Jensen's *Gradiva* (1907 a) and his paper on "Creative Writers and Day-Dreaming" (1908 e).

first motive force, chronologically, for the formation of symptoms is libido. Thus symptoms are *fulfilments of wishes*, just as dreams are.[1]

At later stages the defence against libido has made a space for itself in the *Ucs.* as well. Wish-fulfilment has to meet the requirements of this unconscious defence. And this takes place if a symptom is able to operate as a punishment (for an evil impulse) or as a self-hindrance due to self-distrust. The motive forces of *libido* and of *wish-fulfilment* as a punishment can then act together by way of summation.[2] In this the general tendency towards abreaction and to the irruption of the repressed is unmistakable—a tendency to which the two other motive forces are added. It appears as though at later stages on the one hand complicated structures (impulses, phantasies, motives) are produced by transference from memories, while on the other hand *defence*, arising from the preconscious (the ego), seems to force its way into the unconscious—so that defence as well becomes *multilocular*.

The formation of symptoms by means of identification is linked to phantasies, that is to say, to their repression in the *Ucs.*, and is analogous to the modification of the ego in paranoia [p. 153]. Since the outbreak of *anxiety* is linked to these repressed phantasies, we must conclude that the transformation of libido into anxiety does not proceed by a defence between the ego and the *Ucs.* but within the *Ucs.* itself. For this reason there must also be *Ucs.* libido.

The repression of impulses does not seem to generate *anxiety* but depression, perhaps—melancholia. Thus the melancholias follow the pattern of obsessional neurosis.

Definition of "Saintliness"

"Saintliness" is something based on the fact that, for the sake of the larger community, human beings have sacrificed some of their freedom to indulge in sexual perversions. The horror of incest (as something impious) is based on the fact that, as a result of a common

---

[1] The similarity between the formation of dreams and of symptoms had struck Freud as early as 1895 (see "Project", p. 398), but he only "rediscovered" it, *i.e.*, became fully aware of its significance, in 1899 (Letter 105). See also Introduction, p. 34.

[2] This is the first insight into the nature of the anxiety dream (*cf. The Interpretation of Dreams*, pp. 579 *sqq.*) and to Freud's subsequently developed views concerning the need for punishment.

sexual life (even in childhood), the members of a family hold together permanently and become incapable of contact with strangers. Thus incest is anti-social and civilization consists in a progressive renunciation of it.[1] Contrariwise the " superman ".

65

Tuesday, 12. 6. 97.

My dear Wilhelm,

Your letter amused me greatly, especially the part about the title. At our next congress you shall call me "Herr Professor"—I mean to be a gentleman like other gentlemen. The fact is that we keep pace wonderfully in sufferings, but less so in achievement. I have never yet imagined anything like my present spell of intellectual paralysis. Every line I write is torture. You are flourishing again, while I open all the doors of my senses and take nothing in. But I am looking forward to the next congress. At Aussee I hope and in August. . . .

At Aussee I know a wonderful wood full of ferns and mushrooms, where you shall reveal to me the secrets of the world of the lower animals and the world of children. I am agape as never before for what you have to say—and I hope that the world will not hear it before me, and that instead of a short article you will give us within a year a small book which will reveal organic secrets in periods of 28 and 23.

Your remark about the temporary disappearance of periods followed by their reappearance above the surface again struck me with the force of a correct intuition. That is what has happened with me. Incidentally, I have been through some kind of a neurotic experience, with odd states of mind not in-

---

[1] This seems to be the earliest statement of Freud's views of the conflict between civilization and the instincts, which he further developed in " 'Civilized' Sexual Ethics and Modern Nervous Illness" (1908 d); *Totem and Taboo* (1912-13); and *Civilization and its Discontents* (1930 a); and "Why War?" (1933 b).

telligible to consciousness—cloudy thoughts and veiled doubts, with barely here and there a ray of light.[1] . . .

I am all the more pleased that you are at work again. We share like the two beggars[2] one of whom allotted himself the province of Posen; you take the biological, I the psychological. Let me confess that I have recently made a collection of deeply significant Jewish stories.[3]

During the summer I had to take on two new cases, which are going very well. The latest is a girl of nineteen with almost pure obsessional ideas, who greatly interests me. According to my hypothesis obsessional ideas date back to a later psychical age, and so *a priori* do not point back to the father, who treats the child the more carefully the older it is, but to her slightly older brothers and sisters in whose eyes the child has not become a woman. Now in this case the Almighty was kind enough to remove the father by death before the child was eleven months old, but two brothers, of whom one was three years older than my patient, shot themselves.

Otherwise I am empty and ask your indulgence. I believe I am in a cocoon, and heaven knows what sort of creature will emerge from it.

Heartiest greetings and an early meeting,

Your

Sigm.

66

Dr. Sigm. Freud,
Lecturer in Nervous Diseases
  at the University.

Vienna, 7. 7. 97.

IX. Berggasse 19.

My dear Wilhelm,

I know that I am a useless correspondent just now, with no

---

[1] This passage can be regarded as a sign of the beginning of, or rather of the preparation for, Freud's self-analysis. The subject is more plainly referred to in the next letter and is specifically mentioned in the later letters of this summer. In his letter of August 14th Freud states: "This analysis is harder than any other". It is the principal subject of the following letters. See Introduction p. 30 *sqq.*

[2] [Freud here uses the Jewish word *Schnorrer.*]

[3] [No doubt the first material for what was to become Freud's book on jokes (1905 c).]

right to any claims to consideration, but it was not always so and it will not remain so. I still do not know what has been happening to me. Something from the deepest depths of my own neurosis has ranged itself against my taking a further step in understanding of the neuroses, and you have somehow been involved.[1] My inability to write seems to be aimed at hindering our intercourse. I have no proofs of this, but merely feelings of a very obscure nature. Has anything similar been the case with you? For some days past an emergence from this darkness seems to have been in preparation. I notice that meanwhile my work has made some progress, and every now and then I have started having ideas again. No doubt the heat and overwork have contributed.

I see for instance, that defence against memories does not prevent them from giving rise to higher mental structures, which persist for a while and are then themselves subjected to defence, which, however, is of a highly specific nature, just as in dreams, which in any case contain the whole psychology of the neuroses in a nutshell. The result is all these distortions of memory and phantasies, either about the past or the future. I am learning the rules which govern the formation of these structures, and the reasons why they are stronger than real memories, and have thus learned new things about the characteristics of processes in the unconscious. Side by side with these structures perverse impulses arise, and the repression of these phantasies and impulses which later becomes necessary gives rise to the higher determination of the symptoms resulting from the memories and to new motives for clinging to the illness. I am learning a number of typical cases of the composition of these phantasies and impulses and a number of typical conditions under which repression comes into play against them. My knowledge of all this is not complete yet. So far as technique is concerned I am beginning to prefer one particular way as the natural one.

The firmest point seems to me to be the explanation of dreams; it is surrounded by huge and obstinate riddles. The organological side is waiting for you; I have made no progress with it.

---

[1] See Introduction, p. 43 and preceding letter.

An interesting dream is that of finding yourself half or completely naked surrounded by strangers and feeling anxious and ashamed.[1] The curious thing is that they generally do not notice you, for which you have wish-fulfilment to thank. This dream material, which goes back to exhibitionism in childhood, has been misconstrued and tendentiously worked over in a famous fairy tale (the Emperor's new clothes—"Talisman").[2] The ego habitually misinterprets other dreams in the same way.

The thing that interests me immediately about the summer is when and where we shall meet, for meet we must. Dr. Gattl is becoming much attached to me and my theories. . . . I hope you will find something in him and like him when he comes to Berlin.

All goes well at Aussee. I am very anxious for news of you.

With heartiest regards to the whole family,

Your
Sigm.

67

Aussee, 14. 8. 97.

My dear Wilhelm,

I have to keep reminding myself that I did the right thing yesterday in saying no; otherwise I should feel too sorry about it. But I know that I was right. . . .

This time you are losing nothing in what I have to tell. Things are fermenting inside me, but I have nothing ready; I am very satisfied with the psychology, tortured with grave doubts about the neuroses, very lazy, and have done nothing here to get the better of the turbulence of my thoughts and feelings. That must wait for Italy.

After a spell of good spirits here I am now having a fit of gloom. The chief patient I am busy with is myself. My little hysteria, which was much intensified by work, has yielded one stage further. The rest still sticks. That is the first reason for my

---

[1] See Freud's dream mentioned in Letter 64.
[2] [A play by Fulda, based on the fairy tale.]

mood. This analysis is harder than any other. It is also the thing that paralyses the power of writing down and communicating what so far I have learned. But I believe it has got to be done and is a necessary stage in my work.

My cordial greetings to both of you, and after this brief disappointment please give me something new to look forward to.

Your

Sigm.

68

Aussee, 18. 8. 97

My dear Wilhelm,

. . . I see that I have been rather neglecting our correspondence, because a meeting was in prospect. Now that the prospect is over—in my thoughts—I intend to open the way again to the old, unjustly despised technique of exchanging ideas. My handwriting is more human again, so my tiredness is wearing off. Your writing, I see with pleasure, never varies.

Martha is looking forward to the journey, though the daily reports of train accidents do not make the father and mother of a family look forward to travelling with any pleasure. You will laugh—and rightly—but I must confess to new anxieties, which come and go but last for half a day at a time. Fear of a railway accident deserted me half an hour ago when it occurred to me that Wilhelm and Ida were also on their way. That ended the idiocy. This must remain strictly between us.

. . . This time I hope to go rather more deeply into Italian art. I begin to see your point of view, which looks, not for what is of cultural-historical interest, but for absolute beauty clothed in forms and ideas and in fundamentally pleasing sensations of space and colour. At Nuremberg I was still far from seeing it. By the way, have I already told you that Naples is off, and that the route is *via* San Gimignano, Siena, Perugia, Assisi, Ancona —in other words Tuscany and Umbria?

I hope to hear from you very soon, even if only briefly. For

the next few days I shall be here; from the 25th to September
1st my address will be Venice, Casa Kirsch.

My best wishes for the rest of the summer,

Your
Sigm.

69

21. 9. 97.
IX. Berggasse 19.

Dr. Sigm. Freud,
Lecturer in Nervous Diseases
    at the University.

My dear Wilhelm,

Here I am again—we returned yesterday morning—refreshed, cheerful, impoverished and without work for the time
being, and I am writing to you as soon as we have settled in
again.[1] Let me tell you straight away the great secret which has
been slowly dawning on me in recent months. I no longer believe
in my *neurotica*. That is hardly intelligible without an explanation; you yourself found what I told you credible. So I shall
start at the beginning and tell you the whole story of how the
reasons for rejecting it arose. The first group of factors were the
continual disappointment of my attempts to bring my analyses
to a real conclusion, the running away of people who for a time
had seemed my most favourably inclined patients, the lack of the
complete success on which I had counted, and the possibility of
explaining my partial successes in other, familiar, ways. Then
there was the astonishing thing that in every case . . . blame
was laid on perverse acts by the father, and realization of the
unexpected frequency of hysteria, in every case of which the
same thing applied, though it was hardly credible that perverted

---

[1] A reference to Freud's unusually late return from his summer holidays.

acts against children were so general.[1] (Perversion would have to be immeasurably more frequent than hysteria, as the illness can only arise where the events have accumulated and one of the factors which weaken defence is present.) Thirdly, there was the definite realization that there is no "indication of reality"[2] in the unconscious, so that it is impossible to distinguish between truth and emotionally-charged fiction. (This leaves open the possible explanation that sexual phantasy regularly makes use of the theme of the parents.)[3] Fourthly, there was the consideration that even in the most deep-reaching psychoses the unconscious memory does not break through, so that the secret of infantile experiences is not revealed even in the most confused states of delirium. When one thus sees that the unconscious never overcomes the resistance of the conscious, one must abandon the expectation that in treatment the reverse process will take place to the extent that the conscious will fully dominate the unconscious.

So far was I influenced by these considerations that I was ready to abandon two things—the complete solution of a neurosis and sure reliance on its ætiology in infancy. Now I do not know where I am, as I have failed to reach theoretical understanding of repression and its play of forces. It again seems arguable that it is later experiences which give rise to phantasies which throw back to childhood; and with that the factor of hereditary predisposition regains a sphere of influence from which I had made it my business to oust it—in the interests of fully explaining neurosis.

Were I depressed, jaded, unclear in my mind, such doubts might be taken for signs of weakness. But as I am in just the opposite state, I must acknowledge them to be the result of

---

[1] Freud's attention had for months past been directed to the study of infantile phantasy; he had studied the dynamic function of phantasy and gained lasting insights into this field. See pp. 204 and 207 and Letter 62 *sqq*. He had drawn near to the Oedipus complex, in which he recognized the aggressive impulses of children directed against their parents, but had still remained faithful to his belief in the reality of the seduction scenes. It seems reasonable to assume that it was only the self-analysis of this summer that made possible rejection of the seduction hypothesis.

[2] [See "Project," p. 429.]

[3] The next step from this was insight into the Oedipus complex.

honest and effective intellectual labour, and I am proud that
after penetrating so far I am still capable of such criticism. Can
these doubts be only an episode on the way to further knowledge?

It is curious that I feel not in the least disgraced, though the
occasion might seem to require it. Certainly I shall not tell it in
Gath, or publish it in the streets of Askalon, in the land of the
Philistines—but between ourselves I have a feeling more of
triumph than of defeat (which cannot be right).[1]

How delightful that your letter should come just at this
moment! It gives me the opportunity to make a suggestion with
which I intended to finish this letter. If during this slack period
I slip into the North-West Station on Saturday night I can be
with you by Sunday midday and travel back the next night. Can
you make the day free for an idyll for two, interrupted by one
for three and three-and-a-half? That was what I wanted to ask.
Or have you a visitor in the house or something urgent to do?
Or, if I should have to leave and come home again the same
evening, which would not be worth while, could the same
arrangements apply if I went to the North-West Station on
Friday evening and stayed one-and-a-half days with you? I
mean of course this week.[2]

To go on with my letter. I vary Hamlet's remark about ripe-
ness—cheerfulness is all. I might be feeling very unhappy. The
hope of eternal fame was so beautiful, and so was that of certain
wealth, complete independence, travel, and removing the

---

[1] See Introduction, p. 29 *sqq.* In a footnote dated 1924 to the section on "the
specific aetiology of hysteria" in "Further Remarks on the Neuro-Psychoses of
Defence" (1896 b) Freud states:

"This section was written while I was under the ascendency of an error
which I have since then repeatedly acknowledged and corrected. I had not yet
found out how to distinguish between patients' phantasies about their own
childhood and real memories. I consequently ascribed to the ætiological factor
of seduction an importance and general validity which it does not possess.
When this error was overcome, the door was opened to an insight into the
spontaneous manifestations of infantile sexuality which I described in my
Three Essays on the Theory of Sexuality (1905 d). Nevertheless, there is no need
to reject the whole of what appears in the text above; seduction still retains a
certain ætiological importance, and I still consider that some of the psychological views expressed in this section meet the case."

[2] Freud went to Berlin and returned to Vienna on the 29th.

children from the sphere of the worries which spoiled my own youth. All that depended on whether hysteria succeeded or not. Now I can be quiet and modest again and go on worrying and saving, and one of the stories from my collection[1] occurs to me: "Rebecca, you can take off your wedding-gown, you're not a bride any longer!"

There is something else I must add. In the general collapse only the psychology has retained its value. The dreams still stand secure, and my beginnings in metapsychology have gone up in my estimation. It is a pity one cannot live on dream-interpretation, for instance.

Martha came back to Vienna with me. Minna and the children are staying away for another week. They have all been very well. . . .

I hope to hear from you soon in person—assuming your answer is yes—how things are going with you and whatever else is doing between heaven and earth.

Cordially your

Sigm.

70

Vienna, 3. 10. 97.

My dear Wilhelm,

One advantage of my visit to you is that, as I now know the present outline of your work as a whole, you can keep me informed of the details again. But you must not expect an answer to everything, and in the case of many of my answers you will not, I hope, fail to make allowances for my limitations on your subjects, which are outside my sphere. . . .

Outwardly very little is happening to me, but inside me something very interesting is happening. For the last four days my self-analysis, which I regard as indispensable for clearing up the whole problem, has been making progress in dreams and yielding the most valuable conclusions and evidence. At certain

---

[1] [Of Jewish anecdotes.]

points I have the impression of having come to the end, and so far I have always known where the next night of dreams would continue. To describe it in writing is more difficult than anything else, and besides it is far too extensive. I can only say that in my case my father played no active role, though I certainly projected on to him an analogy from myself; that my "primary originator" [of neurosis] was an ugly, elderly but clever woman who told me a great deal about God and hell, and gave me a high opinion of my own capacities; that later (between the ages of two and two-and-a-half) libido towards *matrem* was aroused; the occasion must have been the journey with her from Leipzig to Vienna, during which we spent a night together and I must have had the opportunity of seeing her *nudam* (you have long since drawn the conclusions from this for your own son, as a remark of yours revealed); and that I welcomed my one-year-younger brother (who died within a few months) with ill wishes and real infantile jealousy, and that his death left the germ of guilt in me. I have long known that my companion in crime between the ages of one and two was a nephew of mine who is a year older than I am and now lives in Manchester; he visited us in Vienna when I was fourteen. We seem occasionally to have treated my niece, who was a year younger, shockingly. My nephew and younger brother determined, not only the neurotic side of all my friendships, but also their depth.[1] My anxiety over travel you have seen yourself in full bloom.[2]

I still have not got to the scenes which lie at the bottom of all this. If they emerge, and I succeed in resolving my hysteria, I shall have to thank the memory of the old woman who provided

---

[1] *Cf. Interpretation of Dreams* (p. 483) where Freud refers to this piece of analytical insight in greater detail.

"My emotional life has always insisted that I should have an intimate friend and a hated enemy. I have always been able to provide myself afresh with both, and it has not infrequently happened that the ideal situation of childhood has been so completely reproduced that friend and enemy have come together in a single individual—though not, of course, both at once or with constant oscillations, as may have been the case in my early childhood."

For the possible bearing of this passage on Freud's relationship with Fliess it may be of importance to mention that Fliess's (dead) sister was named Pauline, as was Freud's niece, the sister of his older nephew John. See Introduction, p. 31.

[2] See Letter 68 and 77.

me at such an early age with the means for living and surviving. You see how the old liking breaks through again. I cannot give you any idea of the intellectual beauty of the work.

The children arrive early to-morrow. The practice is still very bad. I fear that if it gets still worse it may interfere with my self-analysis. My recognition that difficulties of treatment derive from the fact that in the last resort one is laying bare the patient's evil inclinations, his will to remain ill, is growing stronger and clearer. We shall see.

My cordial greetings to you and your little family, and I hope soon to receive some crumbs from your table.

Your
Sigm.

Oct. 4th. The children have arrived. The fine weather is over. Last night's dream produced the following under the most remarkable disguises:

She was my instructress in sexual matters, and chided me for being clumsy and not being able to do anything (that is always the way with neurotic impotence: anxiety over incapacity at school gets its sexual reinforcement in this way). I saw the skull of a small animal which I thought of as a "pig" in the dream, though it was associated in the dream with your wish of two years ago that I might find a skull on the Lido to enlighten me, as Goethe once did. But I did not find it. Thus it was "a little *Schafskopf*".[1] The whole dream was full of the most wounding references to my present uselessness as a therapist. Perhaps the origin of my tendency to believe in the incurability of hysteria should be sought here. Also she washed me in reddish water in which she had previously washed herself (not very difficult to interpret; I find nothing of the kind in my chain of memories, and so I take it for a genuine rediscovery); and she encouraged me to steal "Zehners" (ten-Kreuzer pieces) to give to her.[2] A long chain of association connects these first silver Zehners to the heap of paper ten-florin notes which I saw in the dream as

---

[1] [Literally "sheep's head"; figuratively "blockhead".]
[2] See the "verification" of this interpretation in the next letter.

Martha's housekeeping money. The dream can be summed up as "bad treatment". Just as the old woman got money from me for her bad treatment of me, so do I now get money for the bad treatment of my patients; a special role in it was played by Q, who conveyed through you a suggestion that I ought not to take money from her as the wife of a colleague (he stipulated that I should).

A severe critic might say that all this was phantasy projected into the past instead of being determined by the past. The *experimenta crucis* would decide the matter against him. The reddish water seems a point of this kind. Where do all patients derive the horrible perverse details which are often as alien to their experience as to their knowledge?

71

15. 10. 97.
IX. Bergasse 19.

My dear Wilhelm,

My self-analysis is the most important thing I have in hand, and promises to be of the greatest value to me, when it is finished. When I was in the very midst of it it suddenly broke down for three days, and I had the feeling of inner binding about which my patients complain so much, and I was inconsolable. . . .

My practice, ominously enough, still allows me plenty of free time.

All this is the more valuable from my point of view because I have succeeded in finding a number of real points of reference. I asked my mother whether she remembered my nurse. "Of course", she said, "an elderly woman, very shrewd indeed. She was always taking you to church. When you came home you used to preach, and tell us all about how God conducted His affairs. At the time I was in bed when Anna was being born" (Anna is two-and-a-half years younger) "she turned out to be a thief, and all the shiny Kreuzers and Zehners and toys that had been given you were found among her things. Your brother Philipp went himself to fetch the policeman, and she got ten months." Now see how that confirms the conclusions from my dream interpretation. I have easily been able to explain the one possible mistake. I wrote to you that she got me to steal Zehners and give them to her. The dream really means that she stole herself. For the dream-picture was a memory that I took money from a doctor's mother, *i.e.*, wrongfully. The real meaning is that the old woman stood for me, and that the doctor's mother was my mother. I was so far from being aware that the old woman was a thief that my interpretation went astray.[1] I also asked about the doctor we had in Freiberg, because I had a dream full of animosity about him. In analysing the dream-personage behind whom he was hidden I remembered a Professor von K., my history master, who did not seem to fit in, as I had no particular feelings about him and indeed got on with him quite well. My mother told me that the doctor of my infancy had only one eye, and among all my masters Professor K. was the only one with the same disability!

It might be objected that these coincidences are not conclusive, because I might have heard that the nurse was a thief in later childhood and to all appearances forgotten the fact until it emerged in the dream. I think myself that that must have been the case. But I have another unexceptionable and amusing piece of evidence. If the woman disappeared so suddenly, I said to myself, some impression of the event must have been left inside me. Where was it now? Then a scene occurred to me which for the last twenty-nine years has been turning up from time to time in my conscious memory without my understanding it. I was crying my heart out, because my mother was nowhere to be found. My brother Philipp (who is twenty years older than I) opened a cupboard[2] for me, and when I found that mother was not there either I cried still more, until she came through the door, looking slim and beautiful. What can that mean? Why should my brother open the cupboard for me when he knew that

---

[1] See previous letter.
[2] [*Kasten.*]

my mother was not inside it and that opening it therefore could not quieten me ? Now I suddenly understand. I must have begged him to open the cupboard. When I could not find my mother, I feared she must have vanished, like my nurse not long before. I must have heard that the old woman had been locked, or rather "boxed"[1] up, because my brother Philipp, who is now sixty-three, was fond of such humorous expressions, and still is to the present day. The fact that I turned to him shows that I was well aware of his part in my nurse's disappearance.[2]

Since then I have got much further, but have not yet reached any real resting-place. Communicating the incomplete is so laborious and would take me so far afield that I hope you will excuse me, and content yourself with hearing the parts which are established for certain. If the analysis goes on as I expect, I shall write it all out systematically and lay the results before you. So far I have found nothing completely new, but all the complications to which by now I am used. It is no easy matter. Being entirely honest with oneself is a good exercise. Only one idea of general value has occurred to me. I have found love of the mother and jealousy of the father in my own case too, and now believe it to be a general phenomenon of early childhood, even if it does not always occur so early as in children who have been made hysterics. (Similarly with the "romanticization of origins" in the case of paranoiacs—heroes, founders of religion). If that is the case, the gripping power of *Oedipus Rex*, in spite of all the rational objections to the inexorable fate that the story presupposes, becomes intelligible, and one can understand why later fate dramas were such failures. Our feelings rise against any arbitrary, individual fate such as shown in the *Ahnfrau*,[3] etc., but the Greek myth seizes on a compulsion which everyone recognizes because he has felt traces of it in himself. Every member of the audience was once a budding Oedipus in

---

[1] [*Eingekastelt.*]

[2] Freud did not use this example of a verified reconstruction based on a dream interpretation in any of his published works. But he used the screen-memory of the cupboard in *The Psychopathology of Everyday Life* (1901 b). In subsequent editions he added a reference to the cupboard's symbolic meaning (pregnancy).

[3] [The title of a play by Grillparzer.]

phantasy, and this dream-fulfilment played out in reality causes everyone to recoil in horror, with the full measure of repression which separates his infantile from his present state.

The idea has passed through my head that the same thing may lie at the root of *Hamlet*. I am not thinking of Shakespeare's conscious intentions, but supposing rather that he was impelled to write it by a real event because his own unconscious understood that of his hero. How can one explain the hysteric Hamlet's phrase "So conscience doth make cowards of us all", and his hesitation to avenge his father by killing his uncle, when he himself so casually sends his courtiers to their death and despatches Laertes so quickly? How better than by the torment roused in him by the obscure memory that he himself had meditated the same deed against his father because of passion for his mother—"use every man after his desert, and who should 'scape whipping?" His conscience is his unconscious feeling of guilt. And are not his sexual coldness when talking to Ophelia, his rejection of the instinct to beget children, and finally his transference of the deed from his father to Ophelia, typically hysterical? And does he not finally succeed, in just the same remarkable way as my hysterics do, in bringing down his punishment on himself and suffering the same fate as his father, being poisoned by the same rival?[1]

My interest has been so exclusively concentrated on the analysis that I have not yet set about trying to answer the question whether, instead of my hypothesis that repression always proceeds from the female side and is directed against the male, the converse may hold good, as you suggested. But some time I shall tackle it. Unfortunately I can contribute so little to your work and progress. In one respect I am better off than you. What I have to say about the mental side of this world finds in

---

[1] The views and examples briefly set out here are familiar from the *Interpretation of Dreams* (p. 261-6). This passage, the first in which the Oedipus complex is mentioned as such, enables us to see that Freud either first became aware of it or confirmed his conviction of its universality in his self-analysis. He illustrated the connection between his self-analysis and the analysis of his patients in the following words: "I can only analyse myself with objectively acquired knowledge". (Letter 75).

you an understanding critic; what you tell me about its starry side rouses in me only barren admiration.

My cordial greetings to you, your wife, and my new nephew,

Your

Sigm.

72

Vienna, 27. 10. 97.

Dr. Sigm. Freud,
Lecturer in Nervous Diseases
  at the University.
IX. Berggasse 19.

My dear Wilhelm,

I do not seem to be able to "wait" for your answer. The explanation of your silence certainly is not that you have been whirled back by some elemental power to the times when reading and writing were a burden to you, as happened to me on Sunday, when I wanted to write you a letter to mark your not-yet-fortieth birthday; but I hope it was something just as harmless. As for myself, I have nothing to tell you except about my analysis, which I think will be the most interesting thing about me for you too. Business is hopelessly bad, it is so in general, right up to the very top of the tree, so I am living only for "inner" work. It gets hold of me and hauls me through the past in rapid association of ideas; and my mood changes like the landscape seen by a traveller from a train; and, as the great poet, using his privilege to ennoble (sublimate) things, puts it:—

> *Und manche liebe Schatten steigen auf;*
> *Gleich einer alten, halbverklungnen Sage,*
> *Kommt erste Lieb' und Freundschaft mit herauf* [1]—

as well as first terror and strife. Some sad secrets of life are being traced back to their first roots, the humble origins of much pride

---

[1] ["And the shades of loved ones appear, and with them, like an old, half-forgotten myth, first love and friendship."] From the "Dedication" of Goethe's *Faust*, mentioned by Freud in his "Address delivered in the Goethe House at Frankfurt" (1930 c) as a "quotation that could be repeated for all our analyses".

and precedence are being laid bare. I am now experiencing myself all the things that as a third party I have witnessed going on in my patients—days when I slink about depressed because I have understood nothing of the day's dreams, phantasies or mood, and other days when a flash of lightning brings coherence into the picture, and what has gone before is revealed as preparation for the present. I am beginning to perceive big, general framework factors (I should like to call them) which determine development, and other minor factors which fill in the picture and vary according to individual experiences. Simultaneously a number of my doubts about the interpretation of the neuroses, if not yet all of them, are being resolved. An idea about resistance has enabled me to put back on the rails all the cases of mine which looked like breaking down, with the result that they are now going on satisfactorily again. Resistance, which is in the last resort the thing that stands in the way of the work, is nothing but the child's character, its degenerative character, which has, or would have, developed as a consequence of those experiences which one finds in conscious form in so-called degenerate cases; in these cases, however, the degenerative character is overlaid by the development of repression. In my work I dig it out, it rebels, and the patient, who started by being so civilized and well-mannered, becomes vulgar, untruthful or defiant, a malingerer, until I tell him so, and thus make him able to overcome this degenerative character. Resistance has thus become an objectively tangible thing for me, and I only wish that I had also grasped what lies behind repression.[1]

This infantile character develops in the period of "longing", after the child has been deprived of sexual experiences. Longing is the chief characteristic of hysteria, just as actual anæsthesia (even if only potential) is its chief symptom. During this period of longing phantasies arise and masturbation is (invariably ?) practised, which later gives way to repression. If it does not, no hysteria arises; discharge of sexual excitation largely removes the possibility of hysteria. It has become clear to me that various

---

[1] Many of the phenomena of resistance seem to have become intelligible to Freud through his self-analysis.

obsessional movements are a substitute for abandoned masturbatory movements. That is enough for to-day. I shall send
you details another time, when I have heard good and new
things from you. . . .

Your

Sigm.

73

31. 10. 97.
IX. Berggasse 19.

My dear Wilhelm,

. . . Business with us is such that I think we must look
forward to very bad times; in other fields things have been bad
for a long time. As I have time on my hands, I have decided to
take on two cases without fee. That, including my own, makes
three analyses which bring in nothing.

My own analysis is going on, and it remains my chief interest.
Everything is still dark, including even the nature of the problems, but at the same time I have a reassuring feeling that one
only has to put one's hand in one's own store-cupboard to be
able to extract—in its own good time—what one needs. The
most disagreeable thing about it is one's moods, which often
completely hide reality from one. Also sexual excitation is of no
more use to a person like me. But I am still cheerful with it all.
At the moment another period lacking in results has set in.

Do you think that children's talk in their sleep belongs to
their dreams? If so, I can introduce you to the very latest wish-
dream. Little Anna, aged one-and-a-half, had to fast for a day
at Aussee, because she had been sick in the morning, which was
attributed to eating strawberries. During the night she called
out a whole menu in her sleep: "Stwawbewwies, wild stwawbewwies, omblet, pudden!" I may perhaps already have told
you this.[1]

---

[1] See *Interpretation of Dreams*, p.130 ; and "On Dreams" (1901 a).

Under the influence of the analysis my heart-trouble is now often replaced by stomach-trouble.

Forgive to-day's chatter, which is only intended to keep our correspondence alive.

                                        Cordially your
                                                    Sigm.

74

                                        Vienna, 5. 11. 97.
Dr. Sigm. Freud,   IX. Berggasse 19.
Lecturer in Nervous Diseases
   in the University.

My dear Wilhelm,

I have really nothing to say, but I am writing at a moment when I feel the need of company and encouragement. . . .

It is interesting that writers are now turning so much to child psychology. To-day I received another book on the subject, by James Mark Baldwin.[1] So one still remains a child of one's age, even with something one had thought was one's very own.

Incidentally what horrifies me more than anything else is all the psychology I shall have to read in the next few years. At the moment I can neither read nor think. I am sufficiently absorbed in observation. My self-analysis is stagnating again, or rather it trickles on without my understanding its progress. In the other analyses I am getting more and more help from my latest idea about resistance. Not long ago I had occasion to take up again an old idea—it has appeared in print—about the choice of neurosis—that hysteria is connected with sexual passivity and obsessional neurosis with sexual activity. Otherwise it goes slowly, slowly. As I can do nothing but analyse, and am not fully occupied, I am bored in the evening. My lectures are attended

---

[1] Obviously Baldwin's *Mental Development in the Child and the Race* (1895), of which the German translation appeared in 1898. It is quoted in "Three Essays on the Theory of Sexuality" (1905 d). Baldwin's views on the relation between ontogenesis and phylogenesis and on the relation of the individual to the community agree in many respects with Freud's.

by an audience of eleven, who sit there with pencil and paper and hear damnably little that is positive. I play the part of neuropathological researcher before them and comment on Beard, but my interest is elsewhere.[1]

You have said nothing about my interpretation of *Oedipus Rex* and *Hamlet*. As I have not said anything about it to anyone else, because I can imagine in advance the hostile reception it would get, I should be glad to have some short comment on it from you. Last year you turned down a number of my ideas, with good reason.

Not long ago I was treated to a stimulating evening by my friend Emanuel Löwy, who is professor of archæology in Rome.[2] He has a fine and penetrating mind and is an excellent fellow. He pays me a visit every year and keeps me up till three o'clock in the morning. He spends his autumn holiday in Vienna, where his family lives. He tells me about Rome. . . .

Cordial greetings to you and your wife and child,

Your

Sigm.

75

Dr. Sigm. Freud,   Vienna, 14. 11. 97.
Lecturer in Nervous Diseases   IX. Berggasse 19.
  in the University.

My dear Wilhelm,

"It was November 12th, 1897; the sun was in the eastern quarter, and Mercury and Venus in conjunction—" no, birth

---

[1] Freud took an early interest in Beard, whose works were translated into German. In the years 1894-96 he referred repeatedly to Beard's conceptions of neurasthenia and in his "'Civilized' Sexual Ethics and Modern Nervous Sickness" (1908 d) he criticized Beard's belief that neurasthenia was "a new nervous disease which had developed particularly in America".

On the connection between Beard's researches, which date back to 1869, and those of Freud, see Bunker (1930), pp. 108-114.

[2] Emanuel Löwy (1858-1937) Professor of Archæology in Rome and Vienna, with whom Freud maintained a life-long friendship.

announcements do not begin like that any more. It was on November 12th, a day under the influence of a left-sided migraine, on the afternoon of which Martin sat down to write a new poem[1] and on the evening of which Oli lost his second tooth,[2] when, after the terrible pangs of the last few weeks, a new piece of knowledge was born to me. Truth to tell, it was not entirely new; it had repeatedly shown and then withdrawn itself again;[3] but this time it remained and saw the light of day.[4]

---

[1] I was not supposed to know this; his poetic tonsils seem to have been cut out.

[2] The first was extracted by his nurse on the evening of November 9th; otherwise it might perhaps have lasted to the 10th.

[3] None but tall guardsmen for Sa Majesté le roi de Prusse.

[4] The dates at the beginning of this letter refer to Fliess's period theory. The introductory sentences are, presumably, a parody of Vasari's life of Michelangelo; Freud was familiar with Vasari's *Lives* of the Italian painters. The "discovery" which Freud introduces in this way was that of the development of the libido. In talking of his "advance knowledge" of his discoveries Freud in fact describes his own method of work. In the language of psycho-analysis his preconscious worked over scientific connections before they became conscious: Hence the sudden advances in theory-making of the kind described in this letter. The ideas here expressed where in part taken over unaltered into the *Three Essays on the Theory of Sexuality* (1905 d). Others were developed only in later years. For instance, the idea of the meaning of the transition from walking on four legs to walking on two and the role of the upright stance (first touched on above on p. 186) were carried further only in 1928 in *Civilisation and its Discontents* and also discussed in the case history of the "Rat Man" (1909 d). In this letter Freud does not yet distinguish clearly between the three meanings of the word "repression": (i) the psychological mechanism of repression; (ii) those processes which take place in the course of the child's development towards maturity by means of which cathexis is withdrawn from certain zones of the body; and (iii) alterations in the apparatus which takes place in the course of the development of the species and correspond to Freud's later conception of "organic repression". The picture of the development of moral attitudes given in the letter was later fundamentally altered. What Freud here describes is on the whole still at the level of what he later (in *Three Essays*) regarded as reaction-formation. The influence of environment is only partially recognized, and no attention is paid to the influence of object-relationship on development (identification).

In this letter Freud for the first time puts the mechanism of regression in the centre of his dynamic explanation of the neuroses; previously it had been mentioned only incidentally. The subsequent differentiation between topographical and historical regression is not yet attempted.

On the other hand Freud develops in this letter a point of view to which he held fast in all his later works, though due attention has not always been paid to it in psycho-analytic literature. This is the idea that the effect of specific experiences

In a strange way I am aware of these events some time in advance. Thus I wrote to you once during the summer that I was about to find the source of normal sexual repression (morality, shame, etc.), and then for a long time I did not find it. Before the holidays I mentioned that my most important patient was myself, and after my holiday trip my self-analysis, of which there had previously been no trace, began.[1] A few weeks ago I mentioned that I wanted to get behind repression to the essential that lies behind it, and that is what I am writing to you about now.

I have often suspected that something organic played a part in repression; I have told you before that it is a question of the attitude adopted to former sexual zones, and I added that I had been pleased to come across the same idea in Moll. Privately, I would not concede priority in the idea to anyone; in my case the suggestion was linked to the changed part played by sensations of smell: upright carriage was adopted, the nose was raised from the ground, and at the same time a number of what had formerly been interesting sensations connected with the earth became repellent—by a process of which I am still ignorant. ("He turns up his nose"="he regards himself as something particularly noble.") Now, the zones which no longer produce a release of sexuality in normal and mature human beings must be the regions of the anus and of the mouth and throat. This is to be understood in two senses: first, that the appearance and idea of these zones no longer produce any exciting effect, and secondly, that the internal sensations arising from them no longer make any contribution to the libido like the sexual organs proper. In animals these sexual zones retain their power in both respects; where they do so in human beings the result

on the child's development is dependent on the stage of maturity it has reached. He seems to state this idea clearly in the sentence: "The choice of neurosis probably depends on the nature of the step in development which enables repression to occur".

In the last part of the letter Freud rejects a number of false hypotheses; that of the close connection between libido and anxiety, a problem with which he dealt afresh in *Inhibitions, Symptoms and Anxiety* in 1926; and the proposition, developed in connection with Fliess's period theory, of explaining libido as the masculine factor and repression as the feminine one. See also Introduction, p.39 *sqq.*

[1] See, however, Introduction, p. 30.

is perversion. We must suppose that in infancy sexual release is not so much localized as it becomes later, so that zones which are later abandoned (and possibly the whole surface of the body) stimulate to some extent the production of something that is analogous to the later release of sexuality. The extinction of these initial sexual zones would seem to be a counterpart to the atrophy of certain internal organs during the course of development. Now, the release of sexuality (as you know, I have in mind a kind of secretion, which we correctly perceive as an internal state of libido) comes about not only (1) through peripheral stimulation of the sexual organs and (2) through internal excitations arising from those organs, but also (3) from ideas (from memory traces)—that is to say, by deferred action. (You are already familiar with this train of thought.) [*Cf. e.g.*, p. 410 sqq.] If a child's genitals are irritated, years afterwards the memory of this will produce by deferred action a release of sexuality far more powerful than the original one, because the determining apparatus and the amount of secretion have increased in the meantime. Thus a non-neurotic deferred action can occur normally, and this generates compulsion. (Apart from this, our other memories only produce effects because they have already produced them when they were experiences.) Deferred action of this kind, however, operates also in connection with memories of excitation arising from the *abandoned* sexual zones. The consequence, however, is not a release of libido but a release of unpleasure, an internal sensation analogous to the disgust felt when an object is concerned.

To put it crudely, the current memory stinks just as an actual object may stink; and just as we turn away our sense organ (the head and nose) in disgust, so do the preconscious and our conscious apprehension turn away from the memory. This is *repression*.

Now, what is the outcome of normal repression? Something which can turn free anxiety into psychically "bound" rejection—that is to say, the affective basis of a multitude of intellectual developmental processes, such as morality, shame, etc. The whole of this, then, arises at the cost of extinguished ("virtual") sexuality. From this we can see how, with the progressive steps of a child's development, he becomes invested with piety, shame, etc., and how, in the absence of any such extinction of the sexual zones, "moral insanity" may result as a developmental inhibition. These steps in development have a different chronological arrangement in the male and female sexes. (Disgust appears earlier in little girls than in boys.) But the main distinction between the two sexes emerges at the period of puberty, when a *non*-neurotic distaste for sexuality overtakes girls and libido asserts its hold on men. For at that period a further sexual zone is partly or wholly extinguished in females, which persists in males. What I have in mind is the male genital zone, the region of the clitoris, in which during childhood sexual sensitivity seems to be concentrated in girls as well as boys. This accounts for the flood of shame by which girls are overwhelmed at that time, till the new vaginal zone is awakened, whether spontaneously or by reflex action. Hence too, perhaps, the anæsthesia of women, the part played by masturbation in children predisposed to hysteria, and the cessation of masturbation if hysteria results.

And now for the neuroses. Experiences in childhood which merely affect the genitals never produce neuroses in males (or masculine females) but only compulsive masturbation and libido. But since as a rule experiences in childhood also affect the two other sexual zones, the possibility remains open for males also that libido awakened by deferred action may lead to repression and neurosis. In so far as a memory refers to an experience connected with the genitals, what it produces by deferred action will be libido. But in so far as it refers to the anus, mouth, etc., it will produce internal disgust; and the final result of this will be that a certain amount of libido will be unable to make its way through, as it normally would, to action or to translation into psychical terms, but will be obliged to proceed in a *regressive* direction (as happens in dreams). Libido and disgust would here seem to be associatively linked. We owe it to the former that the memory cannot lead to general unpleasure, etc., but can be employed psychically; while the latter results in this psychical employment producing nothing but symptoms instead of purposive ideas. It ought not to be difficult to take in the psychological side of this; the decisive organic factor is whether the abandonment of the sexual zones takes place according to the masculine or the feminine type of development or whether it does not take place at all.

The choice of neurosis (the decision whether hysteria, obsessional neurosis or paranoia is to emerge) probably depends on the nature (that is, the chronological relation) of the step in development which enables repression to occur, *i.e.*, which transforms a source of internal pleasure into one of internal disgust.

This is where I have got to, then—with all the obscurities involved. I have decided, then, henceforth to regard as separate factors what causes libido and what causes anxiety. I have also given up the idea of explaining libido as the masculine factor and repression as the feminine one. These, at least, are significant decisions. The obscurity lies essentially in the nature of the change which causes the sensation of disgust to develop from the sensation of internal craving. I need not draw your attention to the other obscure points. The main value of my synthesis lies in its linking together the neurotic and normal processes. There is now a crying need, therefore, for a prompt elucidation of common neurasthenic anxiety.

My self-analysis is still interrupted. I have now seen why. I can only analyse myself with objectively acquired knowledge (as if I were a stranger); self-analysis is really impossible,[1] other-

---

[1] Freud later regarded self-analysis as no more than a supplement to an analysis undertaken with an analyst. Exceptionally he showed interest in the attempts of individuals to obtain insight into their childhood history by means of self-analysis. For instance, he advised the editors of the *Internationale Zeitschrift für Psychoanalyse* to publish a paper by Dr. Pickworth Farrow in the following terms: "The author of this book is known to me as a man of strange and independent intelligence who, probably because of a certain wilfulness of character, could not get on well with the two analysts with whom he experimented. He then had recourse to a consistent application of the process of self-analysis which I had once used myself to analyse my own dreams. His results deserve notice, especially because of his special individuality and technique." This recommendation of Freud's was later used with his consent as a preface (Freud, 1926c) to Pickworth Farrow (1942).

wise there would be no illness.　As I have come across some
puzzles in my own case, it is bound to hold up the self-analysis.[1]

76

18. 11. 97.

Dr. Sigmund Freud,　　　　　Consulting hours 3-5 p.m.
IX. Berggasse 19.

My dear Wilhelm,

. . . Early to-day I had a pleasant feeling, as if I had succeeded
in something important. But I do not know what it can be. It was
in some way connected with the idea that one must begin the
analysis of a hysteria by uncovering the actual operative motives
for accepting the illness—of which I certainly know some
already.[2] (The illness is not established until the aberrant libido
is put in touch with such motives, finding a definite employment,
as it were.) But it cannot be just that. I tell you all this because
such feelings after a time usually turn out to have been justified,
and because to-day has been a rather bad-period one (tired
head, and a particularly bad lecture).

Cordial greetings,

Your

Sigm.

77

Vienna, 3. 12. 97.

My dear Wilhelm,

. . . Dec. 5th. A critical day prevented me from going on. In
honour of your wife's visit a piece of explanation came to me,
which she was to have taken back to you. But probably it was
not a favourable day, because the idea which occurred to me
during my euphoria withdrew again, I no longer liked it, and it

---

[1] [This letter, being enclosed with another, was not signed.]
[2] This letter points to insight into the "secondary gain from illness".

must wait to be born again. Every now and then ideas whirl through my head which promise to explain everything, and to connect the normal and the pathological, the sexual and psychological, and then they disappear again, and I make no effort to retain them, because I know that both their appearance in consciousness and their disappearance are not the real indication of their fate. On stagnant days such as yesterday and to-day everything inside me is stagnant and terribly lonely. I cannot talk about it to anyone, and I cannot force myself to work, as other workers can. I have to wait until things move inside me and I experience them. And so I often dream whole days away. All this is only introductory to the subject of our meeting—in Breslau, as Ida suggested, if the train connections suit you. You know that what happened in Prague proved that I was right. When we decided on Prague last time, dreams played a big part. You did not want to come to Prague, and you know why, and at the same time I dreamt I was in Rome, walking about the streets and feeling surprise at the large number of German street and shop names. I awoke and immediately realized that the Rome of my dreams was really Prague (where it is well known that there is a demand for street signs in German). Thus the dream had fulfilled my wish to meet you in Rome rather than in Prague.[1] Incidentally my longing for Rome is deeply neurotic. It is connected with my schoolboy hero-worship of the Semitic Hannibal, and in fact this year I have no more reached Rome than he did from Lake Trasimene.[2]

Since I have started studying the unconscious I have become so interesting to myself. It is a pity that one always keeps one's mouth shut about the most intimate things.

Das beste, was Du wissen kannst,
Darfst Du den Buben doch nicht sagen.[3]

---

[1] This dream is described with further associations in *The Interpretation of Dreams*, p. 195-6.

[2] For the significance of Freud's predeliction for Hannibal and its roots in his relations with his own father, see *The Interpretation of Dreams*, p. 196-8.

[3] ["The best that you know you must not tell to boys."] See *The Interpretation Dreams*, p. 142. This quotation from Goethe's *Faust* arose in the course of

Breslau plays a part in my childhood memories. At the age of three I passed through the station when we moved from Frei-berg to Leipzig, and the gas jets, which were the first I had seen, reminded me of souls burning in hell. I know something of the context here. The anxiety about travel which I have had to over-come is also bound up with it.[1] I am good for nothing to-day. . . .

Kindest regards, and let me have a sensible . . . answer soon,

Your

Sigm.

78

Vienna, 12. 12. 97.

IX. Berggasse 19-6.

Dr. Sigm. Freud,
Lecturer in Nervous Diseases
  in the University.

My dear Wilhelm,

. . . Can you imagine what "endopsychic myths" are? They are the latest product of my mental labour. The dim inner per-ception of one's own psychical apparatus stimulates illusions, which are naturally projected outwards, and characteristically into the future and a world beyond. Immortality, retribution, the world after death, are all reflections of our inner psyche . . . psycho-mythology.[2]

---

associations referring to the resistance that Freud had to overcome before he could expose so much of his "intimate nature" to the public in *The Interpretation of Dreams*. Freud said of Goethe in his "Address delivered in the Goethe House at Frankfort" (1930 e) that "as a poet not only was he a great revealer, but he was also, in spite of the wealth of autobiographical hints, a careful concealer". In con-nection with this statement Freud went on again to quote the same words of Goethe's Mephistopheles.

[1] See Letter 70; also Sachs (1945). According to Bernfeld (1946) E. Simmel informed him that Fliess in conversation years after his estrangement from Freud had remarked that Freud freed himself by his self-analysis from a phobic symptom.

[2] The expression "endopsychic myth" stands for an idea which Freud ex-pressed in another form in "Creative Writers and Day-Dreaming" (1908 e). There he says: "As far as it goes, this material is derived from the popular treasure-house of myths, legends and fairy-tales. The study of these creations of folk psychology is in no way complete, but it seems extremely probable that myths, for example, are distorted vestiges of the wishful phantasies of whole nations—the age-long dreams of young humanity."

Let me recommend you a book of Kleinpaul's, *Die Lebendigen und die Todten.*

May I ask you to bring me the enclosed examples of dreams (in so far as they are on separate sheets) to Breslau? I gave a lecture on dreams to my Jewish society (an audience of laymen) last Tuesday, and it had an enthusiastic reception. I shall continue it next Tuesday.[1] . . .

The *Meistersinger* recently gave me extraordinary pleasure. . . . The *Morgentraumdeutweise* moved me considerably. . . . Real ideas are put into music as in no other opera through the association of feeling-tones to meaning.

Take care of yourself until Breslau,

Your
Sigm.

But I hope to hear from you and to write to you before then.

79

Vienna, 22. 12. 97.

My dear Wilhelm,

I am in good spirits again, and keenly looking forward to Breslau—that is, to you and the fine new things you will have to tell me about life and its dependence on the world-process. I have always been curious about it, but hitherto I have never found anyone who could give me an answer. If there are now two people, one of whom can say what life is, and the other can say (nearly) what mind is, it is only right that they should see and talk to each other more often. I shall now jot down a few novelties for you, so that I shall not have to talk and shall be able to listen undisturbed.

It has occurred to me that masturbation is the one great habit that is a "primary addiction", and that the other addictions, for

---

[1] For Freud's relations to the B'nai B'rith see his letter of 1926 published in his posthumous works (1941 e).

alcohol, morphine, tobacco, etc., only enter into life as a substitute and replacement for it.[1] Its part in hysteria is prodigious, and perhaps my great outstanding obstacle is, wholly or in part, to be found in it. The doubt of course arises whether such an addiction is curable, or whether analysis and therapy must stop short at this point and remain content with transforming a hysteria into a neurasthenia.

It is becoming confirmed that in obsessional neuroses the *verbal idea*, and not the concept dependent on it, is the point at which the repressed breaks through. (More accurately, it is the verbal memory.) Hence in the case of an obsessional idea the most disparate things tend to be brought together under a word with more than one meaning. Ambiguous words serve the break-through tendency as a way of killing several birds with one stone, as in the following case, for instance. A girl attending a sewing class which was soon coming to an end was troubled by the obsession: "No, you mustn't go yet, you haven't finished, you must *do*[2] still more, you must learn all that it's possible to learn." Behind this was the memory of childhood scenes; when she was put on the pot, she did not want to stay on it and was subjected to the same compulsion: "You mustn't go yet, you haven't finished, you must *do* some more". The word "do" permits identification of the later with the infantile situation. Obsessions often clothe themselves in a remarkable verbal vagueness in order to make possible manifold applications of this kind. Looked at more closely, the (conscious) content of this one yields: "You must go on learning". What, later, becomes the fixed, compulsive idea arises from such misinterpretation on the part of the conscious.

All this is not entirely arbitrary. The word *machen* [to "make" or "do"] has itself undergone a similar transformation of meaning.[3] An old phantasy of mine, which I should like to

---

[1] Freud neglected this approach to the problem of addiction in the years that immediately followed, *e.g.*, in his *Three Essays* (1905 d) and did not return to it till "Dostoevsky and Parricide" (1928 b) in the course of an analysis of gambling.

[2] [In German *machen*.]

[3] This discovery of Freud's in connection with obsessional neurosis was later recognized by him as a general property of the primary process.

recommend to your linguistic perception, deals with the derivation of our verbs from such originally copro-erotic terms.

I can hardly tell you how many things I (a new Midas) turn
into—filth.[1] This is in complete harmony with the theory of
internal stinking. Above all, gold itself stinks. I think the association is that "miserliness" is "dirty". Similarly birth, miscarriage, and menstruation are all connected with the lavatory *via*
the word Abort[2] (Abortus[3]). It is quite crazy, but completely
analogous to the process by which words assume a transferred
meaning as soon as new concepts appear requiring definition . . .

Have you ever seen a foreign newspaper after it has passed the
censorship[4] at the Russian frontier ? Words, sentences and whole
paragraphs are blacked out, with the result that the remainder is
unintelligible. A "Russian censorship" occurs in the psychoses,
and results in the apparently meaningless deliria.

Au revoir,

Your

Sigm.

I shall take the eight o'clock train on Saturday as arranged.

80

Vienna, 29. 12. 97.

My dear Wilhelm,

. . . A small piece of interpretation turned up soon after I
got back. Herr E., whom you know, had an anxiety-attack at the
age of ten when he tried but failed to catch a black beetle
[*Käfer*]. The meaning of this attack remained obscure for a long
time. Then, while dwelling on the theme of "being unable to
make up one's mind", he repeated a conversation between his
grandmother and his aunt about his dead mother's marriage,

---

[1] [The German *Dreck* also means excrement.] These and many subsequent
passages in the letters refer to the phenomena of the anal phases of libidinal
development.

[2] [Lavatory. [3] Abortion.]

[4] The first appearance of a conception made public in *The Interpretation of
Dreams*. [See, however, *Studies on Hysteria* (1895), *Ges. Werke*, I, pp. 269 and
284; also "Further Remarks on the Neuro-Psychoses of Defence" (1896)
Ges. Werke I, p. 402.]

from which it emerged that she had not been able to make up her mind about it for a long time. From this he jumped to the black *Käfer*, which had not been mentioned for months, and from that to *Marienkäfer* [Ladybird] (his mother's name was Marie). Then he laughed, and inadequately explained his laughter by remarking that zoologists call these beetles septempunctate, etc., according to their number of spots, though they are all the same insect. At that point we broke off, and at the beginning of the next session he told me that the meaning of *Käfer* had occurred to him. It was *que faire ?*—*i.e.*, being unable to make up one's mind. . . .

No doubt you know that here a woman can be called a "nice *Käfer*". His nurse and first love was a Frenchwoman; he actually learned to speak French before he learned to speak German. You will remember our conversations about the use of the words *hineinstecken, Abort*[1], etc. . . .

What I want now is plenty of material for a mercilessly severe test of the left-handedness theory. I have got the needle and thread ready. Incidentally the question that is bound up with it is the first for a long time on which our ideas and inclinations have not gone the same way.[2] . . .

---

[1] [*Hineinstecken,* to stick into, *Abort,* lavatory.] A continuation of the theme of the primary process. See previous letter.

[2] Fliess took this remark of Freud's amiss; see the next letter. The question of bilateralism, which led to the two men's subsequent estrangement, had arisen during their meeting at Breslau shortly beforehand. Fliess referred to this meeting in a letter written in 1904, three years after their relationship had come to an end, in which he laid emphasis on his having been the first to put forward the theory of bisexuality, as against Otto Weininger (see Introduction, p. 41). It appears from this letter that Fliess took Freud's doubts about his theory of bilateralism as a denial of his ideas about bisexuality.

"We first discussed the subject (*i.e.*, bisexuality) in Nuremberg, while I was still in bed and you were telling me the case-history of somebody who had dreams about enormous snakes", Fliess wrote. "At that time you were very much struck with the idea that under-currents in a woman might derive from the male part of her psyche. That made me all the more surprised at your resistance at Breslau to the idea of bisexuality in the psyche. At Breslau I also mentioned to you that there were such a large number of left-handed married couples among my acquaintances, and from the left-handedness theory I worked out an explanation that corresponds in every detail with Weininger's (who does not mention left-handedness). True, you rejected the left-handedness idea. . . ." (Letter of 26. 7. 1904 in Pfennig (1906), p. 29 and Fliess (1906), p. 16). For Freud's later attitude to the problem of bilateralism see also a letter of his quoted by Saaler (1914), p. 430.

A happy New Year, and may we see each other frequently in
1898!

Your

Sigm.

81

Vienna, 4. 1. 98.

My dear Wilhelm,

. . . It interests me that you should take it so much amiss that
I am still unable to accept your interpretation of left-handedness.
I shall try to be objective—I know well how difficult that is.[1]

The facts of the matter seem to me to be as follows: I seized
eagerly on your notion of bisexuality, which I regard as the most
significant for my subject since that of defence. If I had had
some aversion on personal grounds, because I am a bit neurotic
myself, it would certainly have taken the form of aversion to
the idea of bisexuality, which we hold to be responsible for the
inclination to repression. It seems to me that I object only to the
identification of bisexuality and bilateralism which you demand.
At first I adopted no attitude one way or the other to the idea,
because I still felt that the whole subject was remote from me.
On the second afternoon in Breslau I was feeling rather out of
form . . . or I should have expressed the doubt I felt, or
rather have taken you up when you said that each of the two
halves probably contains both kind of sex-organs. What becomes
of the femininity of the left half of a man if the latter includes a
testicle (and the corresponding lesser male sexual organs) just
as the right half does? Your proposition that for all effective
purposes male and female must unite is satisfied in the one half
by itself!

It also occurred to me that you may have considered me to be
partially left-handed; if so, you should tell me, for there would
be nothing hurtful to me in such a piece of self-knowledge. You
have known me long enough, and you know me well enough,
to know that it is your own fault if there is anything personal

---

[1] See footnote to previous letter. There is no mention of Fliess's hypothesis in
modern literature on left-handedness. See Blau (1946).

about me that you do not know. I am not aware of any preference for the left hand, or that I had any such preference in
childhood: I should rather say that in my early years I had
two left hands. There is only one point on which I cannot
object. I do not know whether it is obvious to other people
which is their own or others' right and left. In my case in
my early years I had to think which was my right; no organic
feeling told me. To make sure which was my right hand I
used quickly to make a few writing movements. To the
present day I still have to work out by their position, etc.,
which is other people's right or left hand. Perhaps that fits in
with your theory; it may be connected with the fact that in
general I have a very poor feeling for space, which made the
study of geometry and all kindred subjects impossible for me.

That is how it seems to me. But I know very well that it may
be otherwise, and that the disinclination I have so far felt to
accepting your ideas about left-handedness may be the result of
unconscious motives. If they are hysterical, they have certainly
nothing to do with the subject itself, but with the word. Perhaps
it suggests to me something "left-handed" or guilty. If that is
the case, the explanation will come some time; heaven knows
when. . . .

You must promise me to expect nothing from the chit-chat
article. It really is nothing but tittle-tattle, good enough for the
public, but not worth mentioning between ourselves.[1]

Cordially,

Your

Sigm.

82

16. 1. 98.

IX. Berggasse 19.

My dear Wilhelm,

. . . All sorts of little things are happening: dreams and
hysteria are fitting in with each other even more neatly. These

---

[1] The reference is to the paper "Sexuality in the Aetiology of the Neuroses"
(1898 a).

details are now standing in the way of the great problems touched on in Breslau. One must take it as it comes, and be glad that it does come. I send you herewith the definition of happiness (or did I tell you a long time ago ?)

Happiness is the deferred fulfilment of a prehistoric wish. That is why wealth brings so little happiness; money is not an infantile wish.

All sorts of other things keep dawning on me and driving their predecessors into the shade. It is not possible yet to piece it all together. . . .

Your
Sigm.

83

Vienna, 9. 2. 98.
Dr. Sigm. Freud,   IX. Berggasse 19.
Lecturer in Nervous Diseases
   in the University.

My dear Wilhelm,

On Sunday I was in Hungary for a consultation. The case was that of a lady of fifty, who imagines she goes about on wooden rollers and that her limbs are limp like a doll's, and that she will soon start crawling on all fours. However, I am exceedingly cheerful, entirely without cause, and have found my interest in life. I am deep in the dream book,[1] writing it fluently and smiling at all the matter for "head-shaking"[2] it contains in the way of indiscretions and audacities. If only one did not have to read! The literature on the subject, such as it is, is too much for me already. The only sensible thing on the subject was said by old Fechner[3] in his sublime simplicity: that the psychical territory on which the dream process is played out is a different

---

[1] *I.e., The Interpretation of Dreams.*
[2] A quotation from the *Jobsiade* of Karl Arnold Kortum.
[3] Fechner (1889, II, 520-1). [The passage is quoted in *The Interpretation of Dreams*, p. 48].

one. It has been left to me to draw the first crude map of it. . . .

Self-analysis has been dropped in favour of the dream book. The hysterical cases are doing rather badly. I shall not finish any this year either; next year I shall have no patients to work on.

I finished the tittle-tattle article to-day.[1] It is fairly trailing my coat; Breuer will say I have done myself a lot of harm.

There is a rumour that we are to be invested with the title of professor at the Emperor's jubilee on December 2nd. I do not believe it, but I had a fascinating dream on the subject; unfortunately it is unpublishable, because its background, its deeper meaning, shuttles to and fro between my nurse (my mother) and my wife. . . . Well, the best that you know, etc.[2]

Zola keeps us breathless. He is a fine fellow, a man with whom one could get on.[3] The disgusting behaviour of the French reminded me of what you said on Breslau bridge about the degeneracy of France, which at first I could not believe.

Schweninger's lecture at the talking shop here was a disgrace.[4] I did not go, of course; instead I treated myself to listening to our old friend Mark Twain in person, which was a great pleasure.[5]

My greetings to the whole family, present and future,

Your

Sigm.

---

[1] "Sexuality in the Aetiology of the Neuroses" (1898 a).

[2] [The quotation from *Faust* used in Letter 77.]

[3] The reference is to Zola's trial in Paris (February 7th-23rd, 1898). Two days after the acquittal of Esterhazy, the principal prosecution witness in the Dreyfus case, Zola published his famous open letter *J'Accuse*, in which he revealed the machinations of the anti-Dreyfusards. The result was that Zola was himself convicted.

[4] On February 5th, 1898, Schweninger, Bismarck's well-known doctor, delivered a lecture in dialogue form jointly with Maximilian Harden in which he advocated medical nihilism. He attacked specialization in medicine, made derogatory remarks about the diagnostic value of X-rays and confessed that he envied veterinaries, because their patients could not talk. The climax of his lecture was the phrase: "The world belongs to the brave, including the brave sick".

[5] Freud attended one of the lectures that Mark Twain gave in Vienna (see *Civilisation and its Discontents*) and used frequently to recall it in later years.

84

Dr. Sigm. Freud,
Lecturer in Nervous Diseases
    in the University.

Vienna, 10. 3. 98.
IX. Berggasse 19.

My dear Wilhelm,

    . . . It was no small feat on your part to see the dream book
lying finished before you.[1] It has come to a stop again, and meanwhile the problem has deepened and widened. It seems to me as
if the wish-fulfilment theory gives only the psychological and
not the biological, or rather metapsychological explanation.
(Incidentally I am going to ask you seriously whether I should
use the term "metapsychology" for my psychology which leads
behind consciousness.) Biologically dream-life seems to me to
proceed directly from the residue of the prehistoric stage of life
(one to three years), which is the source of the unconscious and
alone contains the ætiology of all the psychoneuroses; the stage
which is normally obscured by an amnesia similar to hysteria.
I am beginning to suspect that dreams are the result of things
seen in the prehistoric period; that phantasies are the result of
things *heard*; and that the psychoneuroses are the result of
sexual experiences. The repetition of experiences of the prehistoric period is a wish-fulfilment in itself and for its own sake;
a recent wish leads to a dream only if it can be associated with
material from that period, if the recent wish is a derivative of a
prehistoric wish or can get itself adopted by such a wish. I do

_____

    [1] This remark is obviously connected with a passage in a letter of Fliess's re-
ferred to in *The Interpretation of Dreams* (p. 172). The passage is as follows:
"I had a letter from my friend in Berlin the day before in which he had shown his
power of visualization: 'I am very much occupied with your dream book. I see it
lying finished before me and I see myself turning over its pages'."
This enables one to conclude that the present letter was written on the day
or very soon after the "Dream of the Botanical Monograph" reported in *The
Interpretation of Dreams* was written down. In the interpretation of this dream the
connection with an infantile scene plays an important role. It is evident from this
letter that Freud based one of the fundamental principles of his dream interpretation on the interpretation of this dream.

not know yet to what extent I shall be able to stick to this extreme theory, or let it loose in the dream book.

My course of lectures was particularly lively this year, and the audience included an assistant of Erb's. During the involuntary interruption caused by the closing of the University I went on lecturing in my room over a mug of beer and with cigars. Two newcomers have already enrolled for next term, in addition to the old ones.

I picked up a recent book of Janet's[1] on hysteria and *idées fixes* with beating heart, and laid it down again with my pulse returned to normal. He has no suspicion of the clue.

So I keep on growing older, contentedly on the whole, watching my hair rapidly going grey and the children rapidly growing up, looking forward to Easter, and practising patience in waiting for the explanation of the problem of neurosis.

Rumour has it that R. W. is coming too this year. In that case shall we let him make the children's acquaintace ? . . .

Your

Sigm.

85

Vienna, 15. 3. 98.
IX. Berggasse 19.

Dr. Sigm. Freud,
Lecturer in Nervous Diseases
    in the University.

My dear Wilhelm,

If I ever underestimated Conrad Ferdinand, you converted me long since with the *Himmelsthor*[2] . . .

I do not in the least under-estimate bisexuality either; I am looking forward to further enlightenment about it, particularly

---

[1] Janet (1898).

[2] The reference is to the poem *Am Himmelsthor* by the Swiss poet and novelist Conrad Ferdinand Meyer (1825-1898). Fliess drew Freud's attention to Meyer's works, to which he subsequently paid much attention. See Letters 90 and 91. His predeliction for Meyer remained with him for the rest of his life. See Sachs (1945) p. 50.

since the moment in Breslau market-place when we both said the same thing. Only I feel remote from it at the moment, because I am burrowing in a dark tunnel and can see nothing else. My freshness for work seems to be a function of the distance of our congresses. At this stage I am just plain stupid ... I have no more ideas at all. I really believe that my way of living, nine hours of analysis daily for eight months in the year, is playing havoc with me. Unfortunately the recklessness of mine which would advise a holiday from time to time cannot stand up to the bad earnings of these times and the prospect of still worse. So I go on working like a cab-horse, as we say here.[1] It struck me that you might want to read what I have written about dreams but were too discreet to ask. It goes without saying that I should have sent it to you before sending it to the printer's. But as it is at a standstill I can let you see it in fragments. Here are a few explanations. What I am sending you is intended to be the second chapter. The first, on the literature of the subject, is not yet written. After that there will be:—

3. Dream material;
4. Typical dreams;
5. The psychical process in dreaming.
6. Dreams and the neuroses.[2]

The two dreams described will reappear in later chapters, where the partial interpretations will be completed. I hope you will not object to the candid remarks in the professor-dream.[3] The Philistines here will rejoice at the opportunity of being able to say that I have put myself beyond the pale. The thing in the dream which will probably strike you most will be explained later (my ambition). Remarks about *Oedipus Rex*, the Talisman fairy-tale and perhaps *Hamlet* will also come in. First I must read more about the Oedipus legend—I do not know what yet.

I am reluctant to impose upon you at a time when you feel disinclined to work, but against that I set the idea that the

---

[1] Freud uses the term *Komfortableross*, a Viennese colloquialism.

[2] This arrangement is substantially altered in the published work.

[3] This is obviously a reference to the dream "My friend R. was my uncle", in *The Interpretation of Dreams* (p. 137 *sqq.*).

chapter, with its minimum of speculation, will only cause you some harmless amusement.

I am now completely at sea over hysteria. . . .

With cordial greetings,

Your

Sigm.

86

Dr. Sigm. Freud,   Vienna, 24. 3. 98.
Lecturer in Nervous Diseases   IX. Berggasse 19.
  in the University.

My dear Wilhelm,

You will not be surprised if I write to you to-day about your judgment on my dream manuscript, which made it a good day for me. . . .

Fortunately I can answer your objections by referring to what is to come in the later chapters. I have just reached the one which deals with the somatic stimuli of dreams. It will also mention anxiety-dreams, on which new light will be shed in the last chapter, "Dreams and Neurosis". But in the part you have read I shall put in cross-references which will avoid the impression it gave you that the author was skirting over difficulties.

I certainly do not think of this version as final. First I want to get my own ideas into shape, then I shall make a thorough study of the literature on the subject, and finally make such insertions or revisions as my reading will give rise to. So long as I have not finished my own work I cannot read, and it is only in writing that I can fill in all the details. So far I have finished another twenty-four pages, but no part of the rest of the book will be so entertaining or fundamental as the part that you have read.

I hope to hear by word of mouth what you think of many points of detail. You must not refuse the duties attached to being my first reader and supreme arbiter. . . .

Martin recently described in verse the seduction of the goose by the fox. The wooing went thus:—

> *Ich liebe Dich,*
> > *herzinniglich,*
>
> *komm, küsse mich,*
> *Du könntest mir von allen*
> *Thieren am besten gefallen.*[1]

Do you not think the form is notable? Occasionally he makes verses to which his audience objects, *e.g.*:—

> *Der Fuchsvater sagt: Wir gehen nach Aussee,*
> *Darauf freuen sich die Kinder und trinken Cafe.*[2]

To pacify us he said: "When I make up things like that, it's only like making faces".

And Robert Wilhelm? Are you going to bring him when you come to Vienna?

That there may soon be the best of news is the wish of

> Your
>
> > Sigm.

87

Dr. Sigm. Freud,   3. 4. 98.
Lecturer in Nervous Diseases   IX. Berggasse 19.
   in the University.

My dear Wilhelm,

. . . At odd hours[3] I go on writing the dream book. Another chapter, dealing with the sources of dreams and typical dreams, is nearly finished, but it is much less satisfactory than the first and probably needs rewriting. Apart from that I have no scientific progress to report, and I am not interested in anything but dreams.

---

[1] [I love thee with all my heart, come kiss me. You could be my favourite among all animals.]
[2] [Father fox says: We are going to Aussee, whereupon the children are delighted and drink coffee.]
[3] [These three words are in English in the original.]

The influenza has run its course, doing little harm and showing no favouritism for the male sex. The children are lively and amusing, the womenfolk well, the man of the house moody. . . .

The children want me to play the great travel game of "A Hundred Journeys through Europe" with them to-day. I shall do so, for appetite for work is not always present.

My lecture course bores me; I cannot talk about hysteria so long as I can come to no firm decision on two essential points.

I should love to go to our lovely Italy again this year, but earnings have been very bad. I must economize. . . .

Your

Sigm.

88

Dr. Sigm. Freud,   Vienna, 14. 4. 98.
Lecturer in Nervous Diseases   IX. Berggasse 19.
    in the University.

My dear Wilhelm,

I think it a good rule in letter-writing to leave unmentioned things that the recipient knows already and to tell him something new instead. So I shall pass over the fact that I heard you had a bad time at Easter; you know that anyway. Instead I shall tell you about my Easter trip, which I undertook moodily but from which I returned refreshed.[1]

We (Alexander[2] and I) left the South Station on Friday evening and reached Gorizia at ten o'clock on Saturday morning. We walked in bright sunshine between whitewashed houses, saw trees covered with white blossom, and were able to eat oranges and crystallized fruit. We compared memories—the view from the fortress recalled Florence, the *fortezza* itself recalled San

---

[1] A planned meeting with Fliess had been frustrated by the latter's illness. The trip to Istria described in this letter is specifically mentioned in the "Castle by the sea" dream in *The Interpretation of Dreams* (p. 463 *sqq.*).

[2] Freud's younger brother.

Pietro at Verona and the castle at Nuremberg. The first impression that one always has of the Italian landscape, that of missing meadows and woods, was very vivid, as is natural in any such transition. The Isonzo is a magnificent river. On the way we passed three spurs of the Julian Alps. On Sunday we had to get up early to go by the local Friulian railway to near Aquileia. The former capital is a dump, though the museum possesses an inexhaustible wealth of Roman finds: tombstones, amphorae, medallions of the gods from the amphitheatre, statues, bronzes and jewellery. There are several priapic statues: a Venus indignantly turning away from her new-born child on being shown its penis; Priapus as an old man, with a Silenus covering up his genitals for him—from which point onwards he will devote himself to drink; a stone priapic ornament with—instead of a penis a winged animal with a small penis of its own in the normal place and wings that themselves end in penes. Priapus stood for permanent erection, a wish-fulfilment representing the opposite of psychological impotence.

At ten o'clock, just when it was low water, a little steamer was towed into the Aquileia canal by a remarkable tug. It had a rope round its middle and puffed through a pipe while it was working. I should have liked to have brought it back for the children, but as the only link between the world and the resort of Grado it could not be spared. A two-and-a-half hour trip through the dreariest lagoons brought us to Grado, where we were at last able to gather shells and sea-urchins again on the shore of the Adriatic.

We returned to Aquileia the same afternoon, after a meal in the ship of our own provisions, which we washed down with delicious Istrian wine. Several hundred of the prettiest Friulian girls had just gathered in the cathedral for High Mass. The splendour of the old Romanesque Basilica was comforting in the midst of the modern poverty. On the way back we saw a piece of an old Roman road laid bare in the middle of a field. A modern drunk was lying on the ancient paving-stones. The same evening we got to Divaca on the Carso, where we spent the night, so as to be able to visit the caves on the next and last day, Monday. In the morning we went to Rudolf's Cave, a quarter-of-an-hour from the station, which is filled with all sorts of curious stalactitic formations, giant horsetail, pyramid cakes, tusks growing upwards, curtains, corn-cobs, tents and draperies, hams and poultry hanging from above. Most remarkable of all was our guide, strongly under the influence, but completely sure-footed and humorous and lively. He was the discoverer of the cave, and obviously a genius run to seed. He kept talking about his death, his conflicts with the priests, and his achievements in these subterranean realms. When he said he had already been in thirty-six "holes" in the Carso I recognized him as a neurotic and his *conquistador* exploits as an erotic equivalent. He confirmed this a minute later, because when Alexander asked him how far one could penetrate into the caves he answered: "It's like with a virgin; the farther the better".

The man's ideal is to come to Vienna to get ideas for naming his stalactites from the things in the museums. I over-tipped the "biggest blackguard in Divaca", as he called himself, to help him drink his life away the faster.

The caves of St. Cangian which we saw in the afternoon, are a horrifying freak of nature—a subterranean river running through magnificent vaults, with waterfalls and stalactites and pitch darkness, and a slippery path guarded by iron railings. It was Tartarus itself. If Dante saw anything like this, he needed no great effort of the imagination for his Inferno. The ruler of Vienna, Herr Dr. Carl Lueger,[1] was with us in the cave, which after three-and-a-half hours spewed us all out into the light again.

On Monday evening we began the journey home. Next day I could see from a recurrence of fresh ideas that rest had done the apparatus good. . . .

Your

Sigm.

---

[1] The burgomaster of Vienna. See p. 124, footnote 3.

89

Dr. Sigm. Freud,   Vienna, 1. 5. 98.
Lecturer in Nervous Diseases   IX. Berggasse 19.
   in the University.

My dear Wilhelm,

   ... Herewith Chapter III of the dream-book. You will find me rather uninteresting, I am completely wrapped up in dreams and very dull about them. I have now finished the psychological part, at which I had got stuck, but I do not like it, and it will not stand. The chapter you have now is still quite crude in style and in parts badly, *i.e.*, lifelessly, written. The passages I have left in about the somatic stimuli of dreams need to be brought out still more strongly. I am of course expecting you to give me all sorts of pertinent criticisms when we meet again. I think the conclusions are right.

   I wish a powerful stimulus of some kind were present. As I heard someone say of himself the other day, I am an engine meant to run under a pressure of ten atmospheres, and under a pressure of two atmospheres I run hot. So far I have hardly got to the stage of feeling tired this year, and normally at this time of year I have been gasping for a holiday for a long time. I have little on hand, and what I have taxes me even less.

   I have never been able to force my intellectual processes; so my leisure is wasted. . . .

   My cordial greetings, and I hope to hear from you several times before Whitsun.

Your
Sigm.

90

Dr. Sigm. Freud,   Vienna, 9. 6. 98.
Lecturer in Nervous Diseases   IX. Berggasse 19.
   in the University.

My dear Wilhelm,

   ... The dream-book is dragging.[1] (Ida will explain the word

---

[1] [In the original *hapert's,* a Viennese colloquialism.]

to you). I have reached page 14, but it is impossible to publish
it as it is, and perhaps even to show it to anyone. It is nothing
but a first rough draft. It is abominably difficult to set out the
new psychology in so far as it relates to dreams, as it is necessarily
fragmentary only, and all the obscure parts which I have so far
neglected out of laziness are now crying out for clarification. I
need a lot of patience, cheerfulness and some good ideas. I am
stuck over the relationship between the two systems of thinking;
I must get down to them in earnest. For a time I shall be of no
use for anything again. The tension of uncertainty results in a
state of wretched discomfort, which one feels almost physically....

I am reading C. F. Meyer with great pleasure. In *Gustav
Adolfs Page* I find the idea of deferred action twice: in the place
you mentioned, the incident of the sleeping kiss, and in the
episode of the Jesuit who insinuates himself as little Christine's
teacher. At Innsbruck they actually show the chapel where she
was received into the Catholic faith! But otherwise I find myself
bewildered by the arbitrariness of the assumption on which the
plot rests. The likeness in hand and voice between the page and
the Duke of Lauenburg is in itself so very improbable and is
given no plausible basis.

I shall soon send you a little essay on *Die Richterin*.

Cordial greetings,

Your

Sigm.

91

Dr. Sigm. Freud,   Vienna, 20. 6. 98.
Lecturer in Nervous Diseases   IX. Berggasse 19.
   in the University.

My dear Wilhelm,

. . . I came back this morning from Aussee, where I found
my poor family freezing and suffering from colds. They do not

want to go to Aussee again in spite of its loveliness. I find there is enough work here to last till the end of the month. . . .

Die Richterin[1]

There is no doubt that this is a defence against the writer's memory of an affair with his sister. The only remarkable thing is that this happens exactly as it does in neurosis. All neurotics create a so-called family romance (which becomes conscious in paranoia); on the one hand it serves the need for self-aggrandisement and on the other as a defence against incest. If your sister is not your mother's child, you are relieved of guilt.[2] (The same applies if you yourself are the child of other parents.) Where does the material about adultery, illegitimacy, etc., needed to create these romances come from? Generally from the lower social order of female servants. Such things are so common in that class that there is never any lack of material, and it is made all the easier if the seducer herself was a servant. In all analyses one comes upon the same story twice over; the first time as a phantasy relating to the mother, and the second time as a real memory of the servant. This explains why in *Die Richterin*[3]—who is the mother—the same story appears twice over without modification, which would not normally be considered good literary composition. Mistress and maid end by lying lifeless side by side. In the end the maid leaves the house, which is the usual end of stories about domestic servants, but in the story this is also the maid's punishment. This part of the family romance also serves as an act of revenge for being surprised and scolded by the strict mother. In the family romance and the story alike it is the mother who is surprised, unmasked and condemned. The removal of the horn is a truly infantile subject of complaint and its recovery a plain infantile wish-fulfilment. But in the story the sister's condition, her anorexia, obviously the neurotic consequence of infantile seduction, is not laid to the brother's door, but to the mother's. In paranoia poison corresponds exactly to the anorexia of hysteria, and thus to the form of perversion most usual among

---

[1] Freud's first application of analysis to a work of literature.
[2] For the family romance, see p. 205.
[3] ["The (female) Judge."]

children. Even fear of a "stroke" appears in the story (anxiety about having a "stroke", as a phobia, refers to blows feared in childhood). Also the violence which is never absent from an infantile love affair is represented in the story by the sister who is dashed against the rocks, but here it takes the form of a manifestation of outraged virtue, because the child is too forward. The schoolmaster-figure is introduced in the person of Alcuin. The father-figure makes his appearance in the person of the Emperor Charles, who stands for the father's greatness and remoteness from the world of the child's activities. In another incarnation he appears as he whose life was poisoned by his mother and he whom the family-romance regularly does away with because he stands in the son's way (wishful-dream of the father's death). Parental quarrels are the most fruitful source of infantile romances. Hostility to the mother is expressed in the story by the fact that she is turned into a stepmother. Thus in every single feature it is identical with the revenge-and-exoneration romances which my hysterics compose about their mothers if they are boys.

The psychology is going curiously; it is nearly finished, was written as if in a dream, and certainly is not in a form fit for publication—or, as the style shows, intended for it. I feel very hesitant about it. All its themes come from the work on neurosis, not from that on dreams. I shall not finish any more before the holidays.

The summer will soon be becoming very boring. Let me hear soon about you and your family.

Your

Sigm.

92

Dr. Sigm. Freud,   Vienna, 7. 7. 98.
Lecturer in Nervous Diseases.   IX. Berggasse 19.

My dear Wilhelm,

Here it[1] is. I found it very difficult to make up my mind to let

---

[1] The reference appears to be to another chapter of *The Interpretation of Dreams*, probably to the analysis of a specific dream.

it out of my hands. Personal intimacy would have been an insufficient justification for letting you have it, but our intellectual honesty to each other required it. It was all written by the unconscious, on the well-known principle of Itzig, the Sunday horseman. "Itzig, where are you going?" "Don't ask me, ask the horse!" At the beginning of a paragraph I never knew where I should end up. It was not written to be read, of course—any attempt at style was abandoned after the first two pages. In spite of all that I of course believe in the results. I have not the slightest idea yet what form the contents will finally take.

I am now living in comfortable idleness and enjoying some of the fruits of familiarity with hysterical matters. Everything is easy and transparent. On Sunday and Monday I had a distant, consultant's view of the battlefield of Königgrätz.[1] I am not going to Aussee yet. They are now at last enjoying themselves there. I am free from pain at present, which is exceptional; when I am well I am terribly lazy.

Our author's best novel,[2] and that furthest removed from infantile scenes, seems to me to be *Die Hochzeit des Mönchs*,[3] which illustrates magnificently how in the process of phantasy formation in later years the imagination seizes on a new experience and projects it into the past, so that the new figures are a continuation of the old and provide patterns for them. The secret theme is that of unsatisfied revenge and inevitable punishment, represented by Dante as continuing through all eternity. In the foreground, as by a mild misinterpretation of the conscious content, is the theme of loss of mental balance that takes place when a man has abandoned his firm foundations. Common to both the manifest and the latent theme is that blow follows on blow, as if *Die Richterin* were the reaction to infantile misdeeds which came to light, while this novel is the echo of those which remain undetected. The monk is a *frate*, a brother. It is as if he constructed a phantasy before his wedding, meaning: A

[1] The scene of the Prussian defeat of the Austrians in 1866.
[2] The author is, of course, Conrad Ferdinand Meyer. Freud's interpretation, in which the role of latent and manifest themes is stressed, leads directly to his subsequent analysis of Jensen's *Gradiva*.
[3] ["The Monk's Wedding."]

brother like me should not marry, or my infantile love affair will be revenged on my wife.

Cordial greetings to all three-and-three-quarters of you.

Your
Sigm.

93

Aussee, 20. 8. 98.

My dear Wilhelm,

Your note revived the pleasure of our trip. The Engadine, composed in simple lines out of a few elements, a kind of post-Renaissance landscape, and Maloja, with Italy beyond, wearing an air of Italy—perhaps only because we were looking out for it—were really magnificent. Leprese was also idyllic because of the reception we had there and the contrast with the journey up from Tirano. The road is by no means level, and we travelled up it in an appalling dust-storm, and arrived half-dead. The air made me feel brisk and aggressive—I have seldom felt so aggressive before. The height of 5,000 feet did not affect the soundness of my sleep.

Up to the last day in Maloja the sun did not trouble us. Then it grew hot, even at that altitude, and courage to go down to Chiavenna, *i.e.*, to the lakes, failed us. I think that was sensible, because at Innsbruck a few days later we were both in a state of almost paralysing weakness. Since then it has grown still hotter, and here in our lovely Obertressen we lie about from ten in the morning until six in the evening without venturing a step outside our small domain.

Little Anna has not inappropriately described a small Roman statuette I bought at Innsbruck as "an old child".

Being entirely removed from all intellectual activity, and being barely in a fit state, for instance, to understand your magnificent explanation of the time of life covered by old age, my mind is principally occupied with feelings of regret that so much of the holiday has already gone. My lively regret that both of you have been tied to town during this period is tempered by the thought that your trip is behind you and that Ida has a fine compensation ahead.

Yes, I too have skimmed through Nansen, whom my whole household is now hero-worshipping—Martha because the Scandinavians (grandmother, who is staying with us, still talks Swedish) obviously fulfil a youthful ideal of hers, which she has not realized in life, and Mathilde because she is transferring her allegiance from the Greek heroes she has hitherto been so full of to the Vikings. Martin as usual reacted to the three volumes of adventures with a poem—not a bad one.

I shall be able to make good use of Nansen's dreams; they are practically transparent. I know from my own experience that his mental state is typical of someone who is trying to do something new which makes calls on his confidence and probably discovers something new by a false route and finds that it is not so big as he expected. That is something I know from my own experience. Fortunately, the secure harmony of your nature preserves you from that. . . .

My cordial greetings to you and your wife. I am still not reconciled to the distance which divides us while at work and is so seldom eliminated in the holidays.

Your

Sigm.

94

Aussee, 26. 8. 98.

My dear Wilhelm,

. . . You ask what I am doing here? I am getting a little bored at Aussee, where I know all the walks so well. I cannot do without work altogether. I have set myself the task of making a bridge between my germinating metapsychology and what is in the books, and I have therefore plunged into the study of Lipps,[1] whom I suspect of being the best mind among present-

---

[1] Theodor Lipps (1851-1914) was Professor of Psychology in Munich. Freud was bound to seize on his works with interest, as he worked on the assumption of unconscious mental processes. In the summer of 1898 Freud (see Letter 95) read

day philosophical writers. So far he lends himself very well to comprehension and translation into my terms. This is, of course, a poor time for progress in clarification. My work on hysteria seems to my mind ever more dubious and its value slighter—as if I were still leaving a number of powerful factors out of account—and I dread taking it up again.

I have at last understood a little thing that I have long suspected. You know how you can forget a name and substitute part of another for it, to which you could swear, though it invariably turns out to be wrong.[1] That happened to me not long ago over the name of the poet who wrote *Andreas Hofer* ("*Zu Mantua in Banden . . .*"). I felt it must be something ending in *au*—Lindau, Feldau, or the like. Actually of course, the poet's name was Julius Mosen; the "Julius" had not slipped my memory. I was able to prove (i) that I had repressed the name Mosen because of certain associations; (ii) that material from my infancy played a part in the repression; and (iii) that the substitute names that occurred to me arose, just like a

---

part of his *Grundtatsachen des Seelenlebens* (Lipps, 1883). The following passage, among others, is marked in the copy in Freud's library (p. 149). (We believe) "not only in the existence of unconscious mental processes side-by-side with the conscious ones. We further believe that unconscious processes lie at the bottom of all conscious ones and accompany them. As we have already said, the conscious, when fortune favours, arises from the unconscious and then sinks back into it again." Certainly the words "conscious" and "unconscious" do not have for Lipps the same meaning that they have for Freud. Lipps uses them purely descriptively, without any dynamic implications. In this he follows the tradition of German romanticism, expressed in Eduard von Hartmann's celebrated *Philosophy of the Unconscious*. Freud himself stated in his *Jokes and their Relation to the Unconscious* (1905 c) that he owed "the courage and ability" to deal with problems of the comic to his acquaintance with Lipps's *Komik und Humor* (1898). In his own book on the subject Freud dealt in detail with the differences between his views and those of Lipps. He agreed with the latter's view that it was "not the contents of the conscious but inherently unconscious mental processes" which were of decisive importance (Lipps's *Komik und Humor*, p. 123) and expressed the opinion that he differed with Lipps only in speaking of "the cathexis of psychical paths". Freud added: "It was, in fact, experiences of the displaceability of psychical energy along certain associative paths and of the almost indestructible persistence of the traces of psychical processes that encouraged me to attempt to construct a picture of this kind of the unknown". The experiences to which Freud here appealed were only accessible to a scientist with a knowledge of biology and could only be obtained in the field of psychopathology.

[1] This is the first finding in the field of *The Psychopathology of Everyday Life*. The example quoted here was not used in Freud's published works.

symptom, from both groups of material. The analysis resolved the thing completely; unfortunately, I cannot make it public any more than my big dream. . . .

Best regards. How long shall we still have to wait for little Pauline's arrival?

Your

Sigm.

95

Aussee, 31. 8. 98.

My dear Wilhelm,

At midday to-day I leave with Martha for the Adriatic; we shall decide on the way whether to go to Ragusa, Grado or possibly somewhere else. The way to grow rich, according to an apparently eccentric but wise saying, is to sell your last shirt. The secret of this restlessness is hysteria. In the inactivity here and the lack of any interesting novelty the whole thing has come to weigh heavily on my mind. My work seems to me now to be far less valuable, my disorientation is complete, and time—a whole year has gone by without any tangible advance in the principles of the thing—seems hopelessly inadequate for what the problem demands. On top of it, it is the work on which I have staked my livelihood. True, I have a good record of successes, but perhaps they have been only indirect, as if I had applied the lever in the right direction for the line of cleavage of the substance; but the line of cleavage itself remains unknown to me. So I am running away from myself to gather all the energy and objectivity I can, because I cannot throw the work up.

The psychology is going better. In Lipps I have rediscovered my own principles quite clearly stated—perhaps rather more so than suited me. "The seeker often finds more than he seeks." Lipps regards consciousness as only a sense organ, the contents of the mind as ideation, and all mental processes as unconscious. In details the correspondence is close too; perhaps the divergence on which I shall be able to base my own contribution will come later. I have read only about a third of him. I got stuck at the treatment of tone-relations, with which I have always had trouble, lacking the most elementary knowledge of the subject because of my stunted acoustic sensibility. The great news of the day, the Tsar's manifesto, stirred me personally. I diagnosed the young man years ago as—fortunately for us—suffering from obsessional ideas, being "unable to bear the sight of blood", like Koko, the Lord High Executioner in *The Mikado*. If I could be put in touch with him, two people would be helped. I should go to Russia for a year and cure him sufficiently to prevent him from suffering any more, but leave him with enough to make sure that he would not start a war. After that you and I would have three congresses a year, on Italian soil *only*, and I should treat all my patients for nothing. Incidentally, I believe he is actuated by mixed motives, and that the egotistic side of the manifesto is the intention to gratify himself by securing the peaceful partition of China at the conference.

The most extraordinary thing about the manifesto is its revolutionary language. The use of such language about militarism by a leader-writer in a democratic paper in Austria would lead immediately to its confiscation; in Russia itself he would be sent to Siberia.[1]

My cordial greetings to you, Ida, Robert and little Pauline, and I shall send you further news of our trip.

Your

Sigm.

---

[1] On August 28th 1898, Count Muraviev, the Russian Foreign Minister, handed to the diplomatic representatives accredited to the court of St. Petersburg a Note in which the Tsar summoned to a peace conference all nations genuinely devoted to the ideal of universal peace as a way of overcoming the elements of disharmony and subversion. International solidarity was simultaneously to be reinforced by universal recognition of the principles of equity and justice on which national security and popular welfare depended.

The "revolutionary language" to which Freud refers occurs in the following passages: "The maintenance of universal peace and a possible reduction of the excessive armaments which weigh upon all nations in the present condition of affairs all over the world represent the ideal aims towards which the efforts of all governments should be directed. . . . During the last twenty years aspirations towards general pacification have grown particularly strong in the consciences of civilized nations. The preservation of peace has been made the aim of international

96

Vienna, 22. 9. 98.

My dear Wilhelm,

It was high time that I came home, but I had been back hardly three days when the whole depressing atmosphere of Vienna descended upon me again. It is a misery to live here, and it is no atmosphere in which the hope of completing anything difficult can survive.

I wish you thought less highly of my powers and that you were available in the neighbourhood so that I could hear your criticisms more often. But I am not in the least in disagreement with you, and have no desire at all to leave the psychology hanging in the air with no organic basis. But, beyond a feeling of conviction [that there must be such a basis], I have nothing, either theoretical or therapeutic, to work on, and so I must behave as if I were confronted by psychological factors only. I have no idea yet why I cannot yet fit it together [the psychological and the organic.[1]]

I have explained another instance of name-forgetting even more easily. I could not remember the name of the great painter who painted the Last Judgement at Orvieto, the finest I have seen. Instead Botticelli and Boltraffio occurred to me, with the certainty that they were wrong. Eventually I found out the name, Signorelli, and the fact that I then at once remembered the Christian name, Luca, showed that repression was at work and not true forgetfulness. It is clear why "Botticelli" came up; only *Signor* was repressed; the "Bo" in both substitute-names is

policy; for the sake of peace the great Powers have formed powerful alliances, and for the purpose of establishing a better guarantee of peace they have developed their military forces in an unprecedented degree and continue to develop them in spite of every sacrifice. . . . The ever-increasing financial burdens attack public prosperity at its very roots. The physical and intellectual strength of the people, labour and capital, are diverted for the greater part from their natural application and wasted unproductively. . . . Economic disturbances are caused in great measure by the system of extraordinary armaments, and the danger lying in this accumulation of war material renders the armed peace of to-day a crushing burden more and more difficult for the nations to bear."

[1] See Introduction, p. 43 *sqq.*

explained by the memory responsible for the repression, which concerned something that happened in *Bosnia*, and began with someone saying: "*Herr* [Sir, *Signor*], what can be done about it ?" I forgot the name of Signorelli during a short trip into *Her*zegovina, which I made from Ragusa with a lawyer from Berlin (Freyhau), with whom I got into conversation about pictures. In the course of the conversation, which aroused memories which, as I say, evidently caused the repression, we talked about death and sexuality. "Trafio" is an echo of Trafoi, which I saw on an earlier journey! How can I make this seem credible to anyone ?[1]

I am still alone. The "household", whom I already miss very much, are coming back at the end of the month.

A letter from Gattl, who wants to keep in touch, urges me to come to Berlin because of a patient whom he is to treat. It is one of these half-and-half affairs which I might use as an excuse to come and see you (and the new daughter). But it would conflict with my medical conscience, and I must not provoke gods and men by more travelling, but wait here patiently for the sheep to flock to me.

I hope to hear soon from you how your daughter[2] is getting on and—what interests me specially—how Robert behaves towards his sister. I have heard here already that their mother is doing well.

With cordial greetings,

Your

Sigm.

97

Vienna, 27. 9. 98.

My dear Wilhelm,

. . . I have made a little essay out of Signorelli and sent it to Ziehen (Wernicke).[3] If they reject it I think I shall adopt an

---

[1] Freud used it in "The Psychical Mechanism of Forgetting" (1898 b) and in the first chapter of *The Psychopathology of Everyday Life* (1901 b).

[2] Fliess's second child, Pauline.

[3] Ziehen and Wernicke were the editors of the *Monatschrift für Psychiatrie und Neurologie*, which published a number of Freud's early papers.

old idea of yours and send it to the *Deutsche Rundschau.* . . .

I still have nothing to do, *i.e.*, only two hours a day instead of ten. I have started a new case, so I am approaching it entirely without prejudice. At first, of course, everything fits in beautifully. He is a young man of twenty-five, who can hardly walk because of stiffness in the legs, cramp, trembling, etc. A safeguard against the risk of a wrong diagnosis is provided by the anxiety which makes him cling to his mother's apron-strings, like the baby that lies behind him. The occasion for the outbreak of his condition, which has persisted since his fourteenth year, was provided by the death of his brother and the death of his father in a psychosis. He feels ashamed of being seen walking in the way he does, and thinks that is natural. He patterns himself on a tabetic uncle; the current popular ætiology of tabes (sexual excess) caused him to identify himself with him when he was a boy of thirteen. Incidentally, he is of bear-like physique.

Please note that the shame is only appended to the symptoms, and must refer to other precipitating factors. He says himself that his uncle is not all at ashamed of his gait. The connection between his shame and his gait was a correct one several years ago, when he had gonorrhoea, which was naturally noticeable from his walk, and several years before that, when he was hampered in walking by constant (aimless) erections. There is also a deeper cause for the shame. He told me that last year, when the family was living by the River Wien (in the country), the Danube suddenly started rising, and he had a panic fear that the water would come into his bed, *i.e.*, flood his room, and during the night too. Note the double meaning of the expression; I knew he wetted his bed as a boy. Five minutes later he said spontaneously that in his schooldays he still regularly wetted his bed, and his mother threatened that she would come and tell his master and all the boys about it. He suffered great anxiety over this. So *that* is what the shame applies to. On the one hand the whole story of his youth culminates in the leg-symptoms, and on the other it discharges the affect associated with it; the two things are only welded together in his interior perception.

The whole of his forgotten childhood history has yet to be fitted in between.

Now, a child who regularly wets his bed up to his seventh year (without being epileptic, etc.) must have experienced sexual excitation in infancy. Was it spontaneous or the result of seduction? That is the question, which will also settle the closer determination—about the legs.

You see that if need be I can say of myself: *Zwar bin ich gescheiter als alle die Laffen,*[1] etc., but unfortunately the gloomy consequence is not entirely inapplicable to me either. *Führe meine Leute an der Nase herum und seh', dass wir nichts wissen konnen.*[2]

Who is Lipps? He is a professor at Munich, and he says in his jargon just what I worked out about consciousness, quality, etc. I was studying his *Grundtatsachen des Seelenlebens* until I went on my trip; now I must pick up the thread again.

I am expecting the children back from Aussee in the next few days. . . .

Cordial greetings to you, Ida, Robert and little Pauline,

Your

Sigm.

98

Vienna, 9. 10. 98.

My dear Wilhelm,

My moods, critical faculty, reflections—in short, all my secondary mental activities—have been buried under an avalanche of patients which overwhelmed me a week ago. Being unprepared for it and spoilt by the holiday, at first I felt knocked flat. But now I have recovered my vigour again, though I have no energy left over for anything else. It is all concentrated on

---

[1] ["Though I am cleverer than all the coxcombs. . . ."]
[2] ["I lead my people around by the nose and see that we can know nothing." This and the previous quotation are from the celebrated soliloquy at the beginning of Goethe's *Faust*. The second quotation is slightly distorted.]

work with my patients. Treatments—after two short visits first —begin at nine o'clock and go on till half-past one. From three to five there is a pause for consulting hours; my consulting room is alternately crowded and empty; and then from five to nine treatments again. Another case is definitely coming. That makes ten or eleven psychotherapeutic sessions a day. Naturally by evening I am speechless and half-dead. But Sunday is almost entirely free. I turn things over in my mind, test them and modify them here and there, and I am not entirely without new clues. If I hit on anything, you shall hear about it. Half my patients are now men, of all ages from fourteen to forty-five. . . .

Leonardo, of whom no love-affair is recorded, was perhaps the most famous case of left-handedness. Can you use him?

Cordial greetings,

Your

Sigm.

99

Dr. Sigm. Freud,   Vienna, 23. 10. 98.
Lecturer in Nervous Diseases   IX. Berggasse 19.
   in the University.

My dear Wilhelm,

This letter is intended to reach you on the most important date of all to you, and to bring you good wishes for your happiness from me and mine across the distance between us. These wishes are, as they should be, according to their nature, though not according to human misusage, directed towards the future, and they run like this: May you maintain and extend your present possessions and acquire fresh possessions in children and knowledge, and, finally, may you be spared every vestige of suffering and illness over and above that which a man needs to extend his powers and to stimulate his enjoyment of good things by comparison with bad.

Things are probably going well with you, as there is so little to be said about them. It would be the same with me, had the recent influenza epidemic not left me with an infection which has undermined my good spirits, made it difficult to breathe through my nose and will probably have unpleasant after-effects.

Martha is very well, and Mathilde is putting up with school and enjoying it better than we expected. I no longer find it a burden to work from nine to nine—indeed, if an hour falls free I feel unemployed. I have a glimmer of hope that in the course of the next year I shall be in a position to find my way out of serious mistakes to the truth. But the light has not dawned yet, and I shall not talk about it now, so as not to deliver myself before our meeting, on which I have been counting for so long.

In any case I am not in a state to do anything else, except study the topography of Rome, my longing for which becomes more and more acute. The dream book is irremediably at a standstill. I lack any incentive to prepare it for publication, and the gap in the psychology, and the other gap left by the thoroughly analysed example, are both obstacles to finishing it that I cannot overcome yet. Apart from that I am completely isolated, and have even given up my lectures this year, in order not to have to talk about things I do not yet understand. . . .

One thing I have learned, however, which makes an old man of me. If the ascertaining of the few points required for the explanation of the neuroses involves so much work, time and error, how can I ever hope to gain an insight into the whole of mental activity, which was once something I proudly looked forward to ?

Bearing this in mind, it was with a sad and envious smile that I greeted the first volume of Kassowitz's *Allgemeiner Biologie*. Do not buy it; I shall send you my copy.

With cordial greetings,

Your

Sigm.

100

5. 12. 98.

My dear Wilhelm,

The literature (on dreams) which I am now reading is reducing me to idiocy. Reading is a terrible infliction imposed upon all who write. In the process everything of one's own drains away. I often cannot manage to remember what I have that is new, and yet it is all new. The reading stretches ahead interminably, so far as I can see at present. But enough of that. I marked the passing of our beloved C. F. Meyer[1] by buying the volumes I lacked—*Hutten, Pescara, Der Heilige*. I believe I am now as enthusiastic about him as you are. I can hardly tear myself away from *Pescara*. I should like to know something about his life story and the order in which his books were written, which is indispensable for interpretation.

I am glad that you are well again and making plans just as I am making "programmes". Pain is soon forgotten.

To our next meeting, then. In the meantime we shall exchange a few letters, and you will probably receive a small reprint of mine before you leave Berlin.

Your

Sigm.

101

Dr. Sigm. Freud,
Lecturer in Nervous Diseases
   in the University.

Vienna, 3. 1. 99.
IX. Berggasse 19.

My dear Wilhelm,

. . . [2]First of all I have accomplished a piece of self-analysis which has confirmed that phantasies are products of later periods which project themselves back from the present into

---

[1] Conrad Ferdinand Meyer died on 28. 11. 1898, after nearly five years' illness.
[2] Written after a meeting.

earliest childhood; and I have also found out how it happens, again by verbal association.[1]

The answer to the question of what happened in infancy is: Nothing, but the germ of a sexual impulse was there. The whole thing would be easy and interesting to tell, but it would take many pages to write, so I shall keep it for the Easter congress, with other information about my youthful history.

Also I have discovered another mental factor which I believe to be of general application and a preliminary stage of symptoms (even before phantasy).

4.1. I stopped here yesterday because I was tired, and to-day I cannot go on writing any more in the direction I intended, because the thing is growing. There is something in it. It is dawning. In the next few days there will certainly be something to add. I shall write to you when it has grown clear. All I shall disclose to you is that the dream pattern is capable of universal application, and that the key to hysteria really lies in dreams.[2] I understand now why, in spite of all my efforts, I was unable to finish the dream book. If I wait a little longer I shall be able to describe the mental process in dreams in such a way as to include the process in hysterical symptom-formation. So let us wait.

A pleasing thing which I meant to write to you about yesterday is something from—Gibraltar, from Mr. Havelock Ellis, an author who concerns himself with the subject of sex and is obviously a highly intelligent man, as his paper[3] in the *Alienist and Neurologist* (October, 1898), which deals with the connection between hysteria and sexual life, begins with Plato and ends with Freud. He gives a good deal of credit to the latter, and

---

[1] This new piece of self-analysis enabled Freud to answer the question of phantasy and memory, which occupied him for many years, in the way familiar to us from his later works. [It seems probable that this relates to the screen-memory reported in Freud's contemporary paper on that subject (1899 a). This screen memory, which (as shown in the footnote to Letter 107 below) was one of Freud's own, involves a verbal association. A central episode in the memory was of a little girl having some flowers taken away from her, and this is interpreted by Freud as signifying defloration.]

[2] *Cf.* p. 208.

[3] Havelock Ellis (1898). This essay was the continuation of Havelock Ellis's study of auto-erotism and was intended for the second volume of his *Studies in the Psychology of Sex.*

writes a very intelligent appreciation of *Studies on Hysteria* and later publications. . . . At the end he retracts some of his praise. But something remains, and the good impression is not entirely obliterated. . . .

So you see what happens. I live gloomily and in darkness until you come, and then I pour out all my grumbles to you, kindle my flickering light at your steady flame and feel well again; and after your departure I have eyes to see again, and what I look upon is good. Is that only because the term of the period had not previously been reached? Or could not one of the many days available for all purposes be made into the term by the mental influences by which he who is waiting for the term is affected? Must not some place be left for that, so that the dynamic aspect is not ruled out by the time factor?[1]

My cordial greetings to you and yours,

Your

Sigm.

102

Dr. Sigm. Freud,　　　　　　　　　　Vienna, 16. 1. 99.
Lecturer in Nervous Diseases　　　　　IX. Berggasse 19.
　in the University.

My dear Wilhelm,

. . . If I were not so incapable of writing after ten hours' talking—as you can see from my irregular hand—I could write you a small treatise on the small advances made in the wish-theory, for since the 3rd[2] the light has never quite gone out, nor has the certainty that I have laid hands on something of key importance. But perhaps it is better that I should go on saving and collecting, so as not to appear before you again as a penniless

---

[1] This is Freud's first expression of doubt about Fliess's period theory, which he feared would eliminate the dynamic factors from the psyche. See Introduction, p. 37 *sqq.*
[2] The date of the previous letter.

beggar at the Easter congress with nothing to offer you but promises for the future.

A few other things of less importance have happened. It turns out, for instance, that hysterical headaches are due to a fantastic parallel which equates the head with the other end of the body (hair in both places—cheeks and buttocks—lips and labiae—mouth and vagina); so that a migraine can be used to represent a forcible defloration, the illness thus again standing for a wish-fulfilment. That the sexual is the conditioning factor stands out with ever-increasing clarity. One patient (whom I cured with the help of the phantasy key) was continually plunged into despair by the gloomy conviction that she was useless, good for nothing, etc. I always thought that in early childhood she must have seen her mother in a similar state, in an attack of real melancholia. That was in conformity with the earlier theory, but in two years there was no confirmation of it. It now turns out that at the age of fourteen she discovered an *atresia hymenalis* in herself and despaired of ever being able to function fully as a woman, etc. Melancholia is thus fear of impotence. Similar states in which she could not make up her mind to choose a hat or a dress go back to the time when she had to choose her husband.

With another patient I have convinced myself that there really is a hysterical melancholia and established what its indications are, and I have also noted the great variety of translations of the same memory and gained a first inkling of how melancholia arises through summation. This patient incidentally is totally anæsthetic, as she ought to be according to an idea dating from the time of my earliest work on neurosis.[1]

I have heard of a third case in the following interesting manner. An important and wealthy man (a bank director), aged about sixty, came to see me and talked to me about the peculiarities of a young girl who is his mistress. I threw out the guess that she was probably quite anæsthetic. On the contrary, she has from four to six orgasms during a single coitus. But—she falls into a tremor as soon as he approaches her and immediately afterwards falls into a pathological sleep, in which she talks as if in hypnosis;

[1] See p. 101 *sqq.*

she carries out post-hypnotic suggestions, and afterwards has complete amnesia about the whole thing. He will marry her off, and she will certainly be anæsthetic towards her husband. Her elderly lover, because of the easy identification with the powerful father of her childhood, obviously affects her in such a way as to release the libido attached to her phantasies. Very instructive! . . .

The children and their mother are at last well again. Little Anna woke up one morning and was suddenly cured, and since then has been delightfully cheeky.

Affectionate greetings to your wife and children, and let me have news of you soon.

Your

Sigm.

103

Vienna, 30. 1. 99.

My dear Wilhelm,

. . . My dilatoriness is explained as follows. I wrote a letter to you a week ago, thinking I had made a real find. But doubts arose while I was writing and I decided to wait. I was quite right to do so, because the thing was wrong; that is to say, there was something in it, but it had to be worked out in quite another field of application.

You can have no idea how much your last visit raised my spirits. I am still living on it. The light has not gone out since; little bits of new knowledge glimmer now here, now there, which is truly refreshing after the comfortlessness of last year. What is rising out of the chaos this time is the connection with the psychology contained in the *Studies on Hysteria*, the relationship with conflict and life; I should like to call it clinical psychology. Puberty is coming more and more into the centre of the picture, and the phantasy key is substantiating itself. But I have nothing big and complete yet. I am diligently making notes

of the significant features, to lay before you at the congress. I
need you as my audience.

For relaxation I am reading Burckhardt's *History of Greek
Civilization,* which is providing me with unexpected parallels.
My predilection for the prehistoric in all its human forms re-
mains the same. . . .

3.2. I could not make up my mind to consider that the end of
this short letter and to send it off, but waited for new material.
But nothing came—everything is being noted on the pages I am
filling for the congress, and my interest and energy do not
extend to anything else. To-day, after twelve hours' work and
earning 100 florins, I am again at the end of my strength. All my
mental aspirations are asleep. Just as art only thrives in the midst
of prosperity, so do aspirations only thrive with leisure. I am
only looking forward to what you will say about my notes, which
will give you a better insight than ever before. But there is
nothing of the first rank in them. In any case I know you do not
like making plans long in advance.

Otherwise there is nothing new here. I look forward to good
news of you, your wife and children.

Your

Sigm.

104

Dr. Sigm. Freud,   Vienna, 6. 2. 99.
Lecturer in Nervous Diseases   IX. Berggasse 19.
    in the University.

My dear Wilhelm,

. . . I do not see cases of the kind you ask about, simply
because I see none but my daily patients, with whom my
working day will be fully occupied for a long time ahead. They
provide me with the typical; I hope I shall not have any need

to trouble about the corollary fields myself. I do remember cases of TB with anxiety dating from an earlier age, but they did not leave any special impression on me. . . .

The art of deceiving patients is certainly not very desirable. What has the individual come to, how slight must be the influence of the religion of science, which is supposed to have replaced the old religion, if one no longer dare disclose that it is this man's or that man's turn to die. . . . The Christian at least has the last sacraments administered a few hours in advance. Shakespeare says: "Thou owest Nature [God] a death". I hope that when my time comes I shall find someone who will treat me with more respect and tell me when to be ready. My father knew that he was dying, did not speak about it and retained his composure to the end.

For a long time we have not had a period so devoid of external events. From the point of view of the family that is a good thing, as such events are generally not worth hankering after. Work is progressing slowly, not without certain gains, but for a long time there has been no surprising turn. The secret dossier is getting thicker and thicker, as if it were really looking forward to being opened at Easter. I am curious myself about when Easter in Rome will be possible.

I am perfectly serious about a change of occupation and residence, in spite of all the improvement in my work and income.[1] Taken all round, things are too bad. It is a pity that these plans are just as fantastic as "Easter in Rome". Fate, so colourful and prolific of memorable and surprising things, has quite forgotten your friend in his lonely corner. . . .

Your

Sigm.

I am deep in Burckhardt's *History of Greek Civilization.*

---

[1] The correspondence does not reveal what change of work and residence Freud had in mind. In later letters he speaks of an attempt to secure a connection with a watering place, and he frequently mentions in the course of the correspondence the advantages of Berlin as compared with Vienna.

105

Dr. Sigm. Freud,   Vienna, 19. 2. 99.
Lecturer in Nervous Diseases   IX. Berggasse 19.
  in the University.

My dear Wilhelm,

. . . My last generalization holds good and seems inclined to
spread to an unpredictable extent. It is not only dreams that are
fulfilments of wishes, but hysterical attacks as well. This is true
of hysterical symptoms, but it probably applies to every product
of neurosis—for I recognized it long ago in acute delusional
insanity.[1] Reality—wish-fulfilment: it is from this contrasting
pair that our mental life springs. I believe I now know the determining condition which distinguishes dreams from symptoms
that force their way into waking life. It is enough for a dream to
be the wish-fulfilment of the repressed thought; for a dream is
kept apart from reality. But a symptom, which has its place
in actual life, must be something else as well—the wish-
fulfilment of the *repressing* thought. A symptom arises where the
repressed and the repressing thoughts can come together in the
fulfilment of a wish. A symptom, in its character of a punishment, for instance, is a wish-fulfilment of the repressing thought,
while self-punishment is the final substitute for self-gratification
—for masturbation.[2]

---

[1] [In Section III of Freud's first paper on the neuro-psychoses of defence
(1894a).]

[2] Another step forward in insight; after establishing the bridge between
neurosis and dreams, Freud discerns the meaning of symptoms. He had already
gained insight into the compromise character of symptom-formation (Letters
101 *sqq.*); the forces the interplay of which leads to the compromise are now introduced into the formula. From another point of view the conception of a symptom
as the result of repressed and repressing ideas (as a compromise between the id
and the super-ego) had a fructifying effect on the conception of the "dream-
work" and thus supplemented the central hypotheses of *The Interpretation of
Dreams*.

Here we have the key to many problems. Do you know, for instance, why X.Y. suffers from hysterical vomiting? Because in her imagination she is pregnant, because she is so insatiable that she cannot do without having a baby even from her last imaginary lover. But she also vomits because then she will be starved and emaciated, will lose her looks and cease to attract anyone. Thus the meaning of the symptom is the fulfilment of a pair of contradictory wishes.

Do you know why our old friend E. turns red and sweats whenever he sees a certain class of acquaintance, particularly at the play? He is ashamed, no doubt; but of what? Of a phantasy in which he figures as the "deflowerer" of every person he comes across. He sweats as he deflowers, because it is hard work. Whenever he feels ashamed in someone's presence, an echo of the meaning of his symptom finds voice in him like a growl of defeat: "Now the silly idiot thinks she has made me feel ashamed. If I had her in bed she'd soon see whether I felt embarrassed in front of her!" And the period of his life during which he turned his wishes on to this phantasy has left its traces on the psychical complex which produced the symptom. It was in his Latin class. The theatre auditorium reminds him of the classroom; he always tries to get the same regular seat in the front row. The *entr'acte* corresponds to the "break", and "sweating" was the slang word for *operam dare* ("working"). He had a dispute with the master over that phrase. Moreover, he can never get over the fact that at the University he failed to get through in botany; so he carries on with it now as a "deflowerer". He owes his capacity for breaking into a sweat to his childhood, to the time when (at the age of three) his brother poured some soapsuds over his face in the bath—a trauma, though not a sexual one. And why was it that at Interlaken, when he was fourteen, he masturbated in such a peculiar attitude in the W.C.? It was so that he could get a good view of the Jungfrau [literally, "maiden"]; since then he has never caught sight of another—or at all events not of her genitals. No doubt he has intentionally avoided doing so; for why else does he form liaisons only with actresses? How like "a clever work of fiction", and yet how characteristic of "man with all his contradiction"![1] . . .

Cordially,

Your

Sigm.

106

Dr. Sigm. Freud,   Vienna, 2. 3. 99.
Lecturer in Nervous Diseases   IX. Berggasse 19.
  in the University.

My dear Wilhelm,

"Writing he has quite forgotten." Why? And with a plausible theory of forgetfulness fresh in your mind as a warning!

Perhaps our letters will cross again? Mine shall stand over for another day.

Things are going almost uniformly well with me. I cannot wait for Easter to show you in detail one of the principal features —that of wish-fulfilment and the coupling of opposites. I am getting a good deal of satisfaction from old cases and I have two new ones, not of the most favourable prognosis. The realm of uncertainty is still enormous, problems abound, and I understand theoretically only the smallest fraction of what I do. But every few days light dawns, now here, now there, and I have grown modest and count on long years of work and patient compilation, backed by a few serviceable ideas after the holidays, after our meetings.

Rome is still far away; you know my Roman dreams.

5.3. Life is otherwise incredibly empty of content. Nursery and consulting-room—in these times there is nothing else. But, if all is going well in both of these, enough has been sacrificed

---

[1] From C. F. Meyer's *Hutten's letzte Tage*, quoted by Freud in the "Analysis of a Phobia of a Five-Year-old Boy". (1909 b).

to the envy of the gods in other directions. . . . The weather varies every twenty-four hours between snowstorms and hints of spring. Sunday is still a fine institution, though Martin thinks that Sundays are getting fewer and farther between. Easter really is no longer so distant. Are your plans fixed yet? I am already itching to be off.

Pour revenir à nos moutons, I can very clearly distinguish two different intellectual states in myself. In the first I pay very careful attention to everything that my patients tell me and have new ideas during the work itself, but outside it cannot think and can do no other work. In the other I draw conclusions, make notes, have interest to spare for other things but am really farther away from things and do not concentrate properly on the work with my patients. From time to time I visualize a second part of the method of treatment—provoking patients' feelings as well as their ideas, as if that were quite indispensable. The outstanding feature of the year's work seems to me to have been the solution of the phantasy problem. I have let myself be lured a long way from reality. All this work has done a lot of good to my own mental life. I am obviously much more normal than I was four or five years ago.

I have given up my lectures this year in spite of numerous enrolments, and do not propose to resume them in the immediate future. I have the same horror of the uncritical adulation of the very young that I used to have for the hostility of their elders. Also the whole thing is not ripe yet—*nonum prematur in annum!* Pupils *à la* Gattl are to be had for the asking; as a rule they end by asking to become patients themselves. Also I have a secondary motive; the realization of a secret wish which might mature at about the same time as Rome, so, when Rome becomes possible, perhaps I shall throw up the lectureship. But, as I have said, we are not in Rome yet.

I sorely miss news of you. Must it be so?

Cordially, and with best wishes to your wife,

Your

Sigm.

107

Dr. Sigm. Freud,   Vienna, 28. 5. 99.
Lecturer in Nervous Diseases
   in the University.

My dear Wilhelm,

. . . I have sent the screen-memories to Ziehen at Jena.[1]
. . . The dreams, however, have suddenly taken shape without
any special reason, but this time for good. I have decided that
all the efforts at disguise will not do, and that giving it all up
will not do either, because I cannot afford to keep to myself the
finest—and probably the only lasting—discovery that I have
made. In this dilemma I have followed the rabbi's line in the
story of the cock and the hen. Do you know it ? A man and wife
who owned one cock and one hen decided to celebrate a festival
by having a fowl for dinner, but they could not make up their
mind which to kill, so they consulted the rabbi. "Rabbi, what
are we to do, we've only one cock and one hen. If we kill the
cock, the hen will pine, and if we kill the hen the cock will pine.
But we want to have a fowl for dinner on the festival. Rabbi,
what are we to do ?" "Well, kill the cock", the rabbi said. "But
then the hen will pine." "Yes, that's true; then kill the hen."
"But rabbi, then the cock will pine." "Let it pine!" said the
rabbi.

   So the dreams will be done. . . . Alas! That the gods should
have set up the existing literature on a subject to frighten off
the would-be contributor to it! The first time I tackled it I got
stuck, but this time I shall work my way through it; there is
nothing that matters in it anyway. None of my works has been so
completely my own as this; it is my own dung-heap, my own
seedling and a *nova species mihi* (*sic!*). After the reading will
come the blue-pencillings, insertions, etc., and the whole thing
should be ready by the end of July, when I go to the country. I

---

[1] "Screen Memories" (1899 a). S. Bernfeld (1946) shows that it deals with one
of Freud's own screen memories.

may try a change of publisher if I see that Deuticke is not prepared to pay much, or is not very enthusiastic about it.

The ten analyses have not come off; I now have two-and-a-half! Four possibles failed to materialize, and otherwise a deathly hush prevails. Strangely enough, this leaves me quite cold. Recently my technique has been very satisfactory.

The boys have produced a slight sore throat after two days' temperature. Ernst still has a lot of pain from his apparent dilatation of the stomach; he is to be shown to Kassowitz. On Friday they (Minna and the children, except Mathilde) go to Berchtesgaden.

I have bought myself Schliemann's *Ilios* and enjoyed the account of his childhood. The man found happiness in finding Priam's treasure, because happiness comes only from fulfilment of a childhood wish. This reminds me that I shall not be able to go to Italy this year. Better luck next time!

With cordial greetings to you, your wife, son and daughter,

> Your
>
> Sigm.

108

Dr. Sigm. Freud,   9. 6. 99.
    IX. Berggasse 19.   Consulting hours 3-5 p.m.

My dear Wilhelm,

This is a sign of life! The "silence of the forest" is a roar of traffic compared to that in my consulting-room, in which one can "dream" admirably. Some of the specimens of the literature on the subject make me wish for the first time that I had never had anything to do with it. One of them is named Spitta[1] [2. . . .] I am over the hill now. Naturally one gets deeper and deeper into the thing, and there comes a point where you have

---

[1] Spitta, 1892.
[2] [Freud here interpolates. n parentheses a translation of the English word "spit".]

to break off. Once again the whole thing resolves itself into a commonplace. There is *one* wish that every dream is intended to fulfil, though it assumes various forms. That is the wish to sleep. You dream to avoid having to wake up, because you want to sleep. *Tant de bruit. . . !*

I have begun the analysis of a friend (Frau A.), a very remarkable woman—have I never mentioned her to you?—and once more am able to convince myself how beautifully everything fits in. Otherwise I am resigned. I have enough to live on for a few months yet. . . . This plunging myself up to the neck in psychological literature is depressing. It gives me the feeling that I do not know anything instead of having grasped something new. Another unfortunate thing is that one cannot keep up this reading and note-making activity for more than a few hours a day. So I am wondering whether you really gave me good advice or whether I ought not to be cursing you for it. There is only one possible compensation; as part of your introducing me to biology you must give me something refreshing to read.

Cordial greetings to you all,

Your

Sigm.

109

Dr. Sigm. Freud,   Vienna, 27. 6. 99.
Lecturer in Nervous Diseases   IX. Berggasse 19.
   in the University.

My dear Wilhelm,

  . . . I am tired and greatly looking forward to the four days from June 29th to July 2nd which I am going to spend at Berchtesgaden. The writing goes on—once I wrote enough to fill a signature in a single day. The chapter is getting longer and longer, and will be neither good nor fruitful, but it is a duty to do it. In the process I get no fonder of the subject. . . .

I have passed the first signatures for press and am sending

them in to-morrow. Perhaps others will like it better than I do. "*I* don't like it", as Uncle Jonas might say.[1] My own dreams have taken on an absurd complexity. Recently I was told that little Anna said on Aunty Minna's birthday: "On birthdays I'm usually rather good", whereupon I dreamed my usual school-dream. I found myself in the sixth class and said to myself; "In this sort of dream one usually is in the sixth class." The only possible explanation is that Anna is my sixth child. Brrr. . . .!

The weather is foul. As you see, I have nothing to write about, and am not cheerful. . . .

Your

Sigm.

110

3. 7. 99.

My dear Wilhelm,

. . . The author of the "extremely important book on dreams, which is still, unfortunately, insufficiently appreciated by scientists", greatly enjoyed himself for four days in Berchtesgaden *au sein de sa famille,* and only a remnant of shame prevented him from sending you picture postcards of the Königsee. The house is a little gem of cleanliness, loneliness and beautiful views: the women and children are very happy in it and look very well. Little Anna is positively beautified by naughtiness. The boys are already civilized members of society, able to appreciate things. Martin is a comical creature, sensitive and good-natured in his personal relationships—completely wrapped

---

[1] The reference is to an anecdote, of which there were many variations, to which Freud returns again and again in the following letters. The version referred to here was known as the "marriage of convenience". Uncle Jonas meets his nephew, who has heard of his engagement and congratulates him. "And what is your fiancée like, uncle?" he asks. "Well, that's a matter of taste, but personally I don't like her!" Uncle Jonas replies.

up in a humorous phantasy world of his own. When we passed a little cave in the rocks, for instance, he bent down and asked: "Is Mr. Dragon at home? No? Only Mrs. Dragon? Good morning, Mrs. Dragon! Has your husband flown to Munich? Tell him I'll call again soon and bring him some sweets!" All this was occasioned by seeing the name Drachenloch[1] between Salzburg and Berchtesgaden. Oli makes plans of the mountains here just as he does with the Underground lines and tramways in Vienna. They get on very well and without jealousy.

Martha and Minna are reading Hehn's letters to one Herr Wichmann and, as you have the reputation of knowing everything and have actually lived in the Wichmannstrasse, they want me to ask you who Herr Wichmann was. I have warned them that you have more important things on hand at the moment.

Do you know what this trip vividly reminded me of? Our first meeting at Salzburg in 1890 or 1891, and our walking tour over the Hirschbühel to Berchtesgaden, where you witnessed one of my very finest attacks of travel-anxiety at the station. Your name appears in the visitors' book on the Hirschbühel in my handwriting, and you are described as a "universal specialist from Berlin". Between Salzburg and Reichenhall you as usual had no eyes for the beauties of nature, but waxed enthusiastic about Mannesmann's tubes. At the time you rather oppressed me by your superiority. I had that feeling quite distinctly, and I also had another, vaguer feeling, which I can put into words only to-day; it was suspicion that this man had not yet found his vocation, which later turned out to be shackling life with numbers and formulæ. Also there was no trace of that other vocation of yours then, and if I had started talking to you about Fraulein Ida Bondy you would have said: "Who is she?" Please give my family's cordial greetings to the lady in question.

Your

Sigm.

---

[1] ["Dragon hole."]

111

Dr. Sigm. Freud,   Vienna, 17. 7. 99.
Lecturer in Nervous Diseases   IX. Berggasse 19.
   in the University.

My dear Wilhelm,

   . . . I have finished the big task, but there are still 115 little
ones. Chapter I of the dreams is in type and the proofs are
waiting to be read. . . .
   There are still some farewell visits to be made, tidying up to
be done, bills to be paid, etc., and then I shall be free. On the
whole it has been a triumphant year, with many doubts resolved.
The only surprising thing is that when long-awaited things at
last happen you no longer take pleasure in them. Perhaps it is
the constitution that is beginning to fail. . . .[1] In addition to my
manuscript I am taking the "Lasalle" and a few works on the
unconscious to Berchtesgaden. I have reluctantly given up the
idea of any other travelling. In my good hours I imagine new
works, great and small. No introductory quotation for the dreams
has suggested itself since you condemned the sentimental one
from Goethe. It will have to be just a hint at repression:

   Flectere si nequeo superos, Acheronta movebo.
   Titles from my phantasies are:
      The psychopathology of daily life.
      Repression and wish-fulfilment.
      (A psychological theory of the neuropsychoses).
So much about myself. . . .
   The ancient gods still exist, for I have bought one or two
lately, among them a stone Janus, who looks down on me with
his two faces in very superior fashion.
   My cordial greetings, then, and I hope I shall find news of
you waiting for me at Berchtesgaden.
                                        Your
                                             Sigm.

---

[1] [A reference to the story told in footnote 1, p. 183.]

112

Dr. Sigm. Freud,   Vienna, 22. 7. 99.
Lecturer in Nervous Diseases   IX. Berggasse 19.
   in the University.

My dear Wilhelm,

. . . This is the position with the dream book. It lacked a
first chapter, an introduction to the literature on the subject,
which—unless I am greatly mistaken—you too thought necessary in order to lighten the rest. This is now written, but I found
it very difficult, and it has not turned out very satisfactorily. Most
readers will stick in this thicket and never get through to see the
Sleeping Beauty within. The rest, which you have seen, needs
some not very drastic revision. The parts dealing with the
literature of the subject are to be taken out, references to points I
have only just discovered in various books have got to be put
in here and there, and new examples of dreams are going in. All
this does not amount to very much. Then the final psychological
chapter has yet to be written, as well as the wish theory, which
will provide the link with what follows, some hypotheses about
sleep, a discussion of anxiety dreams, and the relation between
the wish to sleep and suppressed material. Perhaps I shall do all
this more by way of allusion.

Now, I am not sure what you want to see, and when. Am I to
send you Chapter I ? And the revised version of the rest, before
I send it to the printer ? You would be assuming a very un-
profitable burden. For me of course it would be all profit if you
would take the trouble. So far as the publisher is concerned,
there is no change. Deuticke did not want to let the book go, and
so I decided not to betray how much I dislike having decided to
leave it with him. At any rate I shall have finished with a part of
the first third of the great task of obtaining a scientific understanding of the neuroses and psychoses by the theory of repression and wish-fulfilment. (1) The organic-sexual; (2) the factual-
clinical; (3) the metapsychology. The work is now in its second

third, and we still have a lot to discuss about the first. When the final third is reached (and Rome or Karlsbad)[1] I shall be glad to have a rest. I always find something extremely comforting in relying on your judgment, which has a stimulating effect on me for a long time.

I should like to hear some definite news about you and your family soon. I shall write from Berchtesgaden as often as the spirit moves me, and that will not be seldom.

With cordial greetings,

Your

Sigm.

113

Dr. Sigm. Freud,
Lecturer in Nervous Diseases
   in the University. Riemerlehen, 1. 8. 99.
Vienna,
IX. Berggasse. 19

My dear Wilhelm,

I am sending you two envelopes with the proofs of the introductory chapter (on the literature) by the same post. If you find anything you do not like, send me the proof back with your observations on it; there will be two or three further proofs, so there is time to make alterations. I cannot tell you how much good your keen interest in the work does me. Unfortunately this chapter will be a hard test for the reader.

Things are ideal here. We go for long and short walks and are all very well, except for the states I fall into at times. I work at finishing off the dreams in a big, quiet ground-floor room with a view of the mountains. My grubby old gods, of whom you think so little, take part in the work as paper-weights. The gap made by the big dream which you took out is to be filled by a small collection of dreams (innocent and absurd dreams, calculations and speeches in dreams, affects in dreams). Real revision

---

[1] See footnote 1, 183.

will only be required for the last, psychological chapter, which
I shall perhaps tackle in September and send you in manuscript
—or bring it with me. All my interest is in that.

There are mushrooms here, though not many yet. The
children naturally join in the fun of looking for them. The
housewife's birthday was celebrated on a big scale, among other
things by a family outing to Bartholomäe. You should have seen
little Anna on the Königsee. Martin, who lives entirely in his
phantasy world here, has built himself a Malepartus den in the
woods. Yesterday he announced: "Actually I don't believe my
so-called poems are really good". We have not contested this
piece of self-knowledge on his part. Oli goes on with his exact
registration of routes, distances and names of places and mountains. Mathilde is a complete little human being, and of course
completely feminine. They are all having a fine time. . . .

The more the work of the past year recedes into perspective,
the better pleased I am with it. Now for bisexuality! I am sure
you are right about it. And I am accustoming myself to the idea
of regarding every sexual act as a process in which four persons
are involved. We shall have a lot to discuss about that.

A good deal of what you said in your letter distressed me
greatly. I wish I could help.

Give my cordial greetings to the whole family, and think of
Riemerlehen where I am.

Cordially,

Your

Sigm.

114

Dr. Sigm. Freud,   Berchtesgaden,
Lecturer in Nervous Diseases   Riemerlehen, 6. 8. 99.
  in the University.

My dear Wilhelm,

As usual, you are right. You have said exactly what I have
been thinking myself, that the first chapter may put many

readers off. But there is not much to be done about it, except to put a note in the preface, which we shall write last of all. You did not want me to deal with the literature in the body of the book, and you were right, and you do not want it at the beginning, and you are right again. You feel about it as I do; the secret must be that we do not want it at all. But, if we do not want to put a weapon into the hands of the "learned", we must put up with it somewhere. The whole thing is planned on the model of an imaginary walk. First comes the dark wood of the authorities (who cannot see the trees), where there is no clear view and it is very easy to go astray. Then there is a cavernous defile through which I lead my readers—my specimens with its peculiarities, its details, its indiscretions, and its bad jokes—and then, all at once, the high ground and the prospect, and the question: "Which way do you want to go ?"

There is no need to return the proof-sheets I am sending you. As you have not objected to anything in Chapter I, I shall pass the proofs of it. None of the rest is yet in type. You will get the proofs as soon as they are pulled, with the new parts marked. I am putting in a lot of new dreams, which I hope you will not delete. *Pour faire une omelette il faut casser des oeufs.* Besides, they are *humana* and *humaniora*, and not really private, *i.e.*, personally sexual. . . . During the last few days I have liked the book very much. "I like it", says Uncle Jonas, which, if experience is any guide, augurs ill for its success. With your permission I am putting Robert's dream among the children's hunger-dreams, after little Anna's menu dream[1]. . . . Some

---

[1] This dream (see Letter 116) was eventually used in another context. It is told in *The Interpretation of Dreams* (pp. 267-8) as follows:—

"A boy not yet four years old described the following dream. He saw a plate in front of him with a big portion of roast meat and vegetables on it. Suddenly he saw that the meat had all been eaten up, without having been cut up, but he did not see the person who ate it up.

"Who could this stranger be who helped himself to this lavish meat meal in our little boy's dream ? He had been on a milk diet under doctor's orders for several days, and that evening he had been naughty, and was given no supper as a punishment. He had experienced an involuntary fast of this nature once before, and had behaved very bravely. He knew he would get nothing to eat, but refused to betray that he was hungry by the slightest word. Education was beginning to have its effect on him; it expressed itself in his dream, which

time attention must be paid to "bigness" in children's dreams: it is connected with the wish to be big and to be able to do things like eating a whole dish of salad like Papa; a child never has enough, even of repetitions. For a child, like a neurotic, the hardest thing is moderation.

Conditions are ideal here, and I feel correspondingly well. I only go out mornings and evenings, and the rest of the time I sit over my work. On one side of the house it is always delightfully shady when the other is blazing hot. I can easily imagine what it is like in town. . . .

We find mushrooms daily. But on the next rainy day I shall walk down to my beloved Salzburg; the last time I was there I picked up a few old Egyptian things. Those things cheer me and remind me of distant times and countries.

J. J. David[1] came to see me several times in Vienna. He is an unhappy man and a not inconsiderable writer. . . .

With cordial greetings and thanks for your co-operation in the Egyptian dream book,

Your
Sigm.

115

Dr. Sigm. Freud,   Berchtesgaden, 20. 8. 99.
Lecturer in Nervous Diseases
  in the University.

My dear Wilhelm,

I have been here for four weeks now, and am regretting that

---

shows the beginning of dream-distortion. There is no doubt that he himself was the person who wanted a lavish spread of roast meat. But, knowing this to be forbidden, he did not sit down to eat it himself, as hungry children do in dreams (see the strawberry dream of my little Anna). The eater in his dream remains anonymous."

The passage in the letter not reproduced here refers to the content of this dream.

[1] Jacob Julius David (1859-1906) was, according to a passage in *The Interpretation of Dreams*, a friend of Alexander Freud's. He came from Freiberg, Moravia, Freud's birthplace. He subsequently reviewed *The Interpretation of Dreams*.

this happy time is passing so quickly. In another four weeks my holiday will be over, and it is all too short. I have got on so well with my work here, in peace and with nothing to disturb me, and in almost complete health; and in between times I have gone for walks, and enjoyed the mountains and woods. You must be lenient with me, because I am completely wrapped up in my work and cannot write about anything else. I am deep in the chapter on the "dream-work" and have replaced—I think to advantage—the complete dream that you deleted by a small collection of dream-fragments. Next month I shall begin the last, philosophical chapter. I dread it; it means doing some more reading.

The setting is going on slowly. I sent you the latest proofs yesterday. Please send back only the proof-sheets on which there is something to which you object and with your comments in the margin; and later on, when you are in a position to, correct any wrong quotations or references which you may come across; here, of course, I have no books available.

After five hours work to-day I have a trace of writer's cramp. The brats are making an unholy row in the meadow; only Ernst is laid up with a bad insect bite. . . . Since he lost a front tooth he has been continually hurting himself, and is as full of wounds as Lazarus, and at the same time reckless and almost anæsthetic. I ascribe it to a slight hysteria. He is the only one whom the former nurse treated badly. . . .

Alexander was here for four days. He has a lectureship on tariffs at the Export Academy, and after a year will have the title and rank of professor extraordinary—long before me, in fact. . . .

My hand refuses to do any more work to-day. I shall write again soon. Cordial greetings from

Your

Sigm.

116

Dr. Sigm. Freud,　　　　　　　　　　　　B., 27. 8. 99.
Lecturer in Mental Diseases
　　in the University.

My dear Wilhelm,

Thank you for the two pages received to-day from Harzburg.
When the revised proofs come back your amendments will of
course be carefully copied into them. You will no doubt have
further occasion to cross out superfluous subjectivity. Your
looking through the work is a great comfort to me.

I am completely absorbed in the dreams, and am useless for
anything else, as you will easily understand. Yesterday I took
a heap of paper in manuscript form (including fifty-six new
pages, dream-interpretations, examples) to the post, and notes
are already beginning to pile up for the last and most ticklish
chapter, the psychological one, the scope and arrangement of
which I still do not see. I also still have to do some reading for it.
The psychologists will have enough to rail at in any case, but a
thing like this must take its own course. Any attempt to make
it better than it is in itself only gives it a forced quality. So it will
contain 2,467 mistakes—which I shall leave in it.[1]

I have never regretted the shortness of the holidays so much
as this year. In three weeks it will all be over, and then troubles
will begin again. . . .

You will find Robert's dream later on, in connection with the
egoism of dreams. Everything here is fine, it is a hot, un-
interruptedly fine summer. A little Italy would round it off
beautifully. But that cannot be.

---

[1] In a postscript to this letter, not contained in the collection of MSS. here
published, Freud explained what determined his choice of this number. He
asked Fliess to return it to him and used it in *The Psychopathology of Everyday
Life.*
　　" 'I at once tried to explain this number,' he wrote, 'and am adding this little
piece of analysis as a postscript to my letter. The best thing is to quote it as I
wrote it down at the time, just after I had caught myself in the act:
　　" 'Let me quickly add a contribution to the psychopathology of everyday

What would you think of ten days in Rome at Easter (the two of us, of course) if all goes well, if I can afford it and have not been locked up, lynched or boycotted on account of the Egyptian dream book? I have looked forward to it for so long. Learning the eternal laws of life in the Eternal City would be no bad combination.

I expect you are back in Berlin. I am delighted that you managed to have a few free days for a visit to Harzburg with all the children. . . .

You must leave me some scope for my "venom" in the dream-interpretations. It is good for the constitution to let fly.

My cordial greetings; during the next few weeks I shall impose on you only too much with the things that I shall send you.

Your

Sigm.

---

life. In the letter I put down the figure 2,467 as an arbitrary estimate of the number of mistakes to be found in the dream book. All I meant was some very big figure, but I put down that particular one. However, nothing that happens in the mind is arbitrary or undetermined. You will therefore rightly conclude that the unconscious had hastened to determine the figure the choice of which had been left open by the conscious. Now, immediately beforehand I had read in the newspaper that General E. M. had retired as Master of the Ordnance. I should explain that I am interested in the man. While I was serving as a medical officer cadet he came to the sick quarters one day (he was then a colonel) and said to the medical officer: "You must cure me in a week, because I have some work to do for which the Emperor is waiting." After that episode I took it upon myself to follow his career, and behold! now he has reached the end of it, having become the Master of the Ordnance and now being put on the retired list. I worked out how long he had taken over this. Assuming that it was in 1882 that I saw him in hospital, it must have been seventeen years. I told my wife this, and she remarked: "You ought to have retired too!" "Heaven forbid!" I exclaimed. Immediately after this conversation I sat down to write to you. But the earlier train of thought went on in my mind, and with good reason. I had miscalculated; I have a fixed point in my memory to prove it. I celebrated my majority, *i.e.,* my twenty-fourth birthday, under military arrest (having been absent without leave). That was in 1880, or nineteen years ago. That gives you one half of the figures in 2,467. Now take my present age—43—add 24, and you have 67. In other words, my answer to the question whether I should have liked to retire myself was to say that I should like another twenty-four years' work first. On the one hand, I am obviously annoyed at having failed to get very far myself during the period during which I have followed Colonel M.'s career, while on the other I celebrate a kind of triumph that his career is now over, while I still have everything in front of me. So one can say with justice that not even the casually scribbled figure 2,467 was without its determination by the unconscious'."

117

Dr. Sigm. Freud,   B., 6. 9. 99.
Lecturer in Nervous Diseases
   in the University.

My dear Wilhelm,

To-day is your wedding day, which I remember well. But you must be lenient with me for a little longer. I am completely absorbed in the dreams, I am writing eight to ten pages a day, and I have just got over the worst in the psychological chapter— under great torment. I dare not think how it has turned out. You must tell me whether it will do, but in the galley-proof stage, because reading manuscript is too great an imposition, and in the galley-proof stage everything can still be altered. I ended by putting more into it than I intended—one always goes deeper and deeper as one goes on—but I am afraid it is rubbish. And the things I shall be told about it! When the storm breaks I shall fly to your spare room. You will find something to praise in it anyway, because you are as prejudiced in my favour as the others are against me.

I have received sixty more galleys, which I am sending you by the same post. I am almost ashamed of exploiting you in this way, because in biology you can discriminate for yourself and do not need any *quid pro quo* from me, you deal in light, not darkness, with the sun and not the unconscious. But please do not tackle the whole thing all at once, but send me the galleys on which you find something to censor when you have a number ready; then I shall get your corrections before sending off my own; they can all go in together. There are a lot of new things in it which I can mark for you. I have avoided sex, but "dirt" is unavoidable, and craves your indulgence. Do not bother, of course, with ordinary literals, but if you detect incorrect quotations or bad similes, please mark them. If only someone could tell me the real worth of the whole thing.

It has been lovely here, and perhaps I shall yet manage a few free days. My style has been bad, unfortunately, because physically I have been feeling too well. I have to feel a little unwell to write well. But enough of all that. Everyone here is in fine fettle, growing and flourishing, particularly the little one. I do not like thinking about the coming working season.

That is all for to-day; I always come back to the same thing. My cordial greetings and thanks.

Your
Sigm.

Do you know David ? And Friedjung's history of 1859-1866 ?[1]

118

Dr. Sigm. Freud,   B., 11. 9. 99.
Lecturer in Nervous Diseases
  in the University.

My dear Wilhelm,

Thank you very much for your trouble. I had myself noticed some things that were carelessly phrased, or obscure because of omissions. The other amendments will be faithfully inserted. . . . Unfortunately, another bundle of thirty galleys is going off to you to-day, and it is by no means the last.

I have finished; that is to say, the last of the manuscript has gone off. You can imagine the state of mind I am in—the increase of normal depression after the elation. Perhaps you do not read *Simplicissimus*, which I regularly enjoy. The following is a conversation between two officers. "Well, so you've got yourself engaged, have you ? And is your fiancée charming, beautiful, witty, sweet-natured ?" "Well, that's a matter of taste, but personally I don't like her !" That is my position entirely.[2]

As for the psychological part, I am leaving it to your judgment whether I should revise it again or let it go as it is.[3] The matter

---

[1] Friedjung (1897). For David see footnote, p. 291.
[2] See footnote, p. 284.
[3] The reference is obviously to Chapter VII of *The Interpretation of Dreams*.

about dreams I believe to be unassailable; what I dislike about it is the style. I was quite unable to express myself with noble simplicity, but lapsed into a facetious, circumlocutory straining after the picturesque. I know that, but the part of me that knows it and appraises it is unfortunately not the part that is productive.

It is certainly true that the dreamer is too ingenious and amusing, but it is not my fault, and I cannot be reproached with it. All dreamers are insufferably witty, and they have to be, because they are under pressure, and the direct way is barred to them. If you think so, I shall insert a remark to that effect somewhere.[1] The ostensible wit of all unconscious processes is closely connected with the theory of jokes and humour.[2]

Greetings to your wife and children. Perhaps we really shall see each other soon.

Your
Sigm.

119

Dr. Sigm. Freud,   Vienna, 21. 9. 99.
Lecturer in Nervous Diseases   IX. Berggasse 19.
   in the University.

My dear Wilhelm,

Here I am after a horrible thirty-two hour journey through water, sitting again in the familiar place with seven signatures of proofs in front of me, and no call from patients, and feeling very pleased over your letter with its good news. I find a kind of

---

[1] See the reference to this remark of Fliess's in *The Interpretation of Dreams*, p. 297n.
[2] What is meant is the relationship of jokes and the comic to the primary process and infantile life. This is the first hint of Freud's next interest, which was to be expressed in *Jokes and their Relation to the Unconscious* (1905 c). The origins of this interest can be traced even further back. See for instance the final footnote on the case history of Elizabeth von R. in *Studies on Hysteria*.

substitute for our frustrated meeting in the increased liveliness of our correspondence, and I hope that you will often still think of the living while you are excavating for the dead. As you rightly suspected, my depression left me, not after one migraine, but after a whole series of such states. But I do not think that my self-criticism was wholly unjustified. Somewhere inside me there is a feeling for form, an appreciation of beauty as a kind of perfection; and the tortuous sentences of the dream-book, with its high-flown, indirect phraseology, its squinting at the point, has sorely offended one of my ideals. And I do not think I am going far wrong if I interpret this lack of form as a sign of deficient mastery of the material. You must have felt this just as much as I did, and we have always been too honest with each other for either of us to have to resort to pretence in front of the other. The consolation lies in its inevitability—it just did not turn out any better. I am still sorry that I had to spoil it for my best and favourite reader by giving him the proofs to read, for how can one enjoy anything one has to read as a proof-reader? But unfortunately I cannot do without you as the representative of "other people", and—I have another sixty galleys for you.

And now for another year of this extraordinary life, in which one's state of mind is the only thing that really matters. Mine is wavering, but as you see, as it says on the city-arms of our dear Paris

Fluctuat nec mergitur.[1]

A patient with whom I have been in negotiation has just announced herself, whether to decline or accept treatment I do not know. My state of mind also depends very much on my earnings. . . . A thing I remember from my boyhood is that when wild horses on the pampas have been once lassoed, they retain a certain nervousness for life. In the same way I once knew helpless poverty and have a constant fear of it. You will see that my style will improve and my ideas be better when this town affords me a prosperous livelihood.

Do not trouble this time over checking quotations, etc., I

---

[1] Quoted below the title of *On the History of the Psycho-Analytic Movement* (1914 d).

have all the necessary literary aids at hand again. The climax of my achievements in dream interpretation comes in this instalment. Absurdity in dreams! It is astonishing how often you appear in them. In the *non vixit* dream I find I am delighted to have survived you;[1] is it not hard to have to hint at such things—to make them obvious, that is, to everyone who understands?

My wife and the children are staying in Berchtesgaden until the end of September. I still have not met little Pauline!

Cordial greetings,

Your

Sigm.

120

Dr. Sigm. Freud,   Vienna, 9. 10. 99.
Lecturer in Nervous Diseases   IX. Berggasse 19.
   in the University.

My dear Wilhelm,

. . . Just imagine it—I have been moved by obscure inner forces to read more psychological literature, and have found myself more at home in it than before. Recently I had the pleasure of finding a part of my hypothetical pleasure-unpleasure theory in an English writer, Marshall.[2] Other authors who come my way, however, are, I find, quite unfathomable.

My spirits are still holding up. Unburdening myself in the dream book must have done me good. . . . I should like to point out in reply to your remark about the acceleration of the practice that there are [not only expresses but] slow trains too. . . . The position is this. Even if my practice picks up to such an extent that I am fully occupied in November, for instance, my income this year, with the lean period from May 1st to the end of October (six months) will have been insufficient to cover our expenses. I have got to look round for something else, and I have now taken a step in a definite direction. During the summer

---

[1] *The Interpretation of Dreams*, p. 421 *sqq.*
[2] Marshall (1894 and 1895).

I propose to attach myself to some hydropathic establishment, and take rooms for the family near it. One such place is going to be opened on the Kobenzl, and the director suggested to me last year that I should take lodgings on the Bellevue (both are in the Kahlenberg neighbourhood.[1]) So I have written to him. In any case we shall have to give up the long summer holiday because of the children's schooling.

In this year's promotions (five professors at the end of September) our group, Königstein, myself, etc., were again passed over. . . .

All but three signatures of the dreams have been printed. The preface which I once showed you stands. . . .

With my cordial greetings to you all,

Your

Sigm.

121

Dr. Sigm. Freud,   11. 10. 99.
  IX. Berggasse 19.   Consulting hours 3-5 p.m.

My dear Wilhelm,

Mental apparatus. Φ

Hysteria—clinical.

Sexual-organic.

Curious things are at work in the bottom storey. A sexual theory may be the immediate successor to the dream book. Several very curious things struck me to-day, which I still do not properly understand. With me there can be no talk of steady deliberation. This kind of work advances intermittently. Heaven alone knows the date of the next surge—unless you have discovered my formula. If more comes of it, discussion and co-operation with you will be practically indispensable. The most extraordinary things are in prospect, some of which I suspected before and during the first stormy productive spell.

Ihr naht Euch wieder, schwankende Gestalten.[2] According to an

---

[1] In the suburbs of Vienna.

[2] ["Wavering phantoms, you approach again." The first line of the "Dedication" of Goethe's *Faust*.]

earlier calculation of yours 1900-1901 ought to be a productive
period for me (every seven-and-a-half years).

Your

Sigm.

122

Dr. Sigm. Freud,   Vienna, 27. 10. 99.
Lecturer in Nervous Diseases   IX. Berggasse 19.
   in the University.

My dear Wilhelm,

Thank you for the kind things you said on receipt of the
dream book. I have long since made my peace with the thing,
and I am awaiting its fate with—resigned curiosity. If the book
did not reach you punctually on your birthday, as I intended it
to, it was because of the unexpected circumstance that the post
office would accept it only as parcel post. We timed sending it off
as if it were a registered letter. So perhaps it arrived too late—
for others it would surely be too early. Incidentally, it is not yet
published, and only our two copies have so far seen the light.

Now, about the other five books I have in mind—we must
allow them time—a long stretch of time, and material, and
thought, and freedom from the most acute disturbances, and
heaven knows what else, besides an occasional mighty push
from "a friendly quarter". For the time being the thread is
broken again, hence the failure to answer your question. I am
seeking for the right point of attack. Pathological phenomena
are in the sexual field often compromise-formations, and are not
suitable for resolution. . . .

I shall startle you again with some enigmatic lines when something moves again in the sexual theory. Meanwhile I wish both
of you all happiness in what the year—and the century—may
bring. I mean in December!

With cordial greetings,

Your

Sigm.

123

Dr. Sigm. Freud,   5. 11. 99.
  IX. Berggasse 19.   Consulting hours 3-5 p.m.

My dear Wilhelm,

You cannot be called excessively communicative. I shall not imitate you, though a grievous uniformity does not make it any easier to write. The book at last came out yesterday. Hannibal's father's name—as I always knew and suddenly remembered recently—was Hamilcar, not Hasdrubal.[1] Practice and children are ailing alike. . . .

I should have liked to have written you something about the sexual theory, because I have something that looks plausible and is confirmed in practice; but I am baffled by the (*absit omen!*) feminine side, and that makes me mistrust the whole thing. Otherwise explanation comes slowly, now here, now there, as the day permits, on the whole rather indolently. One titbit is the explanation of how premonitory dreams arise and what they mean.[2] I hope to hear from you soon about yourself and how your wife and the children are,

                    Cordially,
                              Your
                                    Sigm.

124

Dr. Sigm. Freud,   12. 11. 99.
  IX. Berggasse 19.   Consulting hours 3-5 p.m.

My dear Wilhelm,

. . . . I shall of course arrange accommodation and nursing for Fräulein G., as I do for all foreign patients. Nothing seems

---

[1] The analysis of this and other errors deriving from the father-son relationship in *The Interpretation of Dreams* is given in *The Psychopathology of Everyday Life* (Chapter X). See also Letter 124.
[2] [No doubt a reference to the "premonitory dream" reported in a posthumously published paper dated 10. 11. 1899. [1941 c.]

to have come of the other two. I have heard no more of them.

People keep on pointing out comic mistakes in the dream book. I called Schiller's birthplace Marburg instead of Marbach, and I have already written to you about Hannibal's father, whom I called Hasdrubal instead of Hamilcar. They are of course not the results of defective memory but displacements, symptoms. The critics will find nothing better to do than to fasten on these pieces of carelessness—which they are not.

Everyone is at last well again for once.

Now that all danger is over, please write and tell me what was the matter with the child.

Cordially,

Your

Sigm.

125

Dr. Sigm. Freud,   Vienna, 9. 12. 99.
Lecturer in Nervous Diseases   IX. Berggasse 19.
   in the University.

My dear Wilhelm,

My thirst for personal details about you having been some-what assuaged by your recent presence here, I can apply myself contentedly again to things of the mind.

Perhaps I have recently achieved a first glimpse into something new. I am up against the problem of the "choice of neurosis". What makes a person a hysteric instead of a paranoiac? My first crude answer, at the time when I was still trying to take the citadel by storm, was that I thought it depended on the age at which the sexual traumas occurred—on the time of the experience.[1] I gave that up long ago, and have been without any clue until the last few days, when a connection with sexual theory opened up.

The lowest of the sexual strata is auto-erotism, which re-nounces any psychosexual aim and seeks only local gratification.

---

[1] See p. 163 *sqq.*

This is superseded by allo-erotism (homo- and hetero-), but undoubtedly survives as an independent tendency. Hysteria (and its variant, obsessional neurosis) is allo-erotic; the main highway it follows is identification with the loved person. Paranoia dissolves the identification again, re-establishes all the loved persons of childhood (compare the discussion of exhibitionistic dreams) and dissolves the ego itself into extraneous persons. So I have come to regard paranoia as a surge forward of the auto-erotic tendency, a regression to a former state.[1] The corresponding perverse formation would be so-called primary insanity. The special relation of auto-erotism to the original ego would throw light on the character of this neurosis. At this point the thread has broken again.

Two of my patients have almost simultaneously arrived at self-reproach over the nursing and death of their parents, and shown me that my dreams about this were typical. The guilt is in such cases connected with revenge feelings, malicious pleasure at the patient's sufferings, the patient's excretory difficulties (both urine and stools). Truly an unsuspected corner of mental life. . . .

14.12.   It is indeed unusual that you should have written before I did. The dreariness of the last few days prevented me from finishing. A Christmas time at which one must refrain from buying things is rather depressing. We know that Vienna is not the right place for us. Decency required my not taking you from your family too much. The older claim and the more heartfelt one were in conflict. So my good-bye at the station was only a symbol.

Your news of the dozen Berlin readers pleases me greatly. I have readers here too; the time is not yet ripe for followers. There is too much that is new and incredible, and too little strict proof. I did not even convince my philosopher,[2] even while he was providing me with the most admirable confirmatory

---

[1] This statement is a pointer towards the subsequently recognized connection between narcissism and the group of schizophrenic psychoses.

[2] Dr. Heinrich Gomperz, subsequently professor of philosophy in Vienna and Los Angeles, with whom Freud discussed problems of dream interpretation. Gomperz died in 1939.

material. Intelligence is always weak, and it is easy for a philosopher to transform resistance into discovering logical refutations.

There is an immediate prospect of a new case.

Health reigns among us, except for my cold. I shall write
again before your new arrival comes.

Cordial greetings to them all,

Your

Sigm.

126

Dr. Sigm. Freud,   Vienna, 21. 12. 99.
Lecturer in Nervous Diseases   IX. Berggasse 19.
    in the University.

My dear Wilhelm,

Another line of best wishes for Christmas—which used to be
one of our congress-times. I am not without *one* happy prospect.
You remember (among the absurd dreams)[1] my dream which so
daringly promised an end of E.'s treatment, and you can
imagine how important this one continuing patient has become
to me. Well, the dream now seems to be coming true. I say
cautiously "seems" so, but I am pretty confident about it.
Buried deep beneath all his phantasies we found a scene from
his primal period (before twenty-two months) which meets all
requirements and into which all the surviving puzzles flow. It
is everything at the same time—sexual, innocent, natural, etc.
I can hardly bring myself to believe it yet. It is as if Schliemann
had dug up another Troy which had hitherto been believed to be
mythical. Also the fellow is feeling shamelessly well. He has

---

[1] "Another absurd dream about a dead father." See *The Interpretation of
Dreams*, p. 435.

demonstrated the truth of my theories in my own person, for with a surprising turn [in his analysis] he provided me with the solution of my own railway phobia (which I had overlooked). . . . My phobia, if you please, was a poverty, or rather a hunger phobia, arising out of my infantile gluttony and called up by the circumstance that my wife had no dowry (of which I am proud). You will hear more about all this at our next congress.[1]

Otherwise there is little news. The book has had just one notice, in the *Gegenwart*. As criticism it is empty and as a review inadequate. It is just a bad patchwork of my own fragments, but I forgive it everything because of the one word "epoch-making". Otherwise the attitude of people here in Vienna is very negative. I do not believe I shall get a review here. We are terribly far ahead of our time. . . .

I lack the strength for theoretical work at the moment, so I am dreadfully bored in the evening. This year I am learning what it means to freeze, an experience which had previously escaped me. I can hardly write for the cold in my cellar.

This last page is added only to ask how things are with you and yours, particularly little Pauline. I hope her thriving period has begun. . . .

Oscar[2] comes daily to see Mathilde because of an abscess. The children are otherwise well and vigorous. Martin is putting up well with school and Oli is at the top of his form and taking everything in his stride.

So I am growing old, patiently waiting for fresh developments. A congress would be a magnificent break—but on Italian soil for once.

Cordial greetings from

Your

Sigm.

---

[1] See also Letter 70 of 3. 10. 97.
[2] Dr. Oscar Rie, a former collaborator of Freud's.

127

Dr. Sigm. Freud,   Vienna, 8. 1. 1900.
Lecturer in Nervous Diseases   IX. Bergasse 19.
  in the University.

My dear Wilhelm,

I am delighted to hear news of my friend Conrad.[1] I should like to announce straight away after this first small test of his behaviour that he is a fine fellow. Whether he models himself on his name as he goes through life or on the remarkable circumstances of his birth as celebrated by me, I believe I can foresee that there is something capable and reliable about him, and that he will succeed in whatever he undertakes. I propose to make his personal acquaintance as soon as he is over the worst.

The new century—the most interesting thing about which for us is, I dare say, that it contains the dates of our death—has brought me nothing but a stupid review in the *Zeit*[2] by Burckhard, the former director of the Burgtheater (not to be confused with our old Jacob). It is unflattering, uncommonly lacking in understanding and—most annoying of all—is to be continued in the next number.

I do not count on recognition, at any rate in my lifetime. May you have better luck! At least you can address yourself to a better-mannered audience, trained to think in your subject. I have to deal in dark matters with people I am ten to fifteen years in advance of, who will never catch me up. So all I seek is peace and a little material comfort. I am not working, and it is quiet inside me. If the sexual theory comes up, I shall listen to it.[3] If

---

[1] Fliess's son Conrad had recently been born.

[2] Max Burckhard's review, an ironic and malicious journalistic distortion of Freud's ideas, appeared in *Die Zeit*, a Vienna daily newspaper, on January 6th and 13th, 1900, under the heading "A New Dream Book".

[3] Freud had gained insight into the way his mind worked and its relation to the preconscious. He experienced the surge forward from the preconscious as a process similar to that of "inspiration"; see Kris (1940 and 1952). In a letter to Karl Abraham of 11.12.1914 Freud wrote: "Previously my way of working was different. I used to wait for an idea to come to me. Now I go and meet it, and I do not know whether I find it any faster on that account."

not, not. In the evenings I read prehistory, etc., without any serious purpose, and otherwise my only concern is to lead my cases calmly further towards solution. . . . In E.'s case the second real scene is coming up after years of preparation, and it is one that it may *perhaps* be possible to confirm objectively by asking his elder sister. Behind it there is a third, long-suspected scene. . . .

It is sad how things keep going downwards here. Just imagine it, on January 1st, when the krone currency was introduced,[1] no postcards (which were to cost five hellers) were available. But the post office insisted on a surcharge for use of the old ones with the two-kreuzer stamps, though no one-heller stamps were available to put on them. The new five and ten kroner gold pieces will not be in circulation till the end of March. That is Austria in a nutshell. Some day you will have to take a few of my sons to Berlin for my sake, to give them a chance of getting on in the world.

Now do not let another long interval like this happen again (December 24th—January 7th$=14=\frac{28}{2}$), and give cordial greetings from all of us to your wife as the happy mother of three.

Your
Sigm.

128

Vienna, 26. 1. 1900.
IX. Berggasse 19.

Dr. Sigm. Freud,
Lecturer in Nervous Diseases
  in the University.

My dear Wilhelm,

. . . Nothing is really happening. When I think that since May '99, I have had only one new case, which you know about, and that I am going to lose four patients between April and May, I cannot feel exactly cheerful. How I am to get through

---

[1] The krone currency was introduced on January 1st, 1900, to take the place of the gulden currency at the rate of two kronen for one gulden.

I do not yet know, but I am determined to stick it out. Dislike of grumbling has been another reason for writing less often. Nothing else has happened about the book since the review in the *Zeit*, which showed no understanding but unfortunately also no respect. For the summer we are arranging to go to the Bellevue at Grinzing again; I have dropped the idea of summer work as hopeless.

The work is going well; it is not so strenuous as it used to be. . . .

New ideas come slowly, but there is always something moving. E. is marking time again, in a darker region; the earlier acquisitions still stand. I am collecting material for the sexual theory and waiting for a spark to set fire to the pile.

We are reading a book (by Frey) on the life of your C. F. Meyer. He does not know the intimate side, or withholds it through discretion, and there is little to be read between the lines.

It only remains to say that we want to know how things are going with you and your no longer little family. While waiting for news of them, cordial greetings from

Your

Sigm.

129

Dr. Sigm. Freud,   Vienna, 12. 2. 1900.
Lecturer in Nervous Diseases   IX. Berggasse 19.
   in the University.

My dear Wilhelm,

If at present I keep suppressing my need of a more frequent exchange of ideas with you, it is to avoid troubling you with my complaints while you are still under the influence of your mother's continuing illness. . . .

I feel almost ashamed of writing to you only about myself. There is so much that can be said but not written.

During the past week I have been a little busier. The period in which I saw only one patient in five consulting hours (and five altogether) seems to be over. To-day I actually started another treatment, though I cannot tell if it will last. Also my depression lifted to-day. If I could once tell you what changes I still have to keep making in my ideas *i.e.*, what errors I still find to correct, and how difficult it all is, you would probably feel very lenient about my neurotic vacillations, particularly if you also took my financial worries into account. . . .

I have not the slightest objection to learning the piece of nasal therapy from you when we find the opportunity for it one day, but it is very difficult to carry through anything new here, and there is a difficulty in myself as well. You have no idea how hard I find it to learn anything, and how easy it strikes you when you can do it.

On the whole I am further away from Rome than at any time since we met, and the freshness of youth is notably declining. The journey is long, the stations at which one can be thrown out are very numerous, and it is still a matter of "if I can last out".

Best wishes, and write soon to

Your
Sigm.

130

Vienna, Sunday, 11. 3. 1900.
IX. Berggasse 19.

Dr. Sigm. Freud,
Lecturer in Nervous Diseases
  in the University.

My dear Wilhelm,

A long letter from you at last! I had not heard from you since February 15th, it was your turn to write, and apparently you did not receive a card I sent you at the beginning of March, mentioning the book by Jonas on nasogenous reflex neuroses. . . .

Now I am delighted to hear so much about you, because I think you would be just as sorry as I should be if our correspondence dried up and our meetings came to an end. I was astonished to read that three weeks had passed since I had written. Time has been slipping by so unnoticeably, almost comfortably under my new régime, of which you shall hear.

The children have all been well, Martha has been brighter than usual, and my health has been excellent—regulated by a slight migraine on Sundays. I have been seeing the same people every day, and last week actually started a new case, which is still in the trial stage and perhaps will not get beyond it. I have been as good as cut off from the outside world; not a leaf has stirred to show that the interpretation of dreams meant anything to anyone. But yesterday I was astonished to find a really friendly *feuilleton* article in a newspaper, the *Wiener Fremdenblatt*. . . .

On the whole things are going well with my patients. It is my busy time now, 70 to 80 florins a day, about 500 a week. This, to judge by experience, will be cut short at Easter. I could not fix anything up for the summer. There was nothing to be done, and that is true in general. It is a pity to waste one's energy. That is the key to the situation.

I should like to go away for three days at Easter, and most of all I should like to see you. But I am as hungry as a young man for the spring, and sun, and flowers, and a stretch of blue water. I hate Vienna with a positively personal hatred, and, just the contrary of the giant Antaeus, I draw fresh strength whenever I remove my feet from the soil of the city which is my home. For the children's sake I shall have to renounce distance and mountains, and enjoy the constant view of Vienna from Bellevue. I do not know whether I shall be able to afford a trip in September, so I very much want to get a taste of the beauty of the world at Easter. . . .

If you want to hear any more about me, listen to this. After the exaltation and feverish activity in which I finished the dreams last summer, I was stupid enough to be intoxicated with the hope that it meant a step towards freedom and prosperity. The book's reception, and the silence since, have once more destroyed any budding relationship with my environment. My second iron in the fire is my daily work, the prospect of reaching an end somewhere, solving many doubts, and then knowing what to think of the therapeutic outlook. Prospects seemed most favourable in E.'s case, and it was there that I had the heaviest blow. Just when I thought I had the solution it eluded my grasp, and I was confronted with the necessity of turning everything upside down and putting it together again afresh, losing in the process all the hypotheses that until then had seemed plausible. I could not stand up to the depression of all this. I soon found that it was impossible to continue the really difficult work in the face of depression and lurking doubts. When I am not cheerful and master of myself, every single one of my patients is a tormenting spirit to me. I really thought I should have to give in. I adopted the expedient of renouncing working by conscious thought, so as to grope my way further into the riddles only by blind touch. Since I started this I have been doing my work, perhaps more skilfully than before, but I do not really know what I am doing. I could not give an account of how matters really stand. In my spare time I take care to avoid thinking. I abandon myself to my phantasies, play chess, read English novels; everything serious is banned. For months past I have not written down a line of anything I have learned or suspected. When my work is over I live like a pleasure-seeking Philistine. You know how limited my pleasures are. I must not smoke heavy cigars, alcohol does not mean anything to me, I have finished with begetting children, and I am cut off from contact with people. So I vegetate harmlessly, carefully diverting my attention from the contents of my daily work. Under this régime I keep cheerful and can deal with my eight victims and tormentors.

On Saturday evenings I indulge in an orgy of taroc, and I spend every other Tuesday evening among my Jewish brethren, to whom I recently gave another lecture.[1] So I am all right

---

[1] Freud remained faithful throughout his life to his weekly game of cards—taroc. He described his relations with the B'nai B'rith as follows in his reply to an address on the occasion of his seventieth birthday (1941 e):

"It happened that in 1895 I was subjected simultaneously to two powerful convergent influences. On the one hand I had obtained my first glimpses into the depths of the instinctual life of man, and had seen things calculated to sober or even to frighten me. On the other hand the publication of my disagreeable discoveries led to the severance of the greater part of my human contacts: I felt as though I were despised and shunned by everyone. In this loneliness I was seized with a longing for a circle of chosen men of high character who would receive me in a friendly spirit in spite of my temerity. Your society was pointed out to me as the place where such men were to be found."

until Easter, when several treatments will be broken off and another time of discomfort will begin.

By now you will have had enough. If I ever meet you in Rome or Karlsbad, I shall ask you to forgive me for the many complaints which I have scattered on the way.

Give my cordial greetings to your wife and children. . . .

Your

Sigm.

131

Dr. Sigm. Freud,   Vienna, 23. 3. 1900.
Lecturer in Nervous Diseases   IX. Berggasse 19.
  in the University.

My dear Wilhelm,

I must write to you at length again. Otherwise what would you think of me ? First of all, many thanks for your hospitality to Minna. At last I have some real information about your family again: that your mother is well again—contrary to my expectation and so doubly a relief—and how pretty little Pauline is, and how sturdy Conrad is getting, to say nothing of our old friend Robert and his *apta dicta*. Now I feel again that I have a good picture of it all. I heard with great satisfaction that your interest in my dream-child is unabated, and that you lent your hand to stirring up the *Rundschau* and its indolent reviewers. After a good deal of wavering, I have now come down on the side of being very grateful to you for standing godfather to it, and of thinking it good and sound. It has been a consolation to me in many a gloomy hour to know that I have this book to leave behind me. True, its reception—certainly the reception it has had so far—has not given me any pleasure. It has met with the most meagre understanding, any praise that has been bestowed has been as meagre as charity, most people clearly dislike it, and I have not yet seen any trace that anyone has detected what is important in it. I tell myself that this is because I am fifteen or twenty years ahead of my time. Then of course I feel the usual qualms associated with forming a judgment about oneself.

There has never been a period in which the wish that we lived in the same place as you and your family has affected me so deeply and constantly as in the past six months. You know I have been going through a deep inner crisis, and if we met you would see how it has aged me. So I was deeply touched when I was told of your proposal that we should meet at Easter. Anyone who did not understand the more subtle resolution of contradictions would think it incomprehensible that I am not hastening to assent to the proposal. In point of fact it is more probable that I shall avoid you—not only because of my almost childish yearning for the spring and the beauties of nature, which I should willingly sacrifice for the pleasure of your company for three days. But there are other, inner reasons, an accumulation of imponderables, which weigh heavily on me. . . . Inwardly I am deeply impoverished. I have had to demolish all my castles in the air, and I have just plucked up enough courage to start rebuilding them. During the catastrophic collapse you would have been invaluable to me; in the present stage I should hardly be able to make myself intelligible to you. I conquered my depression with the aid of a special intellectual diet, and now, under the influence of the distraction, it is slowly healing. In your company I should inevitably attempt to grasp everything consciously and tell you all about it, we should talk rationally and scientifically, and your fine and positive biological discoveries would rouse my innermost (impersonal) envy. The upshot would be that I should unburden my woes to you for the whole five days and come back agitated and dissatisfied for the summer, for which I shall probably need all my composure. No one can help me in what oppresses me, it is my cross, which I must bear, and heaven knows my back is getting noticeably bent under it. . . .

My plan for Easter is to go with Alexander to Trent and from there to Lake Garda, and to snatch a few glimpses of spring in travelling such a long way. We shall set off three weeks to-day, if nothing intervenes, and live for four days as students and tourists, as we always do. . . .

Last week we heard a lecture by G. Brandes,[1] on reading. The subject was nothing out of the way, the lecture difficult, the voice harsh, the pronunciation foreign—but the man was refreshing. The whole thing must have seemed pretty outlandish to the worthy Viennese; he treated them to nothing but raw home-truths. Such a severe conception of life is unknown to us; our petty logic, and our petty conventionality, are different from their northern equivalents. I revelled in it, and Martha . . . persuaded me to send a copy of the dream book to his hotel. So far there has been no response—perhaps he actually took it home to read.

Best wishes to you and Ida and the children. I hope to hear from you soon and to write several times again before Easter.

Your devoted
Sigm.

132

Dr. Sigm. Freud,   Vienna, 4. 4. 1900.
Lecturer in Nervous Diseases   IX. Berggasse 19.
   in the University.

My dear Wilhelm,

Expression of one's feelings can be delayed, but practical matters have to be attended to. So let me tell you at once that I have no intention of writing a miniature dream book for the *Rundschau*. I have a number of reasons. In the first place, after the big work it would be a difficult and disagreeable task. Secondly, I have promised an essay of the kind for Löwenfeld,[2] so I cannot send it anywhere else. In the third place it would clash with the principle of division of labour by which one man writes a book and another reviews it, which gives the reader the

---

[1] Georg Brandes, the Danish author and critic (1842-1927).
[2] See p. 321.

benefit of criticism and the author of seeing what effect his work has on the mind of a stranger. Fourthly, and lastly, the *Rundschau* should not, after all, be forced to carry a review against its will. An unwilling reviewer turns at once into a hostile one. That seems to have been the secret of Burkhard's review in the *Zeit*, which, in spite of all its stupidity, killed the book in Vienna. Fifthly, I want to avoid anything that savours of advertisement. I know that my work is odious to most people. So long as I behave perfectly correctly, my opponents are at a loss. If I once start doing the same as they do, they will regain their confidence that my work is no better than theirs. It was for reasons such as these that I refrained some time ago from reviewing your book, which otherwise I should very much have liked to do. People shall not say that we scratch each other's backs. So I think the most advisable course is quietly to accept the *Rundschau's* refusal as an incontrovertible sign of public opinion.

Mathilde is in bed with chicken-pox, and is accordingly feeling not very ill; the others are all well. Thanks to Minna's visit, we are informed about the minor misfortunes in your household. . . . E. finishes at Easter, having derived great benefit, I hope. I am still too lazy to write anything. I had to send my last new case away after a fortnight—it was a paranoia.

With my cordial greetings to you, your wife, daughter and sons,

Your

Sigm.

133

Dr. Sigm. Freud,   Vienna, 16. 4. 1900.
Lecturer in Nervous Diseases   IX. Berggasse 19.
    in the University.

My dear Wilhelm,

Herewith greetings, as arranged, from the land of sunshine. Once more I have failed to get there. . . .

E. at last concluded his career as a patient by coming to supper in my house. His riddle is *almost* completely solved, he feels extremely well, and his nature is entirely changed; for the moment a residue of symptoms remains. I am beginning to see that the apparent endlessness of the treatment is something of an inherent feature and is connected with the transference.[1] I am hoping that this residue will not detract from the practical success. I could have continued the treatment if I had wanted to, but it dawned on me that such prolongation is a compromise between illness and health which patients themselves desire, and that the physician must therefore not lend himself to it. I am not in the least worried by the asymptotic conclusion of the treatment; it is more a disappointment to outsiders than anything else. In any case I shall keep my eye on the man. As he had to participate in all my technical and theoretical mistakes, I think that another similar case would take only half the time. May the Lord send it soon. . . .

At the moment I feel some stirrings towards synthesis, but I am holding them down.

Otherwise Vienna is Vienna, that is to say extremely revolting. If I closed with "Next Easter in Rome",[2] I should feel like a pious Jew. So until we meet in the summer or autumn, in Berlin or where you will,

Cordial greetings,

Your Sigm.

---

[1] This is the first insight into the role of transference in psycho-analytic therapy. Freud had been familiar with the difficulties arising from transference phenomena ever since the days when he still practised hypnotic therapy (see *An Autobiographical Study*, 1925 d). We know from the *Fragment of an Analysis of a Case of Hysteria* (1905 e), which gives us information about Freud's technique during the period when this letter was written, that he had not yet learned technically how to overcome the transference. Freud for the first time developed the theory of the transference in the postscript to that paper. The lack of a complete understanding of the dynamics of the transference accounts for the personal contacts with several of his patients which Freud was having at about this time.

[2] [At the end of the Passover service orthodox Jews wish each other: "Next year in Jerusalem! "]

134

Dr. Sigm. Freud,   Vienna, 7. 5. 1900.
Lecturer in Nervous Diseases   IX. Berggasse 19.
   in the University.

My dear Wilhelm,

Many thanks for your kind words. They are so pleasant to
hear that—if I were in your company—I might almost believe
some of them. However, I look at things a little differently. I
should have no objection to the fact of splendid isolation,[1] if it
were not carried too far and did not come between you and me.
On the whole—except for one weak point, my fear of poverty—I
have too much sense to complain, and at present I feel too well
to want to do so; I know well what blessings I have, and I know
how little, if one takes the statistics of human want into account,
one has a right to lay claim to. But there can be no substitute for
the close contact with a friend which a particular—almost a
feminine—side of me calls for, and the inner voices to which I
am accustomed to listen suggest a much more modest estimate
of my work than that which you proclaim. When your book[2] is
published none of us will be able to pass the judgment on it
which, as in the case of all great new achievements, is reserved
for posterity; but the beauty of the conception, the originality of
the ideas, the simple coherence of the whole and the conviction
with which it is written will create an impression which will
provide the first compensation for the arduous wrestling with
the demon. With me it is different. No critic . . . can see more
clearly than I the disproportion there is between the problems
and my answers to them, and it will be a fitting punishment for
me that none of the unexplored regions of the mind in which I
have been the first mortal to set foot will ever bear my name or
submit to my laws. When breath threatened to fail me in the
struggle I prayed the angel to desist, and that is what he has
done since then. But I did not turn out to be the stronger,

---

[1] [These two words in English in the original.]
[2] *Die Periodenlehre,* Fliess's book on the period theory.

though since then I have been noticeably limping. Well, I really am forty-four now, a rather shabby old Jew, as you will see for yourself in the summer or autumn. My family insisted on celebrating my birthday. My own best consolation is that I have not stolen a march on them in respect of the whole future. The world is still there for them to conquer, so far as may be in their power. I leave them only a foothold; I have not led them to a mountain-peak from which they could climb no higher.

On Saturday I start the lecture on dreams. In ten days we shall be going to Bellevue. . . .

My state of health is now tolerable. It has suddenly grown unbearably hot in Vienna. . . . I have a new patient, probably only for the summer; he is psychologically impotent. Also there are a number of prospects which have not yet matured. Generally speaking, things are stirring a little.

With cordial greetings to the whole family,

Your

Sigm.

135

Dr. Sigm. Freud,   Vienna, 16. 5. 1900.
Lecturer in Nervous Diseases   IX. Berggasse 19.
   in the University.

My dear Wilhelm,

. . . An evening patient has left me. It was my most difficult case, and the most certain in regard to ætiology; for four years I could not get near it, and it was the only case sent me by Breuer. He kept sending the girl back to me after I had sent her away in blank despair. Last year I at last managed to get on terms with her, and this year I at last succeeded in finding the key, *i.e.*, convinced myself that keys found elsewhere fitted her and, so far as the short time (December until now) permitted, I have deeply and vitally altered her condition. She took leave of me to-day with the words: "You've done wonders for me". She told me that, when she told Breuer of her extraordinary improvement, he clapped his hands and exclaimed again and again: "So he is right after all!" . . .

I have an audience of only three, Hans Königstein, Fräulein Dora Teleky, and a Dr. Marcuse from Breslau. The bookseller complains that the *Interpretation of Dreams* is going slowly. The *Umschau* of March 10th contained a short, friendly and uncomprehending review. But I am naturally dominated only by the work, and I am prepared to be entirely one-idea'd if only I can carry it through. . . .

Cordially,

Your

Sigm.

136

Dr. Sigm. Freud,   Vienna, 20. 5. 1900.
Lecturer in Nervous Diseases   IX. Berggasse 19.
   in the University.

My dear Wilhelm,

. . . The dead season, of which I am afraid—or rather, in which I am afraid of myself, is just starting. The fourth patient said good-bye yesterday, on excellent terms and in a very good state, and gave me Böcklin's "Island of the Dead",[1] as a parting gift. This case gave me great satisfaction, and is perhaps completed. So things have gone well this year. I won in the end. But what am I to do now? I still have three-and-a-half patients, that is to say sessions a day, which is too light a load for the whale. Woe is me when I am bored. All sorts of things might happen to me. I cannot work. I am penetrated through and through with laziness; the kind of work that I have been doing from October until now is so unlike the kind that leads to writing and so

---

[1] Reading uncertain. [Böcklin was a well-known Swiss painter.]

unfavourable to it. I have not even started the little dream pamphlet for Löwenfeld.[1] I do not stick even to my hobbies, but alternate between chess, art history and prehistory, but keep at none of them for long. I should like to disappear for a few weeks to somewhere where science does not exist—apart, of course, from the congress with you. If only I had money or a travelling companion for Italy!

I hope your visit to Vienna will not be at Whitsun, as my eldest brother from Manchester has written and said he is coming then. He is no longer a youth, I think he is sixty-eight, though he is very young in appearance.

My cordial greetings,

Your

Sigm.

137

Dr. Sigm. Freud,   Vienna, 12. 6. 1900.
Lecturer in Nervous Diseases   IX. Berggasse 19.
  in the University.

My dear Wilhelm,

We have had family visitors. My eldest brother Emanuel arrived the day before Whitsun, with his youngest son Sam, who is over thirty-five, and stayed till Wednesday evening. It was very refreshing to have him here, because he is a fine fellow, brisk and vigorous in spite of his sixty-eight or sixty-nine years, and he has always meant a great deal to me. He went off to Berlin, which is now the family headquarters. . . .

Life at Bellevue is turning out very pleasantly for everyone. The evenings and mornings are delightful, the scent of acacia and jasmine has succeeded that of lilac and laburnum, the wild

---

[1] See p. 315. The work referred to is the booklet "On Dreams" (1901 a).

roses are in bloom, and everything, as even I notice, seems suddenly to have burst out.

Do you suppose that some day a marble tablet will be placed on the house, inscribed with these words:

> In this house on July 24th, 1895,
>
> the Secret of Dreams was revealed to
>
> Dr. Sigmund Freud[1]

At this moment I see little prospect of it. But when I read the latest psychological books (Mach's *Analyse der Empfindungen*, second edition, Kroell's *Aufbau der Seele*, etc.) all of which have the same kind of aims as my work, and see what they have to say about dreams, I am as delighted as the dwarf in the fairy tale because "the princess doesn't know".

I have no new cases, or rather I have one, which replaces one that started in May but dropped out again, so I am back where I was before. But the new case is an interesting one, a girl of thirteen whom I am supposed to cure at high speed and who for once displays on the surface the things I generally have to unearth from beneath superimposed layers. I do not need to tell you that it is the usual thing. We shall discuss the child in August, unless the treatment is broken off prematurely. For see you in August I shall, unless I am disappointed of the 1,500 kronen which I expect on July 1st. Or rather I shall come to Berlin anyway and . . . also get myself some refreshment and new energy for 1901 in the mountains or in Italy. A bad mental state is no more productive than economizing is.

News has reached me of Conrad's accident and of the happy outcome. I have a right to hear news about you and yours again.

My cordial greetings to you and to them.

Your

Sigm.

---

[1] In the "Dream of Irma's Injection," *The Interpretation of Dreams*, pp. 106-121.

138

Dr. Sigm. Freud,   Vienna, 10. 7. 1900.
Lecturer in Nervous Diseases   IX. Berggasse 19.
   in the University.

My dear Wilhelm,

It is easily settled after all. As you could not give me a fixed
date and I had one, I suggested postponing our congress to
later in the holidays. Now that you have told me what your
arrangements are, I can only reply that they suit me splendidly.
I can be at Innsbruck on July 31st and stay there with you until
August 4th, when our wives can join us and I can go on with
Martha to Landeck, from where we can drive by carriage to
Trafoi. If no child falls sick, no bridge breaks, etc., that is what
we shall do. My own slight regret is that I shall again miss seeing
the children; also that you will see me at the peak of exhaustion
and staleness. But the great thing is that we shall meet; every
postponement involves further risks. You have told me nothing
about your further intentions, so I do not know whether it
might be possible to fix up anything else during these holidays.
But this is settled anyway, and I am delighted about it, after
having had nothing to be delighted about for a long time. . . .
I am completely exhausted with work and with everything connected with it that is germinating, tempting and threatening.
The summer has not been too bad after all. The question of
getting summer work, which seemed a problem a year ago, has
now settled itself. On the one hand it is quite unnecessary, and
on the other I have not the strength for it. The big problems are
still unsettled. It is an intellectual hell, layer upon layer of it,
with everything fitfully gleaming and pulsating; and the outline
of Lucifer-Amor coming into sight at the darkest centre.

People's opinions on the dream book are beginning to leave
me cold, and I am beginning to bewail its fate. The stone is

apparently not being worn down by the dripping. I have not heard of any more reviews, and the nice things said to me from time to time by people I meet annoy me more than the general silent condemnation. I myself have so far found nothing to alter in it. It is true and remains true. I have postponed the short essay on the subject until October.

At any rate our meeting on July 31st or August 1st is a ray of light. Let us stick to it firmly. Details can be settled later. Perhaps instead of Innsbruck we might choose another place on the same line. But it does not matter.[1]

With cordial greetings to your wife and children,

Your

Sigm.

---

[1] This was the last meeting before the latent estrangement between the two men became manifest.

Freud's reaction to the meeting will be seen from subsequent letters. Fliess subsequently gave his version of it as follows:

"I often used to have meetings with Freud for scientific discussions. In Berlin, Vienna, Salzburg, Dresden, Nuremberg, Breslau, Innsbruck, for instance. The last meeting was at Achensee in the summer of 1900. On that occasion Freud showed a violence towards me which was at first unintelligible to me. The reason was that in a discussion of Freud's observations of his patients I claimed that periodic processes were unquestionably at work in the psyche, as elsewhere; and maintained in particular that they had an effect on those pyschopathic phenomena on the analysis of which Freud was engaged for therapeutic purposes. Hence neither sudden deteriorations nor sudden improvements were to be attributed to the analysis and its influence alone. I supported my view with my own observations. During the rest of the discussion I thought I detected a personal animosity against me on Freud's part which sprang from envy. Freud had earlier said to me in Vienna: 'It's just as well that we're friends. Otherwise I should burst with envy if I heard that anyone was making such discoveries in Berlin!' In my astonishment I told my wife about this exclamation at the time, as well as our friend, Frau Hofkapell-meister Schalk, *née* Hopfen, who was then in Vienna and will gladly confirm it.

"The result of the situation at Achensee in the summer of 1900 was that I quietly withdrew from Freud and dropped our regular correspondence. Since that time Freud has heard no more from me about my scientific findings, but in the same year, 1900, during which he complained about my withdrawal, he made the acquaintance of Weininger's friend Swoboda and treated him for a psycho-neurosis. During this treatment Swoboda became acquainted with the fact of persistent bisexuality which, as Freud himself states, has, since I talked to him about it, come to be regularly discussed in the course of his psychoneurotic treatment." (Fliess, 1906).

139

Dr. Sigm. Freud,   Vienna, 14. 10. 1900.
Lecturer in Nervous Diseases   IX. Berggasse 19.
    in the University.

My dear Wilhelm,

Your wife and child must be back again by now, and you will have heard that I saw and spoke to both of them again for a moment. Robert was enchanting. . . .

I hope to hear your news. I am writing the dream pamphlet without real enjoyment and am becoming an absent-minded professor while collecting material for the psychology of every-day life. It has been a lively time, and I have a new patient, a girl of eighteen;[1] the case has opened smoothly to my collection of picklocks.

For the psychology of everyday life I should like to borrow from you the superb quotation: *Nun ist die Welt von diesem Spuk so voll.*[2]. . . . Otherwise I am reading Greek archæology and revelling in journeys which I shall never make and treasures which I shall never possess. . . .

With cordial greetings,
Your
Sigm.

P.S.—There was a review of the dream book in the *Münchner Allgemeine Zeitung* of October 12th.

140

Dr. Sigm. Freud,   Vienna, 25. 1. 1901.
Lecturer in Nervous Diseases   IX. Berggasse 19.
    in the University.

My dear Wilhelm,

. . . I finished "Dreams and Hysteria" yesterday, and the

---

[1] [This must have been "Dora", whose analysis is referred to in the next letter.]
[2] "The world is now so full of this bogy . . ." This quotation [in its correct form *Nun ist die Luft von solchem Spuk so voll* ("the air is now so full of such a bogy")] from Goethe's *Faust*, Part II, Act 5, appears on the title-page of *The Psychopathology of Everyday Life*.

consequence is that to-day I feel short of a drug. It is a fragment of an analysis of a hysteria, in which the interpretations are grouped round two dreams, so it is really a continuation of the dream book.[1] It also contains resolutions of hysterical symptoms and glimpses of the sexual-organic foundation of the whole. All the same, it is the subtlest thing I have so far written, and will put people off even more than usual. But one does one's duty, and does not write just for the day alone. Ziehen has already accepted it,[2] not suspecting that I shall soon inflict *The Psychopathology of Everyday Life* upon him too. How long Wernicke puts up with these cuckoo's eggs is his business.[3]

My cordial greetings, and I hope to hear soon that your oppression has lifted.

Your devoted

Sigm.

141

Dr. Sigm. Freud,   Vienna, 30. I. 1901.
Lecturer in Nervous Diseases   IX. Berggasse 19.
 in the University.

My dear Wilhelm,

 . . . "Dream and Hysteria" should not disappoint you, so far as it goes. The chief thing in it is again psychology, the

---

[1] It was published as a "Fragment of a Case of Hysteria" (1905 e). Freud mentions in the foreword that the paper had originally been called "Dreams and Hysteria", and that he had deliberately put the utilization of dreams in the foreground. In "On the History of the Psycho-Analytic Movement" and in a footnote added in 1933 to the preface to the "Fragment" Freud says that the analysis of the case described was broken off on December 31st, 1899. Freud also mentions that the case history was written down in the following two weeks. This passage shows that Freud was mistaken and that the analysis ended on December 31st, 1900 [as is also proved by internal evidence in the case history itself.]

[2] Freud mentioned in the letter of May 8th that he could not make up his mind to send off the manuscript. In the end he sent if off (letter of June 9th), but then asked for it to be returned.

[3] Freud is referring to the fact that his recent works (since "Screen Memories") had appeared in the *Monatsschrift für Psychiatrie und Neurologie*, which was edited by Ziehen and Wernicke, though at any rate Wernicke was opposed to his views; Ziehen's opposition developed only later.

utilization of dreams, and a few peculiarities of unconscious mental activity. There are only *glimpses* of the organic background—in connection with the erotogenic zones and bisexuality. But bisexuality is mentioned and specifically recognized once and for all, and the ground is prepared for detailed treatment of it on another occasion. It is a hysteria with *tussis nervosa* and aphonia, which can be traced back to pronounced sucking tendencies, and the chief issue in the conflicting mental processes is the opposition between an inclination towards men and towards women.

The "Every-day life" is at a standstill, half-finished, but will soon be continued. I have also a third small thing in mind; I have a lot of free time on my hands and feel the need to occupy myself. This year it has come down to three or four sessions a day with patients, which means a correspondingly greater mental well-being but a certain financial discomfort. . . .

Do you not think that this would be the right moment to jot down on a few sheets of paper the additions you have to your present subject[1]—Head's zones, the effect of *herpes zoster*, and anything else you may have—and have them published? Keeping your name before the public would, after all, be a way of assuring a certain amount of attention later on for the big, biological things which are more important to you. People only follow authority, and authority can only be acquired by doing things that are within their grasp.

In the midst of this mental and material depression I am haunted by the thought of spending Easter week in Rome this year. Not that there is any justification for it—I have achieved nothing yet, and in any case external circumstances will probably make it impossible. Let us hope for better times. My heartfelt wish is that you may soon have such times to report.

Cordially yours,

Sigm.

---

[1] The reference is to Fliess's interests. Fliess carried out Freud's suggestion. See Letter 147.

142

Dr. Sigm. Freud,   Vienna, 15. 2. 1901.
Lecturer in Nervous Diseases   IX. Berggasse 19.
  in the University.

My dear Wilhelm,

I shall no more get to Rome this Easter than you will. What you say has explained to me the meaning of what would otherwise have remained an unintelligible interpolation in my last letter. Behind it there was, of course, a reference to the promise you once gave me in happier times, to hold a congress with me on classical soil. I was perfectly well aware that such a reference was misplaced at the moment. I was only escaping from the present into the most beautiful of my former phantasies, and it was clear to me which one. Meanwhile the congresses themselves have become relics of the past; I am doing nothing new, and, as you say, I have become entirely estranged from what you are doing.

I can only still rejoice from a distance when you announce that you are at work on the book containing your great solutions and say you are so satisfied with the way it is going. In that case you are certainly right to postpone any more writing on the nasal relationships in favour of the wider synthesis.

I shall finish the every-day psychology[1] during the next few days, and then correct both pieces of work, send them off, etc. It has all been written under a certain cloud, of which it will no doubt show traces. The third thing I have started is something quite harmless—a real piece of beggar's hash. I have begun collecting my notes of things told me by neurotics in my consulting room for the purpose of demonstrating the connection between sexual life and neurosis revealed even by such necessarily fleeting observation, and of adding my own comments. In

---

[1] *The Psychopathology of Everyday Life* first appeared in the *Monatsschrift für Psychiatrie und Neurologie* (1901).

other words I am doing roughly the same sort of thing as Gattl did when he made himself so unpopular in Vienna.[1] As I need fresh cases, and my consulting hours are very sparsely attended, I have only six cases in my collection so far, and those none of the best. I have also started left-handedness tests—threading needles with a dynamometer. . . .

I did not give the lecture announced last Monday in the *Neue Freie Presse*. It was . . . Breuer, who had been badgered by the Philosophical Society, who pestered me to do it. I reluctantly agreed, and then, when I came to preparing it, I found I should have to bring in all sorts of intimate and sexual things which would be quite unsuitable for a mixed audience of people who were strangers to me. So I wrote a letter calling it off. That was the first week. Thereupon a delegation of two called on me and pressed me to deliver it after all. I warned them very seriously to do nothing of the sort, and suggested that they should come and hear the lecture themselves one evening at my house (second week). During the third week I gave the two of them the lecture. They said it was wonderful and that their audience would take no exception to it, etc. The lecture was therefore arranged for the fourth week. A few hours beforehand, however, I received an express letter, saying that some members had objected after all and asking me to be kind enough to start by illustrating my theory with inoffensive examples and then announce that I was coming to objectionable matter and make a pause, during which the ladies could leave the hall. Of course I immediately cried off, and the letter in which I did so at any rate did not lack pepper and salt. Such is scientific life in Vienna!

Hoping to hear good news of you soon,

Your faithful

Sigm.

---

[1] See Gattl (1898).

143

Dr. Sigm. Freud,   Vienna, 8. 5. 1901.
Lecturer in Nervous Diseases   IX. Berggasse 19.
   in the University.

My dear Wilhelm,

You may certainly take my birthday as an occasion for wishing
me the prolongation of your energetic mood and the repetition
of refreshing interludes, and I shall altruistically support the
wish. Your letter lay on the birthday table with other presents
which gave me pleasure and were partly connected with you;
though I had asked that the day be overlooked, as it lies in the
wretched middle period; I am too young for a jubilee and much
too old to be a birthday child. Your letter gave me by no means
the least pleasure, except for the part about magic, which I
object to as a superfluous plaster to lay to your doubt about
"thought-reading". I remain loyal to thought-reading, and
continue to doubt "magic".

I seem to remember having heard somewhere that only
necessity brings out one's best. I have therefore pulled myself
together, as you wished me to—I actually did it a few weeks
before you wished me to—and have come to terms with my
environment. A basket of orchids gives the illusion of luxury
and sunshine, a fragment of a Pompeiian wall with a centaur
and faun transports me to my longed-for Italy.[1]

Fluctuat nec mergitur !

. . . I am correcting the first pages of the every-day life,
which has turned out to be about sixty pages long. I have taken
a tremendous dislike to it, and I hope others will take an even
bigger dislike to it. It is entirely formless and contains all sorts
of forbidden things. I have not yet made up my mind to send off
the other work. ["Dreams and Hysteria"]. A new patient, a girl
who broke off her engagement, has filled the gap left by R.'s

---

[1] A small framed fragment of a Pompeiian fresco which forms part of Freud's
collection.

departure, and the case is resolving itself in the most satisfactory manner. In other ways too things are not so quiet as they were a few weeks ago. . . .

Progress in my work is obviously only to be expected from the four-thousandfold repetition of the same impressions, and I am quite ready to submit to it. So far everything is proved to be correct, but I still cannot survey the full extent of the riches laid bare and cannot master them intellectually.

Your "Relations"[1] shall find an attentive reader. You cannot have avoided including some new things.

Cordial greetings from

Your

Sigm.

144

Dr. Sigm. Freud,   Vienna, 4. 7. 1901.
Lecturer in Nervous Diseases   IX. Berggasse 19.
   in the University.

My dear Wilhelm,

. . . You ask so many questions that this is bound to be a long answer. So my consulting hour will be a letter-writing hour.

I cannot say for certain yet where we are going. After all sorts of plans had miscarried, we hit on something unexpected, which will probably come off. I spent the two-day holiday at the end of June with Mama and Minna[2] at Reichenhall, went on a carriage outing to the Thumsee, which is not far away, and lost my heart to the little place—with Alpine roses coming right down to the roadway, a little green lake, magnificent woods all around, as well as strawberries, flowers, and (we hope) mushrooms. I was so delighted with it that I asked whether there was

---

[1] The reference is to Fliess's monograph on the relations between the nose and the sexual organs (Fliess, 1902), the title of which had not yet been settled.
[2] Freud's mother-in-law and sister-in-law.

any accommodation available at the only inn. They are letting rooms there for the first time this year, as the owner, a Bad Kirchberg doctor and property owner, who used to live there himself, has just died. So now negotiations are under way and will probably come off. . . .

The father of one of my patients has taken zealously to sending me every cutting and article in which there is a reference to me or the dream book, including an article on "Dreams and Fairy-tales" which the author, a Munich lecturer, subsequently sent me himself.[1] [The patient's father] keeps writing to me about what can be made public about the treatment in the interests of "propaganda". Whether much, little, or nothing at all comes of it, it all goes back to the moment when you mentioned my name to him. . . .

Things are going very satisfactorily this year with my other clients. There have been fewer of them than last year and, as the strain has been less I am feeling incomparably better than at this time a year ago, but I am rather tired mentally all the same. No new ideas are occurring to me, and I do not really know how to fill in my free time.

Dr. van der Leyen of Munich has called my attention to a book by L. Laistner, *The Riddle of the Sphinx* (1889),[2] which argues vigorously that myths are traceable back to dreams. I read the introduction, which is interesting, but have been too lazy to go on with it. I see that he knows nothing of what is *behind* dreams, though he seems to have a very good idea of *anxiety* dreams. . . .

The every-day life will see the light in a few days, but it will apparently only be half-delivered, so it will be August before I can send you a complete reprint. It is too long for a single number of the *Monatsschrift*.

Martin now writes fewer poems, but draws and paints,

---

[1] The author was Friedrich van der Leyen, who corresponded with Freud for a time and in a letter of May 17th, 1902 (Warburg Institute, London University) drew the attention of Roscher, the author of the celebrated mythological dictionary, to Freud's researches. Leyen regarded Freud's subsequent works with reserve and scepticism.

[2] Laistner (1889).

mostly animal phantasies, with signs of humour, and is beginning to represent movement, etc. What perhaps matters more is that he has gone up to the second class at school with a comparatively good report. Oli's entrance exam will keep us here until the 15th of this month. All my big children will have to stay until then. . . .

Have you read that the English have excavated an old palace in Crete (Knossos) which they declare to be the original labyrinth of Minos?[1] Zeus seems originally to have been a bull. The god of our own fathers, before the sublimation instigated by the Persians took place, was worshipped as a bull. That provides food for all sorts of thoughts which it is not yet time to set down on paper. . . .

Your devoted

Sigm.

145

Thumsee, 7. 8. 01.

My dear Wilhelm,

The weather is horrible to-day for the first time in three weeks, and makes it impossible to do anything else; to-morrow we are going to Salzburg for a performance of *Don Giovanni* . . . that is how I come to be answering you at once, or at any rate beginning an answer.

First some professional matters, then something serious, then pleasant things to finish up with.

Frau D. would be an excellent substitute for G. To judge from your reports she would be a suitable person for treatment, and it would be reasonable to set the chances of success rather higher than the average. But I am not going back to the grindstone before September 16th for the sake of any patient, known or unknown, and by then she may have got over her attack. I never count on anyone until I have my hands on him. My

---

[1] The reference is to the first reports of Sir Arthur Evans's excavations at Knossos in Crete, which then as later Freud followed with lively interest.

clients are sick people, and therefore quite peculiarily irrational and unpredictable. Incidentally, the prospects for next season interest me acutely. I have only one "certain" patient, so to speak, a youth with obsessional neurosis, and my good old lady, who was a small but sure source of income to me, died during the holidays.[1] . . .

There is no concealing the fact that we have drawn somewhat apart from each other. By this and that I can see how much. . . . In this you came to the limit of your penetration, you take sides against me and tell me that "the thought-reader merely reads his own thoughts into other people", which deprives my work of all its value.

If I am such a one, throw my Every-day Life unread into the waste-paper basket. It is full of references to you: obvious ones, where you supplied the material, and concealed ones, where the motivation derives from you. Also you supplied the motto. Apart from any permanent value that its content may have, you can take it as a testimonial to the role you have hitherto played in my life. Having said this, I can send it to you as soon as it comes in without adding anything else. . . .

I said I was also going to write to you about pleasant things. Thumsee really is a little paradise, particularly for the children, who are well fed here, fight each other and the visitors for the boats and then vanish on them from their parents' anxious eyes. Living among the fish has made me stupid, but in spite of that I have not yet got the carefree mind that I usually get on holiday, and I suspect that what is required is eight or twelve days in the land of wine and olive oil. Perhaps my brother will be my travelling companion.

And now for the most important thing of all. My next book, so far as I can see, will be called "Bisexuality in Man"; it will tackle the root of the problem and say the last word which it will be granted to me to say on the subject—the last and the deepest. For the time being I have only one thing ready for it, the fundamental principle, which for a long time now has been

---

[1] [She is referred to several times in *The Interpretation of Dreams* and *The Psychopathology of Everyday Life*.]

based on the notion that repression, my crucial problem, is only possible through reaction between two sexual impulses. I shall need about six months to get the material together, and hope to find that the work is really practicable. But then I shall need a long and serious discussion with you. The idea itself is yours. You remember my saying to you years ago, when you were still a nose specialist and surgeon, that the solution lay in sexuality. Years later you corrected me and said bisexuality, and I see that you are right. So perhaps I shall have to borrow still more from you, and perhaps I shall be compelled in honesty to ask you to add your signature to the book to mine; this would mean an expansion of the anatomical-biological part, which in my hands alone would be very meagre. I should make my aim the mental aspect of bisexuality and the explanation of the neurotic side. That, then is the next project, which I hope will satisfactorily unite us again in scientific matters.

My cordial greetings to you and your family. Let me hear something from you.

Your
Sigm.

146

19. 9. 01.

My dear Wilhelm,

I received your card a few hours before I left. I ought to write to you about Rome, but it is difficult. It was an overwhelming experience for me, and, as you know, the fulfilment of a long-cherished wish. It was slightly disappointing, as all such fulfilments are when one has waited for them too long, but it was a high-spot in my life all the same. But, while I contemplated ancient Rome undisturbed (I could have worshipped the humble and mutilated remnant of the Temple of Minerva near the forum of Nerva), I found I could not freely enjoy the second Rome;[1] I was disturbed by its meaning, and, being incapable of putting out of my mind my own misery and all the other misery

---

[1] *I.e.*, mediaeval as distinct from ancient and modern Rome.

which I know to exist, I found almost intolerable the lie of the salvation of mankind which rears its head so proudly to heaven.

I found the third, Italian, Rome hopeful and likeable.

I was modest in my pleasures, and did not try to see everything in twelve days. I not only bribed Trevi,[1] as everyone does, but also—a thing I found out for myself—I dipped my hand into the Bocca della Verità at Santa Maria Cosmedin and swore to come again. The weather was hot but very tolerable until one day—luckily not before, the ninth—the sirocco broke out and quite knocked me up, and I did not recover for the rest of my stay. After getting home I developed a gastro-enteritis, which I think I contracted on the journey, and I am still troubled with it, though it is nothing to complain of. The family arrived home a day before me, and I still have hardly anything to do.

Your last letter was really beneficial. I can now understand the way you have been writing to me during the past year. It was at any rate the first time that you have ever said anything but the truth to me.

I know in myself that what you say about my attitude to your big work is unjust. I know how often I have thought about it with pride and trembling, and how distressed I have felt when I could not follow you in this or that conclusion. You know that I lack the slightest mathematical ability, and have no memory for numbers and measurements; perhaps it was that that gave you the impression that I did not appreciate what you told me. I do not believe that anything qualitative, any point of view which arose out of the calculations, was wasted on me. Perhaps you have been too quick to renounce me as a listener. A friend who has the right to contradict, who because of his ignorance can never be dangerous, is not without value to one who explores such dark paths and associates with very few people, all of whom admire him uncritically and unconditionally.

The only thing that hurt me was another misunderstanding in your letter, when you connected my exclamation[2] "But

---

[1] The tradition is that the traveller who throws a coin into the Fontana dei Trevi will come to Rome again.

[2] At the last meeting at Achensee.

you're undermining the whole value of my work" with my therapy. . . . I was sorry to lose my "only audience", as our Nestroy called it. For whom shall I write now? If as soon as an interpretation of mine makes you feel uncomfortable you are ready to conclude that the "thought-reader" perceives nothing in others but merely projects his own thoughts into them, you really are no longer my audience, and you must regard the whole technique as just as worthless as the others do.

I do not understand your answer about bisexuality. It is obviously very difficult to understand one another. I certainly had no intention of doing anything but get to grips, as my contribution to the theory of bisexuality, with the thesis that repression and the neuroses, and thus the independence of the unconscious, presuppose bisexuality.

You will have seen from the reference to you as the discoverer of the idea in the "Everyday life"[1] that I have no intention of exaggerating my share in it. But some linking up with the general biological and anatomical aspects of bisexuality would be indispensable and, as nearly all my biological and anatomical knowledge comes from you, there is nothing for it but to ask your aid or leave the whole of the introductory matter to you. But I am not in the least hankering after appearing in print at the moment. Meanwhile, we must discuss it some time.

One cannot simply say "the conscious is the dominant, the unconscious the underlying, sexual factor" without grossly oversimplifying the very complicated nature of the case, though it is, of course, the basic fact. I am working at a more psychological essay, "Forgetting and Repressing",[2] which I shall also keep to myself for a long while to come.

The date for your "relations" lecture has gone by, and I am awaiting it with keen interest; has it been postponed?

My cordial greetings, and I hope for good news of you and yours.

Your

Sigm.

---

[1] See Introduction, p. 38.
[2] Not published.

147

Dr. Sigm. Freud,   20. 9. 01.
   IX. Berggasse 19.   Consulting hours 3-5 p.m.

My dear Wilhelm,

Tableau! Our letters crossed. I was enquiring about it yesterday and now it has come. I have given it a first reading and say with pleasure that you have never before produced anything so clear, so concise, and so rich in substance. And what a blessing that there is no doubt about the truth of it! Thank you also for the little reference to me.[1] I was also delighted with the "Herpes". Throughout one feels that there is more behind you, but that you are able to put your riches aside and confine yourself within the limits laid down. I think that is the hallmark of the classic style.

Does not the title fall disappointingly short of the "causal" connection between the nose and the sexual organ? I expect it is an abbreviation of "modifications in the nose and sexual organ". But it is all right as it is, and I do not want to be pedantic.

My cordial thanks,

Your

Sigm.

148

Dr. Sigm. Freud,   Vienna, 7. 10. 01.
Lecturer in Nervous Diseases   IX. Berggasse 19.
   in the University.

My dear Wilhelm,

It is three weeks since Frau D., whom you sent, came to me, so a report to you about her is overdue.

She is, of course, just the person I need; a difficult constitutional case, in which all the keys fit and all the strings respond. Painless work with her is hardly possible, because she is too

---

[1] The passage in Fliess's latest work referred to states: "The typical cause of neurasthenia in young people is masturbation (Freud), which in older people is frequently replaced by *onanismus conjugalis*". The chapter on *herpes zoster* is connected with the work of Head and Campbell (1900). See Letter 141.

fond both of feeling and of inflicting pain for that. But success with her ought to be certain and lasting.

Unfortunately there are other things in the way. Her husband . . . is still unco-operative. He allowed her three months for treatment, to which I naturally did not agree, but even this concession was none really, because he wanted to pack her off the same evening, and she is daily expecting him to come and fetch her. She will, of course, go with him. She already cannot stand being without him.

If the time-factor is so uncertain, the money-factor seems hardly less so. I do not know whether it is really so unfavourable or whether she has only succeeded in deceiving me about it. In short, it is quite within the bounds of possibility that I shall shortly declare that it is better not to try building on such insecure foundations. With all her intelligence, it is very unlikely that she will get anywhere worth-while in three months. Her husband approached me with such obvious jealous mistrust that I cannot hope to make any impression on him by having a talk with him.

Perhaps everything may yet come right, but I only wanted to prepare you for the possibility that you may see her again sooner than you expected, and to justify myself in advance in case the great trouble you have taken comes to nothing.

Now that we write to each other so seldom, I have not been able to thank you before.

With cordial greetings,

Your

Sigm.

149

Dr. Sigm. Freud,   Vienna, 2. 11. 01.
Lecturer in Nervous Diseases   IX. Berggasse 19.
   in the University.

My dear Wilhelm,

You are certainly entitled to hear from time to time about how matters stand with your patient, and I write about her the more gladly because I am in no mood to write about anything else.

You have, indeed, found me just the case for this therapy. I can say that so far it has gone extremely well—partly, perhaps, because it is easy for me to take an interest in her character. I shall tell you more some time by word of mouth when I can discard discretion. But everything is going smoothly and it all fits in—at any rate with my new point of view—and the instrument responds willingly to the instrumentalist's confident touch. Not that she does not make enough attempts to make my life difficult; that sort of thing has happened already and will happen again. My worried letter, which you answered with the true information, was the result of a tremendous deception she practised on me in raising mountains of difficulties. I shall be less easily deceived a second time, or such at least is my intention. In any case she is an interesting and valuable personality.

I am happy to be able to report this to you and send you my cordial greetings.

Your
Sigm.

150

Dr. Sigm. Freud,   Vienna, 7. 12. 01.
Lecturer in Nervous Diseases   IX. Berggasse 19.
   in the University.

My dear Wilhelm,

Frau D. has taken her departure. The doubts I expressed to you after the first fortnight were not altogether unjustified. As you know, her husband forcibly interrupted the treatment, ascribing his intervention to considerations of time and money, though these—consistently with the information you gave me—were put forward only to serve as a mask for his jealousy. Finally he sent me a letter which made it impossible to prolong the treatment until the 19th of this month, as agreed. The man behaved so offensively towards me that it needed a good deal of self-control on my part to go on so long as we did.

The treatment was so short—only ten weeks—that there can

be no question of a permanent cure. And I cannot foresee how things will shape for the patient in the immediate future. On the other hand the whole thing went so swimmingly that it is inconceivable that the work should bear no fruit. When the storm now unleashed has run its course it should be possible to see what has been effected.

In any case she was the most suitable and most interesting person for whom I have ever had to thank you for recommending to me. It is no fault of either of us that things did not turn out better. Professor D. did not manage to transfer his confidence from you to me. I am going through an unlucky patch, in which mainly unpleasant things happen to me. I am continually practising patience.

Again many thanks,

Your

Sigm.

151

Dr. Sigm. Freud,   8. 3. 02.
  IX. Berggasse 19.   Consulting hours 3-5 p.m.

My dear Wilhelm,

I am glad to be able to tell you that at last the long-withheld and recently really desirable professorship has been conferred on me. The *Wiener Zeitung* will next week announce the fact to the public, which I hope will take note of this seal of official approval. It is a long time since I have been able to send you any news with which pleasant anticipations could be associated.

With cordial greetings,

Your

Sigm.

152

Dr. Sigm. Freud,   Vienna, 11. 3. 02.
Lecturer in Nervous Diseases   IX. Berggasse 19.
   in the University.

My dear Wilhelm,

Just think what an "excellency" can do! He can even cause me again to hear your welcome voice in a letter. But as you talk about such grand things in connection with the news—recognition, mastery, etc.—my usual compulsion to honesty which is so detrimental to my interests makes me feel it incumbent on me to tell you exactly how it finally came about.

It was my own doing, in fact. When I got back from Rome, my zest for life and work had somewhat grown and my zest for martyrdom had somewhat diminished. I found that my practice had melted away and I withdrew my last work from publication because in you I had recently lost my only remaining audience.[1] I reflected that waiting for recognition might take up a good portion of the remainder of my life, and that in the meantime none of my fellow-men were likely to trouble about me. And I wanted to see Rome again and look after my patients and keep my children happy. So I made up my mind to break with my strict scruples and take appropriate steps, as others do after all. One must look somewhere for one's salvation, and the salvation I chose was the title of professor. For four whole years I had not put in a word about it, but now I betook myself to my old teacher, Exner.[2] He was as disagreeable as could be, almost rude,

---

[1] Nestroy, looking through the peep-hole before a benefit performance and seeing only two people in the stalls, is said to have exclaimed: "I know one of the 'audiences', he has a complimentary ticket. Whether the other 'audience' has one too I don't know!"

[2] Sigmund R. von Exner (1846-1926), Professor of Physiology in the University of Vienna, succeeded Brücke in 1891, and since 1894 had been in the Ministry of Education.

did not want to let out anything about the reasons for my having been passed over, and generally played the high official. Only after I had really roused him by a few disparaging remarks about the activity of those in high office did he let fall something obscure about personal influences which appeared to be at work against me with his Excellency,[1] and he advised me to seek a personal counter-influence. I was able to tell him that I could approach my old friend and former patient, the wife of Hofrat Gomperz.[2] This seemed to impress him. Frau Elise was very kind and took up the matter warmly. She called on the Minister and the reply to what she said was a look of astonishment and the answer: "Four years ? And who is he ?" The old fox acted as if I were unknown to him. In any case it would be necessary to have me proposed all over again. So I wrote to Nothnagel and to Krafft-Ebing[3] (who was about to retire) and asked them to renew their previous proposal. Both behaved delightfully. Nothnagel wrote a few days later and said that they had sent it in. But the Minister obstinately avoided Gomperz, and it looked as if nothing was going to come of it again.

Then another force came into play. One of my patients . . . heard about the matter and went into action on her own. She did not rest until she had made the Minister's acquaintance at a party, made herself agreeable to him, and secured a promise from him through a mutual woman friend that he would give a professorship to the doctor who had cured her. But, being sufficiently well-informed to know that a first promise from him meant nothing at all, she approached him personally, and I believe that if a certain Böcklin had been in her possession instead of in that of her aunt . . . I should have been appointed three months earlier. As it is, his Excellency will have to satisfy

[1] The Minister of Education was Wilhelm Freiherr von Hartel (born 1839), formerly Professor of Philology in the University of Vienna.

[2] Elise Gomperz was the wife of Theodor Gomperz (1832-1912), who was appointed Professor of Philology at the same time as Hartel in 1869 and became famous for his *Greek Thinkers*. Freud while still a student had translated a volume of the German edition of the works of John Stuart Mill, which was edited by Gomperz. For Freud's relations with Gomperz see Merlan (1945) and Bernfeld (1949).

[3] See Letter 58 *sqq.*

himself with a modern picture for the gallery which he intends to open, naturally not for himself.[1] Anyway, in the end the Minister most graciously announced to my patient while he was having dinner at her house that the appointment had gone to the Emperor for signature, and that she would be the first to hear when the matter was completed.

So one day she came to her appointment beaming and waving an express letter from the Minister. It was done. The *Wiener Zeitung* has not yet published it, but the news spread quickly from the Ministry. The public enthusiasm is immense.[2] Congratulations and bouquets keep pouring in, as if the role of sexuality had been suddenly recognized by His Majesty, the interpretation of dreams confirmed by the Council of Ministers, and the necessity of the psycho-analytic therapy of hysteria carried by a two-thirds majority in Parliament.

I have obviously become reputable again, and my shyest admirers now greet me from a distance in the street.

I myself would still gladly exchange five congratulations for one good case coming for extensive treatment. I have learned that the old world is governed by authority just as the new is governed by the dollar. I have made my first bow to authority, and am entitled to hope to reap my reward. If the effect in a wider circle is as great as in the immediate one, I may well hope so.

In the whole affair there is one person with very long ears, who was not sufficiently allowed for in your letter, and that is myself. If I had taken those few steps three years ago I should have been appointed three years earlier, and should have spared myself much. Others are just as clever, without having to go to Rome first. That, then, was the glorious process to which, among other things, I owe your kind letter. Please keep the contents of this one to yourself.

> Thanks and cordial greetings,
>
> > Your
> >
> > Sigm.

---

[1] According to H. Sachs's somewhat abbreviated account of this incident (Sachs, 1945) the picture concerned was Böcklin's "Ruined Castle", which Hartel wished to have presented to the Moderne Galerie, which was then being established in Vienna.

[2] [A German journalistic catchphrase often quoted in the Freud household.]

153

(Picture postcard of the temple of Neptune, Paestum)

10. 9. 02.

Cordial greetings from the culminating point of the journey.

Your

Sigm.

PROJECT FOR A

SCIENTIFIC PSYCHOLOGY [1]

---

[1] [The title has been chosen by the translator. The title in the German edition "Entwurf einer Psychologie" was chosen by its editors.] Freud's manuscript bears no title; in his letters he speaks of "the note-books" or "the psychology" [as well as of "the psychology for neurologists" and "the ΦΨω "] For the position occupied by the "Project" in Freud's development, see the Introduction, p. 25 ff.

Editorial Note

The following manuscript dates from the Autumn of 1895. The first and second parts (p. 355 ff., p. 405 ff.) were begun by Freud in the train after a meeting with Fliess. (Letter of September 23, 1895; part of the manuscript [up to the end of section 2 of Part I] is written in pencil.) They were finished on September 25 (see the date at the beginning of Part II). The third part (p. 417 ff.) was begun on October 5, 1895 (see the date at the beginning of the manuscript). All three parts were despatched to Fliess on October 8.

A fourth part, which was to deal with the psychology of repression, regarded by Freud as "the heart of the riddle", was evidently never completed. As he worked at this problem, Freud's doubts as to the fruitfulness of the line of approach attempted in the "Project" grew stronger. These doubts began to arise soon after he had concluded the work which he had begun with such feverish interest. He was already feeling sceptical on November 29, 1895 (Letter 36): "I no longer understand the state of mind in which I concocted the psychology". In his letter of January 1, 1896 (Letter 39), he attempts to give a revised account of his hypotheses on the interrelations of the three kinds of neurones, which, in particular, clears up the position of the "perceptual neurones". More than a year after he had written the "Project", his views had so far developed that he sketched out a diagram of the psychical apparatus with a sense similar to that contained in the seventh chapter of *The Interpretation of Dreams* (Letter 52, of December 6, 1896). From that time onwards, Freud lost interest in the question of representing the psychical apparatus in terms of neuro-physiology. Years later he alluded to the failure of his efforts in that direction in the following terms: "Research has afforded irrefutable proof that mental activity is bound up with the function of the brain as with that of no other organ. The discovery of the unequal importance of the different parts of the brain and their individual relations to particular parts of the body and to intellectual activities takes us a step further—we do not know how big a step. But every attempt to deduce from these facts a localization of mental processes, every endeavour to think of ideas as stored up in nerve-cells and of excitations as travelling along nerve-fibres, has completely miscarried". (Freud, 1915 *e*.) Recent research into the physiology of the brain on the whole shares these views. (Cf. E. D. Adrian's brilliant paper on "The Mental and Physical Origins of Behaviour", 1946.)

Under the cloak of brain physiology, however, the "Project" reveals a wealth of concrete psychological hypotheses, of general theoretical assumptions and of various suggestive hints. Many of these thoughts, after the modifications necessitated by the abandonment of the abortive physiological attempt, were carried over into Freud's later writings, and some of them are numbered among the permanent stock-in-trade of psycho-analytic hypotheses. Other portions of the "Project" (such, for instance, as the treatment of the psychology of intellectual processes in the third part, p. 439ff.) received no similar consideration in Freud's published writings, though certain of the notions which he here develops could be fitted without difficulty into the system of psycho-analytic theories.

The immediate continuation of the "Project" among Freud's published writings is to be found in *The Interpretation of Dreams*. But the fresh formulation of the nature of the psychical apparatus which is attempted in the seventh chapter of that work falls short in one point at least of the hypotheses put forward in the "Project": the position of the perceptual function could not be fully explained in the later work. (Cf. Freud 1917 *d*.) The solution of this problem was only made possible by Freud's hypotheses on psychical *structure*, developed in *The Ego and the Id* (1923 *b*) and subsequently. But this very development was foreshadowed in the "Project" by the elaborately sustained hypothesis of a permanently cathected "ego organization", a hypothesis which was revived in Freud's mind after an interval of thirty years.

At the period in which Freud drew up his "Project" his interests were mainly focused on its connections with neuro-physiology. When his hypotheses on that subject broke down, he simultaneously dropped for the time being others of the topics dealt with. And this may have been true in particular of his hypotheses about the ego, which, in the "Project", were attached to a specially designated group of neurones.

Immediately after Freud had written the "Project", his interests were diverted to other problems. With his return to clinical work during the autumn, the theory of the neuroses moved into the foreground of his thoughts, and his principal discovery of the autumn of 1895 related to the distinction between the genetic factors in obsessional neurosis and hysteria (Letter 34, etc.).

In order to make it easier for readers to follow the extremely condensed train of thought, we have drawn up a table of contents and, where a given topic is broken off, we have indicated in footnotes the point at which it is later resumed.

[A few further elucidations have been inserted in the text by the English translator and some footnotes have also been added by him. These additions are enclosed in square brackets. It will be understood that all other footnotes are by the editor of the German edition. In the English translation the sections have been numbered for purposes of reference.]

CONTENTS

PART I
General Scheme

PART II
Psychopathology
The Psychopathology of Hysteria

PART III

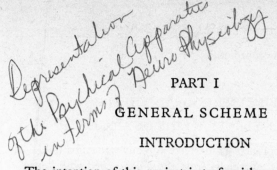

PART I

GENERAL SCHEME

INTRODUCTION

The intention of this project is to furnish us with a psychology which shall be a natural science: its aim, that is, is to represent psychical processes as quantitatively determined states of specifiable material particles and so to make them plain and void of contradictions. The project involves two principal ideas:—

1. That what distinguishes activity from rest is to be regarded as a quantity (Q) subject to the general laws of motion.

2. That it is to be assumed that the material particles in question are the neurones.

N and $Q\dot\eta$ [neurones and quantity][1].—Experiments of a

---

[1] In the manuscript Freud made use of numerous abbreviations, the majority of which have been filled out in the printed version. Apart, however, from customary or easily explicable abbreviations, he employed a certain number of fixed tokens: thus N stands regularly for "neurones" and Φ, Ψ and ω indicate the three systems of neurones (Φ being often used adjectivally). The system of ω-neurones is also frequently referred to as the system of "perceptual neurones" [or "W-neurones", *cf.* footnote, p. 370]. In such cases the abbreviations used by Freud have been added in round brackets. The term "quantity" is represented by Freud by two different abbreviations: Q and $Q\dot\eta$. Towards the end of the draft (p. 110) he gives criteria for distinguishing between them: Q relates to "external" quantity and $Q\dot\eta$ to "psychical" quantity. The distinction is not always maintained consistently and is entirely dropped in Letter 39 of January 1, 1896, p. 140ff.). In the present printed text both Q and $Q\dot\eta$ have been replaced by the word "quantity"; but the abbreviation used by Freud is in each case added in round brackets. Where no abbreviation is added, it should be assumed that Freud did not employ either symbol but wrote out the word in full.—[The translator is inclined to think, however, that Freud's use of the abbreviations Q and $Q\dot\imath$ might be more accurately distinguished as follows. Q seems to be used by Freud quite generally for quantity—including quantity in the external world—when he is not particularly concerned to characterize it more precisely. $Q\dot\imath$ seems to be used by him primarily to mean quantity as it occurs in neurones; thus $Q\dot\imath$ is ascribed to the Φ-system of neurones (e.g., p. 385) and to the ω-system (e.g., p. 373) as well as to the Ψ-system. The Translator also ventures to hazard an explanation of the enigmatic symbol $Q\dot\imath$. As will be seen below (footnote p. 370) Freud jokingly used the Greek ω to stand for the W of *Wahrnehmung* (perception); it seems not impossible that he made similar use of the fact that the Greek $\dot\eta$ is only an "n" with a long tail. If so $Q\dot\eta$ would be an appropriate symbol for "neuronic quantity".]

similar kind are now common.[1]

[1] FIRST PRINCIPAL THESIS:

THE QUANTITATIVE LINE OF APPROACH

This line of approach is derived directly from pathological clinical observations, especially from those concerned with "excessively intense ideas". (These occur in hysteria and obsessional neurosis, where, as we shall see, the quantitative characteristic emerges more plainly than in the normal. [See Part II, p. 405 ff.]) Processes such as stimulus, substitution, conversion and discharge, which had to be described in connection with these disorders, directly suggested the notion of viewing neuronic excitation as quantities in a condition of flow.[2] It seemed legitimate to make an attempt at generalizing what had been found in these particular instances. With this as a starting-point, it was possible to lay down a basic principle of neuronic activity in relation to quantity (Q) which promised to be highly enlightening, since it seemed to cover the entire [neuronic] function. What I have in mind is *the principle of neuronic inertia*, which asserts that neurones tend to divest themselves of quantity (Q). On this basis it becomes possible to understand

---

[1] It is not possible to say definitely what "experiments" Freud had in mind. See, however, as regards views upon brain physiology, the collected papers of E. Fleischl von Marxow (1893), with a biographical sketch by Sigmund von Exner, and, as regards the relations between physiology and psychology, Exner's own writings, particularly his *Outline of a Physiological Explanation of Psychical Phenomena* (1894). In the latter the following passage occurs (p. 225): "All the phenomena of quality and quantity in conscious sensations, perceptions and ideas can be traced back to variable quantitative excitations of various portions of this totality of paths". As regards the theory of memory, Freud may have derived suggestions from the French writers on the subject as well as from a lecture on "Memory and its Abnormalities" (1885) by A. Forel, which he read attentively.

[2] Freud's statement that the successful application of dynamic ideas to the problems of hysteria directly suggested his present line of approach reminds us that *Studies on Hysteria* had appeared only a short time before this draft was written. It is plausible to suppose that Freud was attempting in this "Project" to solve difficulties which Breuer had been unable to solve in his theoretical contribution to the *Studies*. Freud's starting-point is sharply opposed to that of Breuer, who wrote: "In what follows there will be little said of the brain and nothing at all of molecules. Psychical processes will be discussed in the language of psychology: indeed, there is no alternative".

the structure and development of neurones as well as their functions.

The principle of inertia accounts, in the first place, for the division of neurones into two classes, motor and sensory, as a contrivance for counteracting the reception of quantity ($Q\dot{\eta}$) by getting rid of it. Reflex movement now becomes intelligible as an established method of thus getting rid of quantity. The principle of inertia provides the reason for reflex movement. If we look still further back, we can in the first instance link the neuronic system (as inheritor of the general susceptibility of protoplasm to stimulus) with the irritable outer surface of protoplasm which is interspersed with considerable stretches of non-irritable [substance].[1] A primary neuronic system, having thus acquired a quantity ($Q\dot{\eta}$), employs it only in order to get rid of it through the connecting path leading to the muscular mechanism, and thus keeps itself free from stimulus. This process of discharge is the primary function of neuronic systems.

At this point there is an opportunity for the development of a *secondary* function. For among the various methods of discharge those are preferred and retained which involve a cessation of the stimulus—*i.e.*, *flight* from the stimulus. A balance is observed here between the quantity of the excitation and the effort required for flight from that stimulus; so that the principle of inertia is not disturbed in this case.

From the very first, however, the principle of inertia *is* upset by another set of circumstances. As the internal complexity of the organism increases, the neuronic system receives stimuli from the somatic element itself—endogenous stimuli, which call equally for discharge. These have their origin in the cells of the body and give rise to the major needs: hunger, respiration and sexuality. The organism cannot withdraw itself from them as it does from external stimuli; it cannot employ their quantity (Q) for the purpose of flight from the stimulus. They only cease if certain definite conditions are realized in the external world. (Take, for example, the case of the need for nourishment.) To carry out an action [that will bring these conditions about]—an action which deserves to be called "specific"— requires an effort which is independent of endogenous quantities ($Q\dot{\eta}$) and is generally greater than they are, since the individual is

---

[1] Word omitted in the manuscript.

placed under conditions which may be described as "the exigencies of life". The neuronic system is consequently obliged to abandon its original trend towards inertia (that is, towards a reduction of its level of tension to zero). It must learn to tolerate a store of quantity ($Q\dot\eta$) sufficient to meet the demands for specific action. In so far as it does so, however, the same trend still persists in the modified form of a tendency to keep the quantity down, at least, so far as possible and avoid any increase in it (that is, to keep its level of tension constant). All the performances of the neuronic system are to be comprised under the heading either of the primary function or of the secondary function imposed by the exigencies of life.[1]

[2] SECOND PRINCIPAL THESIS:
THE NEURONE THEORY

The idea of combining this "quantity ($Q\dot\eta$) theory" with the knowledge of neurones which has been arrived at by modern histology is a second pillar of our theory. The essence of this new knowledge is that the neuronic system consists of distinct but similarly constructed neurones which only have contact with one another through an intervening foreign substance and which terminate on one another in the same manner as on a piece of foreign tissue; that certain lines of conduction are laid down in them, in so far as they receive excitations through a cell-process [or dendrite] and discharge them through an axis-cylinder [or axone]; and furthermore, that they have numerous ramifications with diameters of various dimensions.

If we combine this account of neurones with an approach on the lines of the quantity ($Q\dot\eta$) theory, we arrive at the idea of a "cathected" neurone (N) filled with a certain quantity ($Q\dot\eta$), though at other times it may be empty. The principle of inertia [p. 356] finds expression

---

[1] The thoughts developed in this passage find a continuation in Freud's discussion of the "two principles of mental functioning" (1911 *b*). Between these two lay the discussions in the seventh chapter of *The Interpretation of Dreams* (1900 *a*; *trans.*, 1953, p. 509 ff.). The distinction between a trend in the psychical apparatus towards reducing its level of tension to zero and the modification of this trend into one towards keeping the level of tension as low as possible—the distinction, that is, between the "Nirvana principle" and the "pleasure principle"—is discussed in *Beyond the Pleasure Principle* (1920 *g*; *trans.*, 1950, p. 76).

in the hypothesis of a *current*, passing from the cell-processes or dendrites to the axone. Each single neurone is thus a model of the neuronic system as a whole, with its division into two classes of neurones—the axone being its organ of discharge. The secondary function [p. 357], which requires quantity ($Q\dot\eta$) to be stored up, is made possible by supposing that there are resistances which oppose discharge; and the structure of the neurone makes it probable that these resistances are all to be found in the *contacts* [between the neurones] which thus function as *barriers*. The hypothesis of "contact-barriers"[1] is fruitful in many directions.

[3] THE CONTACT-BARRIERS

The first justification for this hypothesis lies in the consideration that at this point conduction passes through undifferentiated protoplasm, instead of through differentiated protoplasm (as it does elsewhere within the neurone) which is probably better adapted for conduction. This gives us a hint that there may be a connection between differentiation and capacity for conduction, so that we may expect to find that the process of conduction itself may create a differentiation in the protoplasm and consequently an improved capacity for *subsequent* conduction.

The theory of contact-barriers has, moreover, the following advantages. One of the chief characteristics of nervous tissue is that of "memory": that is, speaking generally, a susceptibility to permanent alteration by a single process. This offers a striking contrast to the behaviour of a material that allows a wave-movement to pass through it and then returns to its former condition. Any psychological theory deserving consideration must provide an explanation of memory. Now any such explanation comes up against the difficulty that, on the one hand, it must be assumed that after an excitation neurones are permanently different from what they were before, while, on the other hand, it cannot be denied that, in general, fresh excitations meet with the same conditions of reception as did the

---

[1] [The term "synapses" was not introduced (by Foster and Sherrington) till 1897, two years after Freud wrote the present paper.]

earlier ones. Thus the neurones would appear to be both influenced and also unaltered—"unprepossessed". We cannot off-hand imagine an apparatus capable of such complicated functioning. The situation is accordingly saved by assigning the characteristic of being permanently influenced by excitation to *one* class of neurones, and the immutability—the characteristic of being fresh for the reception of new excitations—to *another* class. Thus has arisen the current distinction between "sense cells" and "memory cells", a distinction, however, which fits into no other context and has nothing to support it.

The theory of contact-barriers can make use of this way out of the difficulty by expressing it in the following terms. There are two classes of neurones. First there are those which allow quantity ($Q\dot{\eta}$) to pass through them as though they had no contact-barriers, which accordingly, each time an excitation has passed, are left in the same condition in which they were before. And secondly, there are those whose contact-barriers make themselves felt, so that they allow quantity ($Q\dot{\eta}$) to pass through them only with difficulty or partially. This second class may be left in a modified condition after each excitation, and thus afford *a possibility of representing memory*.[1]

Thus there are *permeable* neurones (offering no resistance and retaining nothing) which serve the function of perception, and *impermeable* neurones (offering resistance and retaining quantity [$Q\dot{\eta}$]) which are the vehicles of memory and presumably, therefore, of psychical processes in general. Henceforward, accordingly, I shall call the former system of neurones Φ and the latter Ψ.[2]

---

[1] Freud has made use of some of these ideas in *Beyond the Pleasure Principle* (*trans.*, 1950, p. 27 ff.). He there states specifically that he has "adopted the views on localization held by cerebral anatomy". According to the analysis made by Dorer (1932, p. 128 ff. and especially p. 151) of Freud's relations to Meynert's theories, there can be no doubt that Freud had Meynert in mind when he wrote these words. Meynert's influence is to be suspected at several points in the development of the argument in the "Project", though it is not always possible to distinguish it at once from views which were generally held by the neurology of the 'nineties.

[2] From what follows below we shall find that the attributes of the two groups of neurones respectively are these: the Φ-neurones are "permeable", that is, offer no resistance, serve the purpose of mastering stimuli from the external world, and are to be identified with the grey matter of the spinal cord; the Ψ-neurones are retentive, serve the purpose of mastering internal stimuli, and are to be identified with the super-imposed grey matter of the brain.

At this point it will be advisable to make it clear what assumptions we must lay down concerning the Ψ-neurones if the most general characteristics of memory are to be covered. Here is the argument. These neurones are permanently altered by the course of an excitation; or (if we introduce the theory of contact-barriers) their contact-barriers are brought into a permanently altered condition. And since psychological experience tells us that there is such a thing as progressive learning based on recollection, this alteration must consist in the contact-barriers becoming more capable of conduction—less impermeable—becoming, that is, more like those of the Φ-system. We shall describe this condition of the contact-barriers as their degree of "facilitation" ["*Bahnung*"]. We can then assert that *memory is represented by the facilitations existing between the Ψ-neurones.*

If we were to suppose that all the Ψ-contact-barriers had equally good facilitations or, what is the same thing, offered equal resistances, the characteristics of memory would evidently not be brought out. For memory is obviously one of the determining and directing forces in relation to the path taken by excitations, and if facilitation were everywhere equal there would be nothing to explain why one path should be preferred to another. It is therefore more correct to say that memory is represented by the *differences* in the facilitations between the Ψ-neurones.

Now what does the facilitation in the Ψ-neurones depend on? Psychological experience shows that memory (that is, the persisting force of an experience) depends on a factor that is described as the "magnitude" of the impression and on the frequency of the recurrence of the same impression. Or, translated into our theory, facilitation depends on the quantity ($Q\dot\eta$) which passes through a neurone in the excitatory process and on the number of repetitions of that process. Thus we see that quantity ($Q\dot\eta$) is the operative factor, but that quantity ($Q\dot\eta$) can be replaced by quantity *plus* the facilitation resulting from quantity [Cf. p. 380].

In this connection we are reminded (almost involuntarily) of the primary effort of neuronic systems, retained through all their modifications, to avoid being burdened with quantity ($Q\dot\eta$) or to diminish it so far as possible. Under the pressure of the exigencies of life, the neuronic system has been obliged to lay up a store of quantity ($Q\dot\eta$)

[p. 358]. For this purpose it has had to increase the number of its neurones and these have had to be impermeable. But it now avoids, to some extent at least, being filled with quantity ($Q\dot\eta$)—avoids cathexis, that is,—by setting up facilitations. It will be seen, therefore, that *facilitations serve the primary function.*

The necessity for finding a place for memory in the theory of contact-barriers calls for something further. Every Ψ-neurone must in general be presumed to have several paths of connection with other neurones—that is, several contact-barriers. It is on this that the possibility depends of the excitation having a choice of path, determined by facilitation. This being so, it is quite clear that the condition of facilitation of each contact-barrier must be independent of that of all the others in the same Ψ-neurone. Otherwise there would once again be no possibility of one path being preferred to another—no motive, that is. From this we can draw a negative inference as to the nature of the condition of "facilitation". If we imagine a neurone filled with quantity ($Q\dot\eta$)—i.e., cathected—we can only suppose that this quantity (Q) is uniformly distributed over all the regions of the neurone, including all its contact-barriers. On the other hand, there is no difficulty in supposing that, in the case of a quantity ($Q\dot\eta$) in a condition of flow, it will take only one particular path through the neurone; so that only one of the contact-barriers will be influenced by that quantity ($Q\dot\eta$) and acquire facilitation from it. Therefore facilitation cannot be based upon a cathexis that is retained, for this would not produce the differences of facilitation in the contact-barriers of the same neurone.

It remains to be seen in what, apart from this, facilitation *does* consist. Our first idea might be that it consists in an absorption of quantity ($Q\dot\eta$) by the contact-barriers. Perhaps more light will be thrown on this later. The quantity ($Q\dot\eta$) which has left behind the facilitation is no doubt discharged, precisely on account of the facilitation, which increases permeability. Incidentally, we need not suppose that the facilitation remaining after the passage of the quantity ($Q\dot\eta$) is necessarily as great as it was during the actual passage. [Cf. p. 378.] Perhaps only a quotient of it is left in the form of *permanent* facilitation. In the same way we cannot yet tell whether an equivalent effect is produced by the passage of a given quantity ($Q\dot\eta$)

three times and by the passage of a quantity $(Q\dot\eta)$ three times as great once only.[1] All these points remain to be considered in the light of later applications of the theory to the psychical facts.

[4] THE BIOLOGICAL STANDPOINT

Thus one peculiarity of neuronic systems—their capacity to retain and at the same time to remain receptive—seems to be explained by the hypothesis of there being two neuronic systems, Φ and Ψ, of which the former consists of permeable elements and the latter of impermeable. All psychical acquisition would on this basis consist in the organization of the Ψ-system through partial and locally determined suspensions of the resistance in the contact-barriers which distinguishes Ψ from Φ. As this organization proceeds, the capacity of the neuronic system for the reception of fresh impressions would in fact reach a limit.

Anyone, however, who is occupied in the scientific construction of hypotheses will only begin to take them seriously if they can be fitted into our knowledge from more than one direction and if the arbitrariness of a *constructio ad hoc* can thus be mitigated. It will be objected against our hypothesis of contact-barriers that it assumes the existence of two classes of neurones having a fundamental difference in the conditions of their functioning, whereas there is at present no other ground for making such a differentiation. From the morphological (that is, the histological) point of view, at any rate, there is no known evidence in support of this distinction.

Where else can we look for grounds for this division into two

---

[1] This question is answered on p. 383. Some of this section is carried further in a modified form in Freud's hypotheses on memory and consciousness. See in this connection *The Interpretation of Dreams* (trans., 1953, p. 538 ff.), and the theory that "in the Ψ-systems memory and the quality that characterizes consciousness are mutually exclusive". Subsequently Freud formulated this idea even more drastically in the supposition that "consciousness arises *instead of* a memory-trace" (*Beyond the Pleasure Principle*, 1920 g, trans., 1950, p. 29 [where the whole line of thought is explicitly attributed to Breuer] and "A Note on the 'Mystic Writing-Pad'," 1925 a, *Coll. Papers*, V, p. 177; see also Letter 52 of December 6, 1896). A similar view had been expressed by Breuer in his theoretical chapter of the *Studies on Hysteria*, 1895, p. 164: "This perceptual apparatus, including the sensory spheres of the cortex, must be distinct from the organ which stores up and reproduces sense impressions in the form of memory-images. . . ."

classes? If possible, to the *biological* development of the neuronic system, which, like all else, is regarded by the natural scientist as something that has come about step by step. We should like to know whether the two classes of neurones may have had some different biological significance, and, if so, by what mechanism they may have developed two such different characteristics as permeability and impermeability. The most satisfactory solution would of course be that the mechanism we are looking for should actually itself arise from the primitive biological part played [by the two classes of neurones]. We should thus have found a single answer to both questions.

Let us recall that from the very first the neuronic system had two functions: to receive stimuli from without and to discharge excitations of endogenous origin. It was from this latter duty, it will be remembered [p. 358], that a need for further biological development emerged under the pressure of the exigencies of life. The suspicion now arises that our systems Φ and Ψ may each have taken over one of these two primary duties. The system Φ might be the group of neurones which receive external stimuli, while the system Ψ might contain the neurones which receive endogenous excitations. If that were so, we should not have *invented* Φ and Ψ; we should have *discovered* them. It would only remain to identify them with what is already known. And in fact we know from anatomy that there is a system of neurones (the grey matter of the spinal cord) which is alone in contact with the external world, and a superimposed system (the grey matter of the brain) which has no direct peripheral contacts but which is responsible for the development of the neuronic system and for the psychical functions. The primary brain gives no bad picture of the characteristics we have attributed to the system Ψ, if we may assume that paths lead directly, and independently of Φ, from the brain to the interior of the body. The derivation and original biological significance of the primary brain is unknown to anatomists; on our theory it must have been neither more nor less than a sympathetic ganglion. Here is a first possibility of testing our theory by factual material.[1]

We shall provisionally regard the Ψ-system as identified with the

---

[1] Cf. p. 366 for a further such possibility.

grey matter of the brain. It will now be easily understood from my introductory biological remarks [p. 358] that it is precisely Ψ that is subject to further development through an increase in the number of its neurones and through an accumulation of quantity. It will also be seen how expedient it is that Ψ should consist of impermeable neurones, since otherwise it would be unable to fulfil the requirements of specific action. But how did Ψ acquire the characteristic of impermeability? After all Φ too has contact-barriers; and if *they* perform no function, why should those of Ψ perform one? To suppose that there was an original difference between the value of the contact-barriers of Φ and Ψ has once again a dubious appearance of arbitrariness, even though it would be possible, pursuing a Darwinian line of thought, to claim that impermeable neurones are indispensable and consequently bound to survive.

Another way out of the difficulty would seem more fruitful and less ambitious. Let us recall that the contact-barriers even of Ψ-neurones are in the end subject to facilitation [p. 361] and that what gives them facilitation is quantity $(Q\dot{\eta})$ [p. 361]. The greater the quantity $(Q\dot{\eta})$ concerned in the passage of the excitation, the greater is the facilitation—but that means the closer is the approach to the characteristics of the Φ-neurones. Let us therefore attribute the difference not to the neurones but to the quantities with which they have to deal. There is then reason to suspect that quantities pass through the Φ-neurones against which the resistance offered by the contact-barriers is negligible, but that the Ψ-neurones are only reached by quantities which are of the same order of magnitude as that resistance. If that is the case, a Φ-neurone would become impermeable and Ψ-neurone would become permeable if their locality and connections could be exchanged: they retain their characteristics because the Φ-neurones are connected only with the periphery and the Ψ-neurones only with the interior of the body. A distinction in their essence is thus replaced by a distinction in the *milieu* to which they happen to be allocated.

Now, however, we must examine our assumption that the quantities of stimulus reaching the neurones from the external periphery of the body are of a higher order than those from the internal periphery.

There is in fact much that speaks in favour of that view. In the first place, there can be no question but that the external world is the source of all major quantities of energy, for physical science informs us that it consists of powerful masses in violent movement and that this movement is transmitted by them. The system Φ, which is turned towards this external world, will have the task of discharging as rapidly as possible the quantities $(Q\dot{\eta})$ impinging on the neurones; but it will in any case be subjected to the influence of major quantities (Q).

To the best of our knowledge, the system Ψ is out of contact with the external world; it receives quantities (Q) only, on the one hand, from the Φ-neurones, and, on the other hand, from cellular elements in the interior of the body; and it is now a question of making it probable that these quantities of stimulus are of a comparatively low order. We may be disturbed at first by the fact that two such different sources of stimulus have to be attributed to the Ψ-neurones as Φ and the cells of the interior of the body; but precisely at this point we receive conclusive assistance from the recent histology of the neuronic systems. This shows us that the *endings* of neurones and the *connections* between neurones are constructed according to the same type, and that neurones terminate on one another in the same manner as they terminate on somatic elements [p. 358]; the functional side of the processes in both cases is also probably of the same kind. It is thus probable that similar quantities are dealt with at nerve endings and at intercellular connections. It is also reasonable to suppose that endogenous stimuli are of the same intercellular order of magnitude. And here, incidentally, we have a second opportunity for putting our theory to the test [p. 364].

[5] THE PROBLEM OF QUANTITY

I know nothing of the absolute magnitude of intercellular stimuli, but I venture to assume that it is of a comparatively small order and of the same order as that of the resistances of the contact-barriers. If this is so, it is easily understandable. The hypothesis I have been discussing preserves the essential sameness of Φ- and Ψ-neurones, while their difference in respect of permeability is biologically explained.

In the absence of evidence, it is all the more interesting to consider certain points of view and possibilities opened up by this hypothesis. To begin with, if we have formed a correct impression of the magnitude of the quantities (Q) in the external world, we may ask whether the original trend of the neuronic system towards keeping its quantity ($Q\dot{\eta}$) down to zero (for what it seeks is rapid discharge) may not already be in operation in the process of reception of stimuli.[1] We find, in fact, that the Φ-neurones do not terminate in an unattached manner at the periphery, but end in cell-structures; and it is these and not the Φ-neurones which receive the exogenous stimulus. A "nerve-ending apparatus" of this kind (using the term in the most general sense) might well serve the purpose of not allowing exogenous quantities (Q) to impinge upon Φ in undiminished magnitude but of damping them down. Such pieces of apparatus would then have the function of screens against quantity (Q) which would only allow *quotients* of the exogenous quantities (Q) to pass through.

This would fit in with the fact that the other type of nerve-ending —the unattached kind, without any terminal organ—is by far the commoner at the *internal* periphery of the body. A screen against quantity (Q) seems to be unnecessary there, presumably because the quantities ($Q\dot{\eta}$) which have to be received there do not need to be reduced to the intercellular level, since they are already at that level in the first instance.

Since we can calculate the quantities (Q) which are received by the endings of the Φ-neurones, this may perhaps afford us a means of forming some notion of the magnitudes which pass between the Ψ-neurones and which will also be of the same order as the resistances of the contact-barriers.

Here, moreover, we have a glimpse of a trend which may determine the fact that the neuronic system is built up of *several* systems: a constantly increasing tendency to hold back quantity ($Q\dot{\eta}$) from the neurones. Thus the *structure* of the neuronic system would serve the purpose of *holding back* quantity ($Q\dot{\eta}$) from the neurones, while its *function* would serve the purpose of *discharging* it.

---

[1] See p. 358 and footnote.

[6] PAIN

Every contrivance of a biological nature has limits to its efficiency, beyond which it fails. Such failures exhibit themselves in phenomena bordering on the pathological—in what may be described as normal prototypes of the pathological. We have seen that the neuronic system is contrived in such a way that the major external quantities (Q) are held back from Φ and even more from Ψ. This purpose is served by the screens provided by the nerve-endings and by the fact that Ψ is only indirectly connected with the external world. Is there a phenomenon which can be made to coincide with a failure of these contrivances? Such a phenomenon is, I think, to be found in *pain*.

Everything that we know about pain fits in with this view. The neuronic system has the most decided inclination to fly from pain. In this we can see a manifestation of its primary inclination towards avoiding any increase in its quantitative $(Q\dot\eta)$ tension, and we can conclude that pain consists in *the irruption of large quantities* (Q) *into* Ψ. The two inclinations are thus one and the same.

Pain sets both the Φ-system and the Ψ-system in motion. There are no obstacles to its conduction; it is the most imperative of all processes. The Ψ-neurones seem to be permeable to it, and it must therefore consist in the action of quantities of a relatively high order.

The exciting cause of pain may, on the one hand, be increase in quantity; all sensory excitations (even those of the highest sense organs) tend to turn into pain if the stimulus increases. This can without hesitation be interpreted as failure. On the other hand pain may occur where the external quantities are *small*. Where this is so, it is regularly associated with a breach of continuity: that is to say, if an external quantity (Q) acts directly on the endings of the Φ-neurones and not through the "nerve-ending apparatus", pain results. Pain is thus characterized by the irruption of excessively large quantities (Q) into Φ and Ψ —that is, of quantities (Q) which are of a higher order than the Φ-stimuli.

It is easy to understand the fact that pain passes along all the paths of discharge. On our theory that quantity (Q) produces facilitation [p. 361], pain no doubt leaves behind permanent facilitations in Ψ— like a stroke of lightning. It may be that these facilitations do away entirely with the resistance of the contact-barriers and establish a path of conduction like those in Φ.[1]

[7] THE PROBLEM OF QUALITY

Hitherto we have made no mention of the fact that any psychological theory must, in addition to meeting the demands made by natural science, fulfil another major obligation. It must explain to us the things that we know, in the most puzzling fashion, through our "consciousness"; and, since this consciousness knows nothing of what we have so far been assuming—quantities and neurones—our theory must also explain to us this lack of knowledge.

A postulate by which we have all along been guided at once becomes explicit. We have been treating psychical processes as something that can dispense with being known by consciousness, something that exists independently of it; we are prepared to find that some of our assumptions are not confirmed by consciousness. If we refuse to let ourselves be confused by this, that is because we have postulated that consciousness gives us neither complete nor trustworthy information about the neuronic processes; the whole of these are to be regarded in the first instance as unconscious and are to be inferred in the same way as other natural phenomena.

We have, however, to find a place in our quantitative Ψ-processes for the content of consciousness. Consciousness gives us what we call "qualities"—sensations which show a great variety of "differences" and whose differences depend on relations to the external world. Among these differences there are series, similarities and so on, but there is nothing quantitative about them. We may ask *how* qualities originate and *where* qualities originate. These are questions that need the most careful investigation, but they cannot be exhaustively treated here.

Where do qualities originate? Not in the external world; for out there (according to the views of natural science, to which, in this discussion, psychology too must submit) there are only masses in motion and nothing else. In the Φ-system perhaps? This would tally

[1] This topic is developed further in Section 12 on "The Experience of Pain".

with the fact that qualities are connected with perception, but it is contradicted by everything that rightly speaks in favour of the seat of consciousness being in the higher levels of the neuronic system. In the Ψ-system then? There is an important objection to this. The Φ- and the Ψ-systems are in action together in perception; but there is one psychical process which is no doubt performed exclusively in Ψ—reproduction or recollection. This process, however, is, speaking generally, *devoid* of quality. Recollection normally brings about nothing that has the peculiar character of perceptual quality. Thus we must summon up enough courage to assume that there is a *third* system of neurones—"perceptual neurones" they might be called—which are excited along with the others during perception but not during reproduction, and whose states of excitation give rise to the different qualities—are, that is to say, conscious sensations.[1]

If we stick firmly to the view that our consciousness furnishes only *qualities* whereas science recognizes *quantities*, a characteristic of the perceptual neurones emerges—almost as though it were by rule of three. For whereas science has set itself the task of tracing back all the *qualities* of our sensations to external *quantity*, it is to be suspected from the structure of the neuronic system that that system consists in contrivances for changing external *quantity* into *quality*. In this latter fact the original trend towards holding off quantity seems to triumph once more. The nerve-ending apparatus was a screen for allowing only a quotient of the external quantity to become operative, while at the same time Φ dealt with the discharge of quantity in the rough. The system Ψ was already shielded from higher orders of quantity and had only to do with intercellular magnitudes. Carrying the process further, the system W[2] is moved, we may suppose, by still smaller quantities. It may be that the characteristic of quality

---

[1] The part played by the perceptual neurones and their relation to the Φ- and Ψ-neurones is formulated afresh in Letter 39 (of January 1, 1896): "In my new scheme I insert the perceptual neurones between the Φ-neurones and the Ψ-neurones; so that Φ transfers its quality to ω and ω transfers neither quality nor quantity to Ψ, but merely excites Ψ—that is, indicates the direction to be taken by the free psychical energy".

[2] [W stands for "*Wahrnehmung*" "perception". The "System W" has usually been translated in Freud's later works the "system *Pcpt*." Here the "W" is kept because, as will be seen shortly, Freud jokingly changes the "W" into a Greek *omega* ("ω") to fit in with the Φ and Ψ.]

(that is, conscious sensation) only appears where quantities have so far as possible been excluded. They cannot be got rid of entirely, since these perceptual neurones must, like the rest, be regarded as cathected with quantity ($Q\dot\eta$) and striving to bring about discharge.

But at this point we are faced by what seems to be an immense difficulty. We have seen that permeability depends on the effects produced by quantity ($Q\dot\eta$) and that already the Ψ-neurones are impermeable. Since the quantity ($Q\dot\eta$) concerned is still smaller, the perceptual neurones must be still more impermeable. We cannot, however, attribute this characteristic to the vehicles of consciousness. The mutability of their content, the transitoriness of consciousness, the easy combination of simultaneously perceived qualities—all these tally only with complete permeability of the perceptual neurones coupled with full *restitutio in integrum* [return to their former state]. The perceptual neurones behave like organs of perception; and we could find no place in them for memory. Here then we have permeability, complete facilitation, which does not arise from quantities. Where, then, does it arise from?

I can see only one way of escape: to revise our basic hypothesis on the passage of quantity ($Q\dot\eta$). Hitherto I have regarded it only as a transference of quantity ($Q\dot\eta$) from one neurone to another. It must have another attribute, however—of a *temporal* character; for the mechanics of the physicists have assigned this temporal attribute even to the motions of masses in the external world. I shall describe this attribute briefly as "period". Thus I shall assume that the resistance of the contact-barriers applies only to the transference of quantity (Q), but that the *period* of neuronic motion is transmitted without inhibition in every direction, as though it were a process of induction.

Much remains to be done here in the way of physical clarification, for here as elsewhere the general laws of motion must apply without contradiction. But my hypothesis goes further, and asserts that the perceptual neurones are incapable of receiving quantities ($Q\dot\eta$), but that they assimilate the *period* of an excitation and that this condition of theirs of being affected by a period, while being filled with only a minimum of quantity ($Q\dot\eta$), is the fundamental basis of consciousness. The Ψ-neurones, too, have of course their period, but this is devoid of quality, or, to put it more accurately, is monotonous. Deviations from this specific psychical period reach consciousness as qualities.

Where do these differences in period originate? Everything points to the sense-organs, whose qualities must be represented by different periods of neuronic motion. The sense organs operate not only as screens against quantity (Q)—like every nerve-ending apparatus—but as *sieves*; for they only let through stimuli from certain processes that have a particular period. They probably transfer these differences to Φ by communicating to the neuronic motion periods with differences that are in some way analogous [to those of the processes in the external world]—specific energy; and it is these modifications which pass from Φ through Ψ to W, and there, where they are almost devoid of quantity, generate conscious sensations of qualities.[1] This transmission of quality is not durable; it leaves no traces behind it and cannot be reproduced.

[8] CONSCIOUSNESS

Only by means of these complicated and far from self-evident hypotheses have I so far succeeded in introducing the phenomena of consciousness into the structure of quantitative psychology.

No attempt can be made, of course, to explain how it is that excitatory processes in the perceptual neurones (ωN) involve consciousness. Our only task is to find varying processes in the perceptual neurones which are parallel to the characteristics of consciousness that are known to us. And this is not difficult to do in some detail.

First, however, a word upon the relation of this theory of consciousness to others. According to a modern mechanistic theory, consciousness is no more than an appendage added to physiologico-psychical processes, an appendage whose absence would make no difference to the course of psychical events. According to another theory consciousness is the subjective side of all psychical events and is thus inseparable from physiologico-mental processes. The theory which I have

---

[1] [This is discussed more fully below, p. 374-5.]

here propounded lies between these two. According to it consciousness is the subjective side of a *part* of the physical processes in the neuronic system—namely, of the *perceptual* processes (ω-processes); and its absence would *not* leave psychical events unchanged but would imply the absence of any contribution from the W (ω)-system.

If we represent consciousness by perceptual neurones (ωN), several consequences follow. These neurones must have a discharge, small though it may be; and there must be some means of filling the perceptual neurones with quantities ($Q\dot\eta$) of the necessary small amount. As in all other cases, this discharge will be in the direction of motility; and it is to be observed that, with the change-over into motion, obviously every characteristic of quality, every periodic peculiarity, is lost. The perceptual neurones must, no doubt, be filled with quantity only from Ψ, for we should wish to exclude any direct connection between this third system and Φ. It is impossible to suggest what may have been the original biological value of the perceptual neurones.

So far, however, we have only given an incomplete description of the content of consciousness. Apart from the series of sensory qualities, it presents another and very different series—the series of sensations of pleasure and unpleasure. And these we must now interpret. Since we have certain knowledge of a trend in psychical life towards *avoiding unpleasure*, we are tempted to identify that trend with the primary trend towards inertia. In that case *unpleasure* would coincide with a rise in the level of quantity ($Q\dot\eta$) or with a quantitative increase of pressure; it would be the perceptual sensation when there is an increase of quantity ($Q\dot\eta$) in Ψ. *Pleasure* would be the sensation of discharge. Since the system W is presumed to be filled from Ψ, it would follow that the cathexis in W increases when the level in Ψ rises, and diminishes when that level falls. Pleasure and unpleasure would be the sensations of W's own cathexis, of its own level, while W and Ψ would function to some extent like inter-communicating pipes. Thus the quantitative processes in Ψ would reach consciousness in this way too, once again as qualities. [Cf. pp. 371-2.] Along with sensations of pleasure and unpleasure, the capacity disappears for perceiving sensory qualities which lie, so to speak, in the indifferent zone between pleasure and unpleasure.[1] This must be translated thus: the perceptual neurones (ωN) show an optimum capacity for receiving the period of neuronic motion when they have a particular amount of cathexis; if the cathexis becomes stronger, unpleasure arises, if it becomes weaker, pleasure arises—till, when there is *no* cathexis, the capacity for reception vanishes. The form of motion in question would have to be constructed in accordance with these data

[9] THE FUNCTIONING OF THE APPARATUS

We can now form the following picture of the functioning of the apparatus constituted by $\Phi\ \Psi\ \omega$.

Sums of excitation impinge from outside upon the endings of the Φ-system. They first come up against the nerve-ending apparatus and are broken up by it into quotients, which are probably of a higher order than intercellular stimuli (or possibly of the same order?). Here we have a first threshold. Below a certain quantity no effective quotient at all comes into being. So that the effectiveness of stimuli is restricted more or less to the *medium* quantities. At the same time the nature of the nerve-coverings acts as a sieve, so that not every kind of stimulus can be effective at the various endings. The stimuli which actually reach the Φ-neurones have a quantity and a qualitative characteristic[2]; in the external world they form a series possessing the same quality [as the stimuli] and increasing [degrees of] quantity, rising from the threshold up to the limit of pain.

The *processes* in the external world form a continuum in two directions—according to quantity and period (quality); whereas, the *stimuli* corresponding to those processes are, as regards quantity,

---

[1] [This point is expanded in the third paragraph of Section I of *Beyond the Pleasure Principle* (1920 *g*). It is there attributed to Fechner.]

[2] [For the sake of clarity, it may be pointed out that neither the "processes" in the external world, nor the "stimuli" that pass through the "nerve-ending apparatus" into Φ, nor the cathexes in Φ or Ψ possess quality, but only a *characteristic*—"period"—which, when it reaches ω, *becomes* quality.]

firstly *reduced* and, secondly *limited* by excision, and are, as regards quality, *discontinuous*, so that certain periods do not operate at all as stimuli. [Fig. 12.]

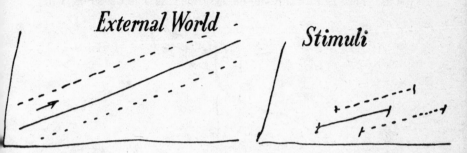

Fig. 12

The characteristic of quality in the stimuli now proceeds without hindrance through Φ by way of Ψ to ω, where it generates sensation; it is represented by a particular period of neuronic motion which is certainly not the same as that of the stimulus but has some relation to it, determined according to a reduction formula that is unknown to us. This period does not persist for long and vanishes in the direction of motility; nor, since it is allowed to pass through, does it leave any memory behind it.

The *quantity* of the Φ-stimulus excites the trend towards discharge in the nervous system, and it is converted into a proportional motor excitation. (The apparatus of motility is directly attached to Φ.) The quantities thus converted produce an effect which is quantitatively far superior to themselves; for they enter the muscles, glands, etc., and act in them as a *release* [of quantity], whereas between the neurones there is only a *transference* [of quantity].

Further, the Φ-neurones terminate in the Ψ-neurones, to which a part of the quantity ($Q\dot\eta$) is transferred, but only a part—a quotient, perhaps, corresponding to the magnitude of intercellular stimuli. At this point we may ask whether the quantity ($Q\dot\eta$) transferred to Ψ may not increase in proportion to the quantity (Q) of the current in Φ, so that a larger stimulus will produce a stronger psychical effect. A special contrivance seems to operate here, which once again holds back quantity (Q) from Ψ. For the sensory paths of conduction in Φ have a peculiar structure. They constantly send out branches and exhibit thicker and thinner paths, which terminate at numerous end-points. This is probably to be explained as follows. [Fig. 13].

Fig. 13

A stronger stimulus pursues different paths from a weaker one. For instance, $Q\dot{\eta}1$ will only pass along path I and will transfer a quotient to Ψ at end-point α. $Q\dot{\eta}2$ [*i.e.*, a quantity twice as great as $Q\dot{\eta}1$] will not transfer a *double* quotient at α, but will be able to pass along path II, which is a narrower one, as well as along path I, and will open up a second endpoint to Ψ [at β]; $Q\dot{\eta}3$ will open up the narrowest path and will transfer through the end-point γ [see fig.] as well. In this way the single path will be relieved of its charge and the *larger* quantity in Ψ will be expressed by the fact that *several* neurones will be cathected in Ψ instead of a single one. Each of the cathexes of the different Ψ-neurones may, in such a case, be of approximately equal magnitude. If $Q\dot{\eta}$ in Φ produces a cathexis in Ψ, then $Q\dot{\eta}3$ will be expressed by a cathexis in $\Psi_1 + \Psi_2 + \Psi_3$. Thus *quantity* in Φ is expressed by *complexity* in Ψ. And by this means quantity (Q) is held back from Ψ, within certain limits, at least. This is very reminiscent of Fechner's law,[1] which might in this way be localized.

In this way Ψ is cathected from Φ with quantities (Q) which, in the normal course of things, are small. While the *quantity* of the Φ-excitation is expressed in Ψ by complexity, the *quality* is expressed

---

[1] [A formulation of the relation between changes in the intensity of a stimulus and changes in the resultant sensation. Freud appears to be suggesting that Fechner's law comes into operation at this particular point in the neuronic system.]

topographically, since, in accordance with the anatomical relations, the different sense organs communicate only with particular Ψ-neurones. But Ψ also receives cathexes from the interior of the body, and it seems reasonable to divide the Ψ-neurones into two groups: the neurones of the pallium[1] which are cathected from Φ, and the nuclear neurones which are cathected from the endogenous paths of conduction.

[10] THE Ψ PATHS OF CONDUCTION

The nuclear portion of Ψ is connected with the paths by which endogenous quantities (Q) of excitation ascend. Without excluding the possibility that these paths may be connected with Φ, we must nevertheless adhere to our original assumption that a direct pathway leads from the interior of the body to the Ψ-neurones [p. 364]. But this implies that Ψ is exposed without protection to quantities (Q) from this direction, and in this fact [as we shall see (p. 379)] lies the driving force of the psychical mechanism.

What we know of the endogenous stimuli can be stated in the hypothesis that they are of an intercellular nature, that they arise continuously, and that it is only periodically that they become psychical stimuli. We cannot avoid supposing that they accumulate, and the intermittent nature of their psychical effect must lead to the view that in their path of conduction they come up against resistances which are only overcome when the quantity of excitation increases. The paths of conduction are thus arranged in a series, with several contact-barriers, leading up to the nucleus of Ψ. When they are above a certain quantity (Q) the endogenous stimuli act continuously, and every increase of quantity (Q) is perceived as an increase of the Ψ-stimulus. This, therefore, implies a state of affairs in which the path of conduction has become permeable. Experience further shows that after the discharge of the Ψ-stimulus the path of conduction once more resumes its resistance.

A process of this kind is termed "summation". The Ψ-paths of

---

[1][Mid-nineteenth century histologists had distinguished two main strata of nerve-cells in the cerebral cortex, and gave the name of "pallium" ("mantle") to the outer layer. Recent neuro-anatomy has revealed a far more complex stratification.]

conduction are filled by summation until they become permeable. It is evidently the smallness of the separate stimuli that enables summation to occur. Summation is also found in the Φ-paths of conduction—for instance, in the case of the conduction of pain; but it applies in their case only to small quantities. The minor part played by summation on the Φ side argues in favour of the fact that there we are concerned with quantities (Q) of considerable magnitude. Very small ones seem to be held back by the operation of the nerve-ending apparatus as a threshold, whereas on the Ψ-side there is no such apparatus and only small quantities $(Q\dot\eta)$ are operative.

It should be noticed that the Ψ-conduction-neurones can alternate between the characteristics of permeability and impermeability, since they can almost completely resume their resistance in spite of the passage of quantity $(Q\dot\eta)$. This is in complete contradiction to the property which we have attributed to the Ψ-neurones of becoming permanently facilitated by a current of quantity $(Q\dot\eta)$ [p. 361]. How is this contradiction to be explained? By supposing that a resumption of resistance after a current has ceased is a general attribute of contact-barriers. There is then not much difficulty in bringing this into harmony with the fact that the Ψ-neurones are influenced [by the passage of quantity] in the direction of facilitation. We need only suppose that the facilitation which remains after the quantity (Q) has passed consists not in the removal of *all* resistance but in its reduction to a necessary minimum. During the passage of the quantity (Q) the resistance is suspended, but afterwards it is restored—but only to a particular height, according to the quantity (Q) that has passed; so that next time a smaller quantity will be able to pass, and so on. When the most complete facilitation has been established, there will remain a certain resistance, equal in amount in the case of all contact-barriers; so that quantities (Q) will have to increase above a certain threshold in order to be able to pass it. This resistance would be a constant. Accordingly, the fact that endogenous quantities $(Q\dot\eta)$ operate by summation means no more than that these quantities are composed of very small magnitudes of excitation, less than the constant; and there is complete facilitation in the endogenous paths of conduction.

It follows from this, however, that the Ψ-contact-barriers are in general higher than the barriers in [the endogenous] paths of conduction, so that a fresh accumulation of quantity $(Q\acute{\eta})$ can occur in the nuclear neurones. [See p. 384.] From the time when the path of conduction is filled up, no limit is set to this accumulation. Here (Ψ) is at the mercy of quantity (Q), and it is thus that there arises in the interior of the system the impulsion which sustains all psychical activity. We are familiar with this force as the "will"—the derivative of the "instincts". [Cf. p. 399.]

[11] THE EXPERIENCE OF SATISFACTION

The filling of the nuclear neurones in Ψ has as its consequence an effort to discharge, an impetus which is released along motor pathways. Experience shows that the first path to be followed is that leading to *internal change* (e.g., emotional expression, screaming, or vascular innervation). But, as we showed at the beginning of the discussion [p. 357], no discharge of this kind can bring about any relief of tension, because endogenous stimuli continue to be received in spite of it and the Ψ-tension is re-established. Here a removal of the stimulus can only be effected by an intervention which will temporarily stop the release of quantity $(Q\acute{\eta})$ in the interior of the body, and an intervention of this kind requires an alteration in the external world (e.g., the supply of nourishment or the proximity of the sexual object), and this, as a "specific action", can only be brought about in particular ways. At early stages the human organism is incapable of achieving this specific action. It is brought about by extraneous help, when the attention of an experienced person has been drawn to the child's condition by a discharge taking place along the path of internal change [e.g., by the child's screaming]. This path of discharge thus acquires an extremely important secondary function— viz., of bringing about an understanding with other people; and the original helplessness of human beings is thus the primal source of all moral motives. [Cf. p. 422-3.][1]

When the extraneous helper has carried out the specific action in

---

[1] In none of Freud's later formulations of this idea has the present one been equalled or surpassed: it indicates the part played by object-relations in the transition from the pleasure to the reality principle. See also p. 390 ff.

the external world on behalf of the helpless subject, the latter is in a position, by means of reflex contrivances, immediately to perform what is necessary in the interior of his body in order to remove the endogenous stimulus. This total event then constitutes an "experience of satisfaction", which has the most momentous consequences in the functional development of the individual. For three things occur in his Ψ-system: (1) A lasting discharge is effected, so that the urgency which had generated unpleasure in W is brought to an end. (2) A cathexis corresponding to the perception of an object occurs in one or more neurones of the pallium [p. 377]. (3) At other points of the pallium a report is received of the discharge brought about by the release of the reflex movement which followed the specific action. A facilitation is then established between these cathexes [(2) and (3)] and the nuclear neurones [which were being cathected from endogenous sources during the state of urgency].

(The report of the reflex discharge comes about owing to the fact that every movement, as a result of its collateral consequences, gives rise to fresh sensory excitations—of the skin and muscles—which produce a *motor [or kinaesthetic] image.*)

The facilitation arises in a manner which gives a deeper insight into the development of Ψ. Hitherto we have learned that the Ψ-neurones are influenced from the Φ-neurones and through the endogenous paths of conduction, while the separate Ψ-neurones are cut off from one another by contact-barriers with powerful resistances. There is, however, a fundamental law of *association by simultaneity,* which operates during pure Ψ-activity (during reproductive recollection); and this is the basis of all connections between Ψ-neurones. We find that consciousness (that is, quantitative cathexis) passes from one Ψ-neurone a to another β, if a and β have at some time been simultaneously cathected from Φ (or elsewhere). Thus the simultaneous cathexis a—β has led to the facilitation of a contact-barrier. It follows, in the language of our theory, that a quantity $(Q\dot{\eta})$ passes more easily from a neurone to a cathected neurone than to an uncathected one. Thus the cathexis of the second neurone operates in the same way as an increase in the cathexis of the first one; and in this case once again *cathexis is seen to be equivalent, in respect of the passage of quantity $(Q\dot{\eta})$, to facilitation.* [Cf. p. 361.]

Here then we learn of a second important factor in directing the course taken by a quantity ($Q\dot{\eta}$). A quantity ($Q\dot{\eta}$) in neurone a will go not only in the direction of the barrier which is best facilitated, but also in the direction of the barrier which is cathected on its further side. These two factors may support each other or may in some cases operate against each other.

Thus the experience of satisfaction leads to a facilitation between the two memory-images [of the object wished-for and of the reflex movement] and the nuclear neurones which had been cathected during the state of urgency. (No doubt, during [the actual course of] the discharge brought about by the satisfaction, the quantity ($Q\dot{\eta}$) flows out of the memory-images as well.) Now, when the state of urgency or wishing re-appears, the cathexis will pass also to the two memories and will activate *them*. And in all probability the memory-image of the object will be the first to experience this wishful activation.

I have no doubt that the wishful activation will in the first instance produce something similar to a perception—namely, a hallucination. And if this leads to the performance of the reflex action, disappointment will inevitably follow.

[12] THE EXPERIENCE OF PAIN

Ψ is normally exposed to quantity (Q) from the endogenous paths of conduction, and abnormally (though not yet pathologically) in cases where excessively large quantities (Q) break through the screening contrivances into Φ—that is to say, in cases of *pain* [p. 368]. Pain gives rise in Ψ to (1) a large rise in the level [of quantity], which is felt as unpleasure by W [p. 373] (2) an inclination to discharge, which can be modified in various directions and (3) a facilitation between this inclination to discharge and the memory-image of the object that generated the pain. Moreover there is no question but that pain has a special quality which makes itself felt alongside the unpleasure.

If the memory-image of the (hostile) [i.e., the pain-giving] object is in any manner freshly cathected (e.g., by fresh perceptions), a condition arises which is not pain but has a similarity to pain. It includes unpleasure and the inclination to discharge corresponding to the experience of pain. Since unpleasure implies a heightened level [of quantity], the question arises of where this quantity $(Q\acute{\eta})$ comes from. In the experience of pain proper, it was the irrupting external quantity (Q) which raised the level in Ψ. In its reproduction—in the affect—the only quantity $(Q\acute{\eta})$ arising is the quantity (Q) cathecting the memory; and it is obvious that this is of the same nature as any other perception and cannot result in a general increase in quantity $(Q\acute{\eta})$.

We are thus driven to assume that unpleasure is *released* from the interior of the body—is freshly provoked—by the cathexis of memories. The mechanism of this release can only be pictured as follows. Just as there are motor neurones which, when they are filled up to a certain degree, conduct quantities $(Q\acute{\eta})$ into the muscles and thus discharge them, so too there must be "secretory" neurones which, when they are excited, cause the generation in the interior of the body of something which acts as a stimulus on the endogenous paths of conduction to Ψ. These secretory neurones must influence the production of endogenous quantities $(Q\acute{\eta})$ and accordingly do not *discharge* quantity $(Q\acute{\eta})$ but *introduce* it in roundabout ways. We shall give the name of "key neurones" to these secretory[1] neurones. Evidently they are only excited when a certain level has been reached in Ψ. The experience of pain provides an excellent facilitation between the memory-image of the hostile object and these key neurones; and by virtue of this facilitation an unpleasurable affect is now released.

Support is lent to this puzzling but indispensable hypothesis by what happens in the case of the release of sexual feeling. At the same time a suspicion forces itself on us that in both these examples the endogenous stimuli consist of chemical products, of which there may be a considerable number. Since the release of unpleasure can be extraordinarily large where there is only quite a slight cathexis of the hostile memory, we may conclude that pain leaves behind it specially abundant facilitations. And in this connection we may suspect that facilitation depends entirely on the [magnitude of the]

---

[1] [The manuscript reads "motor"—evidently a slip of the pen.]

quantity $(Q\dot\eta)$ attained: so that the facilitating effect of $3Q\dot\eta$ may be far greater than that of $Q\dot\eta$ 3 times repeated. (See p. 363.)

[13] AFFECTS AND WISHFUL STATES

The residues of the two kinds of experiences [of satisfaction and of pain] which we have been discussing are *affects* and *wishful states*. These have in common the fact that both of them involve a heightening of the quantitative tension in Ψ: in the case of an affect this is brought about by a sudden release, and in that of a wish by means of summation. Both these states are of the greatest importance in relation to the passage of quantity in Ψ, since they leave motive forces behind them which affect that passage in a compulsive fashion. A wishful state produces what amounts to a positive *attraction* to the object of the wish, or rather to its memory-image; an experience of pain results in a repulsion, a disinclination to keep the hostile memory-image cathected. Here we have primary *wishful attraction* and primary *defence* [or fending-off].[1]

Wishful attraction can easily be explained by supposing that the cathexis of the friendly memory in a state of desire is far greater in quantity $(Q\dot\eta)$ than it is in the case of mere perception; so that in the former case there is a particularly good facilitation between the Ψ-nucleus and the corresponding neurones of the pallium.

It is more difficult to explain primary defence or "repression"— the fact that a hostile memory-image has its cathexis removed as soon as possible.[2] The explanation may nevertheless be that the primary experiences of pain were brought to an end by reflex defence. The emergence of some other object in place of the hostile one acted as a signal for the fact that the experience of pain was at an end; and the Ψ-system, learning from biological experience, seeks to reproduce the state in Ψ which indicated the cessation of the pain. The phrase "learning from biological experience" introduces a fresh basis of

---

[1] [These states are further discussed in Part III, pp. 428 and 433 ff.]

[2] Further on in the present paper (p. 408) Freud already distinguishes between primary defence and repression. He later separated the reaction to pain from repression. (See his paper on "Repression", 1915 *d*; *trans. Coll. Papers* IV, p. 85.)

explanation which must carry independent weight of its own, though at the same time it does not exclude (but indeed requires) a recourse to mechanical principles—that is, to quantitative factors.[1] In the case before us it may well be the increase in quantity ($Q\dot\eta$), invariably arising when hostile memories are cathected, which forces an increase in the activity of discharge and so at the same time a flow of quantity away from the memories as well.

[14] INTRODUCTION OF THE CONCEPT OF AN "EGO"[2]

With our hypothesis of "wishful attraction" and of a tendency to repression we have in fact already touched upon a state of Ψ which has not yet been discussed. For both these processes indicate that an organization has been formed in Ψ whose presence interferes with the passage [of quantities] if that passage occurred for the first time in a particular manner [i.e., if it was accompanied by satisfaction or pain]. This organization is called the "ego". It can easily be pictured if we consider that the constantly repeated reception of endogenous quantities ($Q\dot\eta$) in certain neurones (of the nucleus) and the consequent facilitating effects of that repeated reception will produce a group of neurones which retains a constant cathexis [p. 378-9] and which thus constitutes the vehicle for the store of quantity required by the secondary function [p. 358].[3] The ego may thus be defined as the totality of Ψ-cathexes at any given time; and in these a permanent portion may be distinguished from a changing one. [Cf. p. 390.] It is easy to see that the facilitations between the Ψ-neurones form part of the domain of the ego, since they represent possibilities of determining the extent of the changing ego from one moment to another.

---

[1] [The topic of "learning from biological experience" recurs frequently in Part III, *e.g.*, on pp. 417 and 428.]

[2] [This topic is further discussed in Part III, on p. 426 ff.]

[3] A constant cathexis of energy, the function of inhibiting or postponing certain discharges, and a connection with the secondary process—all of these are also among the characteristics of the "ego organization", as Freud uses the term in his structural theory. (See *The Ego and the Id*, 1923 *b*. and Freud's later writings.)

While it must be the ego's endeavour to get rid of its cathexes by the method of satisfaction, it (the ego) must inevitably influence the repetition of experiences of pain and affects; and it must do so in the following manner, which is generally called "inhibition".

A quantity $(Q\dot\eta)$ which enters a neurone from anywhere will pursue its path through the contact-barrier which shows the greatest facilitation, and will give rise to a current flowing in that direction. To put this more accurately: the current of quantity $(Q\dot\eta)$ will divide its course towards the different contact-barriers in inverse ratio to the resistance which they offer; and where a quotient of quantity comes up against a contact-barrier whose resistance is superior to it, nothing will in practice pass through. This distribution may easily be different for every difference in quantity $(Q\dot\eta)$ there may happen to be in the neurone, for quotients may appear which rise above the threshold of still other contact-barriers. Thus the course taken depends on the quantities $(Q\dot\eta)$ and the relative strength of the facilitations. We have, however, come to know a third powerful factor [p. 380]. If an adjoining neurone is simultaneously cathected, this acts like a temporary facilitation of the contact-barriers between the two neurones, and modifies the course of the current, which would otherwise have followed the direction of the only facilitated contact-barrier. A "lateral" cathexis thus acts as *an inhibition on the passage of quantity* $(Q\dot\eta)$. Let us imagine the ego as a network of cathected neurones, well facilitated in relation to one another [See Fig. 14]. Then suppose a quantity $(Q\dot\eta)$ enters neurone *a* from the outside (Φ). If it were uninfluenced it would have proceeded to neurone *b*. But it is in fact so much influenced by the lateral cathexis in neurone

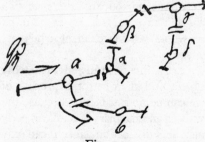

Fig. 14

α that it only passes on a quotient to *b*, or may even not reach *b* at all. Where, then, an ego exists, it is bound to inhibit psychical processes.

But inhibition of this kind is decidedly to Ψ's advantage. Let us

suppose that a is a hostile memory and b a key neurone [p. 382] for unpleasure. Then, if a is aroused, the primary effect will be the release of unpleasure, which might perhaps be pointless—at all events in its full amount. But as a result of the inhibitory effect of α the release of unpleasure is very small and the neuronic system is spared the development and discharge of quantity without suffering damage in any other way. We can now easily see how, with the help of a mechanism which draws the ego's *attention*[1] to an imminent fresh cathexis of the hostile memory-image, the ego can succeed in inhibiting the passage of quantity from the memory-image to the release of unpleasure, by a copious lateral cathexis which can be increased as circumstances dictate. Indeed, if we assume that the initial unpleasurable release of quantity $(Q\dot{\eta})$ is received by the ego itself, it will have within itself the source of the quantity whose expenditure is necessary for the purpose of the inhibitory lateral cathexis.

Thus the stronger the unpleasure, the stronger will be the primary defence.

[15] THE PRIMARY AND SECONDARY PROCESSES IN Ψ

It follows from what we have so far made out that there are two situations in which the ego in Ψ (which we can treat in regard to its trends like the nervous system as a whole) is liable to fall into a helpless state in which it is exposed to damage.

The first of these arises if, while it is in a wishful state, it freshly cathects the memory of the object and then sets the process of discharge in motion, where there can be no satisfaction because the object is not present *really* but only as an imaginary idea. At an early stage Ψ is not in a position to make this distinction, since it can only work on the basis of the sequence of analogous states between its neurones [i.e. on the basis of its previous experience that the cathexis of the object was followed by satisfaction]. Thus it requires a criterion

---

[1] [The function of attention is discussed at great length in Part III (p. 418 ff.).]

from elsewhere in order to distinguish between perceptions and ideas.[1]

In the second place, Ψ is in need of an indication that will draw its attention to the re-cathexis of a hostile memory-image and enable it to avoid, by means of a lateral cathexis, the consequent release of unpleasure. If Ψ is able to effect this inhibition soon enough, both the release of unpleasure and the defence against it will be slight; whereas otherwise there will be immense unpleasure and an excessive primary defence.

Both a wishful cathexis and a release of unpleasure when there is a fresh cathexis of the memory concerned can be biologically damaging. This is true of a wishful cathexis whenever it oversteps a certain limit and thus encourages discharge; and it is true of a release of unpleasure at all events whenever the cathexis of the hostile memory-image arises from Ψ itself (by association) and not from the external world. Thus, in the latter case too what is needed is an indication which will distinguish a perception from a memory (or idea).

In all probability it is the perceptual neurones which furnish this indication—an "indication of reality". In the case of every external perception a qualitative excitation occurs in W. But this, as such, is of no importance to Ψ. We must therefore add that the perceptual excitation leads to a perceptual *discharge*, and that a report of this (as of all other kinds of discharge) reaches Ψ. *It is this report of a discharge coming from W (ω) that constitutes an indication of quality or reality to* Ψ.

If the wished-for object is fully cathected, so that it is activated in a hallucinatory manner, the same indication of discharge or reality will follow as in the case of an external perception. In this instance the criterion fails. But if the wishful cathexis is subjected to *inhibition*, as will be possible if the ego is cathected, a quantitative case may occur in which the wishful cathexis will not be intense enough for an indication of quality to be produced, as it would be in the case of an

---

[1] What follows contains the earliest formulation of a notion to which Freud gave frequent and varying expression and to which he finally gave shape in his statement that "reality-testing" is a function of the ego. Earlier formulations, which immediately follow upon the account given in the "Project", will be found in *The Interpretation of Dreams* and in Freud's paper on the two principles of mental functioning (1911 *b*; *trans. Coll. Papers* IV, especially p. 14).

external perception. In this instance, then, the criterion retains its value. The distinction between the two instances resides in the fact that, whereas indications of quality derived from outside make their appearance *whatever* the intensity of cathexis, those derived from Ψ only do so if the intensities are large. Accordingly, *it is the inhibition brought about by the ego that makes possible a criterion for distinguishing between a perception and a memory.* Biological experience will then teach the lesson that discharge must not be initiated until an indication of reality has arrived, and that for this reason the cathexis of the desired memories must not be carried beyond a certain degree.

On the other hand, the excitation of the perceptual neurones can also serve to protect the Ψ-system in the *second* situation: namely, by drawing the attention of Ψ to the fact of the presence or absence of a perception. For this purpose we must assume that the perceptual neurones (ωN) were originally connected anatomically with the paths of conduction from the different sense organs and that their discharge was directed back again to the motor apparatus belonging to these same sense organs. Then the report of this latter discharge (the report, that is, of *reflex attention*) will act as a biological signal to Ψ to send out a quantity of cathexis in the same direction.

To sum up. Where inhibition is operated by a cathected ego, the indications of ω-discharge serve in general as indications of reality which Ψ learns, by biological experience, to make use of. If the ego is in a state of wishful tension at the moment when an indication of reality emerges, it will allow discharge to follow along the lines of the specific action [p. 379]. If an increase of unpleasure coincides with the indication of reality, Ψ will institute a defence of normal magnitude by an appropriately large lateral cathexis at the point indicated. If neither of these is the case [i.e., if there is neither a wishful state nor an increase of unpleasure at the moment when an indication of reality is received], the cathexis will be allowed to proceed unhindered, according to the nature of the facilitations prevailing. Wishful cathexis carried to the point of hallucination and a complete generation of unpleasure, involving a complete expenditure of defence, may be described as "psychical primary processes". On the other hand, those processes which are only made possible by a good cathexis of the ego and which represent a moderation of the primary processes may be described as "psychical secondary processes". It will be seen that the *sine qua non* of the latter is a correct exploitation of the indications of reality and that this is only possible when there is inhibition on the part of the ego.[1]

[16] COGNITIVE AND REPRODUCTIVE THOUGHT[2]

We have thus put forward a hypothesis to the effect that, during the process of wishing, inhibition on the part of the ego leads to a moderation of the cathexis of the object wished-for, which makes it possible for that object to be recognized as not being a real one. Let us now carry our analysis of this process further; and here there is more than one different possibility.

In the first case, the wishful cathexis of the memory-image may be accompanied by a simultaneous perception of it [that is, of the object to which the memory relates]. The two cathexes will then coincide (a situation from which no biological profit can be derived). In addition to this, an indication of reality arises from W, which, as we have seen, is followed by a discharge that is successful.[3] Thus this case is easily disposed of.

In the second case, the wishful cathexis that is present may be

---

[1] For purposes of comparison with this section, we may quote a passage from *The Interpretation of Dreams* (trans., 1953, pp. 598-600): "A current of this kind in the apparatus, starting from unpleasure and aiming at pleasure, we have termed a 'wish'.... The first wishing seems to have been a hallucinatory cathecting of the memory of satisfaction ... All that I insist upon is the idea that the activity of the *first* Ψ-system is directed towards securing the *free discharge* of the quantities of excitation, while the *second* system, by means of the cathexes emanating from it, succeeds in *inhibiting* this discharge and in transforming the cathexis into a quiescent one, no doubt with a simultaneous raising of its level. I presume, therefore, that under the dominion of the second system the discharge of excitation is governed by quite different mechanical conditions from those in force under the dominion of the first system. When once the second system has concluded its exploratory thought-activity, it releases the inhibition and damming-up of the excitations and allows them to discharge themselves in movement".

[2] [The topics of this and the two next sections are further elaborated in Part III.]

[3] Compare in connection with this and with what follows a later formulation dealing with this extended group of problems: "Thus the first and immediate aim of the process of testing reality is not to discover an object in real perception

accompanied by a perception which agrees with it only partly and not wholly. This is the moment at which to recall the fact that perceptual cathexes are never cathexes of single neurones but always of complexes. Hitherto we have neglected this feature and the time has come to take it into account. Let us suppose that the *wishful* cathexis, speaking quite generally, is attached to neurone a+neurone b; whereas the *perceptual* cathexis is attached to neurone a+neurone c. This being the commoner case—more common than that of identity—it deserves close study. Here, too, biological experience teaches that it is unsafe to initiate discharge if the indications of reality confirm only a part of the complex and not the whole of it. Now, however, we come upon a method of turning the similarity into a complete identity. If we compare this W-complex with other W-complexes, we are able to analyse it into two portions: a neurone a which on the whole remains the same and a neurone b which on the whole varies. Language later applies the term "judgement" to this process of analysis, and discovers the resemblance which exists between the nucleus of the ego and the constant portion of the perceptual complex on the one hand and between the changing cathexes in the pallium and the inconstant portion of the perceptual complex on the other [cf. p. 384]; language describes neurone a as a "thing" and neurone b as its activity or attribute—in short, as its "predicate". [Cf. pp. 393 and 423.]

Thus judgement is a Ψ-process which is only made possible by the inhibition exercised by the ego and which is brought about by the difference between the wishful cathexis of a memory and a similar perceptual cathexis. It follows from this that when these two cathexes

---

corresponding to what is imagined, but to *re-discover* such an object, to convince oneself that it is still there. The differentiation between what is subjective and what is objective is further assisted by another faculty of the power of thought. The reproduction of a perception as an image is not always a faithful one; it can be modified by omissions or by the fusion of a number of its elements. The process for testing the thing's reality must then investigate the extent of these distortions. But it is evident that an essential precondition for the institution of the function for testing reality is that objects shall have been lost which have formerly afforded real satisfaction". ("Negation", 1925 *h, trans. Coll. Papers,* V, p. 184.) The connection with an early object relation which is stated in this last sentence is often only implicit in the "Project". But the example used by Freud for his discussion of the establishment of an identity between the image and what is imagined is the infant's image of his mother's breast (pp. 391 and 393).

coincide, the fact will be a biological signal for ending the activity of thinking and for initiating discharge.[1] When they do *not* coincide, an impetus is given to the activity of thinking which will be brought to a close when they *do* coincide.

The process can be analysed further. If neurone *a* is present in both the wishful and the perceptual cathexis but if neurone *c* is perceived instead of neurone *b*, the efforts of the ego follow the connections of this neurone *c* and, by means of a flow of quantity($Q\dot\eta$) along these connections, cause fresh cathexes to emerge until at last the missing neurone *b* is reached. As a rule, what is interpolated between neurone *c* and neurone *b* is a motor image, and, when this image is revived by the actual carrying out of a movement, the perception of neurone *b* is obtained and the desired identity established. Suppose, for instance, that the memory-image wished for is—to take the case of a baby—an image of the mother's breast with a front view of its nipple, but that the baby begins by having a perception which is a *side* view of the same object without the nipple. Now, he has in his memory an experience, made accidentally while he was sucking, of a particular movement of his head which changed the front view into the side view. Accordingly, the side image which he now sees leads to the head-movement, and an experiment will show him that the reverse of the movement must be performed and the perception of the front view will thus be obtained.

This case still has little of judgement about it; but it is an example of the possibility, by reproducing cathexes, of arriving at an action which is one of the chance off-shoots of the specific action.

There is no doubt that what underlies this travelling along the facilitated neurones is quantity ($Q\dot\eta$) from the cathected ego, and that the travelling is not controlled by the facilitations but by an aim. What, then, is this aim and how is it attained?

The aim is to get back to the missing neurone *b* and to release the sensation of identity—that is, the moment at which only neurone *b* is cathected and the travelling cathexis finds its way into *b*. The aim is attained by experimentally displacing the quantities ($Q\dot\eta$) in all directions, and for that purpose sometimes a greater and sometimes a less

---

[1] [Cf. the very similar remarks on judgement in Freud's paper on "Negation" (1925 *h*).]

expenditure of lateral cathexis will clearly be necessary, according to whether one can make use of the existing facilitations or must work against them. The struggle between the fixed facilitations and the changing cathexes is characteristic of the secondary process of reproductive thinking as contrasted with the primary succession of associations.

What is it that directs the course of the travelling? The fact that memory of the wishful idea is kept cathected, all the while the chain of association is followed from neurone c. As we know, the fact of the cathexis of neurone b will increase the facilitation and accessibility of any connections it may have.

In the course of this travelling it may happen that the quantity (Q) comes up against a memory which is related to an experience of pain, and will thus give rise to a release of unpleasure. Since this is a sure sign that neurone b cannot be reached along this path, the current will at once be diverted from the cathexis in question. The unpleasureable paths retain their great value, however, in directing the current of reproduction.

17] REMEMBERING AND JUDGING

Thus reproductive thinking has a practical purpose and a biologically established end: namely, to lead a quantity $(Q\dot\eta)$ that is travelling away from the undesired perception back to the missing neuronic cathexis. Identity is then achieved together with a right to discharge—provided that the indication of reality appears from neurone b. But the process can make itself independent of the second of these aims [i.e., discharge] and can strive for identity alone. In that case what we have before us is a pure act of thought, though it can always be put to practical use subsequently. Moreover, in such cases the cathected ego behaves in exactly the same fashion.

We will now turn to a third possibility which can arise in a wishful state. [For the first two see above p. 389.] With a wishful cathexis present, a perception may emerge which does not coincide in *any* way with the memory-image that is wished for (which we will call *Mem* +). It will then become a matter of interest to cognize—to get to know—this perceptual image, so that in spite of everything it may perhaps be possible to find a way from it to $Mem+$. For this purpose the [whole] perception is presumably hypercathected from the ego, just as happens in the former case with the portion of the perception constituted by neurone c [p. 391]. If the perception is not an absolutely new one, it will now recall and revive the *memory* of some perception with which it will have at least something in common. And now the process of thought that I have previously described will be repeated in connection with this memory-image, though to some extent without the aim provided by the cathected wishful idea.

In so far as the cathexes coincide, they give no occasion for activity of thought. But the differing portions of the cathexes "arouse interest" and may give occasion for thought-activity of two sorts. The current will either be directed on to the revived memories and set an aimless activity of *memory* at work (which will thus find its motive in differences and not in resemblances), or it will remain concentrated on the newly presented portions of the perception and so set at work an equally aimless activity of *judgement*.

Let us suppose that the object presented by the perception is similar to the [percipient] subject himself—that is to say, a fellow human-being. The theoretical interest taken in it is then further explained by the fact that an object *of a similar kind* was the subject's first satisfying object (and also his first hostile object) as well as his sole assisting force. For this reason it is on his fellow-creatures that a human being first learns to cognize. The perceptual complexes arising from this fellow-creature will in part be new and non-comparable—for instance, its features (in the visual sphere); but other visual perceptions (for instance, the movements of its hands) will coincide in the subject with his own memory of quite similar visual impressions of his own body—a memory with which will be associated memories of movements experienced by himself. The same will be the case with other perceptions of the object; thus, for instance, if the object screams, a memory of the subject's own screaming will be aroused and will consequently revive his own experiences of pain. Thus the complex of a fellow-creature falls into two portions. One of these gives the impression of being a constant structure and remains as a coherent "thing"; while the other can be *understood* by the activity of memory—that is, can be traced back to information about the subject's own body.[1] This process of analysing a perceptual complex is described as "cognizing" it; it involves a judgement and is brought to an end when that has been achieved. Judging, as will be seen, is not a primary process, and presupposes a cathexis from the ego of the disparate (non-comparable) portion of the complex. Judging has in the first instance no practical purpose; and, in the process of judging, the cathexis of the disparate portions is probably discharged, for this would explain why the activities or "predicates" have only a loose path of connection with the "subject" portion of the complex. [Cf. pp. 423 and 440 f.]

This might lead us deep into the analysis of the act of judging; but it would be a diversion from our theme.

Let us be satisfied with bearing firmly in mind that it is the original interest in establishing the situation of satisfaction that produces in the one case *reproductive reflection* and in the other case *judging* as methods of proceeding from the perceptual situation that is really presented to the situation that is wished for. It remains a *sine qua non* for this that the Ψ-processes shall not run their course without inhibition, but shall be subject to the activity of the ego. The eminently practical bearing of all thought-activity will thus be demonstrated.

[18] THOUGHT AND REALITY

Thus the aim and end of all processes of thought are the establishment of a *state of identity*, the transportation of a cathectic quantity ($Q\dot\eta$) emanating from outside into a neurone cathected by the ego. Cognitive or judging thought seeks for an identity with a somatic cathexis; reproductive thought seeks for an identity with a psychical cathexis (an experience of the subject's own). Judging thought

---

[1] These reflections on the roots of our understanding of other people's expressive actions were never adequately pursued in Freud's later writings. A section in his book on jokes (1905 *c*) makes use of the hypothesis that a recollection of one's own expenditure of nervous energy is what enables one to understand the facial play and gestures of other people. (Cf. p. 395.) Recent investigations of the "body schema" place these formulations of Freud's in a fresh light. Cf. Schilder, 1942. For the relation between earliest body contacts and identification, see Kris, 1952.

operates in advance of reproductive thought, since the former furnishes the latter with ready-made facilitations to assist further associative travelling. If at the conclusion of the act of thought the indication of reality also reaches perception, then a *judgement of reality*, a *belief*, is achieved and the aim of the whole activity is attained.

There is this more to be said about judgement: its basis is evidently the presence of somatic experiences, sensations and motor images of the subject's own. So long as they are absent the variable[1] portion of the perceptual complex cannot be understood; that is, it can be reproduced but cannot point a direction for further paths of thought. For instance (a fact which will be of importance later [in Part II]) no sexual experiences can produce any effect so long as the subject has no sexual feelings—that is, generally speaking, until the beginning of puberty.

Primary judgement seems to presuppose a lesser degree of influence by the cathected ego than do reproductive acts of thought. Though it may happen that an association is followed owing to there being a partial coincidence [between the wishful and the perceptual cathexes] and no need for modification, there are also instances in which the associative process of judging is performed with a full current of quantity. Perception may be said to correspond to a nuclear object *plus* a motor image. While one is perceiving *W*, one copies the movements oneself; that is to say, one innervates one's own motor image (which has been aroused to coincide with the perception) so strongly that one actually performs the movement. Thus one can speak of a perception as having an "imitative value". [Cf. p. 423.] Or the perception may arouse the memory-image of a sensation of pain of one's own, so that one feels the corresponding unpleasure and repeats the appropriate defensive movements. Here we have the "sympathetic value" of a perception.

No doubt these two cases show us the primary process at work in judging; and we may assume that all secondary judging has come about through a mitigation of these purely associative processes. Thus judging (which later becomes a means of cognizing an object that may be of practical importance) is in its origin a process of

---

[1] [So in the MS. Wrongly printed *"verarbeitende"* in the German edition of 1950.]

association between cathexes arriving from without and cathexes derived from one's own body—an identification between reports or cathexes coming from Φ and from the interior. It is perhaps justifiable to suspect that judging also indicates the way in which quantities coming from Φ can be transmitted and discharged. What we term "things" are residues that have evaded judgement.

The example of judgement gives us a hint of the quantitative difference which must be presumed to exist between thinking and the primary process. It is reasonable to suppose that in the act of thinking a small stream of motor innervation passes from Ψ—but only, of course, if during that act a motor or a key [i.e., secretory, see p. 382] neurone is innervated. Yet it would be wrong to regard this discharge as the thought-process itself—of which it is merely an unintended subsidiary result. The thought-process consists of the cathexis of Ψ-neurones accompanied by a change in the previously operative facilitations brought about by a lateral cathexis from the ego. It is intelligible from a mechanical standpoint that in this process only a portion of the quantity ($Q\dot\eta$) is able to follow the facilitations and that the magnitude of this portion is constantly regulated by the cathexes. But it is equally clear that in this way enough quantity ($Q\dot\eta$) is at the same time economized to make the reproduction profitable. Otherwise the *whole* of the quantity ($Q\dot\eta$) which is needed for final discharge would be given off to the points of motor outlet during its passage. Thus, *the secondary process is a repetition of the original course of excitation in* Ψ, *but at a lower level and with smaller quantities.*

With quantities, it may be asked, even smaller than those which normally pass through the Ψ-neurones? How is it possible for such small quantities ($Q\dot\eta$) to make their way along paths which are, indeed, only passable by larger ones than Ψ usually receives? The only possible answer is that this must be a mechanical consequence of the lateral cathexes. We must conclude that matters are so constituted that when there is a lateral cathexis small quantities ($Q\dot\eta$) can flow through facilitations which could normally be passed only by large ones. The lateral cathexis, as it were, "binds"[1] a certain amount of the quantity ($Q\dot\eta$) passing through the neurone.

---

[1] [This term is explained in Part III, p. 425 f., where this whole question is further discussed.]

Thought must further satisfy another condition. It must make no essential change in the facilitations laid down by the primary processes, or otherwise it would falsify the traces of reality. It is enough to say of this condition that facilitation is probably the result of the single passage of a major quantity, and that cathexis, though very powerful at the moment, leaves behind it no comparably lasting effect. The small quantities (Q) that pass during thought-processes cannot in general prevail over the facilitations.

Nevertheless there can be no doubt that thought-processes *do* leave permanent traces; since thinking something over a second time demands so much less effort than the first time. Therefore, in order that reality may not be falsified, there must be special traces (indications of thought-processes) which constitute a "thought-memory"— something which it has not so far been possible to formulate. We shall hear presently of the means by which traces of thought-processes are distinguished from traces of reality.[1]

[19] PRIMARY PROCESSES—SLEEP AND DREAMS

The question now arises as to the *source* of the quantitative means by which the primary Ψ-process is carried out. In the case of the experience of *pain* the source is obviously the quantity (Q) which irrupts from without; and in the case of *affect* it is the quantity released by facilitation. In the case of the secondary process of *reproductive thinking* a greater or less quantity can be transferred to neurone c from the ego [p. 391];[2] this may be described as "thought interest" and it is proportional to the "affective interest" where this is able to develop. The only question is whether there are Ψ-processes of a primary nature for which the quantity $(Q\dot\eta)$ contributed from Φ suffices, or whether the Φ cathexis of a perception is automatically supplemented by a contribution from Ψ (namely, attention), and that

---

[1] [This whole question is discussed much more fully in Part III, p. 436 ff.]
[2] [What Freud here describes as "thought interest" seems to be the same as what is termed "attention" in the next sentence and on p. 399, as well as in Part III, where this subject is dealt with at greater length (p. 417 ff.).]

this alone makes a Ψ-process possible. This question remains an open one, though it may perhaps be decided by reference to some particular psychological facts.

One such important fact is that primary Ψ-processes, of a kind that have been gradually suppressed by biological pressure in the course of the evolution of Ψ, are daily presented to us during sleep. A second fact of equal importance is that the pathological mechanisms which are revealed by the most careful analysis in the psychoneuroses bear the greatest similarity to dream-processes. The most momentous conclusions follow from this comparison, which I shall discuss later. [See also p. 402.][1]

But first the fact of sleep must be fitted into our theory. The essential precondition of sleep is easily recognizable in children. Children sleep so long as they are not tormented by physical needs or external stimuli (e.g., by hunger or by sensations of cold from wetting). They fall asleep when they have obtained satisfaction (at the breast). So, too, adults fall asleep easily *post coenam et coitum* [after eating and copulating]. Accordingly the precondition of sleep is *a lowering of the endogenous charge in the Ψ-nucleus*, which renders the secondary function unnecessary. In sleep the subject is in the ideal state of inertia, with the store of quantity ($Q\dot{\eta}$) discharged.

In the waking state this store is collected in the "ego", and we may assume that it is the discharging of the ego which is the precondition and characteristic of sleep. And here, we can see at once, we have the precondition of primary psychical processes.

It is not certain whether, in adults, the ego is *completely* relieved of its charge in sleep. In any case it withdraws a large number of its cathexes, though on awakening these are re-established immediately and without trouble. This contradicts none of our presuppositions; but it draws attention to the fact that we must assume that between neurones which are effectively interconnected there must be currents which affect the total level [of cathexis] as happens in intercommuni- cating pipes—although the height of the level in the different

---

[1] Cf. in this connection *The Interpretation of Dreams*, particularly (*trans.* 1953) p. 597 f. It seems as though Freud lost sight of the discovery which he here reveals of the "similarity" between dream-processes and the mechanisms of the psychoneuroses, and did not rediscover it till the beginning of 1899 [in Letter 105]. See also p. 410 and the footnote to p. 209.

neurones need only be proportional [see p. 427] and is not necessarily uniform.

The characteristics of sleep reveal some things which could not have been guessed.

Sleep is characterized by motor paralysis, a paralysis of the will. [See below, p. 400.] The will is the discharge of the total Ψ-quantity ($Q\acute{\eta}$). [Cf. p. 379.] In sleep the spinal tonus is partly relaxed (it seems likely that motor Φ-discharge is manifested in tonus); other innervations persist, together with the sources of their excitation.

It is a highly interesting fact that the state of sleep begins and is evoked by the closing of those sense organs that are capable of being closed. Perceptions should not be made during sleep and nothing disturbs sleep more than the emergence of sense impressions, cathexes entering Ψ from Φ. This seems to indicate that in daytime a constant, though displaceable, cathexis (i.e., "attention")[1] is sent into the neurones of the pallium which receive perceptions from Φ; so that it is quite possible that the primary Ψ-processes may be performed with this contribution from Ψ. [Cf. p. 397-8.] (It remains to be seen whether the pallium neurones themselves or the adjoining nuclear neurones are already pre-cathected.) If Ψ withdraws these pallium cathexes, the perceptions reach uncathected neurones and are slight and may perhaps even be unable to give an indication of quality.[2] And as we have just hinted, along with the emptying of the perceptual neurones (ωN), an innervation of discharge that increases attention comes to a stop. At this point, too, we might approach the enigma of hypnosis. The apparent unexcitability of the sense organs in that condition would seem to rest on this withdrawal of the cathexis of attention.

Thus, by an automatic mechanism which is the opposite of the mechanism of attention, Ψ excludes Φ-impressions so long as it itself is uncathected.

But what is strangest of all is that during sleep there occur Ψ-processes—dreams which have many characteristics that are not understood.

---

[1] [See footnote, p. 397.]
[2] [So in the MS. Wrongly printed "*Quantität*" in the German edition of 1950.]

[20] THE ANALYSIS OF DREAMS[1]

Dreams exhibit every degree of transition to the waking state and of admixture with normal Ψ-processes; nevertheless, their essential character can easily be extracted.

1. Dreams are devoid of motor discharge and, for the most part, of motor elements. We are paralysed in dreams.

The easiest explanation of this characteristic is the absence of spinal pre-cathexis owing to the cessation of Φ-discharge. Since the neurones are uncathected, the motor excitation cannot pass over the barriers. In other dreamlike conditions movement is not excluded. This is not the essential characteristic of dreams.

2. The connections in dreams are partly nonsensical, partly feeble-minded or even meaningless or strangely demented.

The last of these attributes is explained by the fact that the compulsion to associate prevails in dreams, as no doubt it does primarily in all psychical life. Two cathexes that are simultaneously present must, so it seems, be brought into connection with each other.[2] I have collected some amusing examples of the dominance of this compulsion in waking life. (For instance, some provincial spectators who were present in the French Chamber during a bomb outrage concluded that whenever a deputy made a successful speech a shot was fired as a sign of applause.)[3]

The two other attributes, which are in fact identical, show that a part of the dreamer's psychical experiences have been forgotten. In

---

[1] The following first attempt at a theory of dreams is fragmentary in so many essential portions that it seems scarcely worth while to compare it in detail with the hypotheses developed in *The Interpretation of Dreams*. We can see that Freud approached the study of dreams from two directions: his attempts to establish the nature of the psychical apparatus enabled him to understand the general mechanisms of dream-formation, but it was only the analysis of his own dreams—and the concrete experience of his self-analysis—that made it possible for him to take the step forward which carried him from the views expressed in the 'Project' to those in *The Interpretation of Dreams*.

[2] [This point was insisted on by Freud in the course of a long footnote to the case history of Emmy von N. (under the date of May 15), in Breuer and Freud's *Studies on Hysteria* (1895). He recurs to it in Chapter V, Section A, of *The Interpretation of Dreams* (1900a).]

[3] Freud made use of these examples in *The Interpretation of Dreams* (trans. 1953, p. 500), and explained them as "efforts at making an intelligible pattern of the sense-impressions that are offered to us".

fact, all those biological experiences have been forgotten which normally inhibit the primary process, and this is due to the insufficient cathexis of the ego. The senseless and illogical nature of dreams is probably attributable to the same fact. It seems as though Ψ-cathexes which have not been withdrawn find their level partly in the adjoining facilitations and partly in neighbouring cathexes. If discharge from the ego were complete, sleep would necessarily be dreamless.

3. Ideas in dreams are of a hallucinatory nature; they awaken consciousness and meet with belief.

This is the most important characteristic of dreams. It becomes obvious at once in alternate fits of sleeping and waking. One shuts one's eyes and hallucinates, one opens them and thinks in words.[1] There are several explanations of the hallucinatory nature of the cathexes in dreams. In the first place, it might be supposed that the current from Φ to motility [in waking life] acts as an obstacle to any retrogressive cathexis of the Φ-neurones from Ψ, but that when that current ceases, Φ is retrogressively cathected and the conditions fulfilled for the production of quality.[2] The only argument against this is the consideration that the Φ-neurones should be protected from cathexis from Ψ by the fact of their being uncathected (just as motility is so protected [p. 400]). It is characteristic of sleep that it reverses the whole situation: it stops the motor discharge from Ψ and makes the retrogressive one to Φ possible. It is tempting to assign the determining role to the great waking current of discharge from Φ to motility. In the second place, we might turn back to the nature of the primary process and point out that the primary recollection of a perception is always a hallucination [cf. p. 402] and that it is only inhibition on the part of the ego which has taught us never to cathect W in such a way that it can transfer cathexis retrogressively to Φ. This hypothesis can be made more plausible by the consideration that conduction from Φ to Ψ is in any case easier than from Ψ to Φ; so that a Ψ-cathexis of a neurone, even if it is far more intense than the perceptual cathexis of the same neurone, need not involve retrogressive conduction. This explanation is further supported by the fact that in

---

[1] Cf. *The Interpretation of Dreams* (1900a), Chapter I, Section E.]

[2] [This explanation of regression in dreams is considered and criticized in Chapter VII, Section B, of *The Interpretation of Dreams* (1900a).]

dreams the vividness of the hallucination is in direct proportion to the importance (that is, to the quantitative cathexis) of the idea concerned. This indicates that it is quantity (Q) that conditions hallucination. If a perception comes from Φ in waking life, Ψ-cathexis (interest) makes it more distinct but not more vivid; it does not alter its quantitative character.

4. The purpose and meaning of dreams (or at least of normal ones) can be established with certainty. Dreams are *the fulfilments of wishes*[1]—that is, primary processes following on experiences of satisfaction; and they are not recognized as such, merely because the release of pleasure (the reproduction of pleasurable discharges) in them is slight, since in general they run their course almost without affect (*i.e.*, without motor release). But it is very easy to prove that this is their nature. And it is for this very reason that I am inclined to infer that *primary wishful cathexes too are of a hallucinatory character*.

5. It is noticeable how bad the memory is in dreams and how little damage dreams do compared with other primary processes. But this is easily explained by the fact that dreams mostly follow old facilitations and thus cause no changes, that Ψ-experiences are kept back from them and that, owing to the paralysis of motility, they leave no traces of discharge behind them.

6. It is, moreover, interesting that consciousness furnishes quality in dreams as easily as in waking life. This shows that consciousness is not restricted to the ego but can be attached to any Ψ-process. This is a warning against a possible identification of primary processes with unconscious ones. *Here are two invaluable hints for what follows.*

If, when dreams are remembered, we enquire from consciousness as to their content, we shall find that the meaning of dreams as wish-fulfilments is concealed by a number of Ψ-processes all of which we meet with once more in the neuroses and which are characteristic of the pathological nature of those disorders.[2]

---

[1] Freud reached this conclusion after interpreting his "dream of Irma's injection" in July 1895 (see Letter 137). It seems that the analysis of this dream was not yet correlated with his self-analysis. The analysis of the dream was dynamically directed but not genetically.

[2] Cf. p. 398 and footnote. [Cf. also pp. 407 and 410.]

[21] DREAM CONSCIOUSNESS

Our consciousness of dream ideas is above all a discontinuous one. It does not become aware of a whole chain of associations but only of separate points in it; and between them lie unconscious intermediate links which we can easily discover when we are awake. If we investigate the reasons for these leaps, here is what we find. Suppose [Fig. 4] that A is a dream-idea that has become conscious and that it leads to B. But, instead of B, C appears in consciousness and it does so because it lies on the path between B and another cathexis D, which is simultaneously present. Thus there is a diversion owing to a simultaneous cathexis of another kind, which is not, moreover, conscious. C has therefore taken the place of B, though B fits in better with the chain of thought, that is, with the wish-fulfilment.

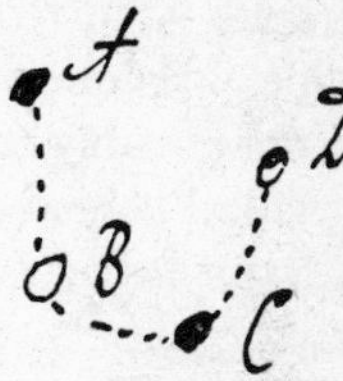

Fig. 15

For instance, [I have a dream that] O. has given Irma an injection of propyl $[A]$[1]. I then see "trimethylamin" very vividly before me, and hallucinate its formula $[C]$. The thought that is simultaneously present is of Irma's illness being of a sexual nature $[D]$. Between this thought and that of propyl lies an association $[B]$ of a conversation on sexual chemistry with W. Fl. [Wilhelm Fliess] in which he drew my special attention to trimethylamin. This latter idea is then pushed into consciousness from both directions. It is a puzzling fact that neither the intermediate link (sexual chemistry $[B]$) nor the diversionary idea (the sexual nature of the illness $[D]$) are also conscious. And this needs explaining. One might suppose that the cathexis of B or D alone would not be intense enough to bring about a retrogressive hallucination, but that C, being cathected from both of them, would be able to do so. But in the example I have given D (the sexual nature of the illness) was certainly as intense as A (the injection of propyl), and the derivative of these two (the chemical formula $[C]$) was prodigiously vivid.

The problem of unconscious intermediate links applies equally to waking life, in which similar events occur daily. But what remains

---

[1] See the discussion of this part of the "dream of Irma's injection" in *The Interpretation of Dreams*, (trans. 1953), p. 115 f.

characteristic of dreams is *the ease with which quantity ($Q\dot\eta$) is displaced* in them and thus the way in which B is replaced by a C which is superior to it quantitatively.

And the like is true of wish-fulfilment in dreams generally. We shall not find, for instance, a wish that is conscious and afterwards its fulfilment hallucinated; but the latter only will be conscious and the intermediate link [the wish] will have to be inferred. It has quite certainly occurred, but without being able to give itself a qualitative shape. It is obvious, however, that the cathexis of the wishful idea cannot possibly be stronger than the motive impelling to it. Thus the psychical course of excitation in dreams takes place in accordance with quantity (Q); but it is not quantity (Q) that decides what shall become conscious.

We may also perhaps infer from dream-processes that consciousness emerges *during the passage* of a quantity ($Q\dot\eta$), that is to say that it is not aroused by a *constant* cathexis. On the other hand we might suspect that an intense current of quantity ($Q\dot\eta$) is not favourable to the emergence of consciousness, since consciousness is attached to the *outcome* of the current—to some extent, that is, to a comparatively quiescent persistence of cathexis. It is hard to find one's way to the real determinants of consciousness in view of these mutually contradictory preconditions. And we must also take into account the circumstances in which consciousness emerges in the secondary process.

This last peculiarity of dream-consciousness may perhaps be explained by supposing that a retrogressive current of quantity ($Q\dot\eta$) towards Φ is incompatible with a relatively energetic current towards the Ψ-paths of association. Other conditions seem to apply to the conscious Φ-processes.

PART II

PSYCHOPATHOLOGY

25 Sept. 95.

The first part of this project included what could, as it were, be inferred *a priori* from its basic hypothesis, moulded and corrected in accordance with a few factual experiences. This second part seeks by an analysis of pathological processes to determine further features of the system founded on the basic hypothesis. A third part, based on the two earlier ones, will endeavour to construct the characteristics of the course of normal psychological events.

THE PSYCHOPATHOLOGY OF HYSTERIA

[1] *Hysterical Compulsion*

I shall start with some things which are to be found in hysteria but are not necessarily peculiar to it.

Every observer of hysteria is at once struck by the fact that hysterical patients are subject to a *compulsion*, which is operated by means of *excessively intense ideas*. An idea may emerge into consciousness with special frequency, without the course of events justifying it; or it may be that the arousing of this neurone is accompanied by psychical consequences which are unintelligible. The emergence of the excessively intense idea has results which, on the one hand, cannot be suppressed and, on the other hand, cannot be understood: releases of affect, motor innervations, inhibitions. The subject is by no means without insight into the strangeness of the situation.

Excessively intense ideas also occur normally. They are what lends an ego its peculiar character. We are not surprised at them, if we know their genetic development (education, experiences) and their motives. We are in the habit of regarding these excessively intense ideas as the product of powerful and reasonable motives. In *hysterics*, on the contrary, excessively intense ideas strike us by their oddity. They are ideas which produce no effects in other people and whose importance we cannot appreciate. They appear to us as intruders and usurpers and accordingly as ridiculous.

Thus hysterical compulsion is (1) incomprehensible; (2) incapable of being cleared up by any process of thought, and (3) incongruous in its structure.

There is a simple neurotic compulsion which may be contrasted with the hysterical kind. For instance, suppose a man runs into danger by being thrown out of a carriage and that afterwards driving in a carriage becomes impossible for him. Such a compulsion is (1) comprehensible, since we know its origin; and (3) not incongruous, since the association with danger makes it justifiable to link driving in a carriage with fear. It, too, however, is incapable of being cleared up by any process of thought. This last characteristic cannot be described as entirely pathological; our *normal* excessively intense ideas as well are often incapable of being cleared up. One would be inclined to regard neurotic compulsions as completely non-pathological, if it were not that experience shows that a compulsion of this kind in a normal person only persists for a short time after its occasion, and then disintegrates by degrees. Thus the persistence of a compulsion is pathological and points to a *simple neurosis*.

Now our analyses show that a hysterical compulsion is cleared up at once if it is explained—that is, made comprehensible. Thus these two characteristics are essentially one and the same. In an analysis we also learn the process by which the appearance of absurdity and incongruity comes about. The result of analysis is, in general terms, as follows.

Before the analysis, A is an excessively intense idea, which forces its way into consciousness too often, and each time it does so leads to tears. The subject does not know why A makes him weep and regards it as absurd; but he cannot prevent it.

After the analysis, it has been discovered that there is an idea B which rightly leads to tears and which rightly recurs often until a certain complicated piece of psychical work directed against it has been completed by the subject. The effect of B is not absurd, is comprehensible to the subject and can even be fought against by him.

B stands in a particular relation to A. For there has been an event which consisted of $B+A$. A was a subsidiary circumstance, while B was well calculated to produce a lasting effect. The production of this event in memory now occurs as though A had taken B's place. A has become a substitute, a "symbol", for B.[1] Hence the incongruity; for *A* is accompanied by consequences which it does not seem to deserve, which are not appropriate to it.

Symbols are formed in this way normally as well. A soldier will sacrifice himself for a piece of coloured cloth on a pole, because it has become the symbol of his native country; and no one considers this neurotic. But a hysterical symbol behaves differently. The knight who fights for a lady's glove *knows*, in the first place, that the glove owes its importance to the lady; and, secondly, his worship of the glove does not in the least prevent him from thinking of the lady and serving her in other ways. But the hysteric who is reduced to tears by *A* is unaware that this is because of the association *A—B*, and *B* itself plays no part whatever in his mental life. In this case the symbol has taken the place of the thing completely.

This assertion is true in the strictest sense. One can convince oneself that whenever a stimulus from outside or an association ought properly to cathect *B*, *A* emerges into consciousness instead. Indeed, one can infer the nature of *B* from the occasions which bring about the emergence of *A* in such a remarkable fashion.

We can sum the matter up by saying that *A* is compulsive and *B* repressed (at least from consciousness).

Analysis has revealed the surprising fact that for every compulsion there is a corresponding repression, that for every excessive irruption into consciousness there is a corresponding amnesia.

The term "excessively intense" points to *quantitative* characteristics. It is plausible to suppose that repression has the quantitative sense of being denuded of quantity, and that the sum of the two [*i.e.*, of the compulsion *plus* the repression] is equal to the normal. If so, only the *distribution* of quantity has been altered. Something has been added to *A* that has been subtracted from *B*. The pathological process is one of *displacement*, such as we have come to know in dreams, and is hence a primary process.

[2] *The Genesis of Hysterical Compulsion*

Several significant questions now arise. Under what conditions

---

[1] After *Studies on Hysteria* Freud only rarely used the word "symbol" in this sense.

does a pathological formation of a symbol such as this occur (or, conversely, a repression)? What is the operating force concerned? What is the state of the neurones of an excessively intense or of a repressed idea?

Nothing could be discovered about this and nothing further could be inferred from it, if it were not that clinical experience teaches us two facts. Repression is exclusively brought to bear on ideas that, firstly, arouse a distressing affect (unpleasure) in the ego, and that, secondly, relate to sexual life.

We may at once suspect that it is this unpleasurable affect which brings about repression. Indeed, we have already assumed the existence of a "primary defence", which consists in a reversal of the current of thought as soon as it comes up against a neurone the cathecting of which releases unpleasure [pp. 383 and 392].

The justification for this assumption lay in two observations: (1) that a neuronic cathexis of this latter kind is certainly not what is being sought for when the original purpose of the thought-process was to establish a Ψ-situation of satisfaction, and (2) that when an experience of pain is brought to an end in a reflex manner the hostile perception is replaced by another [p. 383].

We can, however, convince ourselves in a more direct manner of the part played by defensive affects. If we investigate the condition of the repressed [idea] *B*, we find that this idea can easily be found and brought into consciousness. This is surprising, for we might well have supposed that *B* was really forgotten and that no trace of it remained in Ψ. But no; *B* is a memory-image like any other. It is not extinguished; but if, as is usually the case, *B* is a complex of cathexes, then an uncommonly strong *resistance*, and one that cannot easily be eliminated, opposes any activity of thought in relation to *B*. This resistance to *B* can at once be recognized as a measure of the *compulsion* exercised by *A*, and we can conclude that the force which originally repressed *B* is at work once more in the resistance. And at the same time we learn something else. We had only known so far that *B* could not become *conscious*; we knew nothing of *B*'s behaviour in regard to thought-cathexis. But we now find that the resistance is directed against any occupation of one's thoughts with *B*, even though it has already been made partly conscious. So that instead of "excluded from consciousness", we can say "excluded from thought-processes".

Thus it is a defensive process emanating from the *cathected ego* that results in hysterical repression and at the same time in hysterical compulsion. To this extent the process seems to be differentiated from the primary Ψ-processes.

[3] *Pathological Defence*

Nevertheless we are far from having found a solution. As we have seen, the outcome of hysterical repression differs very widely from that of normal defence, about which we have very accurate knowledge. It is a general fact that we avoid thinking about things that only cause us unpleasure, and that we achieve this by directing our thoughts to something else. But even though we contrive that the intolerable B idea shall rarely emerge in our consciousness, we never succeed in forgetting B to such an extent that we can never be reminded of it by some fresh perception. Nor can a re-awakening of the idea in this manner be precluded even in hysteria. The difference lies only in the fact that in hysteria what becomes conscious (*i.e.*, what is cathected) is always A instead of B. Thus it is this immovable symbolization which constitutes the function that is so far in excess of normal defence.

The most obvious explanation of this excessive function would be to attribute it to a greater intensity of the defensive affect. Experience shows, however, that the most distressing memories, which must necessarily arouse the greatest unpleasure (memories of remorse over bad actions), cannot be repressed and replaced by symbols. The existence [p. 408] of a second necessary precondition of pathological defence—sexuality—suggests that the explanation must be looked for elsewhere.

It is out of the question to suppose that disagreeable sexual affects so greatly exceed all other unpleasurable affects in intensity. There must be some other attribute of sexual ideas to explain why they alone are subject to repression.

One further remark must here be made. Hysterical repression clearly takes place by the help of symbolization—of *displacement* on to other neurones. It might be supposed that the riddle lies in this displacement and that the repression itself requires no explanation. But we shall find when we come to analyse (for instance) obsessional neurosis that there repression occurs *without* symbolization, and, indeed, that repression and substitution are there separated in time. Accordingly, the process of repression remains the core of the riddle.

[4] *The Hysterical* Πρῶτον Ψεῦδος [*First Lie*]

As we have seen, hysterical compulsion originates from a peculiar kind of quantitative movement (symbolization), which is probably a primary process since it can easily be seen at work in dreams.[1] The motive force in this process is defence on the part of the ego, which, however, is here performing nothing in excess of a normal function. What we need to explain is how an ego-process can be accompanied by consequences which we are accustomed to meet with only in primary processes. We must expect to find special psychical conditions in operation. Clinical observation tells us that all this happens only in the sexual sphere. Perhaps, then, the special psychical conditions are to be explained by the natural characteristics of sexuality.

As it happens, a special psychical concatenation is to be found in the sphere of sexuality which might serve our purpose. It is known to us empirically, and I will illustrate it by an example.[2]

Emma is at the present time under a compulsion not to go into shops *alone*. She explained this by a memory dating from the age of twelve (shortly before her puberty). She went into a shop to buy something, saw the two shop-assistants (one of whom she remembers) laughing together, and rushed out in some kind of *fright*. In this connection it was possible to elicit the idea that the two men had been laughing at her clothes and that one of them had attracted her sexually.

Both the relation of these fragments to one another and the effect of the experience are incomprehensible. If she felt unpleasure at her

---

[1] For the primary process see p. 386 ff.
[2] This example is not used in Freud's published writings.

clothes being laughed at, this should have been corrected long ago
—ever since she began to dress as a lady. Nor does it make any difference to her clothes whether she goes into a shop alone or in company.
It is not simply a question of being protected, as is shown by the fact
that (as happens in cases of agoraphobia) the company of a small
child is enough to make her feel safe. Then there is the totally disconnected fact that one of the men attracted her. Here again nothing
would be changed if she had someone with her. Thus the memories
aroused explain neither the compulsion nor the determination of the
symptom.

Further investigation brought to light a second memory, which she
denies having had in mind at the moment of Scene I. Nor is there
any evidence to support its presence there. On two occasions, when
she was a child of eight, she had gone into a shop to buy some sweets
and the shopkeeper had grabbed at her genitals through her clothes.
In spite of the first experience she had gone to the shop a second time,
after which she had stopped away. Afterwards she reproached herself
for having gone the second time, as though she had wanted to provoke
the assault. And in fact a "bad conscience" by which she was
oppressed could be traced back to this experience.

We can now understand Scene I (with the shop-assistants) if we
take it in conjunction with Scene II (with the shopkeeper). All we
need is an associative link between them. She herself remarked that a
link of this kind was provided by the *laughter*. The shop-assistants'
laughter had reminded her of the grin with which the shopkeeper had
accompanied his assault. The whole process can now be reconstructed
thus. The two shop-assistants *laughed* in the shop, and this laughter
(unconsciously) aroused the memory of the shopkeeper. The second
situation had the further point of similarity with the first that she
was once again in a shop alone. The shopkeeper's grabbing through
her clothes was remembered; but since then she had reached puberty.
The recollection aroused (what the event when it occurred could
certainly not have done) a sexual release, which turned into anxiety.
In her anxiety she was afraid the shop-assistants might repeat the
assault, and ran away.

It is quite certain that here we have a series of Ψ-processes of two
sorts, and that the recollection of Scene II (with the shopkeeper)

took place in a different state from the first one. The course of events can be represented as follows [Fig. 5]:—

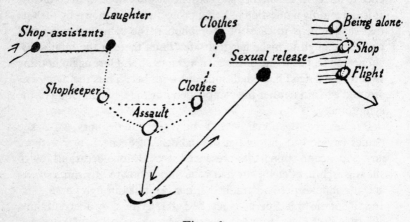

Fig. 16

Here the ideas represented by black dots are perceptions which were recollected. The fact that the sexual release entered consciousness is proved by the otherwise incomprehensible idea that she was attracted by the laughing shop-assistant. Her final conclusion not to remain in the shop because of the danger of being assaulted was quite logically constructed having regard to all the elements of the process of association. But none of the process represented above entered consciousness except the element "clothes"; and the *consciously* functioning thoughts made two false connections in the material concerned (shop-assistants, laughter, clothes and sexual feeling)—namely, that she had been laughed at on account of her clothes and that she had been sexually excited by one of the shop-assistants.

The whole complex (indicated by broken lines) was represented in consciousness by the one idea "clothes"—obviously its most innocent element. At this point a repression accompanied by symbolization had occurred. The fact that the final conclusion—the symptom—was quite logically constructed, so that the symbol played no part in it, was a special peculiarity of the case.

It may be said to be quite usual for an association to pass through a number of unconscious intermediate links before arriving at a conscious one, as happened in this case. The element that enters consciousness is probably the one that arouses special interest. But in our example the remarkable thing is that what entered conscious-ness was not the element that aroused interest (the assault) but another which symbolized it (the clothes). If we ask what the cause of this interpolated pathological process may have been, we can only point to a single one—the sexual release, of which there was also evidence in consciousness. This was linked to the memory of the assault; but it is a highly noteworthy fact that it was not linked to the assault when it was actually experienced. Here we have an instance of a memory exciting an affect which it had not excited as an ex-perience, because in the meantime the changes produced by puberty had made possible a new understanding of what was remembered.

Now this case is typical of repression in hysteria. We invariably find that a memory is repressed which has only become a trauma *after the event*. The reason for this state of things is the retardation of puberty as compared with the remainder of the individual's development.[1]

[5] *The Determinants of the* Πρῶτον Ψεῦδος ὑστ. [*First Hysterical Lie*]

Although it is unusual in mental life for a memory to arouse an affect which the actual experience has not produced, this is nevertheless what quite ordinarily happens in the case of sexual ideas, precisely because the retardation of puberty is a general characteristic of the organization. Every adolescent carries memory-traces which can only be understood after his own sexual feelings have appeared; every adolescent, accordingly, must carry within him the germ of hysteria. Other, concurrent factors must, of course, also be present, if this general tendency is to be restricted to the small number of people who actually become hysterics.

Now analysis shows that what is disturbing in a sexual trauma is

---

[1] Freud's later discovery of the importance of infantile sexuality has not com-pletely invalidated this view; it points to the regressive cathexis of infantile material at puberty.

clearly the release of affect; and experience teaches us that hysterics are persons of whom we know in some cases that they have become precociously excitable sexually through mechanical and emotional stimulation (by masturbation) and of whom we can assume in some cases that they have a predisposition to precocious sexual release. A precocious *onset* of sexual release and a precociously *intense* sexual release are obviously equivalent. This factor is reduced to a quantitative one.

What, then, is the significance of this precocity of sexual release? All the stress must be laid on the precocity, since it cannot be maintained that sexual release in general gives rise to repression. For this would once more make repression into a process of normal frequency.

[6] *The Disturbance of Thought by Affects*

We have been unable to avoid the conclusion that disturbance of the normal psychical process depends on two conditions: (1) on the sexual release being attached to a memory instead of to an experience; and (2) on the sexual release occurring precociously.

If these two conditions are present, it seems, a disturbance will be produced which exceeds the normal amount though it is foreshadowed in normal cases.

We know from everyday experiences that the generation of affect inhibits the normal course of thought, and that it does so in various ways. In the first place, many trains of thought may be forgotten which would otherwise be taken into account—as occurs, that is, in dreams [p. 402]. For instance, it has happened to me that in the agitation caused by a great anxiety I have forgotten to make use of the telephone, which had been introduced into my house a short time before. The recently established path succumbed to the state of affect. The facilitation—that is to say, what was old-established— won the day. Such forgetting involves the loss of the power of selection, of efficiency and of logic, just as happens in dreams. In the second place, without forgetting, paths may be followed which would otherwise be avoided: in particular, paths leading to discharge— actions, for instance, performed under the influence of the affect.

In a word, the affective process approximates to the uninhibited primary process.

Several things follow from this: first, that, when affect is released, the releasing idea itself becomes intensified, and secondly, that the chief function of the cathected ego lies in avoiding fresh affective processes and in reducing the old affective facilitations. The position can only be pictured as follows. Originally a perceptual cathexis, being the heir to an experience of pain, released unpleasure; the cathexis became intensified by the quantity $(Q\dot{\eta})$ thus released and proceeded towards discharge along paths which were already in part pre-facilitated. After the formation of a cathected ego, the function of "attention" to fresh perceptual cathexes developed in the manner we know [p. 399], and this attention now follows with lateral cathexes the course taken by the quantity from W.[1] In this way the release of unpleasure is restricted in quantity, and its start acts as a signal to the ego to set normal defence in operation. Thus the generation of fresh experiences of pain, with their facilitations, is made more difficult. But the more intense the release of unpleasure the harder becomes the ego's task; for it is only up to a certain limit that it is able, by means of its lateral cathexes, to provide a counterweight to the quantities $(Q\dot{\eta})$ concerned, and accordingly it cannot wholly prevent the occurrence of a primary process.

Furthermore, the greater the quantity that is endeavouring to pass through, the more difficult does the ego find thought-activity, which, as everything goes to show, consists in an experimental displacing of small quantities $(Q\dot{\eta})$ [p. 396]. "Reflection" is an activity of the ego which demands time, and it becomes impossible when the affective level involves large quantities. Hence it is that where there is affect there is hastiness and a choice of methods similar to that made in the primary process.

Thus it is the business of the ego to permit no release of affect, since this would at the same time permit a primary process. Its best instrument for this purpose is the mechanism of attention. If a cathexis which releases unpleasure were able to escape attention, the ego's intervention would come too late. And this is precisely what

---

[1] [This process is described at much greater length in Part III, e.g., p. 419 ff.]

happens in the case of the hysterical *proton pseudos* [first lie]. Attention is focused on perceptions, which are the normal occasions for the release of unpleasure. But here it is not a perception but a memory-trace which unexpectedly releases unpleasure, and the ego discovers this too late. It has permitted a primary process, because it did not expect one.

There are, however, other occasions on which memories release unpleasure; and in the case of recent memories this is quite normally so. If a trauma (an experience of pain) occurs for the first time when there is already an ego in existence—the very first traumas of all escape the ego entirely—there is a release of unpleasure; but the ego is simultaneously at work creating lateral cathexes. If there is afterwards a cathexis of the *memory-trace*, the unpleasure is repeated; but the ego-facilitations are already present, and experience shows that the second release of unpleasure is less—until, after further repetition, it is reduced to no more than a signal of an intensity acceptable to the ego.[1] Thus the essential thing is that there should be an inhibition by the ego on the occasion of the *first* release of unpleasure, so that the process does not occur as a "posthumous" primary affective experience. But this is precisely what *does* occur when, as in the case of the hysterical *proton pseudos*, the release of unpleasure is occasioned by a *memory*.

This confirms the importance of one of the preconditions that were indicated by clinical experience: *the retardation of puberty makes possible the occurrence of posthumous primary processes.*

---

[1] [Discussed in greater detail in Part III, p. 437 ff.]

PART III

AN ATTEMPT AT AN ACCOUNT OF NORMAL Ψ-PROCESSES

5 Oct. 95.

[1]

It must be possible to give a mechanical explanation of what I have termed "secondary processes" based on the effects produced by a group of neurones with a *constant* cathexis (the ego) upon other neurones with *changing* cathexes. I shall begin by attempting to give a psychological description of these processes.

On the one hand we have the ego, and on the other hand W (perceptions)—that is, cathexes in Ψ arising from Φ (from the external world). We now have to find a mechanism which shall cause the ego to follow perceptions and influence them. This mechanism lies, I believe, in the fact that, according to my hypotheses, a perception invariably excites ω^1, that is, passes on indications of quality.[2] To put it more accurately, it excites consciousness (consciousness of a quality) in W; and the discharge of the perceptual excitation furnishes Ψ with a report which in fact constitutes the indication of quality. I therefore suggest that it is such indications of quality which *interest* Ψ in the perception. [Cf. p. 397.] Here we seem to have the mechanism of *psychical attention*.[3] I find it hard to give any mechanical (automatic) explanation of its origin. I believe, therefore, that it is *biologically* determined: that is, that it has been left over in the course of psychical evolution because any other behaviour on the part of Ψ has been excluded owing to its generating unpleasure. The effect of psychical attention is to cathect the same neurones which are the bearers of the perceptual cathexis. This state of attention has a prototype in the "experience of satisfaction" [p. 380] (which is of such

---

[1] The system W.

[2] [So in the M.S. The 1950 German edition reads wrongly *Quantität*.]

[3] The part played by attention in the following discussion explains how it is that it contains relatively few points of connection with Freud's later writings. He already insists in *The Interpretation of Dreams* (trans. 1953, p. 593), that "the most complicated achievements of thought are possible without the assistance of consciousness" and that "becoming conscious is connected with the application of a particular psychical function, that of attention". See also p. 430 below.

importance for the whole course of development) and the repetitions of that experience—states of craving which developed into states of wishing and states of expecting. I have shown [Part I, Sections 16-18] that these states contain the biological justification of all thought. The psychical situation in these states is as follows. The craving involves a state of tension in the ego; and as a result of it the idea of the loved object (the "wishful idea") is cathected. Biological experience has taught us that this idea must not be cathected so intensely that it might be confused with a perception, and that its discharge must be postponed till indications of quality arise from it which prove that it is real—that the cathexis is a perceptual one. If a perception arises which is identical with or similar to the wishful idea, the perception finds its neurones precathected by the wish— that is to say, some or all of them are cathected, according to the degree to which the idea and the perception tally. The difference between the idea and the perception then gives rise to the process of thought; and this reaches its conclusion when a path has been found by which the discordant perceptual cathexes can be merged into ideational cathexes. *Identity* is then attained.[1]

Attention consists in the situation of expectation being established even in regard to perceptions that do not even *partly* coincide with wishful cathexes. For it has become important to send out a cathexis to meet *all* perceptions. Attention is biologically justified; the question is merely one of how to give the ego guidance as to *which* expectant cathexis it is to establish : and this purpose is served by the indications of quality.

The process of setting up a psychical *attitude* [of attention] can be followed with more exactitude. At the start, it seems, the ego is not forewarned. A perceptual cathexis arises, followed by its indication of quality. The close facilitation between these two reports intensifies the perceptual cathexis still more and a cathexis of attention now

---

[1] See in this connection a passage in *The Interpretation of Dreams* (trans. 1953, p. 566) in which, after discussing the relation between perception and wish-fulfilment, Freud goes on: "Thus the aim of this first psychical activity was to produce a 'perceptual identity'—a repetition of the perception which was linked with the satisfaction of the need". The "Project" enters into greater detail. Freud attempts here to trace back thinking and reality-testing to the tension to which a child is subjected while it is waiting for satisfaction. See also p. 389 ff.

becomes attached to the perceptual neurones. The next perception of the same object results (in accordance with the second law of association) in a fuller cathexis of the same perception and it is only this latter perception which will be available psychically.

(This piece of description already yields a highly important conclusion. The first time a perceptual cathexis occurs it is of little intensity and involves only a small quantity; the second time, when there is a Ψ-precathexis, the quantity is greater. Now attention involves no intrinsic change in the judgement made upon the quantitative attributes of the object. Consequently the external quantity (Q) of objects cannot be expressed in Ψ by psychical quantity ($Q\dot{\eta}$). [Cf. p. 429.] Psychical quantity ($Q\dot{\eta}$) signifies something quite different, which is not represented in reality; and external quantity (Q) is in fact expressed in Ψ by something different, namely, by complexity of cathexes. By this means external quantity (Q) is held back from Ψ [p. 376].)

Here is a still more satisfactory account [of the process described in the last paragraph but one]. As a result of biological experience Ψ-attention is constantly directed to indications of quality. These indications thus occur in neurones that are already precathected and they thus attain a quantity that is of adequate magnitude. Thus intensified, the indications of quality are able, by their facilitation, to intensify the perceptual cathexes. And the ego has learnt to arrange that its cathexes of attention shall follow the course of this associative movement as it passes from indications of quality to perception. It is in this way enabled to cathect precisely the right perceptions or their environment. Indeed, if we assume that it is the same quantity ($Q\dot{\eta}$), coming from the ego, which travels along the facilitation from the indication of quality to the perception, we shall actually have found a mechanical (automatic) explanation of the cathexis of attention. Thus attention leaves the indications of quality, and turns to the perceptual neurones, which are thereafter hypercathected.

Let us suppose that for some reason or other the mechanism of attention fails to operate. In that case there will be no Ψ-cathexis of the perceptual neurones, and the quantity (Q) which has reached them will be transmitted (purely associatively) along the best facilitations, so far as the relations between the resistances and the quantity of the perceptual cathexis permit. This passage of quantity will probably finish soon; for the quantity (Q) will split up and in some neurone near-by will become too small to flow any further. The passage of the quantities attached to the perception (Wq) may subsequently, in certain circumstances, attract attention, or it may not. In the latter case it will end, unobserved, in the cathexis of some neighbouring neurones of whose later vicissitudes we know nothing. This is the course of a perception unaccompanied by attention, such as must occur countless times every day.[1] As an analysis of the process of attention will show, the current is not able to travel far, and we may infer from this the small magnitude of the quantities (Wq) attached to perception.

If, however, the system W has received a cathexis of attention, a number of things can happen; in particular, two situations may be noticed—the occurrence of *ordinary* thought and that of purely *observant* thought. The latter case would seem to be the simpler; it may be said to correspond to the state of an investigator who has had a perception and asks himself: "What does this mean? Where does this lead?" What happens is this—but for the sake of simplicity I shall now have to substitute a single neurone for the complex perceptual cathexis. The perceptual neurone is hypercathected. The quantity that is compounded of external and psychical quantity (Q and $Q\dot\eta$) flows away along the best facilitations and will overcome a certain number of barriers, according to the resistance and quantity concerned. It will cathect some further, associated neurones; but it will fail to overcome other barriers, because the quotient which reaches them does not rise above their threshold.[2] It is certain that more numerous and more distant neurones will be cathected than in the caso of a merely associative process occurring without attention. But finally the current will come to an end in this case too in one or more terminal cathexes. The outcome of attention will be that in place of the perception, one or more memory cathexes will appear, connected by association with the initial neurone.

---

[1] What follows is in contradiction to Freud's later view (already developed in *The Interpretation of Dreams*) of the importance of preconscious psychical processes. See, on the other hand, pp. 430-1.

[2] [Nine words in this sentence were accidentally omitted in the German edition of 1950.]

For the sake of simplicity let us suppose that it is a *single* memory-image. If this could once again be cathected (with attention) from Ψ, the game would be repeated, the quantity (Q) would once more begin to flow and would cathect (awaken) a fresh memory-image along the path of best facilitation. Now it is obviously the purpose of observant thought to get to know the paths leading from the system W to the furthest possible extent; and in this way an exhaustive knowledge of the perceptual object can be obtained. (It will be noticed that the method of thought here described leads to *cognition*.) For this reason a Ψ-cathexis is once again required for the memory-images which have been reached; but some mechanism is also required which shall direct that cathexis to the right places. How else are the Ψ-neurones in the ego to know where the cathexis is to be directed to? A mechanism of attention, such as the one described above [p. 419], once more presupposes, however, the presence of indications of quality. Do these appear during the course of association? Normally not, according to our presuppositions. They might, however, be obtained by means of a fresh contrivance of the following kind. Indications of quality normally arise only from perception. Thus it is a question of obtaining a perception from the passage of a quantity ($Q\dot{\eta}$). If, in addition to the mere passage, there were a *discharge* attached to the passage of the quantity ($Q\dot{\eta}$), that discharge like any other movement, would give rise to a *report* of the movement. After all, indications of quality are themselves reports of discharges. (We may later consider what *kind* of discharge.) Now it may happen that during the passage of a quantity (Q) a *motor* neurone may be cathected, which will then discharge quantity ($Q\dot{\eta}$) and give rise to an indication of quality. But what we require is that *all* the cathexes shall give rise to such discharges. They are not all motor neurones, and for this purpose, therefore, they must be brought into a firm facilitation with motor neurones.

This purpose is served by *speech-associations*. These consist in the linking of Ψ-neurones with neurones which are employed by auditory images and are themselves intimately associated with motor speech-images. These speech-associations have the advantage over others of possessing two further characteristics: they are circumscribed (*i.e.*, are few in number) and exclusive. The excitation proceeds from the auditory image to the verbal image, and thence to discharge. If, therefore, the memory-images are of such a kind that a branch stream can pass from them to the auditory images and motor verbal images, then the cathexis of the memory-images is accompanied by reports of a discharge, and these are indications of quality and at the same time indications of the memory being conscious. Now if the ego precathects these verbal images as it earlier precathected the images of the discharge of perceptions, it has created a mechanism for directing the Ψ-cathexis to the memories which emerge during the passage of the quantity $(Q\dot{\eta})$.[1] Here we have *conscious, observant thought*.

Besides making cognition possible, speech-associations effect something else of great importance. The facilitations between the Ψ-neurones are, as we know, the "memory"—the representation of all the influences from the external world which Ψ has experienced. But the ego, too, itself cathects the Ψ-neurones and sets currents in motion which must also certainly leave traces in the form of facilitations. Now Ψ has no means of distinguishing these (the results of thought-processes) from the results of perceptual processes. It may be possible to recognize and reproduce perceptual processes through their being associated with discharges of perception; but the facilitations produced by *thought* leave only their result behind them and not a *memory*. A thought-facilitation may have arisen equally well from a single intensive process or from ten less impressive ones. Now the indications of discharge by way of speech help to make good this lack. They put thought-processes on a level with perceptual processes; they lend them reality and *make it possible to remember them*. [See below p. 436 f.]

It is also worth considering the *biological* development of these highly important speech-associations. The innervation of speech is originally a discharge in the nature of a safety-valve for the benefit of Ψ, serving to regulate the oscillations of quantity $(Q\dot{\eta})$ in it—a

---

[1] In *The Interpretation of Dreams* (trans. 1953, p. 617) we find: "In order that thought-processes may acquire quality, they are associated in human beings with verbal memories." In his later writings Freud chose the following formulation: "A conscious idea comprises a concrete idea *plus* the verbal idea corresponding to it, whereas an unconscious idea is the concrete idea alone." ("The Unconscious", 1915 *e, Coll. Papers*, IV, p. 134.)

part of the path to *internal change*, which is the sole means of discharge until the "specific action" has been discovered [p. 379]. This path acquires a secondary function by attracting the attention of some helpful personage (who is usually the wished-for object itself) to the child's longing and distress, and thenceforward it serves the purpose of bringing about an understanding with other people and is thus absorbed into the specific action.

When (as we have already seen [pp. 390 and 393]) the function of judgement is beginning, perceptions arouse interest on account of their possible connection with the object wished-for, and their complexes are analysed into an unassimilable portion (the "thing") and a portion that is known to the ego from its own experience (the thing's "attributes" or activities). This process, which is known as "understanding", affords two points of contact with expression by means of speech. There are, in the first place, objects (perceptions) which make one scream because they cause pain; and it is an immensely significant fact that this association of a sound (which also gives rise to motor images of the subject's own movements) with a perception that is already a complex one emphasizes the *hostile* character of the object and serves to direct attention to the perception. Where otherwise, owing to the pain, one would have received no clear indications of quality from the object, the report of one's own scream serves to characterize the object. This association is thus a means of making conscious memories that cause unpleasure and of bringing attention to bear on them: the first class of *conscious memories* has been created.[1] It is a short step from here to the discovery of speech. There are objects of a second kind which are themselves constantly giving vent to certain noises—objects, that is, in whose perceptual complex a sound plays a part. In consequence of the impulse to *imitate* which emerges during the process of judging [p. 395], it is possible to find a report of a movement [of one's own] attaching to this sound-image. So that this class of memories too can now become conscious. It remains to associate *deliberately produced* sounds with perceptions.

---

[1] This may be expressed as follows in Freud's later terminology. Situations of frustration in earliest infancy make in general an important contribution to the development of the sense of reality; and in particular they provide a reason for recognizing and identifying the person who is in charge of the child and who is the source both of satisfaction and frustration.

When this is done, the memories that arise when one observes indications of discharges by way of sound become conscious like perceptions and can be cathected from Ψ.

Thus we have found that the characteristic thing about the process of cognitive thought is that the attention is from the start directed to the indications of the discharge of thought—that is, to indications of speech. It is well known that what is known as "conscious" thought is accompanied by a slight motor expenditure.[1]

The process of following the associative course of a quantity (Q) can be continued for an indefinite length of time—usually until terminal associative elements are reached which are "completely familiar". The fixing of this path and of its terminal points constitutes the "cognition" of what was perhaps a new perception.

We should be glad now to have some *quantitative* information about this process of cognitive thought. The perception is in this case hypercathected in comparison with what happens in a simple associative process. The process itself consists in a displacement of quantities $(Q\dot{\eta})$ which is regulated by association with indications of quality. At each halting-point the Ψ-cathexis is renewed, and discharge finally takes place from the motor neurones of the speech-path. We may now ask whether this process involves the ego in a considerable loss of quantity $(Q\dot{\eta})$, or whether the expenditure in the activity of thinking is relatively slight. The answer to this question is suggested by the fact that the current of speech-innervations while thought is proceeding is obviously very small. We do not *really* speak, any more than we *really* move when we picture a motor image. But the difference between imagining and moving is only a quantitative one, as we know from experiments in "thought-reading". When we think intensely, we may even actually speak aloud. But how can such small discharges be effected, since, after all, small quantities $(Q\dot{\eta})$ cannot flow and large ones are levelled down *en masse* through the motor neurones ?

It seems probable that the quantities involved in displacement

---

[1] Thought "is essentially an experimental kind of acting accompanied by displacement of smaller quantities of cathexis together with less expenditure (discharge) of them". ("Formulations on the Two Principles of Mental Functioning", 1911 *b*; *Coll. Papers*, IV, p. 16.)

during the process of thinking are also of no great magnitude. For, in the first place, the expenditure of large quantities $(Q\dot\eta)$ means a loss for the ego which must be kept within the narrowest possible limits, since the quantity $(Q\dot\eta)$ is in fact required for use in the exacting "specific action" [p. 357]. And in the second place, a large quantity $(Q\dot\eta)$ would pass simultaneously along several paths of association, which would leave no time for the thought-cathexis and would cause a large expenditure. Accordingly, the quantities (Q) that flow during the process of thinking must no doubt be small. Nevertheless[1], according to our hypothesis, perception and memory during the process of thinking must be hypercathected [p. 419], and more intense than in simple perception. Moreover, there are various degrees of intensity of attention; and this can only be interpreted as various degrees of intensification of the cathecting quantities $(Q\dot\eta)$. It would then follow that the greater the attention the greater would be the difficulty in the way of the process of following (that is, of observing). And this would be so inexpedient that we cannot suppose it true.

Thus we are faced by two apparently contradictory requirements: a strong cathexis and a weak displacement. If we are to bring these into harmony, we are led to the hypothesis of what may be described as *a "bound"*[2] *condition in the neurones, which, though there is a high cathexis, permits only a small current to flow.* This hypothesis may be made more plausible by the consideration that the current in a neurone is clearly affected by the cathexes surrounding it. Now the ego itself is a mass of neurones of this kind which hold fast to their cathexis (which, that is, are in a bound condition), and this can only occur, no doubt, as a result of their mutual influence. We can therefore imagine that a perceptual neurone which is cathected with attention may on that account be, as it were, temporarily absorbed into the ego, and may thereafter be subject to the same binding of its

---

[1] ["*Dennoch*" in the MS. Wrongly printed "*demnach*" ("accordingly") in the German edition of 1950.]

[2] The distinction between "bound" or "quiescent" psychical energy on the one hand and "free" or "mobile" psychical energy on the other is one of Freud's most fundamental concepts and occurs throughout his later writings. It appears, for instance, in Section E of Chap. VII of the *Interpretation of Dreams* (1900*a*) (*trans.* 1953, p. 601). Freud attributes the distinction to Breuer, who discussed it in the second section of his theoretical contribution to *Studies on Hysteria* (Breuer & Freud 1895) which had been published a few months before Freud wrote the present "Project".]

quantity $(Q\dot\eta)$ as all the other ego-neurones. If it is more strongly cathected, the quantity (Q) of its current may accordingly be *diminished*, and not necessarily increased. We may perhaps suppose that, as a consequence of this binding, the external quantity (Q) remains free to flow, while the cathexis of attention is bound—a state of things which need not, of course, be permanent.

Thus the process of thought would be characterized mechanically by this bound condition, which combines a high cathexis with a small flow of current. We can think of other processes in which the current would run *parallel* to the cathexis—processes with an uninhibited discharge.

I hope that the hypothesis of a bound condition of this kind will turn out to be tenable mechanically. I should like, however, to throw some light on the psychological implications of this hypothesis. It seems at first sight to labour under an internal contradiction. If the bound condition means that, when there is a cathexis of this sort, only small quantities (Q) are left over for displacement, how can it bring about the inclusion of fresh neurones—that is, cause large quantities (Q) to travel into fresh neurones ? And, to push the same difficulty further back, how has it been in any way possible to evolve an ego put together in this same manner ?

Thus we have unexpectedly arrived at the most obscure of problems—the origin of the "ego", a complex of neurones which hold fast to their cathexis, and which thus constitute, for short periods of time, a complex with a constant level.[1] A genetic treatment of the question will be the most instructive. The ego consists originally of the nuclear neurones [p. 377], which receive endogenous quantity $(Q\dot\eta)$ along paths of conduction [p. 377] and discharge it by the method of internal change [p. 379]. The "experience of satisfaction" [p. 380] brings this nucleus into association with a perception (the wishful image) and the report of a movement (the reflex portion of the specific action) [p. 380]. The education and development of this original ego take place in states in which there is a repetition of the craving, in states of *expectation*. The ego learns first that it must not cathect the motor images (with consequent discharge), until certain conditions have been fulfilled on the perceptual side. It learns further that it must not cathect the wishful idea beyond a certain degree, because,

---

[1] [For what follows cf. p. 384 ff.]

if it does, it will deceive itself in a hallucinatory manner. If, however, it respects these two restrictions and turns its attention to the new perceptions, it has a prospect of attaining the desired satisfaction. Clearly, therefore, the restrictions which prevent the ego from cathecting the wishful image and the motor image beyond a certain degree are the cause of an accumulation of quantity ($Q\dot\eta$) in the ego and oblige the ego, it seems, to transfer its quantity ($Q\dot\eta$) within certain limits to the neurones that are accessible to it.

The hypercathected nuclear neurones abut ultimately upon the paths of conduction from the interior of the body, which have become permeable owing to being continuously filled with quantity ($Q\dot\eta$) [p. 377]; and since the nuclear neurones are prolongations of these paths of conduction, they too must remain filled with quantity ($Q\dot\eta$). The quantity in them will flow away in proportion to the resistances met with in its course, until the next resistances are greater than the quotient of quantity ($Q\dot\eta$) available for the current. But at this point the whole cathectic mass is in a state of equilibrium, held back on one side by the two restrictions against motility and wish, on the other by the resistances offered by the furthest neurones attained and towards the interior by the constant pressure of the paths of conduction. In the inside of this structure which constitutes the ego, the cathexis will by no means be everywhere equal; it need only be *proportionally* equal—that is, in relation to the facilitations [cf. p. 399].

If the level of the cathexis in the nucleus of the ego rises, the ego will be able to extend its area; if it sinks, the ego will narrow concentrically. At a given level and a given extension of the ego, there will be no obstacle to displacement taking place within the region of its cathexis.

It only remains now to enquire into the origin of the two restrictions which guarantee the constant level of the ego, and in particular into the origin of the restriction upon motor images, which hinders discharge. Here we find ourselves at a decisive point in regard to our view of the whole organization. All we can say is that at a time when these restrictions were not yet operating and when motor discharge occurred simultaneously with the wish, the expected pleasure failed to make its appearance and the continuing release of endogenous stimuli eventually generated unpleasure. It is only this threat of unpleasure, which became attached to premature discharge, that can correspond to the restrictions we are considering. In the course of subsequent development, facilitation took over a portion of the task [of carrying out the restrictions]. But it still remains an established fact that the quantity $(Q\grave{\eta})$ in the ego refrains from immediately cathecting the motor images because, if it did, a release of unpleasure would follow.

Everything that I describe as a "biological acquisition" of the neuronic system is, I believe, represented by a *threat of unpleasure* of this kind, the effect of which is that neurones which lead to a release of unpleasure are not cathected. This constitutes *primary defence*, and is an intelligible consequence of the original trend of the neuronic system [p. 356-7]. Unpleasure remains the sole means of education. The question of how we are to give a mechanical explanation of primary defence—of non-cathexis owing to the threat of un-pleasure—is, I must confess, one to which I can offer no answer.

From this point onwards I shall venture to omit any mechanical representation of biological rules of this kind; and I shall be content if I can henceforward keep faithfully to a clearly demonstrable course of development.

There is no doubt a second biological rule, derived by abstraction from the process of expectation, to the effect that one must direct one's attention to indications of quality (because they belong to perceptions that may lead to satisfaction) and then allow oneself to be led from the indication of quality to the perception which has emerged. In short, the mechanism of attention must owe its origin to a biological rule of this kind, which will regulate the displacement of ego-cathexes.[1]

Here it may be objected that a mechanism like this, operating by the help of indications of quality, is redundant. The ego, it will be said, might have learnt biologically to cathect the perceptual sphere in states of expectation on its own account, instead of only being led to this cathexis through the agency of indications of quality. There

---

[1] See the continuation of this line of thought in Freud (1911 *b*) where attention is assigned the task of "periodically searching the external world, in order that its data may be already familiar if an urgent internal need should arise". (*Coll. Papers*, IV, p. 15.)

are, however, two points to be made in justification of the mechanism of attention. (1) The sphere of the indications of discharge from the system W (ω) is clearly a smaller one, comprises fewer neurones, than the sphere of perception—that is, of the whole pallium of Ψ which is connected with the sense organs. Consequently the ego saves an extraordinarily large expenditure if it cathects the discharge instead of the perception. (2) The indications of discharge or the indications of quality are also primarily indications of *reality*, and are intended to serve the purpose of distinguishing the cathexes of real perceptions from the cathexes of wishes. Thus we see that we cannot do without the mechanism of attention. But it consists in every case of the ego cathecting those neurones in which a cathexis has already appeared.

The biological rule of attention, in so far as it concerns the ego, runs as follows: *If an indication of reality appears, the perceptual cathexis which is simultaneously present must be hypercathected.*

This is the second biological rule. The first one is that of primary defence.

[2]

From what has been said, we may gather a few hints of a general nature as well as for a mechanical representation—such, for instance, as the one already mentioned [p 419] to the effect that external quantity cannot be represented by $Q\eta$, psychical quantity. For it follows from the representation that has been given of the ego and its oscillations [p. 427] that the level [of cathexis], too, has no relation to the external world—that a general lowering or raising of it makes no difference normally to the picture of the external world. Since this picture is based upon facilitations, this means that general oscillations of level make no difference to the facilitations. A second principle, too, has been mentioned already [p. 427], namely, that small quantities can be displaced more easily when the level is high than when it is low. Here we have a few points which must be borne in mind when we set about describing the characteristics of neuronic motion, which are still quite unknown to us.

Let us now return to our account of observant or cognitive processes of thought. Here, in contradistinction to what occurs in *expectant* processes, perceptions do not light upon *wishful* cathexes. And here, accordingly, it is the first indications of reality that direct the ego's attention to the perceptual region which is to be cathected. The course of association taken by the quantity (Q) brought with them [by the perceptions] passes along neurones that are pre-cathected; and the $Q\Phi$ (the quantity belonging to the Φ neurones) which is displaced [along these precathected neurones] is set free again at each stage. During this course of association the indications of quality (of speech) are generated, and, as a consequence, that course becomes conscious and capable of being reproduced.

Now here once again the usefulness of indications of quality might be questioned. All that they achieve, it might be argued, is to induce the ego to send out a cathexis to the point at which a cathexis emerges in the course of the associations. But they do not themselves provide these cathecting quantities ($Q\dot{\eta}$), or at most they only make a contri-bution to them. And, if so, the ego could cause its cathexis to travel along the course taken by the quantity (Q) without their assistance.

This is no doubt true; but nevertheless mindfulness of the indica-tions of quality is *not* redundant. For it must be emphasized that the biological rule of attention stated above [p. 429] is an abstraction made from *perception* and in the first instance applies only to indica-tions of *reality*. Indications of discharge by way of speech are also in a certain sense indications of reality—indications of *thought*-reality though not of *external* reality[1]; but no biological rule of the kind in question has become established in the case of these indications of thought-reality, since no regular threat of unpleasure would be attached to a breach of it. The unpleasure arising from a neglect of cognition is not so striking as where the external world is ignored, though the two cases are at bottom the same. There is in fact, there-fore, a kind of observant thought-process in which indications of quality are never, or only sporadically, aroused, and which is made possible by the ego following the course of association with its cathexes *automatically*. This kind of thought-process is indeed far the more frequent and by no means abnormal; it is our ordinary kind of

---

[1] [This distinction is often stressed in Freud's later writings: e.g., in the last pages of *The Interpretation of Dreams* (1900*a*).]

thinking, unconscious, but with occasional intrusions[1] into conscious-ness—what is described as conscious thinking with unconscious intermediate links, which can, however, be made conscious.[2]

Nevertheless, indications of quality are of indisputable value for thinking. In the first place, the arousing of indications of quality intensifies the cathexes in the course of association and assures the automatic attention which, we do not know how, is evidently attached to the emergence of cathexis. Moreover—and this seems more important—attention to the indications of quality ensures the impartiality of the course of association. For it is very difficult for the ego to put itself into the situation of pure "research". The ego almost always has purposive or wishful cathexes, whose presence during an investigation has, as we shall see [p. 433 ff.], an influence on the course of association, and thus produces false knowledge about the perceptions. Now there is no better protection against this falsification of thought than by the ego directing a normally dis-placeable quantity $(Q\dot{\eta})$ to a region which cannot produce (that is, provoke) any such diversion of the course of association. There can be only one device of this kind, namely, the directing of attention to the indications of quality; for these are not purposive ideas, but, on the contrary, their cathexis places greater emphasis on the course of association by contributing to the cathecting quantity.

Thus, thought which is accompanied by the cathexis of indications of thought-reality or of indications of speech is the highest and most secure form of cognitive thought-process.

Since the arousing of indications of thought is of undoubted value, we may expect to find contrivances to guarantee their occurrence. For indications of thought, unlike indications of reality, do not arise spontaneously, without the participation of Ψ. Now observation shows that such contrivances are not so effective in the case of all thought-processes as in investigatory ones. It is a *sine qua non* of the arousing of indications of thought that they shall receive a cathexis of attention; they arise when this is so by virtue of the law that where there are two neurones which are connected and simultaneously

---

[1] [The German word is *"Einfall"*—which is also the word commonly rendered in English by the highly ambiguous term "association", especially in the phrase "free association".]

[2] Freud's earliest description of preconscious processes of thought. Cf. p. 420.

cathected the conduction between them is improved [p. 480]. Never-theless, the "enticement" offered by the precathexis of the indications of thought only has a certain degree of power to over-ride other influences. Thus, for instance, every other cathexis (such as purposive or affective cathexes) in the neighbourhood of the course of associa-tion will compete with it [the precathexis of attention] and tend to make the course of association unconscious. A similar effect, as experience confirms, is produced if the quantities involved in the course of association are considerable, for they will increase the current and consequently accelerate the whole course of association. The common assertion that something "happened in one so quickly that one didn't notice it" is no doubt completely correct; and it is also a familiar fact that affects can interfere with the arousing of indications of thought.

All this leads us to a new proposition in our mechanical representa-tion of psychical processes: namely, that the course of association, which is not altered by the level [of cathexis], can be influenced by the magnitude of the quantity (Q) in passage itself. [Cf. p. 436.] *Generally speaking, a quantity* (Q) *of large magnitude takes a different path through the network of facilitations from that taken by a small one.* There is no great difficulty, I think, in illustrating this.

For every barrier there is a threshold of value below which no quantity (Q)—let alone a quotient of that quantity—can pass it. When a quantity (Q) is too small, it will distribute itself along two other paths, of whose facilitations it is large enough to avail itself. But if the quantity (Q) increases, the first path will now come into use and assist the passage of the quantity's quotients; moreover, cathexes lying beyond what has become a surmountable barrier will now be able to make themselves felt. Indeed, yet another factor may become significant. It may perhaps be assumed that the paths through a neurone are not all equally receptive to a quantity (Q), and we may describe this difference as "breadth of path". Breadth of path is in itself independent of resistance; for the latter can be altered by the quantity which is in passage (Abq)[1], whereas the breadth of path remains constant. Let us now suppose that, with the increase of quantity (Q), a path is opened which can make its breadth felt; we

---

[1] [German "*Ablaufsquantität*".]

can then see that it is possible for the course of the quantity (Q) to be fundamentally altered by an increase in the magnitude of the quantity (Q) in passage. Everyday experience seems to lend positive support to this conclusion.

Thus the arousing of indication of thought seems to be bound up with the passage of *small* quantities (Q). This is not to assert that passages of any other sort must remain unconscious—for the arousing of indications of thought is not the only way in which consciousness can be invoked.

How then can we give a clear picture of thinking that becomes *sporadically* conscious—with sudden intrusions into consciousness [p. 430]? Our ordinary purposeless thinking, although it is accompanied by precathexis and automatic attention, lays no stress upon indications of thought. Nor have we found biological grounds for regarding such indications as indispensable for the process. Nevertheless they usually emerge (1) when the whole smooth course of association has reached an end or has come up against an obstacle; and (2) when it has aroused an idea which, for other reasons, gives rise to indications of quality, *i.e.*, consciousness. But here I will break off the present discussion.

[3]

Obviously there are other kinds of thought-process which, instead of the unselfish aim of cognition, have some practical aim in view. The state of expectation, from which thinking in general has developed, is an example of this second kind of thought. In that state there is a wishful cathexis which is firmly retained, while a second cathexis, a perceptual one, emerges and is followed with attention. But the purpose of this is not to discover where it will lead *in general*, but to discover by what paths it will lead to the activation of the wishful cathexis which has meanwhile been retained. This kind of thought-process, biologically the earlier one, can easily be represented on our hypothesis. Let $+ V$ be a wishful idea, which is kept specially cathected, and let W be the perception which is to be followed. Then the first result of the cathexis of W with attention will be that the $Q\,\Phi$ [see p. 430] will pass into the best facilitated neurone a. Thence it would once more pass along the best path if it were not interfered with by the presence of lateral cathexes [p. 385]. If three paths lead from a ... in the order b, c and d, according to their degree of facilitation—and if d lies in the neighbourhood of the wishful cathexis $+ V$, the outcome may be that, in spite of the facilitations, the $Q \Phi$ may flow, not to c and b, but to d, and thence to $+ V$; so that the desired path will be revealed as $W \ldots a \ldots d \ldots + V$. Here we see in operation the principle we have long been familiar with [cf. p. 380-1] that cathexis diverts facilitation and can thus work against it and that accordingly lateral cathexis can modify the course of quantity $(Q\dot\eta)$. Since cathexes can be changed, it lies within the choice of the ego to modify the course taken from W in the direction of any purposive cathexis.

And by purposive cathexis is here to be understood not a uniform one, such as affects a whole region in the case of attention, but an emphatic one, standing out above the level of the ego. We must probably also assume that, in this kind of thinking with purposive cathexes, quantity $(Q\dot\eta)$ also travels out from $+ V$ at the same time, so that the course of association from W may be influenced not only from $+ V$ itself but also from the further points reached by it. In this case, however, the path leading from $+ V$ ... is known and fixed, whereas the path leading from $W \ldots a \ldots$ has still to be discovered. Since in reality our ego always entertains purposive cathexes—and often many at the same time—we can now understand both the difficulty of carrying on purely cognitive thinking, as well as the possibility that, in the case of practical thinking, the most various paths may be traversed at various times, in various circumstances, by various individuals.

We can also appreciate the difficulties in thinking in the case of practical thought, difficulties with which we are familiar from our own experience. Let us return to our earlier example in which the $Q \Phi$ current would naturally flow to b and c, while d is characterized by a close connection with the purposive cathexis or its derivative ideas. Then it may be that the influence of the facilitation from $b \ldots c$ is so great that it far outweighs the attraction of $d \ldots + V$. In order, in spite of this, for the course of association to be directed to $+ V$, it would be necessary for the cathexis of $+ V$ and its derivative ideas to be still more intensified; perhaps, too, it would be necessary for the attention to W to be modified, in order that a larger or smaller degree of "binding" [p. 425] might be attained and a level of current which would be more favourable to the path to $d \ldots + V$. The expenditure required in order to overcome better facilitations and to entice the quantity (Q) into paths that are poorly facilitated but that lie nearer to the purposive cathexis corresponds to the difficulty in thinking.

The part played by indications of quality in practical thinking differs little from that played by them in cognitive thinking. The indications of quality ensure and fix the course of association, but are not absolutely indispensible for it. If we replace the single neurones and the single ideas by complexes of neurones and complexes of ideas, we are brought up against a complication of practical thinking which it is no longer possible to picture, while we can well understand that in such cases rapid conclusions are desirable [cf. p. 440]. But here the indications of quality are as a rule not fully aroused, and indeed their generation serves to slow up and complicate the course of association. Where that course, from a particular perception to particular purposive cathexes, has already been repeatedly followed and has become stereotyped by means of mnemic facilitations, there will usually be no occasion to arouse the indications of quality.

The aim of practical thinking is *identity*—the moment at which the displaced $Q\,\Phi$ cathexis finds its way into the wishful cathexis which has meanwhile been firmly retained. As a purely biological consequence, there then ceases to be any necessity for thinking, and, instead, a complete innervation of the motor images which have been touched on during the passage [of the quantity] becomes permissible —motor images which constitute what is in the circumstances a permissible accessory portion of the "specific action". Since during the passage the cathexis of these motor images was only of a "bound" sort, and since the thought-process started from a perception (W) which was only followed as a memory-image, the whole thought-process is able to make itself independent both of the expectational process and of reality and can proceed to identity without any kind of modification. Thus it starts from what is merely an *idea*, and, after it is completed, does not lead to action; it has, however, produced a piece of *practical knowledge*, which can be used if there is a real occasion for it. For experience shows that it is expedient to have the practical thought-process ready at hand to meet such an occasion and not to have to leave its construction till the very moment when the real need for its use arises.

The time has now come to qualify a statement that I previously made [p. 422] to the effect that the recollection of a thought-process is only made possible by indications of quality, because otherwise its traces could not be distinguished from the traces of a perceptual facilitation. It remains true that a real memory ought not to properly be modified by thinking over it. But on the other hand it is an undeniable fact that thinking over a topic leaves extremely important traces upon any subsequent thinking over the same topic;[1] and it is highly doubtful whether this result is produced only by thought that is accompanied by indications of quality and by consciousness. There must therefore be such things as thought-facilitations; and yet the original paths of association must not be obliterated. But since there can only be one kind of facilitation, it might be supposed that these two conclusions were incompatible. Nevertheless it must be possible to find a means of reconciling and explaining them in the fact that *thought*-facilitations all originated when there was a high level [of cathexis] and also probably make themselves felt once again when the level is high; whereas *associative* facilitations originated in complete or primary passages of quantity and reappear if the conditions characterizing an unbound passage[2] of quantity are re-established. Accordingly it is impossible to dispute the fact that thought-facilitations might have some possible effect upon associative facilitations.

We thus arrive at this further characteristic of the unknown neuronic motion. Memory consists in the facilitations. Facilitations are not changed by a rise in the level [of cathexis], though there are facilitations which function only at a particular level. The direction taken by the passage of quantity is not altered in the first instance by an alteration of level, but it is no doubt altered by the quantity of the current [cf. p. 432 ff.] and by the lateral cathexes. When the level is high, smaller quantities (Q) are more easily displaced.

---

[1] [This subject was touched upon earlier, on p. 397 f.]

[2] [*Ungeb.* for *ungebunden* in M.S. Wrongly given in the 1950 German edition as *umgebenden* ("surrounding").]

Alongside of *cognitive* and of *practical* thought we must distinguish *reproductive or recollecting* thought, which is partly included in practical thought but does not cover it completely. This recollecting is a precondition of any testing carried out by critical thought. It follows a given thought-process in a reverse direction, as far back, it may be, as a perception; and it does so, once again, without an aim (as contrasted with practical thinking), and, in the process, makes use to a great extent of indications of quality. In pursuing this backward course, the process meets with intermediate links which have hitherto been unconscious, which have left no indications of quality behind them but whose indications of quality emerge *ex post facto*. It follows from this that the passage of thought in itself, without any indications of quality, has left traces behind it. In some cases, indeed, it appears as though we are only able to conjecture certain stretches of a train of thought because their starting-points and terminations are given by indications of quality.

In any case, the reproducibility of thought-processes extends far beyond their indications of quality; they can be made conscious subsequently, though perhaps the outcome of a train of thought leaves traces behind it more often than do its intermediate stages.

In the course of thinking—whether it is cognitive, critical or practical—events of all kinds may occur that deserve to be described. Thinking may lead to *unpleasure* or it may lead to *contradiction*.

Let us take the case in which practical thinking, accompanied by purposive cathexes, leads to a release of unpleasure. Everyday experience teaches us that such an event acts as an obstacle to the thought-process. How is it that it can come about at all? If a memory generates unpleasure when it is cathected, this is due, generally speaking, to the fact that the corresponding perception generated unpleasure when it occurred—that is, formed part of an experience of pain [p. 381]. Experience shows that perceptions of this kind attract a high degree of attention, but that they arouse fewer indications of quality belonging to the perceptions themselves than to the reaction which those perceptions generate: they are associated with their own manifestations of affect and defence. If we follow the vicissitudes of perceptions of this kind when they become memory-images, we shall find that their *first* repetitions still arouse affect as well as unpleasure, but that in course of time they lose this capacity. And at the same time they undergo another change. To begin with they retain the characteristic of sensory qualities, but when they cease to be capable of producing affects they also lose these sensory qualities and come to resemble other memory-images. If a train of thought comes up against a memory-image of the still "untamed" sort, its indications of quality (often of a sensory kind) are generated, as well as unpleasurable feelings and an inclination to discharge, the combination of which characterizes some particular affect—and the train of thought is interrupted.

What is it that happens to memories capable of generating affect which leads to their becoming "tamed"? We cannot suppose that "time" weakens their capacity to repeat the generation of affect, since that factor normally contributes rather to *intensify* an association. No doubt something must happen during the "time" in which these repetitions occur which brings about the subjugation of the memories; and this can only be that some relation to the ego or to the ego cathexes obtains power over them. If this takes longer in such cases than it does normally, we can point to a special reason—namely, to the origin of memories that are thus capable of generating affect. Being traces of experiences of pain, they have been cathected (according to our hypothesis about pain [p. 368]) with excessive $Q\Phi$ and have acquired an excessively strong facilitation towards the release of unpleasure and affect. They must therefore receive especially large and repeated "binding" from the ego before this facilitation towards unpleasure can be counterbalanced.

The fact that memories continue for so long to be of a hallucinatory character also calls for an explanation—and this would have an important bearing on our view of hallucinations. It is plausible to suppose that, like the capacity of a memory to generate affects, its capacity to generate hallucinations is a sign that the ego cathexis has not yet acquired any influence over it, that primary methods of discharge and the complete or primary process [p. 388] predominate in it.

We must necessarily suppose that in states of hallucination the quantity (Q) flows back to Φ and at the same time to W (ω). Thus a bound neurone does not permit such a flow-back to occur. It must further be asked whether what makes a flow-back possible is the excessive magnitude of the cathectic quantity of the memory. But here we must bear in mind that a quantity (Q) of this large magnitude is only present on the first occasion, when the actual experience of pain occurs. When it is repeated, we are dealing with a mnemic cathexis of no more than the usual magnitude, and yet it generates hallucination and unpleasure. We can only presume that it does so owing to an unusually powerful facilitation. It follows from this that an ordinary Φ-quantity suffices to bring about flow-back and to excite discharge; and the inhibiting affect of binding by the ego accordingly gains in importance.

It becomes possible in the long run to cathect the memory of the pain in such a way that it can no longer exhibit any flow-back and can only release minimal unpleasure. It has now been "tamed"—and by a thought-facilitation powerful enough to exercise a permanent effect and to operate as an inhibition whenever there is a subsequent repetition of the memory. The path leading to the release of unpleasure, owing to disuse, gradually increases its resistance—for facilitations are subject to gradual decay (that is, to forgetting). Only when this has occurred does the memory become a tamed memory like any other.

Nevertheless, it appears that this process of subjugating a memory leaves permanent traces behind it on the thought-process. Since previously the train of thought was interrupted each time the memory was activated and unpleasure aroused, so now too there is a tendency to inhibit the train of thought as soon as the tamed memory generates its trace of unpleasure. This tendency is very opportune for the purposes of practical thinking, since an intermediate element that leads to unpleasure cannot lie on the desired path to identity with the wishful cathexis. Thus a primary "thought-defence" comes into being, which, in practical thinking, takes the release of unpleasure as a signal that some particular path must be abandoned—that is, that the cathexis of attention must be directed elsewhere.[1] Here, once again, unpleasure directs the flow of quantity $(Q\dot\eta)$, just as it

---

[1] Cf. *The Interpretation of Dreams*, (trans. 1953, p. 602): "It is easy to see, too, that the unpleasure principle, which in other respects supplies the thought-process with its most important signposts, puts difficulties in its path towards establishing 'thought-identity'. Accordingly, thinking must aim at freeing itself more and more from exclusive regulation by the unpleasure principle and at restricting the development of affect in thought-activity to the minimum required for acting as a signal".

does according to the first biological rule [p. 428]. It might be asked why this thought-defence is not directed against the memory while it is still capable of generating affect. Presumably, however, the *second* biological rule [p. 429] comes into operation at that point—the rule which calls for attention when there is an indication of reality—for the untamed memory is still in a position to enforce the production of real indications of quality. As we can see, both of the two rules serve a useful purpose and they are consistent with each other.

It is interesting to observe how *practical* thought lets itself be directed by the biological rule of defence. In *theoretical* (cognitive and critical) thought, the rule is no longer observed. This is intelligible; for in purposive thinking it is a question of finding *some* path and those paths to which unpleasure attaches can be excluded, whereas in theoretical thinking *every* path has to be investigated.

[4]

The further question arises of how *error* can occur during the passage of thought. What is error?

The process of thinking must be considered in still greater detail. Practical thought, in which it originated, remains the final goal of all thought-processes. Every other species branched off from it. It is an obvious advantage if the conduction of thought which takes place in practical thinking can take place in advance, and not be put off until the state of expectation arises. This is so for two reasons: (1) because it saves time in arriving at the specific action; and (2) because the state of expectation is far from being particularly favourable for a train of thought. The value of promptitude during the short interval between perception and action becomes clear when we consider that perceptions change rapidly. If the thought-process lasts too long, its outcome will have become valueless in the interval. For this reason we "think in advance".

The beginning of the thought-processes that branched off from practical thinking lies in the process of making judgements. The ego arrived at this through a discovery made in its organization—through the fact (which has already been indicated [pp. 393 and 423]) that perceptual cathexes partly coincide with reports from the subject's own body. In this way perceptual complexes are divided into a constant, uncomprehended portion—the "thing"—and a changing, comprehensible portion—the attributes or movements of the thing. Then, since the "thing-complex" keeps re-appearing in connection with a variety of "attribute-complexes", and since conversely the latter keep re-appearing in connection with a variety of "thing-complexes", it becomes possible to work out paths of thought that lead from these two kinds of complex to the desired state of the "thing" in a manner which is, as it were, valid *generally* and independently of the perception that happens to be real at the moment. Thus thinking with judgements instead of with single, orderless perceptual complexes is a great economy. We must leave on one side the question whether the psychological unity thus attained is represented by a corresponding neuronic unity in the train of thought (apart from the unity presented by the verbal image).

Error can already make its way in during the making of a judgement. For the thing-complexes (or movement-complexes) are never entirely identical, and there may be some among their divergent portions whose neglect will vitiate the outcome in reality. This defect has its origin in the tendency (which, indeed, we ourselves are imitating here) to substitute a single neurone for a complex—for this is necessitated by the immense complexity of the material. These are *mistaken judgements due to faulty premisses.*

Another source of error may lie in the fact that the real objects of perception were not completely perceived because they were outside the scope of the senses. These are *errors due to ignorance*, which no human being can avoid. But where this is not the case, there may have been defective psychical precathexis (owing to the ego being distracted from the perceptions) and inaccurate perceptions and incomplete trains of thought may result. These are *errors due to insufficient attention.*

If now we take as the material of thought-processes complexes that have been judged and reduced to order, instead of unsophisticated ones, an opportunity will then be found for shortening practical thought-processes themselves. For if it has happened that the path from perception to identity with the wishful cathexis has passed through a motor image *M*, it is biologically certain that after identity has been achieved this M will be fully innervated. The simultaneity of the perception and M will produce an intense facilitation between them, and an immediately subsequent perception will arouse M without any further course of association. (This, of course, presupposes that it is possible at any time to set up a connection between two cathexes.) What was originally a laboriously established thought-connection becomes, as a result of simultaneous full cathexis, a powerful facilitation. The only question about this facilitation is whether it always follows the path that was originally discovered or whether it can form a more direct line of connection. The latter alternative seems both more likely and more expedient, since it avoids the necessity for fixing paths of thought which should remain free for other connections of the most various sorts. If the original path of thought is not followed again, we shall not expect to find it facilitated, and the outcome will be better fixed by a *direct* connection. It remains an open question, however, where the new path originated. The problem would be made easier if the two cathexes, W and M, had a common association with a third one.

The portion of the thought-process that passes from perception to identity through a motor image may also be brought into prominence and will lead to a similar result, if attention fixes the motor image and brings it into association with the perceptions—these having also been fixed once more. Here, too, the thought-facilitation will be set up again when there is a real occurrence.

In this kind of thought-activity the possibility of errors is not at first sight obvious. But no doubt an inexpedient path of thought may be taken or a wasteful movement may be emphasized, since, after all, in practical thinking the choice depends solely on reproducible experiences.

With an increasing number of memories, fresh paths of displacement are constantly coming into existence. For that reason it has been found advantageous to follow out all the different perceptions fully, so that the most favourable of all the paths may be discovered. This is the task of *cognitive* thought, which thus emerges as a preparation for practical thought, though in fact it only developed out of the latter at a late stage. Its findings are of value for more than one kind of wishful cathexis.

The errors that may occur in cognitive thinking are self-evident. They are due to partiality, which may arise unless purposive cathexes have been avoided, and to incompleteness, which may arise unless every path has been investigated. It is clearly an enormous advantage here if indications of quality have been aroused at the same time. When these thought-processes are picked out and introduced into the state of expectation, it becomes possible for the whole course of association from beginning to end to pass by way of the indications of quality instead of through the entire extent of thought; nor is it even necessary for the train of quality to correspond completely to the train of thought.

In theoretical thought no part is played by unpleasure, and for this reason it can be carried on even in connection with "tamed" recollections.

One more species of thought remains to be considered: critical or examining thought. The occasion for this is when, in spite of all the rules being obeyed, the state of expectation, followed by the specific action, has led not to satisfaction but to unpleasure. Critical thought, proceeding in a leisurely manner, without any practical aim, seeks, while calling up all the indications of quality, to repeat the whole passage of quantity $(Q\dot\eta)$[1] in order to trace some intellectual error or some psychological defect. Critical thought is cognitive thought operating on a particular object, namely, on a train of thought. We have already formed an idea as to the nature of the latter [? psychological defects], but in what do *logical errors* consist ?

Briefly, in disregarding the biological rules that govern trains of thought. These rules lay down where it is that the cathexis of attention is to be directed on each occasion, and when the thought-process is to come to a stop. They are protected by threats of unpleasure, they are arrived at from experience and can be directly transposed into the rules of logic. (This will have to be shown in detail.) Thus the intellectual unpleasure of a contradiction, which brings critical thought to a stop, is nothing other than the unpleasure stored up for the protection of the biological rules, which is stirred up by the incorrect thought-process.

---

[1] [So in the original MS. The 1950 German edition wrongly reads *Qualität*.]

The existence of these biological rules can, in fact, be demonstrated from the feeling of unpleasure provoked by logical errors.[1]

Action, again, is to be understood as the full cathexis of the motor images brought into prominence during the thought-process, and also, perhaps, of the motor images which form part of the intentional portion of the specific action (if we are dealing with a state of expectation). Here the "bound" state is abandoned and the cathexes of attention are withdrawn. As regards the former [the abandonment of the "bound" state], what happens is, no doubt, that at the first passage of quantity from the motor neurones the level in the ego falls irresistably. It is not to be expected, of course, that the ego will be *completely* discharged as a result of single actions; this will only occur in the case of actions involving satisfaction of the most abundant kind. It is instructive to observe that action does not take place by reversing the path travelled by the motor images, but along special motor paths. For this reason, too, the affect attaching to the movement is not *ipso facto* the one that is desired, which would necessarily be the case if there were merely a reversal of the original path. A fresh comparison has therefore to be made during the action between the motor reports coming in and the movements which are precathected, and there must be an excitation of corrective innervations until identity has been attained. Here we have the same situation as we found in the case of perceptions, only that here there is less multiplicity, greater speed and an invariably *complete* discharge not found with perceptions. The analogy between practical thought and efficient action deserves notice, however. It shows us that the motor images are *sensory*. But the peculiarity that in the case of action new paths are traversed instead of the far simpler reversal of the original ones seems to show that the line of conduction of the neuronic elements is one that is firmly fixed; so that it is possible that the

---

[1] An approximation, though admittedly not a very far-reaching one, to this idea is to be found in Freud's published writings in his hypothesis of a synthetic function of the ego, which includes a need for getting rid of contradictions. Freud only touched incidentally on this problem in *The Interpretation of Dreams* (trans. 1953, p. 499): "Our waking (preconscious) thinking behaves towards any perceptual material with which it meets in just the same way in which the function we are considering behaves towards the content of dreams. It is the nature of our waking thought to establish order in material of that kind, to set up relations in it and to make it conform to our expectations of an intelligible whole".

neuronic motion in the two cases may have different characteristics.

Motor images are perceptions and as such, of course, they possess quality and arouse consciousness. Nor can it be disputed that they sometimes attract great attention to themselves. But their qualities are not very striking and are probably not so various as those of the external world; and they are not associated with verbal images, but on the contrary are themselves in part employed by such associations. It must be remembered, however, that they do not arise from highly organized sense organs, and that no doubt their quality is monotonous. [Cf. p. 371-2].

BIBLIOGRAPHY

[Titles of books and periodicals are in italics; titles of papers are in inverted commas. Abbreviations are in accordance with the *World List of Scientific Periodicals* (Oxford, 1950). Numerals in thick type refer to volumes; ordinary numerals refer to pages. The figures in round brackets at the end of each entry indicate the page or pages of this volume on which the work in question is mentioned. In the case of the Freud entries, the letters attached to the dates of publication are in accordance with the corresponding entries in the complete bibliography of Freud's writings to be included in the last volume of the *Standard Edition*.

For non-technical authors, and for technical authors where no specific work is mentioned, see the *General Index*.]

A

BIBLIOGRAPHICAL INDEX OF THE WRITINGS OF FREUD REFERRED TO IN THIS WORK

G.S. =Freud, *Gesammelte Schriften* (12 vols.), Vienna, 1924-34

G.W. =Freud, *Gesammelte Werke* (18 vols.), London, from 1940

C.P. =Freud, *Collected Papers* (5 vols.), London, 1924-50

Standard Ed. =Freud, *Standard Edition* (24 vols.), London, from 1953

(1877*a*) "Über den Ursprung der hinteren Nervenwurzeln im Rückenmarke von Ammocoetes (Petromyzon Planeri)", *Sitzb. k. Akad. Wissensch.* (Vienna, Math.-Naturwiss. Kl.), III Abt., **75**, 15. (16)

(1878*a*) "Über Spinalganglien und Rückenmark des Petromyzon", *Sitzb. k. Akad. Wissensch.* (Vienna, Math.-Naturwiss. Kl.), III Abt., **78**, 81. (16)

(1884*a*) "Ein Fall von Hirnblutung mit indirekten basalen Herdsymptomen bei Scorbut", *Wiener med. Wochenschr.*, Nr. 9, 244 and Nr. 10, 276. (16)

(1884*d*) "Eine neue Methode zum Studium des Faserverlaufes im Centralnervensystem", *Archiv. Anat. Physiol.*, Anat. Abt., 453. (16)

(1884*e*) "Über Coca", *Centralbl. ges Therap.*, **2**, 289. (16, 30)
[*Trans.:* (abridged), "Coca", *St. Louis Med. Surg. J.*, **47**, 502.]

(1885*a*) "Beitrag zur Kenntniss der Cocawirkung", *Wiener med. Wochenschr.*, **35**, Nr. 5, 129. (16)

(1885*c*) "Ein Fall von Muskelatrophie mit ausgebreiteten Sensibilitätsstörungen (Syringomyelie)", *Wiener med. Wochenschr.*, **35**, Nr. 13, 389 and 14, 426. (16)

(1885*d*) "Zur Kenntnis der Olivenzwischenschicht", *Neurolog. Centralbl.*, **4**, Nr. 12, 268. (16)

(1886*a*) "Akute multiple Neuritis der spinalen und Hirnnerven", *Wiener med. Wochenschr.*, **36**, Nr. 6, 168. (17)

(1886*b*) "Über die Beziehung des Strickkörpers zum Hinterstrang und Hinterstrangskern nebst Bemerkungen über zwei Felder der Oblongata", *Neurol. Centralbl.*, **5**, Nr. 6, 121. (17)

(1886*c*) "Über den Ursprung des Nervus acusticus", *Monatsschr. Ohrenheilk.*, Neue Folge **20**, Nr. 8, 245 and 9, 277. (17)

(1886*e*) "Beobachtung einer hochgradigen Hemianästhesie bei einem hysterischen Manne (Beiträge zur Kasuistik der Hysterie I)", *Wiener med. Wochenschr.*, **36**, Nr. 49, 1633. (20)

(1886*f*) "Übersetzung mit Vorwort und Anmerkungen zu Charcot *Leçons sur les maladies du système nerveux*, Tome III, Paris, 1887, unter dem Titel *Neue Vorlesungen über die Krankheiten des Nervensystems insbesondere über Hysterie*", Vienna. (16-17, 55)

(1887*d*) "Bemerkungen über Cocainsucht und Cocainfurcht, mit Beziehung auf einen Vortrag W. A. Hammond's", *Wiener med. Wochenschr.*, **37**, Nr. 28, 929. (17, 52)

(1888*a*) "Über Hemianopsie im frühesten Kindesalter", *Wiener med. Wochenschr.*, **38**, Nr. 32, 1081 and 33, 1116. (17, 52, 56)

(1888*b*) "Aphasie", "Gehirn" and "Hysterie" in Villaret's *Handwörterbuch der gesamten Medizin*, **1**, Stuttgart. (56, 59)

(1888-9) "Übersetzung mit Vorrede und Fussnoten zu Bernheim *De la suggestion et de ses applications à la thérapeutique*, Paris, 1886, unter dem Titel *Die Suggestion und ihre Heilwirkung*", Vienna. (17, 53, 56-58)
[*Trans.:* Preface to Bernheim's *Die Suggestion und ihre Heilwirkung*, *C.P.*, **5**, 11; *Standard Ed.*, **1**.]

(1891*a*) With RIE, O. "Klinische Studie über die halbseitige Cerebrallähmung der Kinder", Heft III of *Beiträge zur Kinderheilkunde*, ed. Kassowitz, Vienna. (17, 63)

(1891*b*)   "*Zur Auffassung der Aphasien*, Vienna. (18-19, 30, 44, 52, 61, 173)
[*Trans.: On Aphasia*, London, 1953.]

(1891*c*)   "Kinderlähmung" and "Lähmung" in Villaret's *Handwörterbuch der gesamten Medizin*, **2**, Stuttgart. (56, 59)

(1892*a*)   "Übersetzung von Bernheim *Hypnotisme, Suggestion, Psychothérapie: Etudes Nouvelles*, Paris, 1891, unter dem Titel *Neue Studien über Hypnotismus, Suggestion und Psychotherapie*", Vienna. (17, 53)

(1892-3*a*) "Übersetzung mit Vorwort und Fussnoten zu Charcot *Leçons du Mardi* (1887-8), Paris, 1888, unter dem Titel *Poliklinische Vorträge*", Bd. **1**, Vienna. (17-18, 20-21, 23, 44, 52, 62, 135, 159)
[*Trans.*: "Preface and Footnotes to Charcot's *Poliklinische Vorträge*, Vol. **1**", *Standard Ed.*, **1**.]

(1892-3*b*) "Ein Fall von hysterischer Heilung nebst Bemerkungen über die Entstehung hysterischer Symptome durch den 'Gegenwillen' ", *G.S.*, **1**, 258; *G.W.*, **1**, 1. (20, 70)
[*Trans.*: "A Case of Successful Treatment by Hypnotism", *C.P.*, **5**, 33; *Standard Ed.*, **1**.]

(1893*a*)   With BREUER, J., "Über den psychischen Mechanismus hysterischer Phänomene: Vorläufige Mitteilung", *G.S.*, **1**, 7; *G.W.*, **1**, 81. (12, 20, 63-64, 76)
[*Trans.*: "On the Psychical Mechanism of Hysterical Phenomena: A Preliminary Communication", *C.P.*, **1**, 24; *Standard Ed.*, **2**.]

(1893*b*)   "Zur Kenntniss der cerebralen Diplagien des Kindesalters (im Anschluss an die Little'sche Krankheit)", Heft III, Neue Folge, of *Beiträge zur Kinderheilkunde*, ed. Kassowitz, Vienna. (17, 63, 73, 84)

(1893*c*)   "Quelques considérations pour une étude comparative des paralysies motrices organiques et hystériques", *G.S.*, **1**, 273; *G.W.*, **1**, 37. (23, 56, 59, 73, 75-76, 135)
[*Trans.*: "Some Points for a Comparative Study of Organic and Hysterical Motor Paralyses", *C.P.*, **1**, 42; *Standard Ed.*, **1**.]

(1893*f*)   "Charcot", *G.S.*, **1**, 243; *G.W.*, **1**, 19. (77)
[*Trans.*: "Charcot", *C.P.*, **1**, 9; *Standard Ed.*, **3**.]

(1893*g*)   "Über ein Symptom, das haufig die Enuresis nocturna der Kinder begleitet", *Neurolog. Centralbl.*, **12**, Nr. 21, 735. (80)

(1894*a*)   "Die Abwehr-Neuropsychosen", *G.S.*, **1**, 290; *G.W.*, **1**, 57. (80-81, 180, 277)
[*Trans.*: "The Neuro-Psychoses of Defence", *C.P.*, **1**, 59; *Standard Ed.*, **3**.]

(1895*b*) "Über die Berechtigung, von der Neurasthenie einen bestimmten Symptomenkomplex als 'Angstneurose' abzutrennen", *G.S.*, **1**, 306; *G.W.*, **1**, 313. (23-24, 66, 78, 80, 85, 102, 159)
[*Trans.:* "On the Grounds for Detaching a Particular Syndrome from Neurasthenia under the Description 'Anxiety Neurosis' ", *C.P.*, **1**, 76; *Standard Ed.*, **3.**]

(1895*c*) "Obsessions et phobies", *G.S.*, **1**, 334; *G.W.*, **1**, 343. (81)
[*Trans.:* "Obsessions and Phobias", *C.P.*, **1**, 128; *Standard Ed.*, **3.**]

(1895*d*) With BREUER, J., *Studien über Hysterie*, Vienna. *G.S.*, **1**; *G.W.*, **1**, 75. Omitting Breuer's contributions. (3, 12, 14-15, 19-21, 24-25, 27-28, 44, 62, 64, 71, 81, 87, 95, 110, 115, 156, 240, 272, 274, 297, 356, 363, 400, 407, 425)
[*Trans.: Studies on Hysteria, Standard Ed.*, **2.** Including Breuer's contributions.]

(1895*e*) "Über die Bernhardt'sche Sensibilitätsstörung am Oberschenkel", *Neurolog. Centralbl.*, **14**, Nr. 11, 491. (30, 119)

(1895*f*) "Zur Kritik der 'Angstneurose' ", *G.S.*, **1**, 343; *G.W.*, **1**, 355. (36, 64, 67, 78, 96, 118-19, 168)
[*Trans.:* "A Reply to Criticisms of my Paper on Anxiety Neurosis", *C.P.*, **1**, 107; *Standard Ed.*, **3.**]

(1895*g*) "Über Hysterie", abstracted in *Wienerklin. Rundschau*, **9**, Nos. 42-4. (128, 132)
[*Trans.:* "Lectures on Hysteria", *Standard Ed.*, **1.**]

(1896*a*) "L'hérédité et l'étiologie des Névroses", *G.S.*, **1**, 388; *G.W.*, **1**, 405. (67, 96, 155)
[*Trans.:* "Heredity and the Aetiology of the Neuroses", *C.P.*, **1**, 138; *Standard Ed.*, **3.**]

(1896*b*) "Weitere Bemerkungen über die Abwehr-Neuropsychosen", *G.S.*, **1**, 363; *G.W.*, **1**, 377. (101, 109, 127, 141, 146, 152, 155, 217, 240)
[*Trans.:* "Further Remarks on the Neuro-Psychoses of Defence", *C.P.*, **1**, 155; *Standard Ed.*, **3.**]

(1896*c*) "Zur Ätiologie der Hysterie", *G.S.*, **1**, 404; *G.W.*, **1**, 423. (28, 159, 167)
[*Trans.:* "The Aetiology of Hysteria", *C.P.*, **1**, 183; *Standard Ed.*, **3.**]

(1897*a*) *Die infantile Cerebrallähmung*, **9**, II Theil, II Abt. of Nothnagel's *Specielle Pathologie und Therapie*, Vienna. (17, 124, 129, 131, 133-34, 167, 170, 189)

(1897*b*) *Inhaltsangaben der wissenschaftlichen Arbeiten des Privatdozenten Dr. Sigm. Freud (1877-1897)*, Vienna. *G.W.*, **1**, 461. (24, 36, 167, 200)

[*Trans.: Abstracts of the Scientific Writings of Dr. Sigm. Freud* (1877-1897), *Standard Ed.*, **3**.]

(1898*a*) "Die Sexualität in der Ätiologie der Neurosen", *G.S.*, **1**, 439; *G.W.*, **1**, 489. (46, 243, 245)
[*Trans.:* "Sexuality in the Aetiology of the Neuroses", *C.P.*, **1**, 220; *Standard Ed.*, **3**.]

(1898*b*) "Zum psychischen Mechanismus der Vergesslichkeit", *G.W.*, **1**, 517. (265)
[*Trans.:* "The Psychical Mechanism of Forgetting", *Standard Ed.*, **3**.]

(1899*a*) "Über Deckerinnerungen", *G.S.*, **1**, 465; *G.W.*, **1**, 529. (30, 35, 271, 281)
[*Trans.:* "Screen Memories", *C.P.*, **5**, 47; *Standard Ed.*, **3**.]

(1900*a*) *Die Traumdeutung*, Vienna. *G.S.*, **2-3**; *G.W.*, **2-3**. (3, 13, 20, 30-31, 34, 42-44, 115, 143, 171-74, 183-84, 194, 197, 200, 207-09, 219, 224, 227, 236-37, 240, 244-51, 254-55, 257-58, 269, 271, 277, 281-84, 286, 307, 309, 311, 313-16, 320, 322-25, 332, 334, 349-50, 358, 363, 387, 389, 398, 400-01, 403, 417-18, 420, 422, 425, 430, 439, 444)
[*Trans.: The Interpretation of Dreams*, revised ed., London and New York, 1932; *Standard Ed.*, **4-5**.]

(1901*a*) *Über den Traum*, Wiesbaden. *G.S.*, **3**, 189; *G.W.*, **2-3**, 643. (227, 321, 324-25)
[*Trans.: On Dreams*, London and New York, 1951; *Standard Ed.*, **5**, 629.]

(1901*b*) *Zur Psychopathologie des Alltagslebens*, Berlin, 1904. *G.S.*, **4**; *G.W.*, **4**. (3, 30, 38, 62, 223, 261, 265, 292-94, 302, 325-28, 332, 334, 337)
[*Trans.: The Psychopathology of Everyday Life*, *Standard Ed.*, **6**.]

(1905*c*) *Der Witz und seine Beziehung zum Unbewussten*, Vienna, *G.S.*, **9**, 5; *G.W.*, **6**. (45, 210, 261, 297, 394)
[*Trans.: Jokes and their Relation to the Unconscious*, *Standard Ed.*, **8**.]

(1905*d*) *Drei Abhandlungen zur Sexualtheorie*, Vienna. *G.S.*, **5**, 3; *G.W.*, **5**, 29. (3, 103, 147, 165, 184, 189, 204, 217, 228, 230, 239)
[*Trans.: Three Essays on the Theory of Sexuality*, London, 1949; *Standard Ed.*, **7**, 125.]

(1905*e*) "Bruchstück einer Hysterie-Analyse", *G.S.*, **8**, 3; *G.W.*, **5**, 163. (3, 34, 147, 317, 325, 330)
[*Trans.:* "Fragment of an Analysis of a Case of Hysteria", *C.P.*, **3**, 13; *Standard Ed.*, **7**, 3.]

(1907*a*)   *Der Wahn und die Träume in W. Jensens "Gradiva"*,
       Vienna. *G.S.*, **9**, 273; *G.W.*, **7**, 31. (208, 258)
       [*Trans.: Delusions and Dreams in Jensen's "Gradiva"*,
       Standard Ed., **9**.]

(1908*d*)   "Die 'kulturelle' Sexualmoral und die moderne Nervo-
       sität", *G.S.*, **5**, 143; *G.W.*, **7**, 143. (210, 229)
       [*Trans.:* " 'Civilized' Sexual Ethics and Modern Nervous
       Illness", *C.P.*, **2**, 76; *Standard Ed.*, **9**.]

(1908*e*)   "Der Dichter und das Phantasieren", *G.S.*, **10**, 229;
       G.W., **7**, 213. (199, 208, 237)
       [*Trans.:* "Creative Writers and Day-Dreaming", *C.P.*,
       4, 173; *Standard Ed.*, **9**.]

(1909*b*)   "Analyse der Phobie eines fünfjährigen Knaben",
       G.S., **8**, 129; *G.W.*, **7**, 243. (279)
       [*Trans.:* "Analysis of a Phobia in a Five-Year-Old Boy",
       C.P., **3**, 149; *Standard Ed.*, **10**.]

(1909*d*)   "Bemerkungen über einen Fall von Zwangsneurose",
       G.S., **8**, 269; *G.W.*, **7**, 381. (230)
       [*Trans.:* "Notes on a Case of Obsessional Neurosis",
       C.P., **3**, 293; *Standard Ed.*, **10**.]

(1910*g*)   "Zur Selbstmord-Diskussion", *G.S.*, **3**, 321; *G.W.*, **8**,
       62. (102)
       [*Trans.:* "Contributions to a Discussion on Suicide",
       Standard Ed., **11**.]

(1911*b*)   "Formulierungen über die zwei Prinzipien des psy-
       chischen Geschehens", *G.S.*, **5**, 409; *G.W.*, **8**, 230. (175,
       358, 387, 424, 428)
       [*Trans.:* "Formulations on the Two Principles of
       Mental Functioning", *C.P.*, **4**, 13; *Standard Ed.*, **12**.]

(1911*c*)   "Psychoanalytische Bemerkungen über einen auto-
       biographisch beschriebenen Fall von Paranoia (Demen-
       tia Paranoides)", *G.S.*, **8**, 355; *G.W.*, **8**, 240. (109)
       [*Trans.:* "Psycho-Analytic Notes on an Autobiographical
       Account of a Case of Paranoia (Dementia Paranoides)",
       C.P., **3**, 387; *Standard Ed.*, **12**.]

(1912*d*)   "Über die allgemeinste Erniedrigung des Liebeslebens",
       G.S., **5**, 198; *G.W.*, **8**, 78. (198)
       [*Trans.:* "On the Universal Tendency to Debasement in
       the Sphere of Love", *C.P.*, **4**, 203; *Standard Ed.*, **11**.]

(1912-13)   *Totem und Tabu*, Vienna, 1913. *G.S.*, **10**, 3; *G.W.*, **9**.
       (210)
       [*Trans.: Totem and Taboo*, London, 1950; *Standard
       Ed.*, **12**.]

(1913*i*)   "Die Disposition zur Zwangsneurose", *G.S.*, **5**, 277;
       G.W., **8**, 442. (42)

[*Trans.:* "The Predisposition to Obsessional Neurosis", *C.P.*, **2**, 122; *Standard Ed.*, **12.**]

(1914*d*) "Zur Geschichte der psychoanalytischen Bewegung", *G.S.*, **4**, 411; *G.W.*, **10**, 44. (11-12, 29-30, 33-34, 52, 54, 161, 172, 298, 326)
[*Trans.:* "On the History of the Psycho-Analytic Movement", *C.P.*, **1**, 287; *Standard Ed.*, **14.**]

(1915*d*) "Die Verdrängung", *G.S.*, **5**, 466; *G.W.*, **10**, 248. (383)
[*Trans.:* "Repression", *C.P.*, **4**, 84; *Standard Ed.*, **14.**]

(1915*e*) "Das Unbewusste", *G.S.*, **5**, 480; *G.W.*, **10**, 264. (350, 422)
[*Trans.:* "The Unconscious", *C.P.*, **4**, 98; *Standard Ed.*, **14.**]

(1917*d*) "Metapsychologische Ergänzung zur Traumlehre", *G.S.*, **5**, 520; *G.W.*, **10**, 412. (350)
[*Trans.:* "A Metapsychological Supplement to the Theory of Dreams", *C.P.*, **4**, 137; *Standard Ed.*, **14.**]

(1917*e*) "Trauer und Melancholie", *G.S.*, **5**, 535; *G.W.*, **10**, 428. (102)
[*Trans.:* "Mourning and Melancholia", *C.P.*, **4**, 152; *Standard Ed.*, **14.**]

(1919*e*) " 'Ein Kind wird geschlagen' ", *G.S.*, **5**, 344; *G.W.*, **12**, 197. (39)
[*Trans.:* " 'A Child is Being Beaten' ", *C.P.*, **2**, 172; *Standard Ed.*, **17.**]

(1920*g*) *Jenseits des Lustprinzips*, Vienna. *G.S.*, **6**, 191; *G.W.*, **13**, 3. (42, 108, 130, 173, 358, 360, 363, 374)
[*Trans.: Beyond the Pleasure Principle*, London, 1950; *Standard Ed.*, **18.**]

(1922*a*) "Traum und Telepathie", *G.S.*, **3**, 278; *G.W.*, **13**, 165. (182)
[*Trans.:* "Dreams and Telepathy", *C.P.*, **4**, 408; *Standard Ed.*, **18.**]

(1923*b*) *Das Ich und das Es*, Vienna. *G.S.*, **6**, 353; *G.W.*, **13**, 237. (166, 205, 350, 384)
[*Trans.: The Ego and the Id.*, London, 1927; *Standard Ed.*, **19.**]

(1924*d*) "Der Untergang des Ödipuskomplexes", *G.S.*, **5**, 423; *G.W.*, **13**, 395. (206)
[*Trans.:* "The Dissolution of the Oedipus Complex", *C.P.*, **2**, 269; *Standard Ed.*, **19.**]

(1925*a*) "Notiz über den 'Wunderblock' ", *G.S.*, **6**, 415; *G.W.*, **14**, 3. (173, 363)
[*Trans.:* "A Note upon the 'Mystic Writing-Pad' ", *C.P.*, **5**, 175; *Standard Ed.*, **19.**]

(1925*d*)   "*Selbstdarstellung*", Vienna. *G.S.*, **11**, 119; *G.W.*, **14**, 33. (5, 11, 15, 28, 30, 52, 56, 64, 317)
            [*Trans.: An Autobiographical Study*, London, 1935; *Standard Ed.*, **20.**]

(1925*g*)   "Josef Breuer", *G.S.*, **11**, 281; *G.W.*, **14**, 562. (11)
            [*Trans.*: "Josef Breuer", *Standard Ed.*, **19.**]

(1925*h*)   "Die Verneinung", *G.S.*, **11**, 3; *G.W.*, **14**, 11. (389-91)
            [*Trans.*: "Negation", *C.P.*, **5**, 181; *Standard Ed.*, **19.**]

(1926*c*)   "Bemerkung zu E. Pickworth Farrow's 'Eine Kind-heitserinnerung aus dem 6 Lebensmonat' ", *G.W.*, **14**, 568. (234)
            [*Trans.*: "Foreword" to E. Pickworth Farrow's *A Practical Method of Self-Analysis*, London, 1942; *Standard Ed.*, **20.**]

(1926*d*)   *Hemmung, Symptom und Angst*, Vienna. *G.S.*, **11**, 23; *G.W.*, **13**, 113. (24, 109, 230)
            [*Trans.: Inhibitions, Symptoms and Anxiety*, London, 1936; *The Problem of Anxiety*, New York, 1936; *Standard Ed.*, **20.**]

(1928*b*)   "Dostojewski und die Vatertötung", *G.S.*, **12**, 7; *G.W.*, **14**, 399. (239)
            [*Trans.*: "Dostoevsky and Parricide", *C.P.*, **5**, 222; *Standard Ed.*, **21.**]

(1930*a*)   *Das Unbehagen in der Kultur*, Vienna. *G.S.*, **12**, 29; *G.W.* **14**, 421. (15, 147, 210, 230, 245)
            [*Trans.: Civilization and its Discontents*, London and New York, 1930; *Standard Ed.*, **21.**]

(1930*e*)   "Ansprache im Frankfurter Goethe-Haus", *G.S.*, **12**, 408; *G.W.*, **14**, 547. (225, 237)
            [*Trans.*: "Address delivered in the Goethe House at Frankfort", *Standard Ed.*, **21.**]

(1933*b*)   *Warum Krieg ?*, *G.S.*, **12**, 349; *G.W.*, **16**, 13. (210)
            [*Trans.: Why War ?*, *C.P.*, **5**, 273; *Standard Ed.*, **22.**]

(1935*b*)   "Die Feinheit einer Fehlhandlung", *G.W.*, **16**, 37. (33)
            [*Trans.*: "The Subtleties of a Faulty Action", *C.P.*, **5**, 313; *Standard Ed.*, **22.**]

(1936*a*)   "Brief an Romain Rolland: Eine Erinnerungsstörung auf der Akropolis", *G.W.*, **16**, 250. (30-31, 33)
            [*Trans.*: "A Disturbance of Memory on the Acropolis", *C.P.*, **5**, 302; *Standard Ed.*, **22.**]

(1937*c*)   "Die endliche und die unendliche Analyse", *G.W.*, **16**, 59. (33, 39)
            [*Trans.*: "Analysis Terminable and Interminable", *C.P.*, **5**, 316; *Standard Ed.*, **23.**]

(1937*d*)   "Konstruktionen in der Analyse", *G.W.*, **16**, 43. (190)

[*Trans.:* "Constructions in Analysis", *C.P.*, **5**, 358; *Standard Ed.*, **23**.]

(1939*a*) *Der Mann Moses und die monotheistische Religion, G.W.*, **16**, 103. (190)
[*Trans.: Moses and Monotheism,* London and New York, 1939; *Standard Ed.*, **23**.]

(1940*d*) With BREUER, J., "Zur Theorie des hysterischen Anfalls", *G.W.*, **17**, 9. (21, 64, 135)
[*Trans.:* "On the Theory of Hysterical Attacks", *C.P.*, **5**, 27; *Standard Ed.*, **1**.]

(1941*a*) "Brief an Josef Breuer", *G.W.*, **17**, 5. (62, 64, 135)
[*Trans.:* "A Letter to Josef Breuer", *C.P.*, **5**, 25; *Standard Ed.*, **1**.]

(1941*b*) "Notiz 'III' ", *G.W.*, **17**, 17. (64)
[*Trans.:* "Memorandum 'III' ", *C.P.*, **5**, 31; *Standard Ed.*, **1**.]

(1941*c*) "Eine erfüllte Traumahnung", *G.W.*, **17**, 21. (302)
[*Trans.:* "A Premonitory Dream Fulfilled", *C.P.*, **5**, 70; *Standard Ed.*, **5**.]

(1941*e*) "Ansprache an die Mitglieder des Vereins B'nai B'rith", *G.W.*, **17**, 51. (238, 312)
[*Trans.:* "Address to the Members of the B'nai B'rith", *Standard Ed.*, **20**.]

(1941*f*) "Ergebnisse", *G.W.*, **17**, 151. (197)
[*Trans.: Standard Ed..*, **23**.]

B

BIBLIOGRAPHICAL INDEX OF THE WRITINGS OF AUTHORS OTHER THAN FREUD

ABRAHAM, K. (1912) "Ansätze zur psychoanalytischen Erforschung und Behandlung des manisch-depressiven Irreseins und verwandter Zustände", *Zbl. Psychoanal.*, **2**, 302. (102)
[*Trans.*: "Notes on the Psycho-Analytical Investigation and Treatment of Manic-Depressive Insanity and Allied Conditions", *Selected Papers*, London, 1927, Chap. VI.]

ABRAHAMSEN, D. (1946) *The Mind and Death of a Genius*, New York. (41)

AELBY, J. (1928) Die Fliess'sche Periodenlehre im Lichte biologischer und mathematischer Kritik. (8, 40)

BALDWIN, J. M. (1895) *Mental Development in the Child and the Race*, New York. (228)

BEARD, G. M. (1881) *American Nervousness, its Causes and Consequences*, New York.

(1886) *Sexual Neurasthenia (nervous exhaustion), its hygiene, causes, symptoms and treatment*, New York. (229)

BERNFELD, S. (1944) "Freud's Earliest Theories and the School of Helmholtz", *Psychoanal. Quart.*, **13**, 341.

(1946) "An Unknown Biographical Fragment by Freud", *American Imago*, **4**, No. 1. (30, 236, 281)

(1949) "Freud's Scientific Beginnings", *American Imago*, **6**, No. 3. (343)

(1951) "Sigmund Freud, M.D., 1882-1885", *Int. J. Psycho-Anal.*, **14**, No. 3.

BERNFELD, S., and S. C. (1944) "Freud's Early Childhood", *Bull. Menninger Clin.*, **8**, No. 4. (31)

(1952) "Freud's First Years in Practice", 18—-1887, *Bull. Menninger Clin.*, **16**, No. 2. (20, 22, 52)

BERNFELD, S. C. (1952) "Discussion of Buxbaum, Freud's Dream Interpretation in the Light of his Letters to Fliess", *Bull. Menninger Clin.*, **16**, No. 2. (35)

BERNHEIM, S. (1886) *De la Suggestion et de ses Applications à la Thérapeutique*, Paris. (2nd Ed. 1887.) (16, 17, 56, 58)
Trans.: by Freud as *Die Suggestion und ihre Heilwirkung*, Leipzig and Vienna, 1888-9.]

(1891) *Hypnotisme, Suggestion, Psychothérapie. Etudes Nouvelles*, Paris. (16, 17, 53)

BERNHEIM, S. (*contd.*)
   [*Trans.:* by Freud as *Neue Studien über Hypnotismus, Suggestion und Psychotherapie*, Leipzig and Vienna, 1892.]

BLAU, A. (1946) *The Master Hand*, American Orthopsychiatric Association, Res. Mon. No. 5, New York. (242)

BLEULER, E. (1913) "Der Sexualwiderstand", *Jb. psychoanal. psychopath. Forsch.* **5**, 442.

BRUN, R. (1936) "Sigmund Freud's Leistungen auf dem Gebiet der organischen Neurologie", *Schweiz. Arch. Neurol. und Psychiatrie*, **37**. (17, 56, 61)

BUNKER, H. A. (1930) "Symposium on Neurasthenia, from Beard to Freud, a Brief History of the Concept of Neurasthenia", *Medical Rev. of Rev.* N.Y. **36**, No. 3.

BUXBAUM, E. (1951) "Freud's Dream Interpretation in the Light of his Letters to Fliess", *Bull. Menninger Clin.*, **15**, No. 6. (34)

CHARCOT, J. M. (1886) *Leçons sur les Maladies du Système Nerveux*, Tome III, Paris, 1887. (16, 17, 55)
   [*Trans.* by Freud as *Neue Vorlesungen über die Krankheiten des Nervensystems, inbesondere über Hysterie*, 1886.]
   (1888) *Leçons du Mardi à la Salpêtrière*, Paris. (16, 17, 20, 21, 23, 52)
   [*Trans.* by Freud as *Poliklinische Vorträge*, 1. Bd., Vienna.]

DENKER, A. and KAHLER, O. (Eds.) (1928) *Handbuch der Hals-, Nasen-, und Ohren-Heilkunde*, Vienna. (5, 9, 40)

DORER, M. (1932) *Die historische Grundlagen der Psychoanalyse*, Leipzig. (47)

EISSLER, K. R. (1951) "An Unknown Autobiographical Letter by Freud and a Short Comment", *Int. J. Psycho-Anal.*, **22**, No. 4.

ELLIS, HAVELOCK (1898) "Hysteria in Relation to the Sexual Emotions", *Alien. and Neurol.*

ERB, W. (1882) *Handbuch der Elektrotherapie*, **3** of *Handbuch der allgemeinen Therapie*, edited by W. H. von Ziemssen, Leipzig. [*Trans.:* *Handbook of Electro-Therapeutics*, London 1883.]

EXNER, S. (1894) *Entwurf einer physiologischen Erklärung der psychischen Erscheinungen*, Vienna. (356)

FARROW, PICKWORTH E. (1942) *A Practical Method of Self-Analysis*, London. (American Edition entitled *Psychoanalyse Yourself*, 1945.)

FENICHEL, O. (1945) "Nature and Classification of the So-Called Psychosomatic Phenomena", *Psychoanal. Quart.*, **14**. (45)

FLEISCHL, E. VON MARXOW (1893) *Gesammelten Abhandlungen*, herausgegeben von Otto Fleischl von Marxow, mit biogr. Skisse von Prof. Sigmund Exner, Leipzig. (356)

FLIESS, W. (1892) *Neue Beiträge und Therapie der nasalen Reflexneurose*, Vienna.

FLIESS, W. (*contd.*)

(1893) "Die nasale Reflexneurose", *Verhandlungen des Kongresses für innere Medizin*, Wiesbaden, 384-94.

(1895) "Magenschmerzen und Dysmenorrhöe in einem neuen Zusammenhang", *Wien. klin. Rdsch.*, No. 1, etc.

(1897) *Die Beziehungen zwischen Nase und weibliche Geschlechtsorganen in ihrer biologischen Bedeutungen dargestellt*, Vienna. (37, 158)

(1902) *Über den ursächlichen Zusammenhang von Nase und Geschlechtsorgan, zugleich ein Betrag zur Nervenphysiologie*, Halle. (331)

(1906a) *In Eigener Sache. Gegen Otto Weininger und Hermann Swoboda*, Berlin. (241, 324)

(1906b) *Der Ablauf des Lebens*, 2nd ed. 1923, Vienna. (8, 23)

(1924a) *Vom Leben und vom Tode*, 5th ed., Jena.

(1924b) *Das Jahr im Lebendigen*, 2nd ed., Jena.

(1925) *Gesammelte Aufsätze zur Periodenlehre*, Jena.

FOREL, A. (1885) *Das Gedächtnis und seine Abnormalitäten*. Zürich. (356)

FRESE, O. (1928) "Die Krankheiten der Luftwege und der Mundhöhle" in *Handbuch der Hals-, Nasen-, und Ohren-Heilkunde*, **2**, 51, edited by A. Denker and O. Kahler, Vienna. (40)

FREUND, C. S. (1893) "Über psychische Lähmungen", *Neurol. Zbl.* 938.

FRIEDJUNG, H. (1897) *Der Kampf um die Vorherrschaft in Deutschland*, 1859-66, Stuttgart.

[*Trans.*: (abridged) *The Struggle for Supremacy in Germany*, 1859-66, London, 1935.]

(1908) *Osterreich von* 1848-1860. 2, Aufl., Stuttgart and Berlin.

FROMM, E. (1951) *The Forgotten Language. An Introduction to the Understanding of Dreams, Fairy Tales and Myths*, New York (London, 1952). (34)

GATTL, F. (1898) *Über die sexuellen Ursachen der Neurasthenie und Angstneurose*, Berlin.

GRAY, H. (1948) "Bibliography of Freud's Pre-Analytic Period", *Psychoanal. Rev.*, **35**, No. 4.

HARTMANN, E. VON (1890) *Philosophie des Unbewussten*, 10th ed. Leipzig (1st ed. 1869).

[*Trans.*: *Philosophy of the Unconscious*, by W. C. Coupland, London, 1884.]

HARTMANN, H. (1940) "Ichpsychologie und Anpassungsprobleme", *Int. Z. Psychoanal.*, **26**. (175)

[*Trans.*: in *Organization and Pathology of Thought*, edited by D. Rapaport, New York, 1951.]

HARTMANN, H., KRIS, E. and LOEWENSTEIN, R. (1947) "Some Comments on the Formation of Psychic Structure", *Psychoanalytic Study of the Child*, **2**. (45, 175)

(1953) "The Function of Psychoanalytic Theory" in *The Psychology of Instincts*. Essays in honour of Marie Bonaparte, edited by R. M. Loewenstein, New York. (64)

HEAD, H. and CAMPBELL (1900) "The Pathology of Herpes Zoster and its Bearing on Sensory Localisation", *Brain*, **91**, 3, 353 ff. (327, 338)

HOLMES, T. H., and others (1949) *Nose*. An Experimental Study of Reactions within the Nose in Human Subjects during Varying Life Experiences. With a Foreword by W. T. Longcope, Springfield.

ISAKOWER, O. (1939) "On the Exceptional Position of the Auditory Sphere", *Int. J. Psycho-Anal.* **20**, 340. (30)

JACKSON, C. and C. L. (1945) *Diseases of the Nose, Throat and Ear*, (16)

JACKSON, HUGHLINGS (1879) "On Affections of the Speech from Diseases of the Brain", *Brain*, **1**.

(1880) Ditto, **2**. (19, 44)

JANET, P. (1894) *L'Etat Mental des Hystériques*. *Les Accidents Mentaux*, Paris.

(1898) *Névroses et Idées Fixes*, 2 Vols., **2** with F. Raymond, Paris. (76, 84, 247)

JELLIFFE, S. E. (1937) "Sigmund Freud as Neurologist. Some Notes on his Earlier Neurological and Clinical Studies", *J. Nerv. Ment. Dis.*, **86**, No. 6.

JERUSALEM, W. (1895) *Urteilsfunktion*, Vienna. (120)

JONES, E. (1952) "Letter on Van der Heide", *Bull. Menninger Clin.* **16**, No. 5. (35)

KASSOWITZ, M. (Ed.) (1890) *Beiträge zur Kinderheilkunde an dem ersten öffentlichen Kinderkrankeninstitut*. Vienna. (16)

KNAUS, H. (1938) "Zur Periodizität des menstruellen Zyklus", *Münchner med. Wschr.*, 47 (9, 76)

KRIS, E. (1940) "On Inspiration", *Int. J. Psycho.-Anal.*, **20**. Reprinted in *Psychoanalytic Explorations in Art*, New York, 1952. (307)

(1946) "Review of F. J. Hoffmann's 'Freudianism and the Literary Mind'," *Psychoanal. Quart.*, **15**. Reprinted 1952, as above.

(1947) "The Nature and Validation of Psychoanalytic Propositions". *Freedom and Experience*. *Essays in Honour of Horace Kallen*. (45, 47). New York and London.

(1950a) "The Significance of Freud's Earliest Discoveries", *Int. J. Psycho-Anal.*, **29**, Nos. 1 and 2. (29)

KRIS, E. (*contd.*)

(1950b) "On Preconscious Mental Processes", *Psychoanal. Quart.* **19**, reprinted in the *Yearbook of Psychoanalysis*, edited by S. Lorand, 1951; *also* in *Psychoanalytic Explorations in Art*, New York, 1952. For a slightly different version *see Organization and Pathology of Thought*, edited by D. Rapaport, New York, 1952.

(1951) "The Development of Ego-Psychology", *Samiksa*, **5**, No. 3.

KROELL, H. (1900) *Der Aufbau der menschlichen Seele, eine psychologische Skisse*, Leipzig.

LAISTNER, S. L. (1889) *Das Rätsel der Sphinx, Grundzüge der Mythenforschung*, 2 Vols. Berlin. (332)

LIPPS, T. (1883) *Grundtaschen des Seelenlebens*, Bonn. (261, 267)

(1898) "Komik und Humor" in *Beiträge zur Ästhetik*, Hamburg. (261)

LOWENFELD, S. L. (1895) "Über die Verknüpfung neurasthenischer und hysterische Symptome in Anfallsform nebst Bemerkungen über die Freudsche Angstneurose", *Münchner med. Wschr.*, No. 13. (36)

MARSHALL, H. R. (1894) *Pain, Pleasure and Aesthetics*, London.

(1895) *Aesthetic Principles*, London and New York.

MAYLAN, C. (1930) *Freuds tragischer Komplex*, Munich. (34)

MERLAN, P. (1945) "Brentano and Freud", *J. Hist. Ideas*, **6**, No. 3. (343)

PFENNIG, A. R. (1906) *Wilhelm Fliess und seine Nachentdecker: Otto Weininger und H. Swoboda*, Berlin. (41, 241)

PREYER, A. (1884) *Die chronische nervöse oder reflektorische Diarrhöe (Diarrhoea Chronica Nervosa). Ein Beitrag zur Lehre der Darmerkrankungen*, Basle. (74)

(1888) *Die reizbare Blase oder idiopathische Blasenreizung (Irritable bladder, nervous bladder). Ihre Ursachen, Diagnose und Behandlungen. Eine Studie aus der Praxis*, Stuttgart. (74)

(1889a) "Der Urin bei Neurosen". *Sammlung klinischer Vorträge in Verbindung mit deutschen Klinikern* herausgegeben von R. von Volkmann, **2**, No. 131, 12th series. Leipzig. (74)

(1889b) "Asthma und Geschlechtskrankheiten (Asthma sexuale)". Berliner Klinik. *Sammlung kliniker Vorträge*, Berlin. (74)

(1891) "Die Neurose der Prostata". Berliner Klinik. *Sammlung klinischer Vorträge*, Berlin. (74)

(1893) "Die nervösen Affektionen des Darmes bei der Neurasthenie des männlichen Geschlechtes (Darmneurasthenie)". Wiener Klinik. *Vorträge aus der gesamten praktischen Heilkunde*, **1**, Vienna. (74)

PREYER, A. (*contd.*)
( ) Der unvollständige Beischlaf (Congressus Interruptus, Onanismus Conjugalis) und seine Folgen beim männlichen Geschlechte. Eine Studie aus der Praxis. (67)

RANK, O. (1909) *Der Mythus von der Geburt des Helden*, Leipzig and Vienna. (205)
[*Trans.: Myth of the Birth of the Hero*, New York, 1913.]

RIEBOLD, G. (1942) *Einblick in den periodischen Ablauf des Lebens mit besonderer Berücksichtigung des Menstruationsvorgangs*, Stuttgart. (8, 9, 40)

SAALER, B. (1914) "Die Fliess'sche Periodizitätslehre und ihre Bedeutung für die Sexualbiologie", *Z. Psychoanal. Psychother.* **4**. (241)

SACHS, HANNS (1945) *Freud, Master and Friend*, London. (237, 247, 344)
[*Trans.: Freud, Meister und Freund*, London, 1951.]

SACHS, HEINRICH (1893) *Vorträge über Bau und Tätigkeit des Grosshirns und die Lehre von der Aphasie und Seelenkrankheit*, Breslau. (135)

SCHILDER, P. (1942) *Mind, Perception and Thought*, New York. (394)

SLUDER, GREENFIELD (1927) *Nasal Neurology, Headaches and Eye Disorders*, St. Louis. (6)

SPITTA, W. (1892) *Die Schlaf-und Traumzustände der menschlichen Seele*, Tübingen. (108)

SWOBODA, H. (1906) *Die gemeinnützige Forschung und der eigennützige Forscher*, Vienna. (41)

VAN DER HEIDE, C. (1952) "Discussion of Buxbaum (1951)", *Bull. Menninger Clin.* **16**, No. 2. (35)

VILLARET, A. (1888) *Handwörterbuch der gesamten Medizin*, **I**, Stuttgart.
(1892) Ditto, **2**. (18, 52, 56)

WEININGER, O. (1902) *Geschlecht und Charakter*, Vienna. (41)
[*Trans.: Sex and Character*, London, 1906.]

WITTELS, F. (1924) *Sigmund Freud, der Mann, die Lehre, die Schule*, Vienna. (13, 34)
[*Trans.: Sigmund Freud, his Personality, his Teaching and his School*, London, 1924.]

INDEX

This index includes the names of non-technical authors. It also includes the names of technical authors where no reference is made in the text to particular works. For references to particular technical works, the *Bibliography* should be consulted.

GG*